Conceptual History in the European Space

European Conceptual History

Editorial Board:
Michael Freeden, University of Oxford
Diana Mishkova, Centre for Advanced Study Sofia
Javier Fernández-Sebastián, Universidad del País Vasco, Bilbao
Willibald Steinmetz, University of Bielefeld
Henrik Stenius, University of Helsinki

The transformation of social and political concepts is central to understanding the histories of societies. This series focuses on the notable values and terminology that have developed throughout European history, exploring key concepts such as parliamentarianism, democracy, civilization and liberalism to illuminate a vocabulary that has helped to shape the modern world.

Conceptual History in the European Space
Edited by Willibald Steinmetz, Michael Freeden and Javier Fernández-Sebastián

Parliament and Parliamentarism: A Comparative History of a European Concept
Edited by Pasi Ihalainen, Cornelia Ilie and Kari Palonen

Conceptual History in the European Space

Edited by
Willibald Steinmetz, Michael Freeden and
Javier Fernández-Sebastián

Published in 2017 by
Berghahn Books
www.berghahnbooks.com

© 2017, 2019 Willibald Steinmetz, Michael Freeden and Javier Fernández-Sebastián
First paperback edition published in 2019

All rights reserved. Except for the quotation of short passages
for the purposes of criticism and review, no part of this book
may be reproduced in any form or by any means, electronic or
mechanical, including photocopying, recording, or any information
storage and retrieval system now known or to be invented,
without written permission of the publisher.

Library of Congress Cataloging-in-Publication Data
A C.I.P. cataloging record is available from the Library of Congress

British Library Cataloguing in Publication Data
A catalogue record for this book is available from the British Library

ISBN 978-1-78533-482-5 hardback
ISBN 978-1-78920-494-0 paperback
ISBN 978-1-78533-483-2 ebook

Contents

List of Figures	vii
Introduction. Conceptual History: Challenges, Conundrums, Complexities *Willibald Steinmetz and Michael Freeden*	1
CHAPTER 1 Europe at Different Speeds: Asynchronicities and Multiple Times in European Conceptual History *Helge Jordheim*	47
CHAPTER 2 Multiple Transformations: Temporal Frameworks for a European Conceptual History *Willibald Steinmetz*	63
CHAPTER 3 Concepts and Debates: Rhetorical Perspectives on Conceptual Change *Kari Palonen*	96
CHAPTER 4 Conceptual History, Ideology and Language *Michael Freeden*	118
CHAPTER 5 Transnational Conceptual History, Methodological Nationalism and Europe *Jani Marjanen*	139
CHAPTER 6 Conceptual History: The Comparative Dimension *Jörn Leonhard*	175
CHAPTER 7 Concepts, Contests and Contexts: Conceptual History and the Problem of Translatability *László Kontler*	197

CHAPTER 8 Conceptualizing Spaces within Europe: The Case of
Meso-Regions   212
Diana Mishkova and Balázs Trencsényi

CHAPTER 9 Conceptualizing Modernity in Multi- and Intercultural
Spaces: The Case of Central and Eastern Europe   236
Victor Neumann

CHAPTER 10 Concepts in a Nordic Periphery   263
Henrik Stenius

Conclusions: Setting the Agenda for a European Conceptual History   281
Javier Fernández-Sebastián

Index   299

Figures

5.1	In Google Books' set of texts – consisting of books published in the whole of the English-speaking world – the word 'nationalism', with or without capitalization, only started gaining popularity after the turn of the twentieth century.	150
6.1	A Franco-German Library of Translations, 1770–1815.	184
6.2	Monographs containing 'liberal' in title or subtitle in European comparison, 1801–1880.	185

Introduction

Conceptual History

Challenges, Conundrums, Complexities

Willibald Steinmetz and Michael Freeden

The purpose of this book is twofold. To begin with, it serves as the lead volume to an ambitious series of volumes on conceptual histories in Europe. But it also is an opportunity to reflect on the state of the art of conceptual history in a post-Koselleckian era. Does current conceptual history respect its founders and their intentions? What are its most prominent trends? On what is it still missing out? And how does it have to change when practised on a European scale?

The practice of conceptual history, like its subject matter, is simultaneously discontinuous and intra-referential, scattered and centripetal. In fact, over the past twenty years its study has been experiencing a rebirth. Its practitioners are multiplying; its investigations have spread across many languages and cultures – within Europe and beyond; its assumptions and contentions are becoming more nuanced; and it has entered into a fertile mutual give-and-take with neighbouring disciplines. Moreover, it has embraced the digital age: leafing through yellowing dictionaries has been (partly) replaced by recourse to searchable databases.[1] From being a somewhat esoteric venture within the domain of history it is fast becoming one of the most important avenues to studying not just intellectual history and political thought but a broad spectrum of discourses ranging from comparative religion, emotional lexicons and welfare state policies to the natural sciences and science and technology studies.[2] Before delving deeper into the opportunities offered and challenges posed by conceptual history, two basic questions need to be addressed: Why concepts? And why Europe?

Concepts can be seen as focal points of interpretation and understanding; as identifying regularities and differences in human discourse; as windows through which we can appreciate how comprehensions of the world are organized and brought to bear on action; as milestones in the changing course of the evolution of knowledge; as constraints on the messiness of human thought and enablers of its transformation; and as rational and emotional containers of social logic and imagination. Their history is the history of all this and more, both on the micro-level of human interaction and on the macro-stage of national and international upheavals, revolutions, transactions and order.

The main body of work to which conceptual historians all over the world continue to refer is the volumes of Reinhart Koselleck's monumental *Geschichtliche Grundbegriffe*.[3] These volumes cover in alphabetic order the social and political concepts in the German language in modern times. For Koselleck, basic concepts express what a discourse is talking about, and some concepts attain the status of 'inescapable, irreplaceable part[s] of the political and social vocabulary'.[4] One of Koselleck's main findings is that in the late modern era these concepts became more abstract and general, and also more future-oriented. Conceptual history traces the modifications occurring in the meanings of such concepts, always within a particular social and cultural context, and always in a state of potential contest with one another. It is, in his words, a 'record of how th[e] uses [of past conceptualizations] were subsequently maintained, altered or transformed'.[5] Hence, the method identifies the many layered meanings contained in the actual usages of a concept. Koselleck argued that concepts consist of aggregative meanings that are reflected in later usage, and this was expressed in the famous phrase the 'simultaneity of the non-simultaneous'. While Koselleck was more interested in long-term, diachronic change, the method is equally applicable to shorter time frames and to synchronic comparisons within one community of language users, or between languages.

There is already much debate and research on how to apply conceptual history and what it is that we are conceptualizing, but less on what the practice of conceptualizing concepts itself entails. We need to know what concepts can and cannot deliver, and how they convey information, as part of the discipline of conceptual history. The emphasis on conceptual change should not rule out a parallel emphasis on the performativity of concepts. That means, among others, looking at their intricate structure, at their illocutionary force, and at the emotional clothing in which they are articulated. It even means deducing concepts indirectly from non-textual evidence such as that provided by art, architecture, dance, photography, political emblems or body language.[6] And conceptual absences too demand their own investigation. These are only some of the complexities that make conceptual history so fascinating a topic, and they will be discussed in the present and the following volumes of our European book series.

But why Europe? This question immediately entails another, preliminary one: What is 'Europe' from a conceptual history point of view? Where do we consider the European conceptual space to end, given the fact that, since the onset of modernity, major European languages like Spanish, Portuguese, French, Russian and above all English have been spoken, and are still being used, as second or indeed first languages in many parts of the world? And how do we contend with the fact that European languages have been and continue to be in constant interchange with non-European ones? What is at stake here is the spatial scope of our project. Should we extend our view to the totality of linguistic contacts between speakers of European and non-European languages or, rather, restrict our inquiries to uses of concepts in the political communities which, together, make up the geographical province conventionally called Europe?

Without pretending that the two approaches may be as neatly separable from each other as this alternative suggests we have chosen the second option. Our main reason is a pragmatic one. Jumping immediately to the global level in a discipline that is just about to move beyond single-nation or single-language studies would be rash and could, possibly, overstrain the resources and network-building capacities of the editors and contributors to the book series. The decision to concentrate on conceptual histories in Europe, however, does not preclude looking at how those histories were affected by events happening outside Europe, by people migrating into Europe or by translations and conceptual transfers originating in non-European world regions. Non-European linguistic and extra-linguistic developments will thus have a legitimate place in our volumes in so far as they have had repercussions on European ones. Even with these restrictions in mind the task in front of us is ambitious enough.

Our venture of writing conceptual histories on a European scale fits well with similar projects underway for other world regions. The most advanced, and also the nearest from a cultural point of view, is the *Iberconceptos* project, which explores parallel and diverging uses of concepts in the Spanish- and Portuguese-speaking worlds on both sides of the Atlantic.[7] Also far advanced are two competing South Korean projects on conceptual histories and transfers within the East Asian region and particularly between China, Korea and Japan.[8] More recently, similar attempts have been made to explore the histories of certain clusters of concepts or semantic fields in parts of Asia, the Middle East and Africa.[9] The introduction of Western concepts in the respective Asian and African languages during the colonial and postcolonial periods is an important, though never exclusive, research topic in those projects. Given the present state of research, choosing a world-regional rather than a global approach seems to be the appropriate step.

When we turn to Europe as one among several world regions we do not thereby wish to claim the existence of a European special path, let alone a European model. The assumption from which we start is that the mechanisms and patterns of conceptual change to be discovered in Europe will be as multiple and diverse as in any other world region. One might perhaps argue that since the Middle Ages the European conceptual universe, despite its diversity, has been more homogenous because of the common traditions of Greek, Latin and Judeo-Christian texts;[10] yet a similar point could easily be made with regard to, for instance, common traditions forming the base of the modern Chinese, Korean and Japanese conceptual worlds. Another argument in favour of European exceptionalism might be that a large number of basic concepts that nowadays serve to order our modern worldview – concepts like 'politics', 'religion', 'science', 'law' and 'economy' – happen to be of European origin. This, however, is the result of the contingent fact that, since the 1920s, English has acquired the status of a global *lingua franca*,[11] but it cannot be attributed to any supposed specific quality of European concepts themselves. In short, rather than searching for European exceptionalisms, we will treat Europe as just one interesting case among others from which one might learn more about how to approach transnational and, eventually, global conceptual history. We regard Europe as one of several provinces suitable for studying mechanisms and patterns of conceptual change – no more and no less.

The following paragraphs of this introduction, as well as the entire volume, address the main issues currently preoccupying conceptual historians working on European languages. As the lead volume to a new book series, it has no pretensions to offer an exhaustive panorama of European political and social concepts. Particular concepts such as liberalism, democracy and regionalism are merely mentioned here as brief case studies to illustrate certain controversies. More comprehensive studies on specific concepts and conceptual clusters will be the object of future volumes in the series.[12]

The Times and Speeds of Conceptual Change

Understanding the historicity of temporal concepts like history and time, progress and decline, revolution and acceleration, synchronicity and repetition, contingency and crisis, experience and expectation, modernity and utopia was at the heart of Reinhart Koselleck's interests when, together with Werner Conze and Otto Brunner, he launched the project of writing the history of German key concepts (*Grundbegriffe*).[13] While his co-editors, Conze and Brunner, were more concerned with past and present contests over the vocabularies of social classification, political institutions and constitutional theory, Koselleck saw conceptual history above all as laying the ground for a theory of historical times. He devoted special articles to most of the temporal concepts mentioned, either in the lexicon *Geschichtliche Grundbegriffe* itself or in separate publications.[14] The title of Koselleck's first collection of essays, 'Futures Past' (*Vergangene Zukunft*), was a programmatic statement in this respect. Koselleck was convinced that notions of time, history and future had changed fundamentally in the course of human development, and especially so in the age of enlightenment, revolution and industrialization between the 1760s and the 1840s. In his view, those decades formed an epochal threshold which he designated as *Sattelzeit* (literally: saddle period), a strange metaphor which has ever since been used as a concept in historiography. The *Sattelzeit*, according to Koselleck, was the period in which our own conceptual universe emerged, in which European modernity came, so to speak, into its own by becoming self-reflexive in terms of being a new way of conceptualizing historical time (*Neuzeit*).

One of the processes that Koselleck saw at work during this transformation period, arguably the most important one, was what he called temporalization (*Verzeitlichung*). Concepts in discourse, he argued, now increasingly appeared as 'entimed' concepts – that is, as concepts that were associated either with a bygone past, a transient present or an ideal future. A common way in which temporalization occurred was to reimagine phenomena formerly thought of as static in the form of dynamic processes. The result was a great number of 'movement concepts' (*Bewegungsbegriffe*). In French and, by extension, in many other European languages movement concepts could be created simply by adding the suffix '-ization' to a known term. 'Democracy' thus became 'democratization'; it was no longer assumed to be a fixed constitutional form, but a supposedly ongoing process or even a task ahead. Another way in which movement concepts could emerge, very prominent in the German context, was the creative use of metaphors. Many key concepts that expressed the new, linear vision of history originally had strong metaphorical resonances. Some of them, notably *Fortschritt* (progress), *Aufklärung* (enlightenment) and *Entwicklung* (development or evolution; literally: unfolding), already implied a movement directed towards an open, potentially better future; others, like *Revolution* (revolution), *Krise* (crisis) and *Geschichte* (history; literally: superimposed layers) had originally referred to circular or recurrent natural phenomena, but their conceptual meaning was reoriented towards a linear vision of time.

Debates have been going on among historians, literary scholars and political theorists about whether Koselleck's findings on the *Sattelzeit* can be generalized with regard to other parts of Europe or whether they should be considered a German peculiarity. How we answer this question is important for our European conceptual history project as it touches upon the issue of periodization, which is discussed more extensively by Willibald Steinmetz in Chapter

2.[15] Without going into details here, we may find a variety of answers. There are some scholars who doubt the validity of the *Sattelzeit* hypothesis even for Germany itself. They have discovered that certain conceptual innovations happened much earlier, or query the limited social significance of Koselleck's source materials, or point to the fact that many political, economic and scientific concepts only became contested much later, in the decades around 1900 rather than around 1800.[16] Other critics argue on a European scale and reject the idea of a pan-European *Sattelzeit* to be dated precisely at that period. These comparativists argue that accelerated conceptual changes along the lines described by Koselleck can be observed earlier in some parts of Europe, and later in others.[17] With a view to Europe, then, these critics tend to dissolve Koselleck's hypothesis of the *Sattelzeit* and replace it with a vision of a Europe at different times and speeds – a formula that is often used in debates on European integration but may profitably be applied, as Helge Jordheim demonstrates in Chapter 1, to understand the complex synchronicities and asynchronicities of conceptual change in Europe.[18]

While the latter vision still relies on the background assumption that conceptual innovation in Europe, although discontinuous and stretching over centuries, by and large followed a similar direction, a third line of criticism, only tentatively raised so far, would be to argue that circumstances in European countries differed so widely that it would be misleading to presuppose a common developmental path. For us this is an open question. What we may safely assume is that temporalization, politicization, ideologization and democratization of concepts are certainly not the only modalities of conceptual change worth exploring in a European context. Alternative modalities might be rupture, replacement and distortion. Another mode of conceptual change, prevalent especially in Europe's peripheral regions and in countries ruled by foreigners, may be termed the 'nationalizing' or 'ethnicizing' of sociopolitical language. In such instances local elites might follow an agenda of cultural rejuvenation or nation-state building, consciously rejecting the foreign (Western), and inventing instead an array of indigenous social or political concepts. The Slavophiles in Russia would be a case in point. Such attempts at 'nationalizing' (or 'ethnicizing') sociopolitical language should be looked at more closely in a European conceptual history project. The increasing degree of scientization of sociopolitical language in the later twentieth century would be another. In the event, the conceptual histories discussed in our book series will be no simple replicas of already existing Western or German models, but will present a much greater variety of paths and speeds of conceptual innovation.

An additional reason why we anticipate a wide variety of paths, compared to existing conceptual history projects, is the extension of our temporal focus:

towards the early modern period and the Middle Ages on the one hand, and towards the twentieth and twenty-first centuries on the other. For instance, it is a widely underexplored question how sociopolitical concepts derived from Latin (or Greek) linguistic roots were introduced, redefined and stabilized (or rejected) in the European vernaculars.[19] Is it possible to identify one or just a handful of typical patterns in this process of 'vernacularization'? Or are there as many different paths in Europe as there are languages or even individual concepts? Similar questions may be raised, and have hardly been touched upon in research so far, with regard to the ongoing twentieth- and twenty-first-century processes of scientization, anglicization and globalization of ever-larger parts of diverse professional languages. Can we observe a limited number of patterns here? And what are the repercussions of these changes in professional languages for the use of vocabularies in ordinary public and private communication?

The anglicization and globalization of our contemporary conceptual space is driven not only by professional discourses but even more through the languages of popular culture, of the entertainment industries and of new communicative practices such as blogging and Facebook. These languages percolate into everyday usage and eventually produce new concepts. The 'selfie' as a new vision and technology of the self may be a case in point. Yet how precisely, and why, some of these concepts, mostly created according to English morphological and phonetic rules, become widely used while others remain ephemeral and limited in use to certain groups or communities, is largely unexplored. And so is the question whether the newly created English words are actually understood in the same way when used in the context of non-English languages.

We can be certain, therefore, that even the most recent developments of conceptual innovation, although apparently expressed in terms of one language (English), are not happening in a synchronized way. As in earlier periods of European history, every concept will continue to have its own temporal structure, within each language and between the European languages. Superficial simultaneity of use may conceal a multiplicity of allusions to past experiences and future expectations. Any vision of a one-size-fits-all periodization to contend with Europe's historic and present asynchronicities and different speeds of conceptual change is doomed to failure.

The Spatial Dimension: Nations and Regions, Centres and Peripheries

Closely connected to the issue of different times and speeds of conceptual change is the question of how we divide Europe into spaces – analytically and historically. The present volume examines this problem from various angles. In Chapter 5, on the pitfalls of methodological nationalism, Jani Marjanen discusses the reasons why nation states have long ceased to be the only relevant spatial framework for the writing of conceptual histories. While stressing the need to look at translations and conceptual transfers, he does not go as far as claiming that nation states have become irrelevant.[20] Assuming, as we do in our book series, a long-term historical perspective from the Middle Ages to the twenty-first century, we are well advised to conceive of Europe as a permanently mutable assemblage of differently shaped political, cultural and linguistic units. Each of these may serve as a focal point for conceptual history studies. Nation states are but one possible form within this assemblage – an important one, but historically speaking an exceptional one. For even during the short period of extreme nationalism between the late nineteenth and the mid twentieth centuries the ideal of the nationalists – namely, the perfect territorial overlap between political 'decision space', ethno-cultural 'identity space' and linguistic space – was nowhere fully realized.[21] Sub-national and supra-national regions of various size and shape, from small historic landscapes up to the European Union, will therefore figure as prominently in our book series as nation states.

As we have learned to de-essentialize nations, so we should also denaturalize regions. Both – nations and regions – are social products, and the same holds true for their names. In Chapter 8, Diana Mishkova and Balász Trencsényi remind us that applying the toolkit of conceptual history to explore the historical practice of giving names to nations and regions is perhaps the best antidote we have against falling into the trap of essentializing the spatial units of our research.[22] How the meanings of names such as 'the Balkans' or the 'Nordic countries' changed over time, by whom, when and why they were politicized, how they became associated with political ideologies ('the Nordic model'), and generally how they were disputed among various groups of agents – academics, politicians, intellectuals, journalists, authors of schoolbooks, international organizations – are questions that need to be addressed more thoroughly if conceptual history turns European. There is a promising new field of research opening up here which includes not only the names of specific spatial units (*Mitteleuropa*, the Mediterranean, Scandinavia, the West,[23] the Eastern bloc and so on), but also the abstract terminology used to organize or classify geographical/political spaces: terms such as 'region', 'country', 'territory', 'land', 'city', 'empire', 'colony', 'province', 'centre', 'periphery', 'zone', 'border', 'frontier', 'international community', and of course also 'nation' and 'nation state'.[24]

The field is all the more interesting as it offers excellent opportunities to integrate the study of visual images and symbolic representations in the practice of conceptual history. We need only think of (gendered) figures like Britannia, Germania, Marianne, or the Russian bear, and the 'family romances' (Lynn Hunt) told around them, to realize the field's potential.[25] Names of regions and nations, and the figures symbolizing them, were disputed in language as well as in images, even in music and sounds; they were put on stage, visualized in monuments and the layout of cities, drawn in maps and schoolbooks, displayed in museums, and represented in the architecture of royal palaces and parliamentary buildings. These names and symbols were not just harmless décor, but functioned as emotionally charged political concepts in situations of conflict. This applies to names of nation states as well as to denominations of supra-national or sub-national regions like 'South Eastern Europe', 'the Celtic fringe', 'Catalonia' and 'Transylvania'. Even today such names take hold of peoples' minds because they serve to draw boundaries, create identities, or exclude unwanted strangers. For this reason they rarely appear alone, but more often in quasi-personalized form: as pairs or groups opposing each other, forming alliances, moving in the same direction or drifting apart.

As well as being identified by names or symbolic figures, spatial units may be conceptualized metaphorically with regard to their modus operandi: as melting pots, transit zones, frontiers, federations, empires or national 'containers'. European history provides examples for all of these, and many more, forms of conceptualizing communication within and between political spaces. Again, the concepts (and metaphors) mentioned had very tangible consequences. On the one hand they informed the ways in which rulers, administrators and statisticians organized territories, constructed institutions, and categorized people; on the other hand the governmental and administrative practices often provoked popular or elitist reactions relying on opposite notions.[26] Studying competing notions of ordering spaces and grouping people is a rewarding task for conceptual historians. In Chapter 9, on Central and Eastern Europe, Victor Neumann provides telling examples showing how, and why, the contests were particularly sharp in regions where stable nation states only asserted themselves by the late nineteenth and early twentieth centuries.[27] In these regions, Neumann explains, new visions of ethno-linguistic homogeneity, derived mostly from German intellectuals (Herder), destroyed the benevolent respect for plurilingualism, multiculturalism and multiconfessionalism, which until the mid-nineteenth century had characterized political interactions in the Habsburg monarchy, and to a lesser extent even in the Ottoman and Russian empires.[28] Languages themselves became a dividing issue in the process of hardening ethno-nationalist attitudes; German for instance changed its role from being a meta-language of intra-imperial communication to just one particularist language among others. The language dispute was carried to an extreme in the imperial parliament for the Austrian (Cisleithanian) part of the monarchy: by the 1900s, decision making there was almost brought to a standstill by nationalist parties insisting on using only their own languages in the absence of a translation service. By that time the assumption of the Austrian Germans that their language should be the universal language in the empire had lost all credibility.[29]

The disruption of political communication in the Austrian parliament may serve as a drastic illustration for a problem discussed in more general terms by Henrik Stenius. In his chapter on concepts in a Nordic periphery he posits it as a rule, valid at least for the formative period of modernity in the eighteenth and nineteenth centuries, that speakers of 'central' European languages (French, English, German) tended to use their own concepts as if they were universally valid. Whether these speakers did so consciously (out of arrogance) or unconsciously (out of ignorance) mattered little to the speakers of 'peripheral' languages who in any case, Stenius argues, found themselves in the awkward position of being forced to react. Their reaction would usually take one of two courses: faced with the allegedly universal concepts transmitted from the centres, speakers of peripheral languages could either accept the claims to universality and redefine their own concepts accordingly (for instance by appropriating foreign terms), or they could denounce these claims as nothing but a concealed particularism and, in turn, defend their own parochial concepts against them. As Henrik Stenius explains in Chapter 10, actors in the peripheries were thus constantly 'forced to navigate between universalisms and particularities'.[30] In theory, there existed a third option which would have been to create a meta-language enabling both groups of speakers to find a balance between local contextualizations of key concepts and claims to universality in their respective languages. In practice, however, this was hard to realize, and it may therefore be difficult to find examples for it in modern European history.

Henrik Stenius's core-periphery hypothesis raises several follow-up problems that need to be investigated empirically. First of all it seems reasonable to assume that no country or region, however remote geographically, is *essentially* peripheral, and nor is any language. 'Core' and 'periphery' are terms that describe a non-reciprocal relationship, and it is evident that such relationships are always shifting. What we, as conceptual historians, define as 'core' and 'periphery' depends on the subject areas discussed, on the historical period of course, and on the perspectives taken by the researchers and the historical agents themselves. From the standpoint of a member of the Republic of Letters in late eighteenth-century Paris, the Russian Empire of Catherine II might well have been viewed as peripheral, yet when it came to measuring political power and military strength it was anything else but peripheral, even from a Parisian perspective.

With respect to languages, though, one might argue that native speakers of small languages like Finnish, Latvian or Basque encounter a greater probability of finding themselves in the 'peripheral' position described by Stenius than native speakers of widely used languages like French or German in the eighteenth and nineteenth centuries, and English in the twentieth and twenty-first centuries. Widely used languages may be described as occupying the 'centre' in the sense that their speakers often feel no need to learn small languages (or sometimes any foreign languages at all) and hence need not care about alternative conceptual universes that the smaller languages may contain. Speakers of small languages, on the other hand, are forced to translate more often. They frequently compare their own autochthonous concepts with the foreign ones, and especially so if they aspire to make their own language capable of expressing their political and cultural identity, as was the case with most intellectuals and politicians during the nation-building processes going on in eighteenth-, nineteenth- and early twentieth-century Europe.

The mere size of a speaker community, however, is no guarantee that a language occupies a 'central' position in the sense described. The Russian language in the eighteenth and nineteenth centuries is a pertinent example. Its spread beyond the imperial borders was limited; Russian concepts rarely posed a challenge for speakers of Western languages to revise their own conceptual apparatus. The Russian elites themselves spoke French when they addressed other Europeans. Much more important than size was, and is, the cultural prestige of a language. It is above all that prestige that stimulates foreigners to learn a language and contend with its conceptual universe. On what factors the cultural prestige is founded, when and why languages acquire or lose it, how far the political, economic or military power of the peoples (or rulers) speaking the language enhance or diminish it: these are all questions only to be answered empirically on a case-by-case basis. For our European conceptual history project they are worth studying.

No less important are questions related to the conceptual innovations happening in the 'peripheral' languages. Again, we need to investigate the specific historical conditions for each particular case to ascertain why certain foreign concepts were eagerly accepted as new and meaningful terms, why others were engrafted on existing autochthonous terms and, finally, why some foreign concepts were rejected or simply ignored. The Nordic examples discussed by Stenius point to such specific conditions as explanatory factors, for example when he shows that the sense of strong conformity brought about by the coincidence of political space and (Lutheran) church left little room in the Nordic countries for using concepts like 'opposition' or 'party' as positive self-descriptions. By contrast, it would be interesting to know whether the same concepts met a different fate when introduced in the multiconfessional and multiethnic environments prevailing in large parts of the Habsburg Empire. It is through genuine comparisons like these that we may ultimately be able to write European conceptual histories that are more significant than conventional 'national' histories of key terms put side by side in the form of a lexicon.

Multilinguality and Translation

Anyone who starts practising conceptual history beyond the boundaries of one single language, usually his or her own, will soon realize that the model of homogenous, self-sufficient national languages is more of a myth (rationalist or romantic) than an adequate description of past and present reality. This is most obvious for the so-called peripheral countries, especially in the period before the growth of modern nation states. The coexistence of overlapping linguistic communities was a normal fact of life for those living in the more remote borderlands of Central, Eastern, and South Eastern Europe, but also in the fringe zones of Western and Northern Europe like the Basque country, the Gaelic-speaking parts of the British Isles, and Lapland. Even today, speakers in these areas often grow up with more than one 'native' language and are able to switch between them depending on where they are and what situations they are in: whether, for example, at home, or in school, a market place, a church, or even a police station.

Note how Elias Canetti, Nobel Prize winner in literature in 1981, describes his early childhood in Ruschuk, a small Bulgarian town on the River Danube's border with Romania, still officially belonging to the Ottoman Empire when Canetti was born in 1905. On any day, he writes, 'you could hear seven or eight languages'. He was a descendant of a family of Sephardic Jews, so the first children's songs he heard were in Spanish, but interspersed with a few Turkish words; his wet nurse was Romanian, the servants of the family Bulgarian, Circassian or Armenian, but there were also Ashkenazy Jews, Greeks, Russians, Albanians and Gypsies in the town.[31] With each other Elias's parents spoke German, a language he was not allowed to understand, but tried to learn secretly on his own, 'like a magic formula'.[32] With the children and relatives they spoke Ladino, 'the true vernacular, albeit an ancient Spanish. ... The peasant girls at home knew only Bulgarian'; so he learnt it with them, forgetting it later only to remember the early events of his childhood in German: 'I don't know at what point in time, on what occasion, this or that translated itself. ... It is not like the literary translation of a book from one language to another, it is a translation that happened of its own accord in my unconscious'.[33] For 'peripheral' Europeans like the young Elias Canetti, switching between languages and the necessity to translate were daily experiences. They were common to all social groups and strata, not just ethnic minorities and the learned elites: 'Each person counted up the languages he knew; it was important to master several, [as] knowing them could save one's own life or the lives of other people'.[34]

The necessity of switching between languages was never limited to the European peripheries. It was no less imperative in the 'core' regions of Europe, notably in the most densely populated cities and along major traffic routes. Cultural historian Peter Burke has vividly described how, from the Middle Ages on, the inhabitants of sea ports like Naples, Cadíz, Bordeaux and Antwerp – ordinary people like merchants, dock workers, cart drivers and keepers of boarding houses – had to be conversant in more than one language.[35] No less polyglot were the seamen on the ships, travelling journeymen, officers and soldiers, or young cavaliers on their *tour d'Europe*. Similarly, students and professors in university towns like Heidelberg, Padua, Leiden, Oxford and Krakow had to write and dispute in Latin while at the same time being able to negotiate with local landladies and shopkeepers in one or several vernaculars. The same was true for lawyers, state counsellors, diplomats, clergymen and the juridically trained clerks in the more important cities. The superimposition of languages went furthest, of course, in the late medieval and early modern European metropoles: Paris, London, Amsterdam and, later on, Vienna and St Petersburg. In all those places multilinguality and translation were ubiquitous.

When doing conceptual history on a European scale we should therefore assume that functional and situational multilinguality was the rule, not an exception, in most European regions for most of the time. This is a fact that has rarely been considered systematically in existing 'national' conceptual history projects. Moreover, we should keep in mind that, far into the early modern period and sometimes beyond, people often mixed fragments of several languages in ordinary communication. This resulted in hybrid languages not easily classifiable by later standards. In general, European vernacular languages were less homogenous, their boundaries more porous, and hence the meanings of terms generally more fluid, even in the most elaborated texts of political theory. Only in later times were national standards imposed and linguistic usages 'purified', either by the state and its academies, as in Richelieu's France, or by independent poets, philologists and intellectuals, as in most other European countries.[36] Latin itself was only restored to a supposed 'classical' norm through the efforts of the Renaissance humanists, thus at a time when Latin had already begun to lose its position as the lingua franca of the European elites, except in the universities and the Catholic Church.

Our modern national languages, but also the 'classical' ancient languages, only emerged out of the various standardizing and purifying movements driven in turn by sixteenth century humanists, seventeenth- and eighteenth-century state-builders, lexicographers and poets, and nineteenth-century romantic nationalists. It is only by means of their language-political activities that the meanings of terms and the semantic relations between them became more stable and 'national' languages on the whole more homogenous and more clearly separated from each other. In many European countries this process stretched over several centuries, in others it was condensed in shorter periods, but in general it started somewhere in the sixteenth century and came to a close towards the late nineteenth century. Conceptual historians working on one language have so far preferred to concentrate on the periods that followed the linguistic homogenization processes, and we may assume that this is no accident since conceptual histories in the form of lexicons like the German *Geschichtliche Grundbegriffe* or the Spanish *Diccionario*[37] require a certain degree of (at least temporarily) stable, and hence recognizable, relations between terms and concepts.

We should not forget, however, that even during and after the stabilization of national languages, and even in the most consolidated nation states like France, the correct use of linguistic standards was often limited to written and verbal exchanges in public institutions such as schools, theatres, town halls, courts of law, and parliaments. Below that official level, dialects, patois, and hybrid languages continued to be spoken. Furthermore, functional multilinguality and the need to translate on a day-to-day basis gained a renewed importance through the growing numbers of migrating workers crossing borders within Europe during industrialization, or immigrating into Europe from the overseas colonies (or ex-colonies) in later times.

If there was a period in which, despite ongoing migration, linguistic homogeneity within European national borders was greatest, it may have been during the short era of extreme nationalism between the two world wars. Since the postwar years, however, with prosperity returning and transnational connections increasing on all levels – economic, political and cultural – we are witnessing almost a kind of rapprochement to the late medieval and early modern situation. Overlapping linguistic communities and continuous hybridization of languages are now as omnipresent as then, with the important difference that a dozen or more varieties of English, instead of Latin or French, are now functioning as a default language not only in Europe, but all over the world.[38]

There are plenty of opportunities in our everyday lives that allow us to get an insight into how far the mixing of languages can go today. Take the example of a young German student of Turkish descent speaking on her mobile phone in a bus on its way to the local university. Listening to her can be a fascinating experience. In her talk, bits of Turkish alternate with passages in German, both interspersed by occasional Anglicisms, and all that happens even within single sentences. Obviously, the young woman feels no need to translate. The words pour out of her in an almost natural flow, and one can only guess that she mixes her languages habitually, depending on the subject matter being addressed: job- or university-related issues are discussed in German, family problems in Turkish, leisure activities or love affairs in a curious mixture of both.[39] It remains to be seen whether, and how, such a linguistic formation of everyday experience, which is by no means exceptional, will shape the use-value and semantic stability of the more abstract sociopolitical, moral or scientific terms in which conceptual historians are often interested. We have good reasons to assume that some of these terms – those referring to work, feelings or family, for example – will be affected considerably, possibly by way of a multiplication of terms or an enrichment of meanings, while others – the vocabularies referring to high politics or legal, economic and scientific matters – are more likely to remain unaffected, at least by this kind of everyday communication.

There exists another level of communication, however, at which precisely the expert vocabularies of sociopolitical, legal, economic and scientific affairs will be noticeably affected: the level of European and international institutions. Organizations like UNESCO and the OECD, the European bureaucracies in Brussels, the European Research Council, the European courts of law, the European Central Bank and especially the European Parliament provide an interesting, only recently discovered experimental ground for the study of the practical functioning, or mal-functioning, of multilinguality.[40] Here, the need to translate, in this case abstract legal, economic, scientific and sociopolitical terms, constitutes a permanent challenge. It is felt more acutely by non-native English speakers, but it is by no means unknown to native English speakers. There is a danger of being misled here by the apparent display of linguistic uniformity that is produced through the common use of English terms in international organizations. In fact, the superficial uniformity of *terms* may often hide a plurality of different national *concepts* that will resurface as soon as it comes to interpreting what the participants actually meant while negotiating or consenting to a document in English. Our linguistically eclectic German-Turkish student, and the European institutions as arenas of multilingual negotiation and translation, are only two – contemporary – examples of new research fields that are opened up when conceptual history takes a transnational – in our case, European – turn. Many more examples from contemporary as well as earlier periods in history could be imagined.

Empirical studies on multilingual situations and translation activities are not just fascinating topics in their own right. For conceptual historians they offer a chance to find additional, or better, explanations for the ways in which conceptual innovation functions. László Kontler, in Chapter 7, discusses plenty of examples and critically reviews academic literature on how acts of translation have brought about shifts in meaning.[41] Most studies so far have focused on the receiving end of the translation process, the target culture. Considering the translators' agency, however, should, Kontler insists, go further than this. Translations operate in two directions: they not only introduce innovations into the conceptual universe of a target culture, but their omissions and redescriptions may also highlight peculiarities of the culture of the 'original' text.

Apart from professional translations, contacts between languages generally are an extremely powerful trigger for semantic change. How, exactly, this happens may be described schematically. The process usually starts with foreign words, or strange-looking signs, coming up more or less contingently in written or oral communication. The mere presence of such 'alien' words and signs functions as an irritant in one's own language. Readers and listeners will try to make sense of the alien expressions by finding equivalent words (and signs) in their own language; if purposely extended to entire texts, this becomes translation in the professional sense. But speakers or writers will also use the opportunity, consciously or unconsciously, to 'play' with the foreign terms while their meaning is still unclear. In that case, the foreign words may serve as a stimulus to rearrange, and enrich, semantic fields in one's own language. Douglas Howland calls this process a 'translingual act of transcoding cultural material'.[42] This rearrangement can take different forms. For instance, introducing a foreign word may lead to a 'split' of an original native concept into two: one a negatively connoted concept, now denoted by the foreign term, and the other a positively connoted concept, denoted by the original native term. Such processes of semantic rearrangement by means of irritants derived from another language may be regarded as a translation process in a wider sense, but – as Kontler makes clear – it is recommendable to distinguish the two modes of linguistic contact and their effects; it may be more apposite to call the latter process 'conceptual transfer'. Translation in the professional sense aims at rendering the meaning of foreign terms as faithfully as possible, whereas conceptual transfer in the sense just described is an appropriation of foreign words that may change semantic relations (for example value hierarchies) among concepts in one's own language.

Both kinds of translation studies are highly useful for conceptual historians. The first, more conventional kind of studies looks at historical acts of translation that are explicitly marked as such. Starting points for such inquiries are usually entries in bilingual dictionaries and translations of literary texts or classical works of political theory.[43] These translations may then be interpreted as indicators of semantic congruence or incongruence, and in diachronic perspective as indicators of convergence or divergence, between certain semantic fields in two or more languages at a given time.[44] The second kind of studies looks at transfers of terms between languages. These transfers should then be interpreted as *factors* of conceptual innovation in both the receiving language and the 'original' language.[45] The focus is on the acts of appropriating or redescribing terms, and conceptual historians should read these acts as 'moves' in argumentative games as understood by Quentin Skinner and Kari Palonen.[46] Any kind of text containing lexical items of foreign origin can serve as source material for this kind of inquiry. In practice, historical translation studies often combine both perspectives, and both should have their place in future European conceptual histories. Moreover, as Reinhart Koselleck remarked, even the writing of conceptual histories within one language alone can be seen as a specific form of translation, in this case an attempt to recall into memory and make comprehensible meanings that have been lost over time.[47] Very often, this will require demonstrating in present-day language that no concept remotely equivalent to the modern one with which we are familiar existed, and that the semantic field referring to comparable phenomena or problems was structured in a completely different way.

Finally, a word of caution should be added: reframing, (mis)translation, contestation, and diverse forms of reception have become the nodes around which the study of conceptual history has been increasingly revolving. But it would be wrong to take this too far and to underplay the similarities and conjunctions displayed in human thought. The very act of translation entails an assumption of similarity and of the value of cross-fertilizing cultures with a particular take on knowledge. A concept still remains a marker for a shared specificity and a claim, even when exaggerated, for uniqueness. To be mired in a culture of diversity and fragmentation tells only one story; the other is that of identifying commonalities of the human condition. Both can lead to scholarly extremes; fortunately, that is not evident in the current trajectory of conceptual history studies.

Comparisons: An Outdated Approach?

The unquestionable relevance of cultural transfers, translations and entanglements in modern European (and global) history has induced some scholars, mostly historians, to argue that comparisons between nations, language communities or indeed any other supposed collective entities are not only fraught with difficulties, but should be deemed an improper approach altogether.[48] The allegation of the critics is that practitioners of comparisons all too readily take the unity of the units they compare as granted and tend to essentialize them. The comparers ignore, it is said, how malleable the supposed units of comparison actually are because of the incessant contacts between them.[49] For brevity's sake one may label this kind of unsound comparison 'methodological nationalism', although nation states are only one of many possible entities that may be falsely essentialized. Another reproach is that comparative scholars all too often use the norms, values and concepts of their own culture as a universal yardstick against which they measure the comparative progressiveness or backwardness of other cultures. Historically, this kind of misguided comparison has mainly appeared in the form of 'Eurocentrism' or Western progressivism, although in principle it can also occur elsewhere. Conceptual historians may also be tempted to apply progressivist comparisons to earlier stages in their *own* nation's development. This is what Denis Diderot had in mind when he wrote in the entry 'Encyclopédie' in his and d'Alemberts great work of the same name that *'sur la seule comparaison du vocabulaire d'une nation en différens temps, on se formeroit une idée de ses progrès'*.[50] From Diderot's statement it is only a short step to the idea that comparisons between the vocabularies of different nations might enable us to range them along a temporal scale according to their respective degree of progressiveness.

The criticisms put forward against essentializing and Eurocentric (or progressive) comparisons are no doubt justified. One should be careful however not to forego the opportunities of additional insights that comparisons, if well designed, still have to offer. With regard to conceptual history, the challenge is to devise ways of comparing that bring multilingualism and conceptual transfers, and hence the notorious instability of the compared languages, back into the picture. Similarly, comparisons in conceptual history should explicitly avoid all progressivist undertones when comparing the trajectories of concepts in different linguistic communities or cultures. Thus a statement that a certain community disposes of a certain concept while in another community an exact conceptual equivalent for it does not exist should not be worded in terms of 'already' or 'not yet' or any other formulation that suggests the idea of an alleged 'normal' or ideal development. What seems to be acceptable, though, if carefully worded, are statements of convergences or divergences in the meanings of individual terms or in the configurations of semantic fields.[51]

Even for these kinds of statement, however, considerable methodological pitfalls will have to be surmounted. For, in order to come up with such statements, we need to know in the first place that the terms or vocabularies to be compared are actually the nearest equivalents in the two languages compared. But how can one be sure about this? Bilingual dictionaries may give some clues. Yet the truth is that we would need an intuitive, quasi-divine linguistic knowledge to be confident about where the apex of semantic proximity lies at a given historical moment. Nineteenth-century bilingual dictionaries will tell us, for instance, that the nearest equivalent to the English word 'education' is the German term *Bildung*, although the latter may also be retranslated into English as 'culture' which, in turn, would be retranslated into German as *Kultur*, for which, again, the English term 'civilization' seems to be the most appropriate translation. This chain of translations is an unspectacular example, yet it makes clear why comparisons that start from individual words (semasiological comparisons) will often end up in labyrinths of translations and retranslations and, ultimately, descriptions of untranslatability.[52] The method of 'hopping' through bilingual dictionary entries and contemporary translations of canonical texts combined with intuition may, at best, help to establish charts of vocabularies referring to approximately similar phenomena in the respective linguistic communities at various points in time. Although more than nothing, this is merely a first step.

European conceptual historians working on comparisons may derive additional comfort from the fact that the problem of identifying the lexical equivalents whose meanings are then made the objects of comparisons is much easier to solve in a European context than in a global one. The family resemblances between most European languages are sufficiently large, and hence the probability of coming across truly incommensurable concepts should be quite rare. More important than the morphological resemblances, so fascinating for nineteenth-century comparative philologists, are in this respect the shared vocabularies resulting from uninterrupted chains of translations and conceptual transfers from Antiquity to the present age. Bo Stråth has indeed a good point when he writes that, within Europe, the common foundations of the ancient Greek, the Roman and the medieval Latin languages, as well as the Judeo-Christian intellectual tradition, provided a conceptual reference frame that, in most cases, guaranteed a mutual understanding of the semantic differences that still remained.[53] Stråth's argument holds good especially for the more abstract sociopolitical and philosophical terms that conceptual historians have, so far, usually been interested in: names of institutions ('parliament') and ideologies ('liberalism'), forms of government ('democracy'), historical processes ('revolution'), and fundamental categories of ordering the world like 'religion', 'politics', 'society', 'science' and 'the economy'. Etymologically, large sections of these abstract vocabularies derive from Greek or Latin roots. These terms are common to most European languages, and hence most Europeans, Stråth argues, will have at least roughly similar ideas about what they mean. But are we therefore entitled to say that Reinhart Koselleck's scepticism regarding the feasibility of comparative conceptual histories has been unfounded?[54] Is it true that in the Greek, Latin and Judeo-Christian traditions on the one hand, and English as today's lingua franca on the other hand, we actually dispose of tools that, at least in a European context, come close to the famous 'meta-language' which, according to Koselleck, is necessary to compare different conceptual worlds?[55]

A few caveats against such an over-optimistic view may be in place here. The first and most obvious one concerns the long time lags between the historical moments at which abstract terms derived from Greek or Latin roots became integral parts of the vocabularies of different European languages. While in the Romance languages adaptations of Latin words went on continuously, and while English was enriched by thousands of Latin and Romance loanwords from the Norman Conquest on, similar appropriations happened much later and only in a more sporadic fashion in the Germanic, Slavic and other European languages. Latin (or Greek) terms not only entered these languages much later, but often remained clearly recognizable as 'foreign' for quite some time. The hesitant integration of a word like 'politics' into public discourse in Tsarist Russia from the late eighteenth to the early twentieth centuries is a good example.[56] The process bears more resemblance to analogous attempts of making sense of 'politics' in modern China or India than to conceptualizations of 'politics' in late medieval Italy or early modern France.[57] Our brief discussion on time lags leads to another, more important point: for the periods *before* the abstract terms of Latin (or Greek) origin gained a foothold in the vernaculars, the search for the nearest lexical equivalents will be almost as hard for European as for non-European languages.[58] Neither Latin nor English can serve as substitutes for the much-needed 'meta-language' for these earlier periods.

This last observation leads to a second caveat. There is a danger of falling back into progressivist comparisons of the pattern described above, if research in European comparative conceptual histories focuses too much, or even exclusively, on the vocabularies belonging to the supposed 'common' tradition of Latin, Greek or Judeo-Christian origin. For many regions and periods in European history such an approach would only produce the same kind of deficit- or 'waiting-room' histories that postcolonial historian Dipesh Chakrabarty justly rejected as inappropriate.[59] With regard to our European conceptual history project, we therefore expressly invite contributions dealing with non-Western, non-Greek- or Latin-based terms, terms that do not belong to a supposed common European tradition, even terms that at first sight seem to be unique for one linguistic community only.[60] Finding lexical equivalents for comparisons will thereby not become easier, but this is the only way of truly Europeanizing the practice of conceptual history.

A third caveat against the view that, owing to common lexical traditions, comparative conceptual histories should be easier to realize in a European context than elsewhere in the world is necessary. It is a point elaborated by Jörn Leonhard in Chapter 6 of this volume as well as in his extensive historical studies on the semantics of 'Liberalism' in several Western European political cultures, mainly the Spanish, French, English, Italian and German ones.[61] One of Leonhard's major findings is that the apparent similarity of the *words* 'liberal' and 'liberalism' in these languages concealed many of the differences in the *concepts* conjured up in people's minds in their respective political cultures. At the same time, one might argue that the various conceptions of European liberalisms do not occupy entirely distinct semantic fields. It is indisputable, though, that the historical moments at which the terms became politicized and the ways in which they could be used to name parties across the spectrum between left and right depended not just on national contexts, but also on situational factors. If, then, even a term such as 'liberalism', which is clearly rooted in the Latin-European tradition and seems on the surface easy to translate, has seen different conceptualizations and paths of politicization, we should be all the more sceptical about the allegation that the pitfalls surrounding comparative conceptual histories on a European scale have already been surmounted.

Assuming for the moment that the problem of defining equivalent lexical items as units of comparison may nevertheless be resolved reasonably well, we still need to discuss what the objectives of comparative conceptual histories should be. Why comparisons? As long as we proceed semasiologically (i.e. take words as starting points), the answer seems evident. On a synchronic level the aims are to study similarities and differences in the use-patterns ('meanings') of terms and then, on that basis, to describe the congruities or incongruities of individual concepts; eventually this could lead to comparative descriptions of entire conceptual grids. If we add a diachronic perspective, our search extends to the question of convergence or divergence in the uses of terms and will result in histories of converging or diverging conceptual worlds.

However, it is one thing to elucidate factual changes, and another to *explain* them. One way of approaching explanations has been to embed the conceptual histories in meta-narratives of Europe-wide or world-wide processes such as democratization, secularization, European integration, globalization, and so on. Given the enduring attractiveness of such meta-narratives, which suggest linear and similar developments all over the globe, it is no wonder that comparative conceptual histories have tended to stress convergence more often than divergence. However, there is nothing in the comparative approach as such that obliges scholars to prefer narratives of converging concepts. Comparisons within our European book series will be open for both search directions: those that are about to show convergence as well as those that rather focus on divergence.

Up till now, most comparisons in conceptual history have proceeded semasiologically. Some critics even pretend that conceptual history in principle cannot but use a semasiological approach. But this is unfounded, and confuses the specific method used by Koselleck and others in the *Geschichtliche Grundbegriffe* with the overall research programme of conceptual history. Koselleck has even sketched the inverse method of proceeding onomasiologically in the introduction to the *Grundbegriffe*, although he rarely used the onomasiological method himself.[62] His famous essay on asymmetrical counter-concepts, however, is a fine example of how an onomasiological conceptual history, and a comparative one at that, might be conceived.[63] Basically, the idea is not to begin with words, but to start from phenomena, preferably historical problems – or 'challenges', to use Toynbee's phrase – and then to look for the relevant terms used by historical agents to contend with these problems – the 'responses' to use Toynbee's metaphorical expression again, a metaphor that fits well in our context. In the case of Koselleck's essay on counter-concepts the 'challenge' he explored was the problem of how people in different historical constellations dealt with inclusion and exclusion. And the 'responses' he found were different ways in which groups of human beings were opposed against each other in discourse (and corresponding practice): Hellenes and Barbarians, Christians and heathens, (Arian) humans and (non-Arian) 'sub-humans'. The result of Koselleck's comparative sketch was not only that the concepts used for the 'ins' and the 'outs' varied across time and space, but that the very forms of articulating inclusion and exclusion also changed along with the concepts. Exclusion could be expressed in a way that recognized the human quality of the 'others' although they were considered as inferiors (Barbarians); it could also be articulated so that the 'others' were still recognized as humans in the present, but condemned to hell in the future (heathens); or it could be conceived in a way that denied them even the quality of humans (non-Arian 'sub-humans').[64]

Generally speaking, onomasiological comparisons will never be concerned with just one or a handful of individual concepts; their principal aim is rather to show how concepts within larger semantic networks are interrelated. Onomasiological comparisons are an elegant way around the puzzling difficulties, so typical for semasiological comparisons, of knowing in advance what the relevant and possibly equivalent terms in different languages, communities or circumstances are. Onomasiological comparisons are indeed a way of *finding* the relevant and equivalent terms (and the concepts they refer to) through empirical research on the 'responses' to analogous historical phenomena. These phenomena may be recurrent problems, situations or challenges as, for example, the ways in which societies deal with inclusion and exclusion, organize and conceptualize hierarchies, or position themselves in historical time between past, present and future. What the relevant terms are is then not decided more or less arbitrarily by the researcher, but emerges as a verifiable result of the analysis. And the same applies for the definitions of equivalent terms. They are not preliminarily fixed by intuitive guesses, but can only be identified in the course of the investigation: terms are equivalent when they can be shown to have a similar use-value or position in arguments used to contend with the problem or situation investigated. An additional advantage is that because the relevant terms are not fixed in advance, there can be no Eurocentric or Western progressivist bias in their choice, as happens so easily when proceeding semasiologically. Not least for that reason onomasiological comparisons will have greater potential for surprising findings, a benefit that seems particularly welcome for a multinational and multilingual project like our book series.[65]

For all their advantages, onomasiological comparisons also have their drawbacks. The most serious one is, of course, the identification of suitable phenomena (analogous and recurrent problems, challenges, situations in history) that may be compared. One must not go as far as Koselleck in claiming that human social and political history as a whole is characterized by certain 'repetitive structures' (*Wiederholungsstrukturen*) made possible by 'anthropological' constants. In his view those anthropological constants are, above all, the constant requirements of defining the 'ins' and the 'outs', those being 'above' or 'below', and those who come 'earlier' or 'later'.[66] As Jörn Leonhard points out in his chapter, looking for elementary oppositions like these in discourse may indeed be one point of departure for comparative studies in historical semantics, and we may safely do so without accepting Koselleck's argument that these oppositions have an 'anthropological' quality.

In more limited historical contexts – late nineteenth- and early twentieth-century Europe, for example – other more complex historical problems may be made objects of comparative onomasiological inquiries, for instance debates on electoral reforms, a topic of contestation all over Europe at that time. The difficulty then consists in defining a set of sufficiently abstract test questions that will allow us to *find* the relevant and equivalent vocabularies in the debates compared. In the case of debates on electoral reforms, test questions like the following come to mind: What were the self-descriptions used by those who claimed the right to political participation? How were those who claimed it called by their opponents? What were the legitimating formulas used by those who demanded participation? What were the legitimating formulas used to reject their demands? And so on. The result of such an inquiry would be a set of vocabularies in different national languages that served similar argumentative purposes and could, therefore, be considered as relevant and equivalent with respect to the problem, situation or debate in question.

Onomasiological and semasiological comparisons are by no means mutually exclusive research strategies. They can be used separately or consecutively, the one compensating the shortcomings of the other. Within our European conceptual histories series, both will have their place.

Conceptualizing Concepts

The interrelations and imbrications of concepts may be observed on more than one level. It is not only that concepts are clustered in fluid macro-arrangements such as those that characterize ideologies or professional political theory. Concepts are also located in segmented micro-arrangements that perform a variety of cultural roles, underpinning and mapping understandings that may be peculiar to one society but not to another. The setting of certain concepts in close – and conventionally durable – proximity to one another is one such instance. Thus, the well-worn phrase 'law and order' associates specific meanings of each of the paired concepts, so that the possible link between, say, law and reform is underplayed. Law is there to ensure order rather than, say, to enable innovation or redistribute wealth. The British conservative newspaper the *Daily Telegraph* has an online page on 'law and order' that preponderantly – and ironically – enumerates forms of social disorder, and which, on a particular day, included news on murder, financial fraud, internet trolling, compensation for a medical mishap, drink-driving, and road-rage.[67] But the implicit moralistic and punitive connotations of the pairing are evident.

Another, more recent, pairing, 'truth and reconciliation', narrows down the first concept to a category located in a conceptual terrain that is also populated by 'victimhood', 'historical grievances', 'accountability', 'apology' and 'conflict-resolution', and in which that unusual pairing begins to make sense. But it would only make sense in cultural milieus with strong legal frameworks that entertain the idea of restorative justice, with the invocation of ideologies that recognize ethnic and cultural pluralism, and with an incipient optimism about envisaged futures and the possibility of terminating deep-rooted ill feeling. There are at least ten countries that have set up 'truth and reconciliation' commissions, and many more that employ one term or the other in different pairings. The absence of such commissions in Europe, where in principle they might have been established in some instances, is itself a notable instance of a vacant conceptual space. Note also the ideational distance between that pairing and that of 'law and order', as well as the different future horizons, or levels of expectation, that each of them summons up.

At the level of metaphor, specific phrases have enormous impact on the conceptualization of the ideas and practices with which they are made to relate in professional and vernacular languages. A 'level playing field' – a phrase emanating from rugby or football in British public (i.e. private) schools – is closely connected to notions of fairness, yet is incomprehensible at first glance in many other languages. Indeed, one might ponder the almost complete absence of the word 'fairness' outside anglophone usage, except as a borrowed term (though, significantly, not the absence of the concept). At any rate, the metaphor implies that fairness is about the distribution of equal conditions to different social units, but certainly not about equal results, as the level field supports a competitive game in which there can be clear winners and losers. It underpins a limited, free-market, notion of equality of opportunity.

Likewise, 'holding the ring', in its original sense of keeping order with respect to a boxing or fighting event held within an enclosed space, suggests a norm of social conduct involving non-intervention in the substantive practice in which the combatants are engaged. Simultaneously and necessarily, however, it summons up the impartial monitoring of a practice that is incapable of being entirely self-regulating, and hence one that potentially invites a different kind of intervention, namely, one enabling the practice to run smoothly and correctly (if those are the appropriate phrases for the circumstances!). From there it is but a few steps on towards notions of ostensible state neutrality that update and proscribe state action in certain versions of liberalism.[68] These are instances of the conceptual peculiarities of specific societies with enormous spillover consequences for imagining and managing further sets of social relationships.

Phenomena such as the above alert one to the internal tensions built into conceptual structure. The potential totality they embrace – that is to say, the full interpretative range a concept can call up in its various temporal and spatial manifestations – is effectively inexpressible in concrete 'real-world' understandings and pronouncements, except as a long list of components that may be mutually incompatible. Whereas conceptual historians focus on this issue primarily as a question of continuities and discontinuities, it is simultaneously a question of cultural choice. Employing concepts is always an exercise in selectivity, whether deliberate or unintended, not an exercise in generating the totality of meanings. Disagreement, however gentle, over their connotations is invariably built into the very existence of social and political concepts, because conceptual indeterminacy is their norm, not the exception.[69] Hence the need for semantic parsimony in operationalizing a concept competes with acknowledging the full range of semantic abundance it has carried, is carrying, and can carry. That dualism sharply pinpoints the contest over meaning inherent in language.

There also are issues pertaining to the broader question of conceptual interdependence. In political studies it is now recognized that ideologies constitute clusters of political concepts in varying combinations of flexibility and durability.[70] We have become increasingly aware of the interconnections among concepts and of the limits of studying any concept in isolation from others. But their interrelationships are not best seen as entanglements. When conceptual historians speak of entanglement, that metaphor is more pertinent to cultures than to concepts. Were we to speak of conceptual entanglement, that would imply that intact and autonomous concepts get knotted up with others, as in the sense of having one's clothes caught when walking through a hedge. That kind of trapped enmeshment does not happen in the realm of concepts. Rather, the default position of concepts is that their micro-structure ensures overlap, the sharing of ideational elements, with other concepts. It is more a question of intertwinement. Here word and concept pull in different directions: the word attempts to define, to establish boundaries, even on occasion to finalize – a frequent attribute of political language – but concepts are notably boundary-lacking, or at least boundary-porous.

The potential inter-conceptuality of social and political concepts already exists *ab initio* in a given concept. Different concepts frequently share some components: think of 'power' and 'authority' sharing certain notions of inequality and hierarchy. Yet concurrently, it is a ubiquitous and arguably universal thought-practice that human minds engage in the invention and construction of boundaries – physical and symbolic – and interpret the world through them. Thinking in terms of boundaries is itself a real property of the human imagination, and central to the spatial and temporal mapping exercises people perform in trying to make sense of the world.[71] That is what makes conceptual history so interesting. When we attempt to tell the story of a political or social word, such as 'socialism', a purely lexical approach focusing on the word may run counter to the evidence that breaks socialism down not only into different socialisms, but charts its gravitation towards, or estrangement from, the multiple conceptual environments in which it is located temporally and spatially. Those ideational fields will crucially inform socialism's distinguishing properties and contribute to their constant mutation.

In the series launched by this volume we are keenly aware of the artificial, culturally constructed, nature of concepts. Boundaries and categories function as simplifiers. Naming a constellation of concepts and practices – say, 'liberalism' – is not tantamount to clearing a precise space for that term, but should be seen as a proposal to unpack a linguistic and ideational convention that, on closer inspection, may turn out to be quite slippery – and quite normally so. Both internal semantic pluralism and external cultural contexts and translations contribute to that conceptual malleability.

The requirements of scholarship therefore leave us with a conundrum: how much conceptual detail and diversification do we wish to establish and track down, and how much can we cope with? As a concept begins to accrue multiple meanings and is enriched – or impoverished – by interactions with intersecting concepts, we need a cut-off point, however flexible, so as not to mire ourselves in semantic overload. There is, after all, a limit to the usefulness of minute detail. That is where the notion of a pattern becomes useful. Just because there may be dozens of nuances in the way the concept of liberty is interpreted does not mean that we cannot classify some of them into intelligible categories. Consequently, the distinction to be made is not between the specific and the universal, or the multiple and the singular, but between the unique and the patterned. And there is a danger of over-exaggerating the unique, precisely because conceptual diversity under the umbrella of a given word does not necessarily signal that the particular meanings encompassed in that word have no conceptual affinities. We are always dealing with degrees of similarity, not with identity, unless there is a deliberate attempt to deceive and confuse – the starkest literary version of which is exemplified in George Orwell's *1984*.

In sum, an awareness of conceptual morphology points to new directions conceptual historians can take. In particular, we may distinguish between mass, line and field when analysing concepts. The focus on the concept as if it were a single macro-body of knowledge and understanding downplays the shifting intricacy of its internal semantic composition as a given, and not as imposed by external circumstances. A concept is not a single undifferentiated *mass* which, in the course of its contestation, may change into another single undifferentiated mass. And a concept does not only inhabit a narrative *line* that requires nothing else than the recounting of its own story as it mutates, but is located in complex semantic *fields* in which concepts inform and shape each other. Those features are attributes of language, not merely a result of contestation over time and across space. Identifying the subcomponents of any given concept, and the fluctuating patterns of adjacent conceptual interdependence, may make the task of the conceptual historian more onerous but, as that branch of history gains momentum, the increasing accuracy it can provide to the interpretative task cannot be ignored.

Finally, a word on silences and their impact on meaning. Conceptual historians share with political philosophers an emphasis on articulation, on word, text and utterance. Yet social and political discourses contain significant silences, absences and lacks. The concern here is not the deliberate silencing of individuals and groups – a pervasive occurrence throughout human history. It is, rather, a more intriguing and complex matter, as the unspeakable, the unthinkable, and the unconceptualizable play crucial parts in shaping political communication and debate.[72] Thus, when the concept of consent is understood by Locke also to emanate from verbal tacitness and indicated through performing activities, such as using the highway or taking lodgings, rather than through speech, is that another way of expressing concepts or is it a way of managing silences by superimposing an invented voice on them? In other instances, those superimposed voices may be the voices of future generations or of the war dead, for example. Does the absence, or disappearance, of verbal articulation and of vocabulary open a significant window into the conceptual universe of a society, to which conceptual historians should listen? The absence of conceptual articulation when it might be knowable and would be expected by interlocutors and scholars alike constitutes an interpretative challenge. Can concepts be expressed visually and performatively as well as verbally? Is the insertion of silences and hiatuses that interrupt verbalization a matter of interest to conceptual historians? And how do we approach political silence itself as a social concept? As for the unconceptualizable, here cultural comparisons may be helpful: the presence of a concept in one space- or time-zone and its absence in another can evoke awareness of conceptual lacks that may be crucially important in decoding the semantic potential of a conceptual cluster or chain. That is where comparison comes into its own, and that is where the location of concepts vis-à-vis each other, and the gaps exposed between them, gain enormously in significance.

The Disciplinary Environments of Conceptual History

Conceptual history may, tautologically speaking, have developed within the discipline of history, and to a large extent from the history of ideas, but it is anchored to and linked with intra-disciplinary and extra-disciplinary practices. In the field of history, conceptual historians often count Quentin Skinner as one of their own, his protestations to the contrary. But Skinner's work, spearheading what used to be referred to as the Cambridge school of intellectual history, focuses on a different intellectual enterprise, despite some similarities and overlaps. His emphasis is on intentionality and purpose, on speech-acts, rhetoric and performativity, and on explaining them in the context of the norms and available discourses that justify or challenge beliefs at a point in time and space.[73] It is principally an exercise not in the history of concepts or in detecting continuities or ruptures in their history but in the excavation of meaning, in particular the Austinian illocutionary rendering of an account of what people are doing in engaging in a discourse. That differs from what has primarily preoccupied conceptual historians, not least in its reliance on comparison as a tool of interpretation. What Skinner shares with conceptual historians is sensitivity to context, a curiosity about the particular, and an emphasis on interpretation, rather than the search for truth, a preoccupation with the right and/or the good, or the bestowal of abstract universalism on ideas, as is evidenced by many political philosophers.

That said, in Chapter 3 of this volume Kari Palonen has enlisted Skinner in support of giving discourse and rhetoric their due as instruments of performativity, addressing the question of explaining political action. As is becoming increasingly common among a new generation of conceptual historians, Palonen extends the purview of conceptual history from the concept to the debate – specifically, from the concept of politics to the manner in which it is put into practice in formal parliamentary debates – and utilizes it as a means to investigate conceptual change.[74]

Discourses are of course the focus of discourse analysis, once again placing the single concept within a broader field of terms, expressions and phrases. Directing its concern to language, discourse analysis eschews the concept in favour of linguistic structure – grammar and syntax – identifying deliberate and often concealed meaning contained in word order, frequency, emphasis and metaphor. One of its variants, critical discourse analysis (CDA), exhibits strong normative overtones usually avoided by conceptual historians, and aims at uncovering and combating those discourses that reinforce practices of social domination and discrimination. For some CDA advocates, language is a repository of oppressive power – a perspective that is not in itself misguided, but narrower than the one motivating conceptual historians.[75]

The study of ideologies is perhaps the closest of the disciplines external to conceptual history and, as Michael Freeden contends in Chapter 4 in this volume, intersects with it and can extend it. The analysis of ideologies as a morphological arrangement shares with conceptual history the insistence on the centrality of concepts, not of ideas or discourses. But it elaborates significantly on the casual references to concepts among conceptual historians. It does so through revealing the micro-structure of concepts, composed as they are of conceptions that are not necessarily mutually compatible and, even more so, not necessarily simultaneous. The 'simultaneity of the non-simultaneous' is not the perspective through which we actually access concepts as vernacular, everyday, users. In any given instance some of the past and present meanings of a concept are removed or suppressed in individual speech and text act. The conceptual historian is sensitized to the many layers of a concept, but the vast majority of its users are not. Instead, they engage in the inevitable practice of conceptual decontestation, when one conception of a concept is preferred and given preponderant weight, whether those users be politicians, journalists, bureaucrats or, yes, even scholars. In addition, as noted above, the study of ideologies does not consider concepts in isolation of one another but as always located in conceptual clusters or fields. One of the defining features of ideologies becomes the manner in which these diverse, conceptually decontested clusters compete over the control of public political language, for semantic domination smoothens the path to political control. Significantly, the selected meanings employed in speech and its textual and visual representation may be unintended as well as deliberate.[76]

Here decontestation links into the contingency question. Semantic polysemy is not just the function of temporal or spatial contexts but is built into the essential contestability of concepts, yet societies and individuals cannot endure a state of permanent contestability. Decontestation is a necessary condition of political decision making, an instrument that counters the inevitable contingency of conceptual structure with the alluring illusion of certainty. It achieves that through selecting one of the multiple conceptions contained in social and political concepts, assigning it cultural rather than logical priority, and attempting to associate it with the entire meaning the concept is expected to convey. The study of ideologies examines the application of concepts not only through comparative diachrony, and not only through a focus on how concepts change. It may significantly elaborate the practice of conceptual history by showing what is specifically political about certain concepts and how their subtle flexibility and detailed interface with contexts and events is brought to bear on overcoming the often-assumed gap between idea and practice. And it preaches the normality of conceptual fragmentation and reassembly, while demonstrating the balance of durability as well as change displayed by ideologies.

Finally, a few words on the relationship between political philosophy and conceptual history. Although the two disciplines centre on political and social thought, the mismatch between them seems striking. First, political philosophers and ethicists, and the more conventional practitioners of *Ideologiekritik*, pursue and justify normative value-preferences and tend to examine political ideas and arguments from the perspective of their truth value. In contrast, conceptual historians, historians of ideas of a Skinnerite disposition, and contemporary theories of ideology concentrate on interpretation and meaning, irrespective of the moral attractiveness or political efficacy of their subject matter. Second, the abstract, idealized, universalizing and, until recently, dominant versions of political philosophy – particularly though not exclusively in the anglophone world – have carried little rapport with conceptual historians due to their ahistoricity, their frequent allusion to teleological versions of progress that take change as given, rather than interrogating it, let alone the essentializing predilections of some moral philosophers. Third, the training of many political philosophers is in analytical precision – crucially, not only in their own research but as an expectation directed at the contents of their subject matter. Conceptual historians and students of ideology, to the contrary, acknowledge and even welcome the indeterminacy, slackness and messiness of the languages they explore. Fourth, political philosophers – in particular when they write their own history of ideas – tend to be highly elitist in their choice of voice and argument, though that feature may also be discerned among some conceptual historians. Thus the *Geschichtliche Grundbegriffe* has been criticized as being less socially inclusive and representative of the vocabularies circulating in a society than Koselleckian methodology would seem to indicate. There are still many cross-disciplinary conversations that are not taking place, to the detriment of all potential participants.

Concluding Remarks

Conceptual history is not an orthodoxy, but continuously reinvents itself. As it crosses national and disciplinary boundaries, as it enters different countries and linguistic spaces, as it is applied to new objects of study, the history of concepts is changing and will further develop in practice and theoretical outlook. Moreover, conceptual history necessarily reflects the changing nature of language itself and consequently the ways in which we approach and analyse language. Within this constant flux, there are nonetheless a number of durable assumptions that define conceptual history. Three of them should be emphasized here.

First, there is the idea that 'language matters'; or to put it in more elaborate terms, the idea that the sign systems we use to communicate among each other are neither arbitrary nor merely instruments completely disposable at our will. Rather, taken together, they make up a given structure that imposes certain limits on what is 'sayable' and 'doable' at any point in time.

Second, any conceptualization of the so-called 'reality outside' using language or other sign systems is an inseparable component of that very reality. It is therefore our conviction that the study of past and present politics, society, economics or culture cannot be conducted in any meaningful way without taking into account the conceptualizations of the past or present agents themselves.

Third, when studying language use in time, it is appropriate to distinguish between the linguistic *terms* (or words) of a language and the *concepts* referred to by these terms. As conceptual historians we are convinced that it is possible to make the history of these concepts a worthwhile object of inquiry of its own.

Finally, conceptual historians may also consider the social and political consequences of their enterprise, as Javier Fernández Sebastián suggests in his concluding chapter. In outlining the future perspectives of this book series, he particularly alerts us to the importance of conceptual history studies in the European contests of the present time.[77] One of the most valuable contributions conceptual history could offer in this context is to instil an awareness of the communicative patterns and conceptual challenges involved in the current processes of integration – or disintegration – of Europe.

Michael Freeden is Emeritus Professor of Politics, University of Oxford, and Professorial Research Associate, SOAS, University of London. His books include *The New Liberalism* (Oxford, 1978); *Liberalism Divided: A Study in British Political Thought, 1914–1939* (Oxford, 1986); *Ideologies and Political Theory: A Conceptual Approach* (Oxford, 1996); *Liberal Languages* (Princeton, 2005); and *The Political Theory of Political Thinking* (Oxford, 2013). He is founder-editor of the *Journal of Political Ideologies*, and a Fellow of the Academy of Social Sciences. He was awarded the Sir Isaiah Berlin Prize for Lifetime Contribution to Political Studies by the UK Political Studies Association, and the Medal for Science, Institute of Advanced Studies, Bologna University.

Willibald Steinmetz is Professor of Modern and Contemporary Political History at Bielefeld University and was director of the Collaborative Research Centre *The Political as a Communicative Space in History* (2004–2012). He has published extensively on political languages, parliamentary rhetoric and the use of sociopolitical concepts. His current research interests include the history of comparison as a practice in modern and contemporary Europe. Among his publications in English are *Writing Political History Today* (Campus, 2013), *Political Languages in the Age of Extremes* (OUP, 2011, 2nd edition 2012) and *The Force of Comparison* (Berghahn, 2019).

Notes

1. The use of digitized corpora for purposes that go beyond counting the frequency of words is still at an early stage. There are as yet no internationally agreed standards for extracting and interpreting semantic data from digitized sources. Publications are usually short and scattered across different websites, blogs, working paper series or specialized e-journals often difficult to trace for outsiders. Examples are: Ryan Heuser and Long L-Khac, *A Quantitative Literary History of 2,958 Nineteenth-Century British Novels: The Semantic Cohort*

Method, Pamphlets of the Stanford Literary Lab 4, May 2012; Alix Rule, Jean-Philippe Cointet and Peter S. Bearman, 'Lexical Shifts, Substantive Changes, and Continuity in State of the Union Discourse, 1790–2014', *Proceedings of the National Academy of Sciences (PNAS)*, 1 September 2015, vol. 112, no. 35, 10837–10844; Mike Kestemont, Folgert Karsdorp and Marten Düring, 'Mining the Twentieth Century's History from the Time Magazine Corpus', in Proceedings of the 8th Workshop on Language Technology for Cultural Heritage, Social Sciences, and Humanities, 14th Conference of the European Chapter of the Association for Computational Linguistics (EACL), Gothenburg, 26 April 2014, 67–70 (https://www.aclweb.org/anthology/W/W14/W14-06.pdf); we thank Sinai Rusinek (Jerusalem) for information on these examples. For insights on a project based on digitized medieval Latin texts see: Roberta Cimino, Tim Gelhaar and Silke Schwandt, 'Digital Approaches to Historical Semantics: New Research Directions at Frankfurt University', *Storicamente* 11(7) (2015) (http://storicamente.org/sites/default/images/articles/media/1901/histori cal_semantics.pdf); see also: Tim Geelhaar, 'Talking About *christianitas* at the Time of Innocent III (1198–1216). What Does Word Use Contribute to the History of Concepts?', *Contributions to the History of Concepts* 10(2) (2015), 7–28; Silke Schwandt, 'Virtus as a Political Concept in the Middle Ages', *Contributions to the History of Concepts* 10(2) (2015), 71–90.

2. Marion Eggert and Lucian Hölscher (eds), *Religion and Secularity: Transformations and Transfers of Religious Discourses in Europe and Asia* (Leiden and Boston: Brill, 2013); Thomas Dixon, *The Invention of Altruism: Making Moral Meanings in Victorian Britain* (Oxford: Oxford University Press, 2008); Ute Frevert et al., *Emotional Lexicons: Continuity and Change in the Vocabulary of Feeling 1700–2000* (Oxford: Oxford University Press, 2014); Daniel Béland and Klaus Petersen (eds), *Analysing Social Policy Concepts and Language: Comparative and Transnational Perspectives* (Bristol and Chicago: Policy Press, 2014). On the natural sciences, see the publications of the Centre for Literary and Cultural Research (ZFL) in Berlin at: http://www.zfl-berlin.org/interdisci plinary-conceptual-history.html. On science and technology studies, see Désirée Schauz, 'What is Basic Research? Insights from Historical Semantics', *Minerva* 52 (2014), 273–328.

3. Otto Brunner, Werner Conze and Reinhart Koselleck (eds), *Geschichtliche Grundbegriffe: Historisches Lexikon zur politisch-sozialen Sprache in Deutschland*, 9 vols (Stuttgart: Klett-Cotta, 1972–1997) (hereafter referred to as GG).

4. Reinhart Koselleck, 'A Response to Comments on the *Geschichtliche Grundbegriffe*', in Hartmut Lehmann and Melvin Richter (eds), *The Meaning of Historical Terms and Concepts* (German Historical Institute, Washington DC, 1996), 64.

5. Ibid., 62–63.

6. For a stimulating discussion of this issue, see Margrit Pernau and Imke Rajamani, 'Emotional Translations: Conceptual History beyond Language', *History and Theory* 55 (2016), 46–65.

7. The extensive publications and activities of the *Iberconceptos* network can be traced at http://www.iberconceptos.net/.
8. See Myoung-Kyu Park, 'Conceptual History in Korea: Its Development and Prospects', *Contributions to the History of Concepts* 7(1) (2012), 36–50. Park mainly refers to research done at Seoul National University; another project is underway at Hallym University.
9. For example on 'civilization', 'civility' in Asian and European contexts: Margrit Pernau et al., *Civilizing Emotions: Concepts in Nineteenth-Century Asia and Europe* (Oxford: Oxford University Press, 2015); see also Hagen Schulz-Forberg (ed.), *A Global Conceptual History of Asia, 1860–1940* (London: Pickering & Chatto, 2014); for new ventures in African conceptual history see the website of the project 'Concept Africa' at Helsinki University: http://www.helsinki.fi/conceptafrica/; cf. also: Margrit Pernau and Dominic Sachsenmaier (eds), *Global Conceptual History: A Reader* (London: Bloomsbury, 2016).
10. This is an argument put forward by Bo Stråth in 'Towards a Global Conceptual History'. Paper presented at the seminar 'National and Transnational Notions of the Social', Helsinki, 21 August 2008 (http://www.helsinki.fi/conceptafrica/theory_method_literature/towards_a_global_conceptual_history.html).
11. David Northrup, *How English Became the Global Language* (New York: Palgrave Macmillan, 2013); on twentieth-century projects to construct 'Basic English' as an easy-to-use global language, see Valeska Huber, 'Eine Sprache für alle: Basic English und die Grenzen der Globalgeschichte', in Boris Barth, Stefanie Gänger and Niels P. Petersson (eds), *Globalgeschichten: Bestandsaufnahme und Perspektiven* (Frankfurt and New York: Campus, 2014), 175–204.
12. Already published: Pasi Ihalainen, Cornelia Ilie and Kari Palonen (eds), *Parliament and Parliamentarism: A Comparative History of a European Concept* (New York and Oxford: Berghahn Books, 2016); volumes in preparation: Liberalism, Regions and Regionalism, Democracy, Asymmetric Counterconcepts.
13. The most comprehensive account of the *Grundbegriffe* project, its implications and follow-up projects remains Melvin Richter, *The History of Political and Social Concepts: A Critical Introduction* (New York and Oxford: Oxford University Press, 1995); on Koselleck's work in general, see Niklas Olsen, *History in the Plural: An Introduction to the Work of Reinhart Koselleck* (New York and Oxford: Berghahn Books, 2012).
14. He contributed articles on *Fortschritt* (progress), *Geschichte* (history), *Krise* (crisis) and *Revolution* (revolution) to the *Geschichtliche Grundbegriffe*; the article on *Krise* has been translated into English: Reinhart Koselleck, 'Crisis' [transl. by Michaela W. Richter], *Journal of the History of Ideas* 67 (2006), 357–400. His studies on many other temporal concepts are accessible in English: Reinhart Koselleck, *Futures Past: On the Semantics of Historical Time* [transl. by Keith Tribe] (Cambridge, MA and London: MIT Press, 1985); Reinhart Koselleck, *The Practice of Conceptual History: Timing History, Spacing Concepts* [transl. by Todd Samuel Presner et al.] (Stanford, CA: Stanford University Press, 2002).

15. Steinmetz, below 63–95.
16. See Stefanie Stockhorst, 'Novus ordo temporum: Reinhart Kosellecks These von der Verzeitlichung des Geschichtsbewußtseins durch die Aufklärungshistoriographie in methodenkritischer Perspektive', in Hans Joas and Peter Vogt (eds), *Begriffene Geschichte: Beiträge zum Werk Reinhart Kosellecks* (Berlin: Suhrkamp, 2011), 359–86; Jan Marco Sawilla, 'Geschichte und Geschichten zwischen Providenz und Machbarkeit. Überlegungen zu Reinhart Kosellecks Semantik historischer Zeiten', in ibid., 387–422; Stefan Jordan, 'Die Sattelzeit – Transformation des Denkens oder revolutionärer Paradigmenwechsel?', in Achim Landwehr (ed.), *Frühe Neue Zeiten: Zeitkonzepte zwischen Reformation und Revolution* (Bielefeld: transcript, 2012), 373–88; Christian Geulen, 'Plädoyer für eine Geschichte der Grundbegriffe des 20. Jahrhunderts', *Zeithistorische Forschungen / Studies in Contemporary History* 7 (2010), 79–97.
17. Jörn Leonhard, 'Erfahrungsgeschichten der Moderne: Von der komparativen Semantik zur Temporalisierung europäischer Sattelzeiten', in Joas and Vogt, *Begriffene Geschichte*, 423–48; from a Dutch perspective: Pim den Boer, 'The Historiography of German *Begriffsgeschichte* and the Dutch Project of Conceptual History', in Iain Hampsher-Monk, Karin Tilmans and Frank van Vree (eds), *History of Concepts: Comparative Perspectives* (Amsterdam: Amsterdam University Press, 1998), 21–22.
18. Jordheim, below 47–62.
19. But see some case studies for early modern Sweden, the Netherlands and late medieval Italy and France: Bo Lindberg, *Den antika skevheten: Politiska ord och begrepp i det tidig-moderna Sverige* (Stockholm: Kungl. Vitterhets Historie och Antikvitetsakad, 2006); Pim den Boer, 'La vie politique selon Stevin et Juste Lipse', in Pim den Boer and Catherine Secretan (eds), *Simon Stevin. De la vie civile, 1590* (Lyon: ENS Éditions, 2005), 191–99; Ulrich Meier, Martin Papenheim and Willibald Steinmetz, *Semantiken des Politischen: Vom Mittelalter bis ins 20. Jahrhundert* (Göttingen: Wallstein, 2012), 18–38.
20. Marjanen, below 139–74.
21. We adopt the notions of 'decision space' and 'identity space' from: Charles S. Maier, 'Transformations of Territoriality 1600–2000', in Gunilla Budde, Sebastian Conrad and Oliver Janz (eds), *Transnationale Geschichte: Themen, Tendenzen und Theorien* (Göttingen: Vandenhoeck & Ruprecht, 2006), 35; linguistic spaces may or may not coincide with identity spaces, and therefore it seems appropriate to add that category.
22. Mishkova and Trencsényi, below 212–35.
23. On German conceptualizations of 'the West', see Martina Steber and Riccardo Bavaj (eds), *Germany and 'The West': The History of a Modern Concept* (New York: Berghahn Books, 2015).
24. For a similar approach, cf. Mathias Albert et al. (eds), *Transnational Political Spaces: Agents – Structures – Encounters* (Frankfurt and New York: Campus, 2009).

25. For exemplary studies see: Emma Major, *Madam Britannia: Women, Church, and Nation, 1712–1812* (Oxford: Oxford University Press, 2012); Thomas Dixon, *Weeping Britannia: Portrait of a Nation in Tears* (Oxford: Oxford Unversity Press, 2015); Bettina Brandt, *Germania und ihre Söhne: Repräsentationen von Nation, Geschlecht und Politik in der Moderne* (Göttingen: Vandenhoeck & Ruprecht, 2010); the trilogy by Maurice Agulhon, *Marianne au combat: l'imagerie et la symbolique républicaines de 1789 à 1880* (Paris: Flammarion, 1979), *Marianne au pouvoir: l'imagerie et la symbolique républicaines de 1880 à 1914* (Paris: Flammarion, 1989), *Les métamorphoses de Marianne: l'imagerie et la symbolique républicaines de 1914 à nos jours* (Paris: Flammarion, 2001); and Lynn Hunt, *The Family Romance of the French Revolution* (Berkeley: University of California Press, 1992).
26. See the classic study by James C. Scott, *Seeing Like a State: How Certain Schemes to Improve the Human Condition Have Failed* (New Haven, CT and London: Yale University Press, 1998). Cf. also: Ulrike von Hirschhausen, 'People that Count: The Imperial Census in Nineteenth- and Early Twentieth-Century Europe and India', in Jörn Leonhard and Ulrike von Hirschhausen (eds), *Comparing Empires: Encounters and Transfers in the Long Nineteenth Century* (Göttingen: Vandenhoeck & Ruprecht, 2011), 145–70; Mehmet Hacisalihoglu, 'Borders, Maps and Censuses: The Politicization of Geography and Statistics in the Multi-ethnic Ottoman Empire', in ibid., 171–210.
27. Neumann, below 236–62.
28. Cf. also Martin Schulze Wessel, 'Religion, Politics and the Limits of Imperial Integration: Comparing the Habsburg Monarchy and the Russian Empire', in Leonhard and Hirschhausen, *Comparing Empires*, 337–58; Azmi Özcan, 'Imperial Legitimacy and Unity: The Tradition of the Caliphate in the Ottoman Empire', in ibid., 373–84.
29. On the practice of translation in the Habsburg monarchy, see Michaela Wolf, *Die vielsprachige Seele Kakaniens: Übersetzen und Dolmetschen in der Habsburgermonarchie 1848 bis 1918* (Cologne: Böhlau, 2012).
30. Stenius, below 263–80.
31. Elias Canetti, *The Tongue Set Free: Remembrance of a European Childhood* [transl. from the German by Joachim Neugroschel] (London: Deutsch, 1988), 4–5.
32. Ibid., 24.
33. Ibid., 10.
34. Ibid., 27.
35. Peter Burke, *Languages and Communities in Early Modern Europe* (Cambridge: Cambridge University Press, 2004); for similar stories on the Ottoman/Greek city of Salonica, see Mark Mazower, *Salonica, City of Ghosts: Christians, Muslims, and Jews, 1430–1950* (London: Harper Collins, 2004).
36. On the standardization of French: Francine Mazière, 'La langue et l'État: l'Académie française', in Sylvain Auroux et al. (eds), *History of the Language Sciences / Geschichte der Sprachwissenschaften / Histoire des sciences du langage*, vol. 1 (Berlin and New York: de Gruyter, 2000), 852–62; the volume also con-

tains chapters on the standardization and purification efforts in many other European countries.
37. Javier Fernández Sebastián and Juan Francisco Fuentes (eds), *Diccionario político y social del siglo XIX español* (Madrid: Alianza Editorial, 2002); Javier Fernández Sebastián et al. (eds), *Diccionario político y social del siglo XX español* (Madrid: Alianza Editorial, 2008).
38. For interesting reflections on this – with examples from non-European contexts: Anna Wierzbicka, *Imprisoned in English: The Hazards of English as a Default Language* (Oxford: Oxford University Press, 2014).
39. For a study on the linguistic structure of *'Türkendeutsch'*, see: Yazgül Şimşek, 'Formen und strukturelle Merkmale des Sprachgebrauchs türkisch-deutscher Jugendlicher aus Berlin', in Barbara Jańczak, Konstanze Jungbluth and Harald Weydt (eds), *Mehrsprachigkeit aus deutscher Perspektive* (Tübingen: Narr, 2012), 155–79.
40. See the following publications: Peter A. Kraus, *A Union of Diversity: Language, Identity and Polity-Building in Europe* (Cambridge: Cambridge University Press, 2008); Anne Lise Kjaer and Silvia Adamo (eds), *Linguistic Diversity and European Democracy* (Farnham: Ashgate, 2011); Johann Wolfgang Unger, Michał Krzyżanowski and Ruth Wodak (eds), *Multilingual Encounters in Europe's Institutional Spaces* (London: Bloomsbury, 2014).
41. Kontler, below 197–211.
42. Douglas Howland, 'The Predicament of Ideas in Culture: Translations and Historiography', *History and Theory* 42 (2003), 45.
43. The challenges of translating political theory are discussed in: Martin J. Burke and Melvin Richter (eds), *Why Concepts Matter: Translating Social and Political Thought* (Leiden and Boston: Brill, 2012).
44. An exemplary study is: Fania Oz-Salzberger, *Translating the Enlightenment: Scottish Civic Discourse in Eighteenth-Century Germany* (Oxford: Clarendon Press, 1995); see also: Willibald Steinmetz, 'Gemeineuropäische Tradition und nationale Besonderheiten im Begriff der "Mittelklasse". Ein Vergleich zwischen Deutschland, Frankreich und England', in Reinhart Koselleck and Klaus Schreiner (eds), *Bürgerschaft: Rezeption und Innovation der Begrifflichkeit vom Hohen Mittelalter bis ins 19. Jahrhundert* (Stuttgart: Klett-Cotta, 1994), 161–236 (comparing several translations of Aristotle's Politics into English, German and French around 1800).
45. See, for example, Margrit Pernau, *Ashraf into Middle Classes: Muslims in Nineteenth-Century Delhi* (New Delhi: Oxford University Press, 2013).
46. For Skinner's reassessment of his own rhetorical approach in the light of conceptual history: Quentin Skinner, 'Retrospect: Studying Rhetoric and Conceptual Change', in Skinner, *Visions of Politics, vol. 1: Regarding Method* (Cambridge: Cambridge University Press, 2002), 175–87; for Palonen's take on 'moves' in argument, see Kari Palonen, *Quentin Skinner: History, Politics, Rhetoric* (Cambridge: Polity, 2003), 35–37; see also Kari Palonen's chapter in this volume (Chapter 3).

47. Cf. Melvin Richter, 'Introduction: Translation, the History of Concepts and the History of Political Thought', in Burke and Richter, *Why Concepts Matter*, 11–13.
48. Cf. Michael Werner and Bénédicte Zimmermann, 'Beyond Comparison: Histoire Croisée and the Challenge of Reflexivity', *History and Theory* 45 (2006), 30–50.
49. For an elaboration of these arguments, see Hagen Schulz-Forberg, 'Introduction. Global Conceptual History: Promises and Pitfalls of a New Research Agenda', in Schulz-Forberg, *Global Conceptual History of Asia*, 1–24.
50. Denis Diderot, 'Encyclopédie', in Denis Diderot and Jean Le Rond d'Alembert (eds), *Encyclopédie, ou Dictionnaire raisonné des Sciences, des Art et des Métiers*, vol. 5 (Paris, 1755), 637 [By comparing a nation's vocabulary at different times one can form an idea of its progress].
51. Hagen Schulz-Forberg rejects even this kind of inquiry as 'not a useful question' (Schulz-Forberg, 'Introduction', 8), but we beg to differ. To observe that certain semantic fields in different languages have become more similar (converge) or dissimilar (diverge) over time, for whatever reasons, is not tantamount to maintaining that speakers of one linguistic community have been in any way superior to (or more 'modern' than, or a model for) the speakers of the other language. Whether such statements on convergence and divergence are useful or not depends entirely on what it is we want to know.
52. Good examples, restricted to philosophical vocabulary, can be inspected in: Barbara Cassin (ed.), *Vocabulaire Européen des philosophies: Dictionnaire des intraduisibles* (Paris: Le Robert/Seuil, 2004).
53. Bo Stråth, 'Comparative Conceptual History and Global Translations: An Outline of a Research Agenda', in Rudolf de Cillia et al. (eds), *Discourse, Politics, Identity: Festschrift für Ruth Wodak* (Tübingen: Stauffenburg Verlag, 2010), 216.
54. Koselleck's final thoughts on this issue can be found in an interview he gave in April 2005: Javier Fernández Sebastián and Juan Francisco Fuentes, 'Conceptual History, Memory, and Identity: An Interview with Reinhart Koselleck', *Contributions to the History of Concepts* 2 (2006), 110–12.
55. Ibid., 111; see also: Reinhart Koselleck, Ulrike Spree and Willibald Steinmetz, 'Drei bürgerliche Welten: Zur vergleichenden Semantik der bürgerlichen Gesellschaft in Deutschland, England und Frankreich', in Reinhart Koselleck, *Begriffsgeschichten: Studien zur Semantik und Pragmatik der politischen und sozialen Sprache* (Frankfurt: Suhrkamp, 2006), 413.
56. Cf. Ingrid Schierle, 'Semantiken des Politischen im Russland des 18. Jahrhunderts', in Willibald Steinmetz (ed.), *"Politik": Situationen eines Wortgebrauchs im Europa der Neuzeit* (Frankfurt and New York: Campus, 2007), 226–47; Walter Sperling, 'Vom Randbegriff zum Kampfbegriff: Semantiken des Politischen im ausgehenden Zarenreich (1850–1917)', in ibid., 248–88.
57. On conceptualizations of 'politics' in India and China, see: Sudipta Kaviraj, 'On the Historicity of "the Political": *Rajaniti* and Politics in Modern Indian Thought', in Michael Freeden and Andrew Vincent (eds), *Comparative Political*

Thought: Theorizing Practices (London: Routledge, 2013), 24–39; Rana Mitter, 'Communism, Confucianism, and Charisma: The Political in Modern China', in ibid., 60–69; for Italy and France, see Meier, Papenheim and Steinmetz, *Semantiken des Politischen*.

58. For early modern Russian conceptualizations of 'politics' before the term 'politics' was introduced, see Mikhail Krom, '"Die Sache des Herrschers und des Landes": Das Aufkommen der öffentlichen Politik in Russland im 16. und 17. Jahrhundert', in Steinmetz, *"Politik"*, 206–25.
59. Dipesh Chakrabarty, *Provincializing Europe: Postcolonial Thought and Historical Difference* (Princeton and Oxford: Princeton University Press, 2000), 9.
60. For interesting examples from non-European contexts, see Carol Gluck and Anna Lowenhaupt Tsing (eds), *Words in Motion: Toward a Global Lexicon* (Durham, NC and London: Duke University Press, 2009).
61. See Jörn Leonhard, *Liberalismus: zur historischen Semantik eines europäischen Deutungsmusters* (Munich: Oldenbourg, 2001).
62. Reinhart Koselleck, 'Einleitung', in GG, vol. 1 (Stuttgart: Klett-Cotta, 1972), xxii; Reinhart Koselleck, 'Introduction and Prefaces to the Geschichtliche Grundbegriffe' [transl. by Michaela Richter], *Contributions to the History of Concepts* 6 (2011), 19.
63. Reinhart Koselleck, 'The Historical-Political Semantics of Asymmetric Counterconcepts', in Koselleck, *Futures Past*, 159–97.
64. Kirill Postoutenko is preparing a volume in this book series on 'Hellenes and Barbarians'; cf. also Kay Junge and Kirill Postoutenko (eds), *Asymmetrical Concepts after Koselleck: Historical Semantics and Beyond* (Bielefeld: transcript, 2014).
65. The procedure described here is an extension of what is usually meant by 'onomasiology'.
66. Reinhart Koselleck, 'Structures de répétition dans la langue et dans l'histoire', *Revue de Synthèse* 5(1) (2006), 159–67.
67. http://www.telegraph.co.uk/news/uknews/law-and-order/ (accessed 6 March 2015).
68. For some of the arguments, see R.E. Goodin and A. Reeve (eds), *Liberal Neutrality* (London: Routledge, 1989).
69. For a literary understanding of conceptual indeterminacy, see G. Schwab, 'Introduction', in *Imaginary Ethnographies: Literature, Culture, and Subjectivity* (New York: Columbia University Press, 2012), 1–23. For a discussion of indeterminacy and ambiguity in a political context, see M. Freeden, *The Political Theory of Political Thinking: The Anatomy of a Practice* (Oxford: Oxford University Press, 2013), 69–79.
70. See M. Freeden, L.T. Sargent and M. Stears (eds), *The Oxford Handbook of Political Ideologies* (Oxford: Oxford University Press, 2013).
71. A helpful discussion is to be found in D. Newman, 'Borders and Bordering: Towards an Interdisciplinary Dialogue', *European Journal of Social Theory* 9 (2006), 171–86.

72. See M. Freeden, 'Silence in Political Theory: A Conceptual Predicament', *Journal of Political Ideologies* 20 (2015), 1–9.
73. A succinct rendering of Quentin Skinner's position can be found in his 'Truth, Belief and Interpretation' lecture given at the University of Poznán, 23 October 2014. A similar version is on YouTube, published on 1 December 2014.
74. See also K. Palonen, *Politics and Conceptual Histories: Rhetorical and Temporal Perspectives* (Baden-Baden: Nomos/Bloomsbury, 2014).
75. For differing approaches, see T.A. van Dijk, *Discourse Studies: A Multidisciplinary Introduction*, 2nd edn (London and Thousand Oaks, CA: Sage Publications, 2011); N. Fairclough, *Language and Power*, 2nd edn (Harlow: Longman, 2001); R. Wodak, *The Discourse of Politics in Action* (Houndmills, Basingstoke: Palgrave Macmillan, 2009).
76. For a concise exposition, see Michael Freeden, 'The Morphological Analysis of Ideology', in Freeden, Sargent and Stears, *Oxford Handbook of Political Ideologies*, 115–37.
77. Javier Fernández Sebastián, below 281–297.

References

Agulhon, Maurice, *Marianne au combat: l'imagerie et la symbolique républicaines de 1789 à 1880* (Paris: Flammarion, 1979)

———, *Marianne au pouvoir: l'imagerie et la symbolique républicaines de 1880 à 1914* (Paris: Flammarion, 1989)

———, *Les métamorphoses de Marianne: l'imagerie et la symbolique républicaines de 1914 à nos jours* (Paris: Flammarion, 2001)

Albert, Mathias, et al. (eds), *Transnational Political Spaces: Agents – Structures – Encounters* (Frankfurt and New York: Campus, 2009)

Béland, Daniel, and Klaus Petersen (eds), *Analysing Social Policy Concepts and Language: Comparative and Transnational Perspectives* (Bristol and Chicago: Policy Press, 2014)

Brandt, Bettina, *Germania und ihre Söhne: Repräsentationen von Nation, Geschlecht und Politik in der Moderne* (Göttingen: Vandenhoeck & Ruprecht, 2010)

Brunner, Otto, Werner Conze and Reinhart Koselleck (eds), *Geschichtliche Grundbegriffe: Historisches Lexikon zur politisch-sozialen Sprache in Deutschland*, 9 vols (Stuttgart: Klett-Cotta, 1972–1997)

Burke, Martin J., and Melvin Richter (eds), *Why Concepts Matter: Translating Social and Political Thought* (Leiden and Boston: Brill, 2012)

Burke, Peter, *Languages and Communities in Early Modern Europe* (Cambridge: Cambridge University Press, 2004)

Canetti, Elias, *The Tongue Set Free: Remembrance of a European Childhood* [transl. from the German by Joachim Neugroschel] (London: Deutsch, 1988)

Cassin, Barbara (ed.), *Vocabulaire Européen des philosophies: Dictionnaire des intraduisibles* (Paris: Le Robert/Seuil, 2004)

Chakrabarty, Dipesh, *Provincializing Europe: Postcolonial Thought and Historical Difference* (Princeton and Oxford: Princeton University Press, 2000)

Cimino, Roberta, Tim Gelhaar and Silke Schwandt, 'Digital Approaches to Historical Semantics: New Research Directions at Frankfurt University', *Storicamente* 11(7) (2015) (http://storicamente.org/sites/default/images/articles/media/1901/historical_semantics.pdf)

den Boer, Pim, 'The Historiography of German *Begriffsgeschichte* and the Dutch Project of Conceptual History', in Iain Hampsher-Monk, Karin Tilmans and Frank van Vree (eds), *History of Concepts: Comparative Perspectives* (Amsterdam: Amsterdam University Press, 1998), 13–22

———, 'La vie politique selon Stevin et Juste Lipse', in Pim den Boer and Catherine Secretan (eds), *Simon Stevin. De la vie civile, 1590* (Lyon: ENS Éditions, 2005), 191–99

Diderot, Denis, 'Encyclopédie', in Denis Diderot and Jean Le Rond d'Alembert (eds), *Encyclopédie, ou Dictionnaire raisonné des Sciences, des Art et des Métiers*, vol. 5 (Paris, 1755), 635–48

Dixon, Thomas, *The Invention of Altruism: Making Moral Meanings in Victorian Britain* (Oxford: Oxford University Press, 2008)

———, *Weeping Britannia: Portrait of a Nation in Tears* (Oxford: Oxford Unversity Press, 2015)

Eggert, Marion, and Lucian Hölscher (eds), *Religion and Secularity: Transformations and Transfers of Religious Discourses in Europe and Asia* (Leiden and Boston: Brill, 2013)

Fairclough, Norman, *Language and Power*, 2nd edn (Harlow: Longman, 2001)

Fernández-Sebastián, Javier, and Juan Francisco Fuentes (eds), *Diccionario político y social del siglo XIX español* (Madrid: Alianza Editorial, 2002)

———, 'Conceptual History, Memory, and Identity: An Interview with Reinhart Koselleck', *Contributions to the History of Concepts* 2 (2006), 99–127

Freeden, Michael, 'The Morphological Analysis of Ideology', in Michael Freeden, Lyman Tower Sargent and Marc Stears (eds), *The Oxford Handbook of Political Ideologies* (Oxford: Oxford University Press, 2013), 115–37

———, *The Political Theory of Political Thinking: The Anatomy of a Practice* (Oxford: Oxford University Press, 2013)

———, 'Silence in Political Theory: A Conceptual Predicament', *Journal of Political Ideologies* 20 (2015), 1–9

Freeden, Michael, Lyman Tower Sargent and Marc Stears (eds), *The Oxford Handbook of Political Ideologies* (Oxford: Oxford University Press, 2013)

Frevert, Ute, et al., *Emotional Lexicons: Continuity and Change in the Vocabulary of Feeling 1700–2000* (Oxford: Oxford University Press, 2014)

Geelhaar, Tim, 'Talking About *christianitas* at the Time of Innocent III (1198–1216). What Does Word Use Contribute to the History of Concepts?', *Contributions to the History of Concepts* 10(2) (2015), 7–28

Geulen, Christian, 'Plädoyer für eine Geschichte der Grundbegriffe des 20. Jahrhunderts', *Zeithistorische Forschungen / Studies in Contemporary History* 7 (2010), 79–97

Gluck, Carol, and Anna Lowenhaupt Tsing (eds), *Words in Motion: Toward a Global Lexicon* (Durham, NC and London: Duke University Press, 2009)

Goodin, Robert E., and Andrew Reeve (eds), *Liberal Neutrality* (London: Routledge, 1989)

Hacisalihoglu, Mehmet, 'Borders, Maps and Censuses: The Politicization of Geography and Statistics in the Multi-ethnic Ottoman Empire', in Jörn Leonhard and Ulrike von Hirschhausen (eds), *Comparing Empires: Encounters and Transfers in the Long Nineteenth Century* (Göttingen: Vandenhoeck & Ruprecht, 2011), 171–210

Heuser, Ryan, and Long L-Khac, *A Quantitative Literary History of 2,958 Nineteenth-Century British Novels: The Semantic Cohort Method*, Pamphlets of the Stanford Literary Lab 4, May 2012

Howland, Douglas, 'The Predicament of Ideas in Culture: Translations and Historiography', *History and Theory* 42 (2003), 45–60

Huber, Valeska, 'Eine Sprache für alle: Basic English und die Grenzen der Globalgeschichte', in Boris Barth, Stefanie Gänger and Niels P. Petersson (eds), *Globalgeschichten: Bestandsaufnahme und Perspektiven* (Frankfurt and New York: Campus, 2014), 175–204

Hunt, Lynn, *The Family Romance of the French Revolution* (Berkeley: University of California Press, 1992)

Ihalainen, Pasi, Cornelia Ilie and Kari Palonen (eds), *Parliament and Parliamentarism: A Comparative History of a European Concept* (New York and Oxford: Berghahn Books, 2016)

Jordan, Stefan, 'Die Sattelzeit – Transformation des Denkens oder revolutionärer Paradigmenwechsel?', in Achim Landwehr (ed.), *Frühe Neue Zeiten: Zeitkonzepte zwischen Reformation und Revolution* (Bielefeld: transcript, 2012), 373–88

Junge, Kay, and Kirill Postoutenko (eds), *Asymmetrical Concepts after Koselleck: Historical Semantics and Beyond* (Bielefeld: transcript, 2014)

Kaviraj, Sudipta, 'On the Historicity of "the Political": *Rajaniti* and Politics in Modern Indian Thought', in Michael Freeden and Andrew Vincent (eds), *Comparative Political Thought: Theorizing Practices* (London: Routledge, 2013), 24–39

Kestemont, Mike, Folgert Karsdorp and Marten Düring, 'Mining the Twentieth Century's History from the Time Magazine Corpus', in Proceedings of the 8th Workshop on Language Technology for Cultural Heritage, Social Sciences, and Humanities, 14th Conference of the European Chapter of the Association for Computational Linguistics (EACL), Gothenburg, 26 April 2014, 67–70 (https://www.aclweb.org/anthology/W/W14/W14-06.pdf)

Kjaer, Anne Lise, and Silvia Adamo (eds), *Linguistic Diversity and European Democracy* (Farnham: Ashgate, 2011)

Koselleck, Reinhart, 'Einleitung', in Otto Brunner, Werner Conze and Reinhart Koselleck (eds), *Geschichtliche Grundbegriffe: Historisches Lexikon zur politisch-sozialen Sprache in Deutschland*, vol. 1 (Stuttgart: Klett-Cotta, 1972), xiii–xxvii

———, *Futures Past: On the Semantics of Historical Time* [transl. by Keith Tribe] (Cambridge, MA and London: MIT Press, 1985)

———, 'The Historical-Political Semantics of Asymmetric Counterconcepts', in Reinhart Koselleck, *Futures Past: On the Semantics of Historical Time* [transl. by Keith Tribe] (Cambridge, MA and London: MIT Press, 1985), 159–97

———, 'A Response to Comments on the *Geschichtliche Grundbegriffe*', in Hartmut Lehmann and Melvin Richter (eds), *The Meaning of Historical Terms and Concepts* (German Historical Institute, Washington DC, 1996), 59–70

———, *The Practice of Conceptual History: Timing History, Spacing Concepts* [transl. by Todd Samuel Presner et al.] (Stanford, CA: Stanford University Press, 2002)

———, 'Crisis' [transl. by Michaela W. Richter], *Journal of the History of Ideas* 67 (2006), 357–400

———, 'Structures de répétition dans la langue et dans l'histoire', *Revue de Synthèse* 5(1) (2006), 159–67

———, 'Introduction and Prefaces to the Geschichtliche Grundbegriffe' [transl. by Michaela Richer], *Contributions to the History of Concepts* 6 (2011), 1–37

Koselleck, Reinhart, Ulrike Spree and Willibald Steinmetz, 'Drei bürgerliche Welten: Zur vergleichenden Semantik der bürgerlichen Gesellschaft in Deutschland, England und Frankreich', in Reinhart Koselleck, *Begriffsgeschichten: Studien zur Semantik und Pragmatik der politischen und sozialen Sprache* (Frankfurt: Suhrkamp, 2006), 402–61

Kraus, Peter A., *A Union of Diversity: Language, Identity and Polity-Building in Europe* (Cambridge: Cambridge University Press, 2008)

Krom, Mikhail, '"Die Sache des Herrschers und des Landes": Das Aufkommen der öffentlichen Politik in Russland im 16. und 17. Jahrhundert', in Willibald Steinmetz (ed.), *"Politik": Situationen eines Wortgebrauchs im Europa der Neuzeit* (Frankfurt and New York: Campus, 2007), 206–25

Leonhard, Jörn, *Liberalismus: zur historischen Semantik eines europäischen Deutungsmusters* (Munich: Oldenbourg, 2001)

———, 'Erfahrungsgeschichten der Moderne: Von der komparativen Semantik zur Temporalisierung europäischer Sattelzeiten', in Hans Joas and Peter Vogt (eds), *Begriffene Geschichte: Beiträge zum Werk Reinhart Kosellecks* (Berlin: Suhrkamp, 2011), 423–48

Lindberg, Bo, *Den antika skevheten: Politiska ord och begrepp i det tidig-moderna Sverige* (Stockholm: Kungl. Vitterhets Historie och Antikvitetsakad, 2006)

Maier, Charles S., 'Transformations of Territoriality 1600–2000', in Gunilla Budde, Sebastian Conrad and Oliver Janz (eds), *Transnationale Geschichte: Themen, Tendenzen und Theorien* (Göttingen: Vandenhoeck & Ruprecht, 2006), 32–55

Major, Emma, *Madam Britannia: Women, Church, and Nation, 1712–1812* (Oxford: Oxford University Press, 2012)

Mazière, Francine, 'La langue et l'État: l'Académie française', in Sylvain Auroux et al. (eds), *History of the Language Sciences / Geschichte der Sprachwissenschaften / Histoire des sciences du langage*, vol. 1 (Berlin and New York: de Gruyter, 2000), 852–62

Mazower, Mark, *Salonica, City of Ghosts: Christians, Muslims, and Jews, 1430–1950* (London: Harper Collins, 2004)

Meier, Ulrich, Martin Papenheim and Willibald Steinmetz, *Semantiken des Politischen: Vom Mittelalter bis ins 20. Jahrhundert* (Göttingen: Wallstein, 2012)

Mitter, Rana, 'Communism, Confucianism, and Charisma: The Political in Modern China', in Michael Freeden and Andrew Vincent (eds), *Comparative Political Thought: Theorizing Practices* (London: Routledge, 2013), 60–69

Newman, D., 'Borders and Bordering: Towards an Interdisciplinary Dialogue', *European Journal of Social Theory* 9 (2006), 171–86

Northrup, David, *How English Became the Global Language* (New York: Palgrave Macmillan, 2013)

Olsen, Niklas, *History in the Plural: An Introduction to the Work of Reinhart Koselleck* (New York and Oxford: Berghahn Books, 2012)

Özcan, Azmi, 'Imperial Legitimacy and Unity: The Tradition of the Caliphate in the Ottoman Empire', in Jörn Leonhard and Ulrike von Hirschhausen (eds), *Comparing Empires: Encounters and Transfers in the Long Nineteenth Century* (Göttingen: Vandenhoeck & Ruprecht, 2011), 373–84

Oz-Salzberger, Fania, *Translating the Enlightenment: Scottish Civic Discourse in Eighteenth-Century Germany* (Oxford: Clarendon Press, 1995)

Palonen, Kari, *Quentin Skinner: History, Politics, Rhetoric* (Cambridge: Polity, 2003)

———, *Politics and Conceptual Histories: Rhetorical and Temporal Perspectives* (Baden-Baden: Nomos/Bloomsbury, 2014)

Park, Myoung-Kyu, 'Conceptual History in Korea: Its Development and Prospects', *Contributions to the History of Concepts* 7(1) (2012), 36–50

Pernau, Margrit, *Ashraf into Middle Classes: Muslims in Nineteenth-Century Delhi* (New Delhi: Oxford University Press, 2013)

Pernau, Margrit, et al., *Civilizing Emotions: Concepts in Nineteenth-Century Asia and Europe* (Oxford: Oxford University Press, 2015)

Pernau, Margrit, and Imke Rajamani, 'Emotional Translations: Conceptual History beyond Language', *History and Theory* 55 (2016), 46–65

Pernau, Margrit, and Dominic Sachsenmaier (eds), *Global Conceptual History: A Reader* (London: Bloomsbury, 2016)

Richter, Melvin, *The History of Political and Social Concepts: A Critical Introduction* (New York and Oxford: Oxford University Press, 1995)

———, 'Introduction: Translation, the History of Concepts and the History of Political Thought', in Martin J. Burke and Melvin Richter (eds), *Why Concepts Matter: Translating Social and Political Thought* (Leiden and Boston: Brill, 2012), 1–40

Rule, Alix, Jean-Philippe Cointet and Peter S. Bearman, 'Lexical Shifts, Substantive Changes, and Continuity in State of the Union Discourse, 1790–2014', *Proceedings* of the National Academy of Sciences (PNAS), 1 September 2015, vol. 112, no. 35, 10837–10844

Sawilla, Jan Marco, 'Geschichte und Geschichten zwischen Providenz und Machbarkeit: Überlegungen zu Reinhart Kosellecks Semantik historischer Zeiten', in Hans Joas and Peter Vogt (eds), *Begriffene Geschichte: Beiträge zum Werk Reinhart Kosellecks* (Berlin: Suhrkamp, 2011), 387–422

Schauz, Désirée, 'What is Basic Research? Insights from Historical Semantics', *Minerva* 52 (2014), 273–328

Schierle, Ingrid, 'Semantiken des Politischen im Russland des 18. Jahrhunderts', in Willibald Steinmetz (ed.), *"Politik": Situationen eines Wortgebrauchs im Europa der Neuzeit* (Frankfurt and New York: Campus, 2007), 226–47

Schulze Wessel, Martin, 'Religion, Politics and the Limits of Imperial Integration: Comparing the Habsburg Monarchy and the Russian Empire', in Jörn Leonhard and Ulrike von Hirschhausen (eds), *Comparing Empires: Encounters and Transfers in the Long Nineteenth Century* (Göttingen: Vandenhoeck & Ruprecht, 2011), 337–58

Schulz-Forberg, Hagen (ed.), *A Global Conceptual History of Asia, 1860–1940* (London: Pickering & Chatto, 2014)

——, 'Introduction. Global Conceptual History: Promises and Pitfalls of a New Research Agenda', in Hagen Schulz-Forberg (ed.), *A Global Conceptual History of Asia, 1860–1940* (London: Pickering & Chatto, 2014), 1–24

Schwab, Gabriele, 'Introduction', in *Imaginary Ethnographies: Literature, Culture, and Subjectivity* (New York: Columbia University Press, 2012), 1–23

Schwandt, Silke, 'Virtus as a Political Concept in the Middle Ages', *Contributions to the History of Concepts* 10(2) (2015), 71–90

Scott, James C., *Seeing Like a State: How Certain Schemes to Improve the Human Condition Have Failed* (New Haven, CT and London: Yale University Press, 1998)

Şimşek, Yazgül, 'Formen und strukturelle Merkmale des Sprachgebrauchs türkisch-deutscher Jugendlicher aus Berlin', in Barbara Jańczak, Konstanze Jungbluth and Harald Weydt (eds), *Mehrsprachigkeit aus deutscher Persepktive* (Tübingen: Narr, 2012), 155–79

Skinner, Quentin, 'Retrospect: Studying Rhetoric and Conceptual Change', in Quentin Skinner, *Visions of Politics, vol. 1: Regarding Method* (Cambridge: Cambridge University Press, 2002), 175–87

Sperling, Walter, 'Vom Randbegriff zum Kampfbegriff: Semantiken des Politischen im ausgehenden Zarenreich (1850–1917)', in Willibald Steinmetz (ed.), *"Politik": Situationen eines Wortgebrauchs im Europa der Neuzeit* (Frankfurt and New York: Campus, 2007), 248–88

Steber, Martina, and Riccardo Bavaj (eds), *Germany and 'The West': The History of a Modern Concept* (New York: Berghahn Books, 2015)

Steinmetz, Willibald, 'Gemeineuropäische Tradition und nationale Besonderheiten im Begriff der "Mittelklasse": Ein Vergleich zwischen Deutschland, Frankreich und England', in Reinhart Koselleck and Klaus Schreiner (eds), *Bürgerschaft:*

Rezeption und Innovation der Begrifflichkeit vom Hohen Mittelalter bis ins 19. Jahrhundert (Stuttgart: Klett-Cotta, 1994), 161–236

Stockhorst, Stefanie, 'Novus ordo temporum: Reinhart Kosellecks These von der Verzeitlichung des Geschichtsbewußtseins durch die Aufklärungshistoriographie in methodenkritischer Perspektive', in Hans Joas and Peter Vogt (eds), *Begriffene Geschichte: Beiträge zum Werk Reinhart Kosellecks* (Berlin: Suhrkamp, 2011), 359–86

Stråth, Bo, 'Towards a Global Conceptual History'. Paper presented at the seminar 'National and Transnational Notions of the Social', Helsinki, 21 August 2008 (http://www.helsinki.fi/conceptafrica/theory_method_literature/towards_a_global_conceptual_history.html)

——, 'Comparative Conceptual History and Global Translations: An Outline of a Research Agenda', in Rudolf de Cillia et al. (eds), *Discourse, Politics, Identity: Festschrift für Ruth Wodak* (Tübingen: Stauffenburg Verlag, 2010), 213–20

Unger, Johann Wolfgang, Michał Krzyżanowski and Ruth Wodak (eds), *Multilingual Encounters in Europe's Institutional Spaces* (London: Bloomsbury, 2014)

van Dijk, Teun A., *Discourse Studies: A Multidisciplinary Introduction*, 2nd edn (London and Thousand Oaks, CA: Sage Publications, 2011)

von Hirschhausen, Ulrike, 'People that Count: The Imperial Census in Nineteenth- and Early Twentieth-Century Europe and India', in Jörn Leonhard and Ulrike von Hirschhausen (eds), *Comparing Empires: Encounters and Transfers in the Long Nineteenth Century* (Göttingen: Vandenhoeck & Ruprecht, 2011), 145–70

Werner, Michael, and Bénédicte Zimmermann, 'Beyond Comparison: Histoire Croisée and the Challenge of Reflexivity', *History and Theory* 45 (2006), 30–50

Wierzbicka, Anna, *Imprisoned in English: The Hazards of English as a Default Language* (Oxford: Oxford University Press, 2014)

Wodak, Ruth, *The Discourse of Politics in Action* (Houndmills, Basingstoke: Palgrave Macmillan, 2009)

Wolf, Michaela, *Die vielsprachige Seele Kakaniens: Übersetzen und Dolmetschen in der Habsburgermonarchie 1848 bis 1918* (Cologne: Böhlau, 2012)

Chapter 1

Europe at Different Speeds

Asynchronicities and Multiple Times in European Conceptual History

Helge Jordheim

Over the last ten years or so we have become used to the idea and the formulation of 'Europe at different speeds', in terms of a conceptual and rhetorical response to the fact that the process of European integration towards the goals of a common constitution, a common monetary system, a common foreign policy and so on have not unfolded in the homogenous, linear or synchronous way that was planned. The idea was a reaction to the unwelcome fact that some of the EU countries were unwilling or indeed unable to keep up with the pace of integration set by some of the core countries.[1] The global financial crisis of 2008, the Greek debt crisis and, most recently, the refugee or migration crisis, which hit Europe in the autumn of 2015, have contributed to unveiling the multiple and often conflicting tempi and rhythms, the delays and accelerations in the eurozone, and turned them into a challenge that the EU can no longer ignore. In reaction to a speech by the then British prime minister, David Cameron, in which he announced a revision of the United Kingdom's membership of the EU, the Swedish foreign minister, Carl Bildt, warned: 'Flexibility sounds fine, but if you open up to a 28-speed Europe, at the end of the day there is no Europe at all, just a mess'.[2]

In other, less politically loaded contexts, this 'mess' is called historical contingency, or simply history. The phrase 'Europe at different speeds' is not just a rhetorical device, but corresponds to a fundamental historical reality: that the European countries have indeed never moved at the same speed, or, in other words, they have never been completely synchronous in their social or political development. On the contrary, the history of Europe, including the history of Europe's relationship to the world at large, has always been a history of temporal differences, of forwardness and backwardness, relative to a given goal, of lagging behind and catching up, relative to a perceived avant-garde. Europe has 'multiple modernities', to use a term from S.N. Eisenstadt, or, with an even more general argument, is less dependent on the highly ambiguous idea of 'modernity': Europe has 'multiple times'.[3] Often these various political and social times are even recognized and given labels – such as the German *Sonderweg*, the Nordic model, British insularity – or they are documented, for instance in the EU progress reports.

Multiple Times and Conceptual History

To map how this multiplicity of temporal experiences and horizons, synchronicities and asynchronicities, structures of repetition, and moments of acceleration manifests itself at the level of language is a central task of conceptual history. In the introduction to *Geschichtliche Grundbegriffe* Koselleck famously claims that concepts are both 'indicators' and 'factors' of historical change.[4] In other words, concepts both indicate the speed and rhythm of historical movement specific to a community and contribute to accelerating and slowing down the same movement. At present, the most striking example in a European context is the concept of 'crisis'. On the one hand, 'crisis' indicates to what extent Europeans feel exposed to rapid and accelerating political and social changes that can no longer be anticipated or planned other than in terms of 'risk' and 'risk management'. On the other hand, 'crisis' has also become a factor in bringing about and accelerating the very same changes by evoking both ideas of non-reversible change and imminent catastrophe about to change the face of Europe forever, and ideas of a permanent condition of crisis, which is fast becoming the new and future condition of normality in Europe. For example, the more economists and financial analysts kept warning of a looming financial collapse, prophesized in the concept of 'crisis', the more the collapse itself was accelerated, due to the increasing lack of trust in financial markets. Rhetorically as well as temporally, the advent of the global financial crisis at the beginning of the twenty-first century can be understood as analogous to the political crisis of the French Revolution almost two hundred years earlier. In both cases, the use of a specific language, to which the concept of 'crisis' belongs, made the collapse of the existing political, social and economic order more or less unavoidable, or at least much more imminent.[5] Specific usages and meanings of 'crisis' in different European countries prior to and during the financial crisis, the Greek debt crisis, and the current migration crisis indicate different levels of urgency and immediacy as well as a larger historical narrative, framing the specific moment of crisis. In this way the concepts serve as prisms of asynchronic relations between national and regional histories, but also between different social or political communities, and between different fields and practices of knowledge.

To the extent that concepts are both indicators and factors of historical change, they are interwoven with diverse historical processes, evoking, unfolding and projecting very different pasts and futures. To write the history of these concepts, we have to understand those processes that cannot be reduced to mere empty chronologies, ready-made frameworks for the ordering of lives and events, but have their own times, temporal structures and narratives, as well as principles of succession and causation. To these specific 'historical times' belong, according to Koselleck, 'progress, decline, acceleration or delay, the not-yet and the not-anymore, the before and the after, the too-early and the too-late, the situation and the duration'.[6] As opposed to the categories of chronological time – days, months, years, decades and centuries – with which we cannot grasp the actual temporal dynamics of history, these concepts are 'adequate to historical events and processes' and should thus be deployed to understand historical change and the role of concepts.[7]

The perspective laid out above ties in with, and spells out, certain arguments made in the chapters by Michael Freeden, Willibald Steinmetz and Henrik Stenius. In his suggestion for an expansion of the history of concepts to cover the history of ideologies, Freeden proceeds from the idea that there are indeed 'variable tempi of change' in European history. In similar vein, Steinmetz questions the idea of a single modernity – or *Sattelzeit*, in Koselleck's terms – and argues that this kind of periodization cannot serve as a framework for a European conceptual history. Rejecting the idea of a foundational phase of modernity synchronizing all European cultures and languages, he breaks down the idea of the *Sattelzeit* into processes unfolding at different times in different nations, thus introducing the idea of possible asynchronicities. Following Koselleck in his refusal of the theory of a *Sonderweg*, which applied to one nation, Germany, deviating from the presumed standard path of political and social self-realization for European nations, Steinmetz opens up the possibility of a Europe of multiple paths, all having their particular temporal logics and structures.[8] Finally, the following discussion of the 'asynchronicities' of European history should be read in close conjunction with Stenius's discussion of the asymmetries between language use in centres and peripheries, a discussion that opposes the idea of both spatial and temporal homogeneity within Europe. In many historical instances, temporal differences are indeed due to distances in space, as when we consider the time it takes for a usage or meaning of a concept to travel from the core to the periphery.

To a certain extent, our 'European Conceptual History' book series sets out to realize a set of ambitions central to the project of *Geschichtliche Grundbegriffe*, which the lexicon itself was never really able to make good on. In the theoretical and methodological outlines introducing the first volume, Koselleck explicitly states that one task of conceptual history is to explore the 'synchronicity of the non-synchronous [*die Gleichzeitigkeit des Ungleichzeitigen*] contained in the concepts'.[9] However, in most of the actual articles contained in the lexicon, the long diachronic perspective, ranging from Antiquity to the postwar era, and the success of the idea of the *Sattelzeit*, conceived by Koselleck as a mere 'heuristic tool',[10] led contributors to overlook both synchronicities and asynchronicities, and rather give priority to new and singular conceptual meanings and usages coming to the fore for the first time in a historical event or interval. For our book series a somewhat different time span has been chosen, starting in the late Middle Ages and reaching out into the twenty-first century. At the same time as the time span has been changed, leaving out the origins of Western political culture and language in Greek and Roman Antiquity, the geographical and linguistic range has been expanded to include the entire European continent, both cores and peripheries. As a consequence of these revisions, the project has been given a focus that is less dominated by diachronic narratives and more interested in synchronic entanglements and networks – or to put it another way, in which there is a better balance between diachronic and synchronic perspectives than in the *Geschichtliche Grundbegriffe*. Methodologically, this means that the project will include not only the chronological succession of conceptual meanings and usages in national histories, but also the mapping of synchronicities and asynchronicities across a wide variety of national and cultural traditions and spaces on the European continent, exploring, indeed, a 'Europe at different speeds'.

In the following I will discuss three sets of asynchronicities, or *Ungleichzeitigkeiten*: first, what we could refer to as 'asynchronicities of meaning' that emerge when meanings aggregated in concepts invoke different historical origins, durations, 'spaces of experience' and 'horizons of expectation', to use Koselleck's terms;[11] second, 'asynchronicities of use', when concepts are used in contexts that have their own inherent temporalities, or historical times, through being experienced as moments of progress or decline, of rapid change or permanence, as advanced or belated, as critical or ordinary; third and finally, 'asynchronicities of linguistic plurality', which are involved in both of the already mentioned categories, but demand other methodological approaches and thus need to be discussed separately.

Asynchronicities of Meaning

Conceptual history is not interested in language as linguistic, philosophical or even mathematical abstraction, but always in its uses – in words used in specific historical contexts by specific individuals – to achieve specific goals. But this pragmatic and rhetorical dimension, cultivated to perfection in the studies by Quentin Skinner and others working in the contextualist mode of conceptual history, only allows for one kind of time, the present of a particular moment, the absolutely synchronous present. As soon as we shift our attention to the semantic dimension of language usage, however, the synchronous present begins to break up in different rhythms, tempi and durations. According to Koselleck, what separates a concept from a word is the plurality of meanings that have aggregated over time and can never be reduced to a single definition.[12] On the one hand, these meanings belong to the 'synchronic event',[13] or, in the ubiquitous contextualist idiom, to the context, and can be accessed by means of synchronic analysis, which Koselleck compares to traditional historical *Quellenkritik*, 'source criticism'.[14] On the other hand, concepts come with their own, inherent 'diachronic structures', a 'surplus of meaning', to use Ricoeur's term, which is also a 'surplus of time' in the sense that it cannot be reduced to pure synchronicity or presentism, but contains other times that reach beyond, often far beyond, the immediacy of the present.[15] In modern Europe, a concept such as 'revolution', for example in the case of the so-called 'Orange Revolution' that took place in Ukraine during the winter of 2004/05, never only refers to, or addresses, the context of usage or the situation at hand, but unfolds a 'space of experience' reaching back to the French Revolution and the Communist revolutions, as well as a 'horizon of expectation' that extends way into a more or less utopian future to be anticipated and dreaded at the same time. Among the meanings evoked by the concept 'revolution', some are more than two hundred years old: for example, revolution as the attempt to overthrow an all-powerful elite on behalf of something called 'the people', and imbue the concept with duration and stability. Other meanings, for example revolution as a conflict of generations, have a much shorter history and seem to shift, gaining new and shedding old semantic elements, at a much faster rate.

In order to assemble and organize these multiple meanings and multiple times, Koselleck has suggested the analytic term *Zeitschichten* – 'temporal layers of different durations and different origins' which are inherent in every meaning or usage of a concept, or, with a phrase from the introduction to *Geschichtliche Grundbegriffe*, 'the multiplicity of temporal layers dating from chronologically different times'.[16] There is always more than one temporality at work when a concept is used and, often, these temporalities are in themselves not synchronous with each other. That a concept is asynchronous with itself, however, does not mean that it is less effective in a political or a social context. From traditional German *Begriffsgeschichte* we know that concepts always have more than one meaning, due to their ability to summarize and even synthesize long historical processes and experiences.[17] To these multiple meanings, however, we have to add the presence of multiple temporalities. In this way we are able to approach what Steinmetz refers to as semantic change on the 'micro-diachronic' (situational) or synchronic (comparative) level, which in the articles of *Geschichtliche Grundbegriffe* is all but eclipsed by the long-term diachronic perspective and the emphasis on the emergence of modernity during the *Sattelzeit*.

In many of the concepts to be studied in this book series there are semantic elements that date back to Greek and Roman Antiquity, and that are still at work, still repeated, intentionally or unintentionally, every time a concept like 'democracy', 'tyranny' or 'empire' is used. However, the same concepts also hold far more recent semantic components that are subject to continuous, rapid and even accelerating changes, from one context or one rhetorical situation to another. Take for instance the semantics of toleration, both religious and political, which represents a fundamental part of the Western concept of 'democracy', but which for the last decade seems to have shed old meanings and taken on new ones at a very high speed – to the extent that the exact meaning and possible impact of the concept 'toleration' can only be grasped through an investigation of the particular rhetorical situation in which the concept is used (e.g. the struggle over the use of the *hijab* in French schools, or the fight for gay rights in Norway). At the same time, however, the prominence of such accelerating conceptual changes does not mean that the continuity or the 'structures of repetition' – to use another Kosolleckian phrase,[18] which in this case refers to the semantics of toleration inherited from the Enlightenment – disappears; on the contrary, they may be just as important and effective, only in a different mode.

When Koselleck employs the geological metaphor of 'temporal layers' he seems to assume that older, more stable meanings, changing at a slower pace, are operating at a deeper, more hidden level in the semantic structure of a concept, whereas the more recent, even new or contemporary meanings are much more visible, prominent and effective.[19] As striking and analytically helpful as the *Zeitschichten* metaphor might be, there is a risk that in using it we end up overlooking the political changes generated not by the most recent and immediately recognizable meanings but by the oldest and presumably most hidden and unnoticeable ones. Indeed, there are many recent examples of how the oldest semantic components, going back to Greek or Roman Antiquity, or even further, resurface as rhetorically effective tools in a political situation. To understand the return of the concept of 'empire' as a positive self-description in American foreign policy debates at the beginning of the twenty-first century, or more precisely, in a specific kind of discourse taken up by American Republicans to confer new legitimacy on American military engagements across the globe, it is not sufficient to explore the uppermost temporal layer, in which political events and rhetorical interventions like these are usually contained. What 'surfaces' at that moment, I would argue, is the ancient Roman semantics of 'empire', a semantics that is more stable and durable than both traditional American anti-imperialism going back to the eighteenth-century Wars of Independence, and Communist criticism of imperialism as the ultimate stage of capitalism.[20] In this and other examples, the inference from *Ungleichzeitigkeit* to a vertical, archaeological or even geological structure, where the upper layers appear as new and fast changing, whereas the lower are seen as older and changing at a much slower pace, might prevent us from noticing what is really at work in a particular political situation. Often – as in the example of 'empire' – the impact of certain concepts seems to imply the inverse: that older meanings and usages of concepts are neither deep nor hidden but break through the surface to dominate current discourse. An alternative to analysing concepts according to their temporal layers is to suggest that every concept has its own temporal structure, pointing back at a specific past as well as gesturing towards an expected future in order to make sense of, and intervene in, the present.

Asynchronicities of Use

In his path-breaking book *Imagined Communities*, first published in 1983, the historian and political scientist Benedict Anderson famously argues that the idea of the nation as an 'imagined community' is based on the experience of a shared synchronized time, emerging from the eighteenth century onwards in new media and genres like the novel and the newspaper.[21] As a counterpoint to these synchronized and synchronizing experiences, however, European modernity also features radical asynchronicities between different communities: political, generational, ethnic and professional, to mention only a few. In a similar way, we can observe asynchronicities between fields and practices of knowledge, such as medicine, engineering, theology, philology and literature. Taking my cue from these parallel, often competing and even conflicting, temporal communities, the second set of asynchronicities are what can be called 'the asynchronicities of use', by which concepts used by specific communities or used as part of specific knowledge practices appear to be out of step with other concepts, and even with themselves.

Jean-Jacques Rousseau in his discourse on the arts and the sciences from 1750 already pointed at the asynchronic relationship between the arts and the sciences on the one hand, and morality and politics on the other. Progress in one field, he argued, did not necessarily imply progress in the other; rather the opposite. Rousseau's somewhat 'untimely' intervention, to use a term from one of his avid readers and successors, Friedrich Nietzsche, drew attention to the conflict between the innovations of the scientific or artistic avant-garde and the struggle for political and moral order and stability, which would become one of the characteristics of Western *Kulturkritik* and is based on an experience of asynchronicity between discourses as well as between communities. These 'asynchronicities of use' can be observed in at least two different ways: on the one hand, when the same concepts are used in different and even conflicting discourses – for example, 'progress' or 'future', which seem to contain and deploy very different temporal meanings and structures when used in the context of art and aesthetics than in the context of social and political organization, as shown by Rousseau; on the other hand, when discursive communities and practices, in which there are divergent temporal horizons at work, deploy different concepts to address similar events or experiences – for example, when abortion is justified in terms of 'freedom of choice' by one community and condemned as 'infanticide' by another.

Early attempts to conceptualize these and similar kinds of asynchronicities are found in works by the art historian Wilhelm Pinder, the philosopher Ernst Bloch, and the sociologist Karl Mannheim, who all evoke the trope of the *Gleichzeitigkeit des Ungleichzeitigen*, 'the synchronicity of the non-synchronous' in order to analyse the temporal divergences between different groups in society. In the case of Pinder, the trope is used to conceptualize asynchronicities in art history between generations of artists who produce their art at the same time, but still belong to different epochs of art history, explaining why Romanticist or Classicist art is still produced in the Modernist era.[22] Bloch, on the other hand, evokes the idea of *Ungleichzeitigkeit* to explain the rise of National Socialism, which succeeded in mobilizing the already existing asynchronicities in German society between technological and industrialist avant-garde and rural backwardness.[23] Mannheim, finally, expanded Pinder's analysis of generations in art history to encompass sociocultural patterns in society and dynamics of socialization more broadly, which leave different groups or communities out of step with each other.[24] None of the three authors, however, paid particular attention to language as the vehicle of conflicting temporal experiences and horizons.

In every historical situation or context, members of different communities and participants in different knowledge practices will invest concepts with temporal structures and experiences, depending on what they want to achieve with it. These 'asynchronicities of use' can be made the object of analysis based on theories and methods from conceptual history. If 'use' is understood intentionally and in terms of speech acts, the analysis will move more in the direction of the rhetorical analysis practised by Skinner, for whom the dominating temporal figure is *paradiastole*, 'rhetorical redescription'.[25] If, on the other hand, 'use' is taken to refer to collective practices and shared usages within a group or a community, when a multitude of speech acts, intentions, experiences and events combine to produce meaning, the analysis will have more in common with the fundamentally hermeneutical and sociohistorical approaches pioneered by Koselleck, for whom time is stretched between 'space of experience' and 'horizon of expectation'. One interesting example of the latter is the use of the concept of 'civilization' at the beginning of the twentieth century. Across Europe, 'civilization' had already, and for some time, been a staple in pedagogical and philosophical discourses, which in the tradition starting from Rousseau and the *Kulturkritik* take a critical stance on the ideologies of scientific and technological progress, and evoke conservative, even nostalgic visions of an idealized past, when mankind was really civilized. At the same time, however, advances in biology and eugenics combined with a strong idea of social planning and engineering, produced another concept of 'civilization', which was much more future-oriented and positivist, in the Comtean sense of the term, and with a strong element of Social Darwinism, culminating in the racial state of the Third Reich.[26] Contrasts and conflicts between these discourses or ideologies – which were combined and moulded together in German National Socialism – can be analysed in terms of semantic dislocations in the concept of 'civilization' brought about by 'asynchronicities of use'.

However, as soon as we start discussing how the usages of concepts and their inherent temporal horizons vary between communities and discourses, not just within the 'imagined community' that we call 'nation', often evoking a concurrence of geographical, cultural and linguistic borders, but across the entire European geographic and cultural space, another element comes up, which significantly increases the possibilities for asynchronicities both of use and meaning: language, or rather linguistic plurality. In one way the 'asynchronicities of linguistic plurality', which is discussed in the last part of this chapter, could have been treated under 'meaning' or 'use', but partly because these asynchronicities obviously involve both semantic and pragmatic elements, combined in various ways, and partly to refer to discussions in this book about conceptual history and translation, I will treat them separately.

Asynchronicities of Linguistic Plurality

As we have seen, the different speeds of European conceptual history unfold in part within one and the same language, in part within a plurality of languages. As soon as we expand our horizon to include not one single national language but many, the temporal structures, or to use François Hartog's term, the 'regimes of historicity', tend to multiply across the geographical and cultural spaces that make up 'Europe'.[27] The conceptual history of Europe does not unfold along one linear, homogenous or progressive chronology, as in the Hegelian idea of *Weltgeschichte*, but according to a great variety of national, cultural and regional temporalities – not necessarily in terms of different formal chronologies, but in terms of experienced time, 'spaces of experience' and 'horizons of expectation'. In other words, there is no reason to assume that the concept of 'progress', used around 1800, synthesized the same experiences and expectations when it was employed in Germany, Scandinavia or somewhere on the Balkan peninsula. Furthermore, if we choose to study a concept such as 'freedom' or 'liberalism' we will soon recognize how these concepts, used in different linguistic contexts, are never completely synchronous, that their meanings and ways of usage do not address the same temporal or historical framework, and hence that European conceptual histories are full of asynchronicities caused, or at least amplified, by linguistic plurality.

The question, then, is how to proceed to study these asynchronicities, without explicitly or implicitly making one particular temporal structure or regime, unfolding within one particular cultural and linguistic nation, the 'standard' or 'normal' one, whereas all others are perceived as deviations, *Sonderwege*, following slower, or even faster, historical rhythms. One suggestion would be to start from the entanglements of different national languages and cultures – in other words, the actual interconnections of a *histoire croisée*. Entanglements and interconnections are events that take place within more than one political, social and semantic framework and thus serve to establish a transnational moment of historical experience, a synchronic moment, or even a transnational rhetorical situation, in which certain concepts are used in specific ways. In the moment when transnational events, commercial exchanges, wars, diplomatic scandals, natural catastrophes and so on are conceptualized, they are assimilated into different national histories with different spaces of experiences and horizons of expectation, with different structures of acceleration, progress and decline inherent in them. In this way the synchronicity of the event transforms into a series of linguistic asynchronicities, which can now be identified as such, due to their common origin in a transnational, entangled event. In response to the disclosure of previously hidden US government information by Edward Snowden, concepts such as 'unlawful surveillance', 'patriotism', 'trust', 'allied nations' and 'global espionage' were renegotiated across the entire Western world, and reframed in other national and global narratives with their own specific temporal structures. Obviously, what was perceived by the American government, at least initially, as a setback for global peace, was seen by others as a giant leap towards a more open global society.

Another way to study the asynchronicities of concepts across different languages in the European space is to focus on conceptual transfers – concepts on the move between various linguistic and cultural contexts. This may serve to map how a concept changes its inherent temporality when it moves – or rather, when it is being moved – from one context to another.[28] Breaking with the traditional idea that conceptual history can only be practised within a monolingual framework, because concepts are so intimately linked to the historical experience of the actors using them, concepts can also be seen as the product of ongoing translation practices, which are not unidirectional, from one language and one culture to another, nor can they be conceived in terms of originals and copies, or semantic losses. On the contrary, to study a concept in translation means to follow that concept into a new semantic field and see how this specific field contributes to the meaning of the concept, thus not only learning something about the concept itself, but also about the context into which it has been introduced, and even about the context it came from.[29] In the process of translation the coexistence, the simultaneity of linguistic equivalents and thus of different cultures, is established by means of translation practices, either written or oral. At a closer look, however, this chronological simultaneity exhibits a phenomenological and pragmatic multiplicity of times, invested in the same concept. For example, at the end of the nineteenth century, Norwegian *dannelse*, German *Bildung* and French *civilization* came into use as linguistic equivalents in contemporary debates. But the discourses of which they were part were by no means in step with each other: whereas the German *Bildung* rapidly transformed into a slogan for the young German *Reich*, the Norwegian *dannelse* remained intrinsically linked to pedagogical discourse, by which a certain form of naturalist primitivism was challenged by the process of civilization, and the French *civilization* set out to negotiate the conflicts between civic universalism and cultural supremacism. Thus, the pasts, presents and futures evoked by the three concepts represented obvious asynchronicities within the synchronicity of translation practices.

Conclusion: Tools of Synchronization

Finally, in addition to conceptual entanglements and transfers, studies in conceptual history can focus on what could be called 'the tools of synchronization', that is the procedures and genres used to overcome the asynchronicities between languages and cultures, and to synchronize them, to give them a shared social rhythm.[30] In a European context one of the most obvious recent examples is the many different EU treaties signed – or not signed – by the member countries in order to set the pace and the rhythm for the development of the European Union. From the 1957 Rome treaty to the 2007 Lisbon treaty, these documents were used to align political, social and economic processes in the member countries to the extent that both short-term and long-term developments should follow the same historical patterns, go through the same phases and reach the same milestones. Language, more specifically concepts in these treaties, are used to bring about this temporal alignment, to overcome the asynchronicities of a Europe in which the nations naturally move at different speeds. One obvious example is the so-called 'pillar structure' introduced in the Maastricht treaty of 1992. In this document the semantics of 'pillars', more precisely 'the three pillars of the European Union', were adopted in order to make Europeans think in terms of synchronizing the political, social and financial rhythms of the member states, first and foremost by giving them a common, stable basis and starting point, from which no one would lag behind.

Paradoxically, the phrase 'Europe at different speeds' was in itself an attempt to come to terms with the asynchronicities of European integration. It was coined by the Belgian prime minister, Leo Tindemans, back in 1976, in the so-called Tindemans Report, presenting some initial steps towards an institutional renewal of the European Economic Community (EEC), to counteract the looming stagnation. Envisaging an expansion of the powers of the EEC's existing institutions, Tindemans suggested the possibility of different speeds for member states, depending on their political ambitions and their practical opportunities for progress, hence on their specific national rhythms of political, social and financial development. Even though the idea was rejected politically, it became an important feature of the European Monetary System of 1979.[31] Since then, the phrase 'Europe at different speeds' has served as a conceptual reminder of the asynchronicities at work in European history, as well as the attempts to find ways of containing them semantically.

Helge Jordheim is Professor of Cultural History, University of Oslo, and Visiting Professor, New York University (2015–16). He received his PhD in German literature from the University of Oslo in 2006 for a work on genre and politics in eighteenth-century Germany (*Der Staatsroman im Werk Wielands und Jean Pauls*, Tübingen, 2007). He has published extensively on eighteenth-century intellectual culture in Europe. His latest book is a global history of the concepts of civility and civilization, written with an international team of scholars (*Civilizing Emotions*, 2015). At present he is writing a book on the cultural history of time in the eighteenth century.

Notes

1. Jan Fagerberg and Bart Verspagen, 'Heading for Divergence: Regional Growth in Europe Reconsidered', *Journal of Common Market Studies* 3(34) (1996), 431–48.
2. http://www.spiegel.de/international/europe/cameron-finds-little-support-on-continent-for-referendum-on-eu-a-879441.html (3 Dec. 2014).
3. S.N. Eisenstadt, 'Multiple Modernities', *Daedalus* 1(129) (2000), 1–29; Helge Jordheim, 'Against Periodization: On Koselleck's Theory of Multiple Temporalities', *History and Theory* 51 (2012), 151–71; Helge Jordheim, 'Multiple Times and the Work of Synchronization', *History and Theory* 53 (2014), 498–518.
4. Reinhart Koselleck, 'Einleitung', in Otto Brunner, Werner Conze and Reinhart Koselleck (eds), *Geschichtliche Grundbegriffe: Historisches Lexikon zur politisch-sozialen Sprache in Deutschland*, vol. 1 (Stuttgart: Klett-Cotta, 1972), xiv.
5. Reinhart Koselleck, *Kritik und Krise: Eine Studie zur Pathogenese der bürgerlichen Welt* (Frankfurt/Main: Suhrkamp 1973).
6. Reinhart Koselleck, 'Geschichte, Geschichten und formale Zeitstrukturen' (1973), in Koselleck, *Vergangene Zukunft. Zur Semantik geschichtlicher Zeiten* (Frankfurt/Main: Suhrkamp, 1979), 133.
7. Ibid.
8. Reinhart Koselleck, 'Deutschland – eine verspätete Nation' (1998), in Koselleck, *Zeitschichten. Studien zur Historik* (Frankfurt/Main: Suhrkamp, 2000), 359–79.
9. Koselleck, 'Einleitung', in *Geschichtliche Grundbegriffe*, xxi.
10. Ibid., xv; see also Reinhart Koselleck, 'A Response to Comments on the *Geschichtliche Grundbegriffe*', in Hartmut Lehmann and Melvin Richter (eds), *The Meaning of Historical Terms and Concepts* (Washington, DC: German Historical Institute, 1996), 59–70.
11. Reinhart Koselleck, '"Erfahrungsraum" und "Erwartungshorizont" – zwei historische Kategorien' (1975), in Koselleck, *Vergangene Zukunft*, 349–75.
12. Koselleck, 'Einleitung', in *Geschichtliche Grundbegriffe*, xxii.
13. Reinhart Koselleck, 'Sozialgeschichte und Begriffsgeschichte' (1986), in Koselleck, *Begriffsgeschichten* (Frankfurt/Main: Suhrkamp, 2006), 22.
14. Koselleck, 'Einleitung', in *Geschichtliche Grundbegriffe*, xxi.
15. Koselleck, 'Sozialgeschichte und Begriffsgeschichte', 22; and Paul Ricoeur, *Interpretation Theory: Discourse and the Surplus of Meaning* (Fort Worth: Texas Christian University Press, 1976).
16. Reinhart Koselleck, 'Einleitung', in Koselleck, *Zeitschichten: Studien zur Historik* (Frankfurt/Main: Suhrkamp, 2000), 9.
17. Koselleck, 'Einleitung', in *Geschichtliche Grundbegriffe*, xxii–xxiii.
18. Reinhart Koselleck, 'Wiederholungsstrukturen in Sprache und Geschichte', in Koselleck, *Vom Sinn und Unsinn der Geschichte* (Frankfurt/Main: Suhrkamp, 2011), 96–116.
19. Koselleck, 'Einleitung', in *Zeitschichten: Studien zur Historik*, 9–16.

20. Helge Jordheim, 'Conceptual History between *Chronos* and *Kairos*: The Case of "Empire"', *Redescriptions: Yearbook of Political Thought and Conceptual History* 11 (2007), 115–45; see also Helge Jordheim and Iver Neumann, 'Empire, Imperialism and Conceptual History', *Journal of International Relations and Development* 14 (2011), 153–85.
21. Benedict Anderson, *Imagined Communities: Reflections on the Origins and the Spread of Nationalism* (1983), revised edition (London and New York: Verso, 2006), 9–37.
22. Wilhelm Pinder, *Das Problem der Generation in der Kunstgeschichte Europas* (1926) (Munich: Bruckmann, 1961).
23. Ernst Bloch, *Erbschaft dieser Zeit* (1935), Erweiterte Ausgabe (Frankfurt/Main: Suhrkamp, 1985).
24. Karl Mannheim, 'Das Problem der Generationen', in Mannheim, *Wissenssoziologie* (Berlin and Neuwied: Luchterhand, 1964), 509–65.
25. Quentin Skinner, *Reason and Rhetoric in the Philosophy of Hobbes* (Cambridge: Cambridge University Press, 1996), 150–80.
26. Helge Jordheim, 'The Nature of Civilization: The Semantics of Civilization and Civility in Scandinavia', in Margrit Pernau and Helge Jordheim (eds), *Civilizing Emotions: Concepts in Nineteenth-Century Asia and Europe* (Oxford: Oxford University Press, 2015), 25–44.
27. François Hartog, *Régimes d'historicité: Présentisme et éxperiences du temps* (Paris: Seuil, 2003).
28. Martin Burke and Melvin Richter (eds), *Why Concepts Matter: Translating Social and Political Thought* (Leiden: Brill, 2012).
29. Cf. Chapter 7 in this volume, by Lázló Kontler.
30. Eviatar Zerubavel, *Hidden Rhythms: Schedules and Calendars in Social Life* (Berkeley and Los Angeles: University of California Press, 1981).
31. Bob Reinalda, *Routledge History of International Organizations: From 1815 to the Present Day* (New York: Routledge, 2009), 722.

References

Anderson, Benedict, *Imagined Communities: Reflections on the Origins and the Spread of Nationalism* (1983), revised edition (London and New York: Verso, 2006)

Bloch, Ernst, *Erbschaft dieser Zeit* (1935), Erweiterte Ausgabe (Frankfurt/Main: Suhrkamp, 1985)

Burke, Martin, and Melvin Richter (eds), *Why Concepts Matter: Translating Social and Political Thought* (Leiden: Brill, 2012)

Eisenstadt, Shmuel N. 'Multiple Modernities', *Daedalus* 1(129) (2000), 1–29

Fagerberg, Jan, and Bart Verspagen, 'Heading for Divergence: Regional Growth in Europe Reconsidered', *Journal of Common Market Studies* 3(34) (1996), 431–48

Hartog, François, *Régimes d'historicité: Présentisme et éxperiences du temps* (Paris: Seuil, 2003)

Jordheim, Helge, 'Conceptual History between *Chronos* and *Kairos*: The Case of "Empire"', *Redescriptions. Yearbook of Political Thought and Conceptual History* 11 (2007), 115–45

———, 'Against Periodization: On Koselleck's Theory of Multiple Temporalities', *History and Theory* 51 (2012), 151–71

———, 'Multiple Times and the Work of Synchronization', *History and Theory* 53 (2014), 498–518

———, 'The Nature of Civilization: The Semantics of Civilization and Civility in Scandinavia', in Margrit Pernau and Helge Jordheim (eds), *Civilizing Emotions: Concepts in Nineteenth-Century Asia and Europe* (Oxford: Oxford University Press, 2015), 25–44

Jordheim, Helge, and Iver Neumann, 'Empire, Imperialism and Conceptual History', *Journal of International Relations and Development* 14 (2011), 153–85

Koselleck, Reinhart, 'Einleitung', in Otto Brunner, Werner Conze, and Reinhart Koselleck (eds), *Geschichtliche Grundbegriffe: Historisches Lexikon zur politisch-sozialen Sprache in Deutschland*, vol. 1 (Stuttgart: Klett-Cotta, 1972), xiii–xxvii

———, *Kritik und Krise: Eine Studie zur Pathogenese der bürgerlichen Welt* (Frankfurt/Main: Suhrkamp, 1973)

———, '"Erfahrungsraum" und "Erwartungshorizont" – zwei historische Kategorien' (1975), in Reinhart Koselleck, *Vergangene Zukunft: Zur Semantik geschichtlicher Zeiten* (Frankfurt/Main: Suhrkamp, 1979), 349–75

———, 'Geschichte, Geschichten und formale Zeitstrukturen' (1973), in Reinhart Koselleck, *Vergangene Zukunft: Zur Semantik geschichtlicher Zeiten* (Frankfurt/Main: Suhrkamp, 1979), 130–43

———, 'A Response to Comments on the *Geschichtliche Grundbegriffe*', in Hartmut Lehmann and Melvin Richter (eds), *The Meaning of Historical Terms and Concepts* (Washington, DC: German Historical Institute, 1996), 59–70

———, 'Deutschland – eine verspätete Nation' (1998), in Reinhart Koselleck, *Zeitschichten: Studien zur Historik* (Frankfurt/Main: Suhrkamp, 2000), 359–79

———, 'Einleitung', in Reinhart Koselleck, *Zeitschichten: Studien zur Historik* (Frankfurt/Main: Suhrkamp, 2000), 9–16

———, 'Sozialgeschichte und Begriffsgeschichte' (1986), in Reinhart Koselleck, *Begriffsgeschichten* (Frankfurt/Main: Suhrkamp, 2006), 9–31

———, 'Wiederholungsstrukturen in Sprache und Geschichte', in Reinhart Koselleck, *Vom Sinn und Unsinn der Geschichte* (Frankfurt/Main: Suhrkamp, 2011), 96–116

Mannheim, Karl, 'Das Problem der Generationen', in Karl Mannheim, *Wissenssoziologie* (Berlin and Neuwied: Luchterhand, 1964), 509–65

Pinder, Wilhelm, *Das Problem der Generation in der Kunstgeschichte Europas* (1926) (Munich: Bruckmann, 1961)

Reinalda, Bob, *Routledge History of International Organizations: From 1815 to the Present Day* (New York: Routledge, 2009)

Ricoeur, Paul, *Interpretation Theory: Discourse and the Surplus of Meaning* (Fort Worth: Texas Christian University Press, 1976)

Skinner, Quentin, *Reason and Rhetoric in the Philosophy of Hobbes* (Cambridge: Cambridge University Press, 1996)

Zerubavel, Eviatar, *Hidden Rhythms: Schedules and Calendars in Social Life* (Berkeley and Los Angeles: University of California Press, 1981)

Chapter 2

Multiple Transformations

Temporal Frameworks for a European Conceptual History

Willibald Steinmetz

Periods of accelerated change in the use of vocabulary have attracted conceptual historians' attention ever since the history of concepts was devised as an approach to the past. There are good reasons for focusing on times of rapid innovation. Investigating them may help to understand how and why old terms were superseded by new ones or acquired new meanings that have shaped our own conceptual universe. Moreover, studying such periods may provide insights into how conceptual change works generally; we may learn something about the driving forces likely to provoke semantic changes, and we should be able to discern patterns in the course of those changes. Reflections on periodization are therefore a useful exercise for conceptual historians, not only for the purpose of delimiting research fields, but also for developing hypotheses about the mechanisms of conceptual change in general.

Periodizations tend to become more difficult the larger the scope of the analysis. If the object to be studied is an entity as multifaceted as Europe has been throughout its history, it is all the more questionable whether a common temporal framework can be drawn up at all. Any such attempt at periodization on a European level has to reckon with the fact that sociopolitical units within Europe were always acting at different speeds.[1] This chapter explores solutions for this conundrum. It will be argued that, although a search for synchronized periods of semantic change is a futile enterprise, it is possible to describe a number of basic processes that, although timed differently, have been at work across Europe to effect conceptual changes in similar ways.

As long as the practice of conceptual history remained tied to distinct communities defined in terms of nation states or a shared language, it was fairly easy to know where to look for periods of accelerated change. Depending on the semantic fields historians were interested in, eras of religious reformations and political revolutions, periods of social upheaval, economic crisis, scientific innovation or cultural renaissance almost naturally imposed themselves as preferred objects of study. When, in 1930, Lucien Febvre called for inquiries into the terms of French economic history, terms like *prolétaire, capitaliste* or *ingénieur*, it was the period between the mid eighteenth and the mid nineteenth centuries he envisaged as a starting point.[2] In his brilliant article on the origins of the French term *civilisation*, also published in 1930, Febvre identified the time around 1760 as the formative period, not without noting however that the verb *civiliser* (to civilize) and the participle *civilisé* (civilized) had already been known long before, and that the meanings of *civilisation* were amplified considerably in the decades following the French Revolution.[3] Later on, searching for early conceptualizations of *incroyance* (unbelief), Febvre turned back to the period of religious reform in sixteenth-century France, the age of Rabelais, to look for the semantic fields in which genuine unbelief might first have become conceivable.[4] Almost intuitively Febvre designated the period between sixteenth-century religious reform and the aftermath of the French Revolution up to the mid nineteenth century as the most rewarding temporal framework for studies in French conceptual history. Later research projects conducted by Rolf Reichardt and others followed in his footsteps.[5] More importantly, Febvre's main research interest, although not stated very explicitly, turned around the question of how the contemporary, twentieth-century meanings of the French terms he was studying had seen their breakthrough in the course of that period.

In that respect, Febvre's interests tallied quite nicely with those of Reinhart Koselleck. Koselleck's main goal when setting up the project of *Geschichtliche Grundbegriffe* a generation after Febvre was to elucidate, on a much broader scale, the profound semantic transformations that went along with, and helped to inaugurate, the social and political upheavals leading into the age of modernity as experienced in Germany.[6] Not unlike Febvre, Koselleck saw the history of concepts mainly as a conduit to exploring the genesis (partly interpreted by him as a pathogenesis) of the sociopolitical revolutions he himself and other Germans had experienced in their own lifetimes. There is no need to delve into the intellectual traditions Koselleck relied on to formulate the programme for the handbook *Geschichtliche Grundbegriffe*.[7] More relevant in the context of our search for temporal frameworks is the fact that Koselleck's approach was problem-driven when he elaborated his famous hypothesis of the *Sattelzeit*. As is well known, the core of this hypothesis consists in the idea that, broadly speaking, the decades between 1750 and 1850 should be regarded as the crucial period in which the semantic transformations inaugurating modernity – as far as Germany was concerned – took place. Taking fundamental historical problems such as the genesis of modernity, and not just interesting materials or details, as a point of departure is certainly an objective that today's conceptual historians should aspire to, and the more so if they reach out towards a transnational and comparative level. Yet whether, and if so how, Koselleck's *Sattelzeit* hypothesis might still be of use as a tool for that purpose needs to be critically assessed. This will be done in the following section. In a second section I will discuss a number of problems and long-range processes beyond the *Sattelzeit*, whose implications for semantic change should be made subjects of conceptual history studies on a European scale.

Unpacking the *Sattelzeit*

The *Sattelzeit* hypothesis may be a characteristic feature of *Begriffsgeschichte* as conceived by Reinhart Koselleck in the late 1960s and early 1970s, but it is important to stress that it is by no means essential to its methodology. Even Koselleck himself only thought of it as a point of secondary importance. *Begriffsgeschichte*, the history of concepts, is above all a particular line of historical inquiry, a certain perspective within the broader field of historical semantics.[8] It is a line of inquiry that, in principle, is applicable to all periods of time and all human societies as long as written source materials are available. There is nothing in the theory of *Begriffsgeschichte* as devised by Koselleck, and elaborated by others, that tends to limit its application to certain countries or periods in history.

The reasons why Koselleck chose to concentrate his own work, and the collective efforts of the authors of *Geschichtliche Grundbegriffe*, on the period he called *Sattelzeit* are not difficult to detect. Being a German historian who had lived through the 'Age of Extremes', Koselleck's main interest was to find explanations for what appeared to him as the irrevocable dynamism of modernity. Koselleck was not the only intellectual of his generation who held modernity – and, more particularly, its developmental, future-oriented conception of history – ultimately responsible for the drive towards the totalitarian and potentially genocidal ideologies of the twentieth century. Whether he had a good point in putting forward such a 'pathogenetic' view of modernity, and whether he was right in locating the onset of that modernity in the Enlightenment, need not be discussed in this chapter.[9] Yet it is true that Koselleck used *Begriffsgeschichte* above all to bring home his particular vision of modernity, and it is fair to say that his own contributions to the *Geschichtliche Grundbegriffe* presented strong arguments in support of that vision.[10]

However, to conclude from this that *Begriffsgeschichte* as a line of inquiry should forever be bound to repeat, or be instrumental to prove, that particular Koselleckian view of modern history is nonsense. It is absurd to maintain that the history of concepts in general is now obsolete because the vision of history held by its most prominent founding figure has lost much of its attraction.[11] And it is also misleading to assume that *Begriffsgeschichte*, if applied to other periods or countries outside Western Europe, such as Russia for instance, could achieve nothing else than deficit or catch-up histories of belated entries into a modernity defined in Western terms.[12] That would indeed be a very bad way of practising conceptual history, but there are now plenty of good examples all over the world to demonstrate that the empirical results of conceptual history need not be predetermined by certain visions of modernity or of history in general.[13]

Having said that, one would be mistaken to fall into the opposite extreme of doing conceptual history, as it were, in a blind flight mode. Rather, we should insist on using hypotheses on long-term processes, just as Koselleck did, for *heuristical* purposes – as a source of inspiration for our research, not as a straitjacket. Koselleck was never content merely to describe semantical change. He wanted to explain how it came about and how it was linked to what he called structural change in society and the polity.[14] The *Sattelzeit* hypothesis was part of that venture. Much of its originality consisted in the intention to shed light on the interplay between semantical and social-structural changes. That interplay is what Koselleck alluded to with his famous formula that concepts are at the same time 'indicators' of and 'factors' in the historical process.[15] Critical reviewers have rightly pointed out that due to his preference for a diachronic perspective Koselleck never really got very far in fleshing out how this formula could be translated into an agenda for empirical research. As I have argued elsewhere, we need to adopt a synchronic, or more precisely a micro-diachronic perspective on successive communicative situations in order to show how concepts can indeed fulfil that double function of being indicators and factors simultaneously.[16] Except in his book on Prussia, never translated into English, Koselleck did not spend much thought on such micro-diachronic studies.[17] He thus remained only half-hearted in his aspiration to explain how semantic change actually functioned. In addition, the lexicon format of the *Geschichtliche Grundbegriffe* proved unhelpful in that respect.

For all these legitimate criticisms, Koselleck's *Sattelzeit* hypothesis continues to fascinate conceptual historians, and that is reason enough why it may be useful to assess its valency as a possible reference frame for a European conceptual history project. To begin with, there is no need for a long discussion of its temporal location in the decades between 1750 and 1850. Whereas this periodization holds good for many, yet by no means all, social and political key concepts in German history, it is quite evident that the timing and speed of conceptual change were different even in Germany's neighbouring countries. Lucien Febvre's deviating periodization for the history of French economic, sociopolitical and religious terms is only one example showing the futility of defining a certain period, say the decades around 1800, as the decisive watershed between a premodern and a modern conceptual universe for the whole of Europe.[18] If Koselleck's conception of the *Sattelzeit* in a strong sense (transition to terms and meanings familiar to contemporaries of the mid twentieth century) should be retained at all, then it is clear that it has to be temporally dislocated. We should expect that in many European countries a similar transition might not only have happened earlier or later than in the German case, but also have stretched over a much longer time span or else have been compressed in a much shorter one. The temporal dislocation would go even further, should we consider using the *Sattelzeit* metaphor in a weak sense, designating just any period of accelerated semantic change. In that case we might easily end up finding several *Sattelzeiten* for each European country or language community, including Germany.[19] While it may not be an unrewarding task to chart and compare such periods of accelerated semantic change for all European countries, it does not seem advisable to use the *Sattelzeit* metaphor in such a loose way, because Koselleck's original historiographical conception would thereby be completely obliterated.

But is it sufficient to dislocate the *Sattelzeit* and define separately for each European country the span of time in which concepts acquired the range of meanings corresponding to a mid-twentieth-century (and in that chronological sense 'modern') mindset? My argument is that more can be achieved if we proceed to unpack the *Sattelzeit* further by disaggregating it into its constituent parts. That would entail splitting up the four basic processes that for Koselleck constituted the transition period, and discussing for each of the processes separately and country by country the timing and the impact they might have had on conceptual change.

These processes, he claimed, coalesced in Germany in the decades around 1800 to make this the critical period of profound semantic change ushering in the modern age. Using a somewhat abstract terminology he called those processes politicization, ideologization, democratization and temporalization. To summarize very briefly, politicization meant a process whereby terms formerly deemed unpolitical were increasingly drawn into the sphere of political communication. By ideologization or, more precisely, the 'growing extent to which concepts could be incorporated into ideologies',[20] Koselleck referred to a remarkable increase in the use of abstract sociopolitical concepts, often in the form of collective singulars ('liberty' instead of 'liberties'); these were concepts that one could hardly avoid using, whose meanings were highly contested and which could only be 'decontested' by being related in a fairly regular way to other concepts, thus forming what in Michael Freeden's terms is known as 'an ideology'.[21] Democratization is Koselleck's shorthand formula for two related processes: on the one hand, a wider dissemination of abstract sociopolitical terms in ever-larger publics leading in turn to a more intense participation of these publics in redefining the terms; on the other hand (and more significantly), a growing tendency of the key concepts themselves to become ever-more inclusive and 'universal' in the sense that they transcended ancient barriers of estates, ranks and religious confession and – to a lesser degree and only much later – of gender, race, age and other discriminatory distinctions. Finally, temporalization, or in another translation that in my view is closer to Koselleck's idea of *Verzeitlichung*: 'entiming'.[22] This designates a process whereby key concepts were loaded with notions of a developmental vision of history, thus opening up horizons of expectation towards a hitherto unknown and potentially better future.

Each one of these processes is complicated enough in itself and requires many preconditions. So a concurrence of all four in a rather short period of time, as in Germany around 1800, is therefore a highly contingent event unlikely to have happened anywhere else in the same fashion. With regard to the whole of Europe it is reasonable to expect huge discrepancies in the timing and intensity of the four processes. We may safely assume, though, that no European region or language community has remained completely untouched by those processes in the centuries since 1500. Hence, if taken one by one, Koselleck's brief definitions of the four processes may well serve as valuable heuristical tools, yet without implying the need to postulate a condensed transition period resembling the German *Sattelzeit*.

Analysing politicization, ideologization, democratization and the entiming of concepts separately has another advantage: that of unravelling the problem of singularity, repeatability and reversibility of the four processes. As I have argued elsewhere, politicization especially, but also the incorporation of concepts into ideologies, are repeatable, wave-like phenomena not bound to a specific historical era or constellation.[23] Across Europe there have been recurrent waves of politicization, depoliticization and repoliticization of concepts, sometimes more synchronized, sometimes capturing single countries or regions only. The era of the French revolutionary and Napoleonic wars was certainly a chain of events that had strong politicizing effects on the uses of vocabulary almost everywhere in Europe, no matter whether the revolutionary French principles of citizenship, nationhood, equality, separation of church and state, sovereignty of the people and the plethora of newly coined terms expressing these principles were enthusiastically adopted or consciously rejected. On the other hand, there were also politicization waves that reacted more specifically to particular conditions in one European country alone – for instance, the explicit calls by intellectuals, academics and literati in late Wilhelmine Germany to politicize their pursuits; these calls released a debate with virulent counterreactions and led to a redefinition of the German term *Politisierung* itself.[24] Many more such wave-like politicizations of vocabulary affecting only one, or a handful, or sometimes many European countries can easily be found, the student movements around 1968 and their repercussions on concept formation being an example of the latter case.[25]

If it is sensible, then, to see politicization as a repeatable phenomenon, one might as well argue that it should also be a reversible one. Depoliticizations of extendend semantic fields may be more difficult to detect and describe, not least because conceptual historians so far have rarely paid attention to them. But, again taking Germany as an example, one can point to certain phases in the second half of the nineteenth century, after the revolutions of 1848, and again in the 1950s and 1960s during which certain professional groups – scientists, medical doctors, lawyers, bureaucrats, engineers – were obsessed by the idea of purging their respective languages and practices from anything reminiscent of allusions to the political.[26] There is, however, something paradoxical about such depoliticization attempts generally: the more self-conscious and explicit they become, the less effective they are. Actively demanding the depoliticization of certain vocabularies and fields of practice is itself an extremely political speech act – and a self-defeating one at that. Only tacit, or even unpremeditated, depoliticizations of entire language sectors are likely to result in a durable reversal of previous movements towards politicization.[27] And that is, of course, another reason why it is not easy to detect depoliticizations of language use. In any case, reconfiguring the study of politicization (and depoliticization) processes in that way may be a promising perspective for future comparative studies on semantic fields or certain sectors of language.

A similar argument can be made for ideologization. The process whereby contested concepts are incorporated into ideologies with an intent to decontest their meanings (at least among those who can be brought to believe in the respective ideologies) is certainly a repeatable one. And while the decades of the late Enlightenment, the French Revolution and the Napoleonic expansion in Europe were arguably the first period in which that process gained momentum and was positively observed, resulting even in the coinage of the French terms *idéologue* and *idéologie* themselves and their rapid transmission across Europe,[28] one will easily find many successive waves of ideologization all through the nineteenth and twentieth centuries up until today. Moreover, it can hardly be denied that some of these later ideologization waves penetrated much deeper into the middle and lower strata of European societies – for example, when the lessons of liberal political economy, or socialism, were taught to broad sections of populations, including women and children, through popular catechisms, political dictionaries and other media, including visual materials, that explained the proper meaning of terms in accordance with the ideologies in question.[29] The decontesting of conceptual meanings through ideologization went even further in totalitarian regimes like Nazi Germany and Stalinist Russia. Orchestrated mass campaigns, and ritualized festivals or rallies on the one hand, and crude terror, censorship and repression on the other, ensured that any attempts at contesting the concepts as defined by the ruling ideologists were seen as a life-threatening enterprise.

The brief storyline intimated here might suggest an ever-increasing grip of ideologies on peoples' concept formations, at least until Europe's mid twentieth century – much firmer, of course, in countries with authoritarian or totalitarian regimes, less so in pluralist societies. But this does not mean that reverse movements – relaxations in ideological rigour – were not possible and did not occur, even within totalitarian regimes.[30] As with depoliticizations, however, they have attracted less attention and are more difficult to describe. And as in the case of depoliticization, we also come across paradoxical effects when de-ideologization is positively demanded or declared to be already underway. Those who, beginning in the 1960s, proclaimed the 'end of ideologies', from Daniel Bell to Francis Fukuyama, immediately came under suspicion, and not entirely without reason, of being fabricators of just another ideology or, even worse, of concealing the wished-for dominance of their own ideology by denying it the very name and status of an ideology.[31] While the ideology-sustaining intentions of liberal intellectuals like Bell and Fukuyama were quite transparent, there may nevertheless be some reasons to maintain that the late twentieth and the early twenty-first centuries have seen, if not the end of ideologies, then at least a decrease in their capacity to keep meanings of concepts temporarily stable. The internet and its endless array of border-crossing blogs, social media networks and so on have created an ever-increasing number of overlapping so-called communities whose coherence is in most cases anything but stable, especially as far as the use of concepts is concerned. One could argue, but this is open to debate, that the frequent and fast transfers of concepts from one domain, nation, social sphere or language community to another, facilitated by the internet, bring about an increasing plasticity, or volatility, in the uses of concepts, thus making it more difficult to sustain ideologies.[32]

If ideologization, just like politicization, is a repeatable and reversible phenomenon, what about Koselleck's precise claim that one of the German *Sattelzeit*'s new features was a previously unknown degree of

Ideologisierbarkeit, a growing extent to which concepts could be incorporated into ideologies? His main argument in support of that claim was a linguistical one. It referred to the increasing abstractness of sociopolitical terms in the languages of the German Enlightenment and Idealism, for instance in the shape of collective singulars, as a necessary precondition for *Ideologisierbarkeit*. The argument may appear subtle, but if generalized, it entails that ideologies as such cannot be formed before the language in which they are expressed has reached a certain stage of complexity. With regard to a conceptual history embracing the European space, this argument gives rise to an interesting point to be researched. European languages differed considerably as to the moment of time from which they began to be metamorphosed into instruments capable of conveying abstract sociopolitical concepts, many of them being derivations from Latin or Greek roots. In most European countries this metamorphosis was set in motion by deliberate moves of poets, philologists, historians, theologians, other academics of various disciplines, intellectuals and state institutions to reform their own languages, which they regarded – for one reason or another – as insufficiently elaborated to express complex political or philosophical thoughts. In some countries, such as Russia under Catherine II, state-sponsored translation programmes from Western languages were instituted to expedite this process.[33] In other countries, such as for instance early nineteenth-century Finland, individual academics took on the task to create new autochthonous abstract terms by critically engaging with foreign terms – in this case mostly Swedish, French, or German.[34] What is important here is that the process differed widely with regard to beginnings, duration, modalities and results. If it is true, as Koselleck assumes, that *Ideologisierbarkeit* depends on a certain degree of abstractness of sociopolitical terms, then the differences in the timing and shape of the respective language reform processes need to be taken into account as factors affecting the histories of ideologization in the various European countries.

Let us now turn to the third process included in Koselleck's *Sattelzeit* idea: the democratization of concepts. One may quickly dispose of democratization in the straighter sense of meaning only the increasing dissemination of concepts among ever-larger publics and, along with this, the publics' growing participation in defining and redefining the concepts. In many respects this process is closely related to, or even congruent with, politicization. Hence what has been said above also applies here. The broadening and intensifying of public debate over old or new sociopolitical key concepts is a repeatable phenomenon. It may have occurred at all times in history, long before and long after the time around 1800 which, to be sure, definitely was a period of democratization in this sense almost everywhere in Europe. Public participation in conceptual contests may of course also decrease in breadth and depth; the process is reversible. Tracing and comparing the conjunctures of democratization (in this sense) and reverse movements across Europe can be a worthwile research object, especially if the perspective is extended to include publics both below and above the level of nation states – that is, local and regional publics on the one hand, and imperial or European-wide publics on the other.

More intriguing, however, and difficult to explore is the second aspect of democratization: the ways in which sociopolitical key concepts themselves have become democratized in the various European language spaces. When, why and how concepts designating sociopolitical units took on universalized meanings that were able to transcend traditional segmentations into ranks, orders, estates and religious denominations, and how these potentially universal concepts then contended with discriminations by gender, age, race, class or other features, are still underresearched questions. Sure enough, there is much ongoing research about languages of class, citizenship or people/nation in quite a number of individual European and non-European countries.[35] One may even say that this has been one of the preferred study objects of conceptual historians all over Europe. Yet these studies have rarely embraced the entire semantic field of concepts designating sociopolitical units in the respective languages. Without such an encompassing overview, however, the paths along which the vocabularies of societal self-description have become democratized will remain obscure. More perhaps than in other fields, a single-word (semasiological) approach – for example, a focus on the words for 'citizen' alone – will not lead very far, because what is at stake here is always the *relation* between concepts designating the particular and the more 'universal' sociopolitical entities.

'Universal' has been set in quotation marks since one of the complexities to be disentangled here is to distinguish between the proclaimed universal applicability of concepts and their effective exclusivity, an effect that speakers often try to conceal. Moreover, paradoxical as it may seem, claims to universality in concept usage will always remain only a *relative* affair, as it will always be possible to name groups or social entities that are not yet included. Even ostensibly all-inclusive notions like 'humanity' or 'mankind' may be challenged: Why not include animals and other living species? Why use the term 'mankind' which might be interpreted by some as excluding women? And so on. Democratization of concepts in the sophisticated sense given to it by Koselleck is a potentially never-ending process. And there is certainly more to it than just the desire for politically correct uses of speech. What happened during the *Sattelzeit* in Germany, and in similar ways earlier or later in other European countries, was only one small step in the direction of that still open-ended process. There are, of course, plenty of counter movements to be observed here as well. It has always been possible, and will remain so in the future, to invent new discriminatory categories (or recycle old ones) to reverse a democatization of concepts judged by some to have gone too far or too fast.

What democratization of concepts is, or might have been, or should be in the future, becomes even more difficult to figure out when the viewpoint is elevated from the national to the European or even global level. For here the rights of each individual to be equally recognized in the polity almost inevitably come into conflict with claims of collective entities (peoples, nations, minorities, etc.) to have at least an equal right to be heard, to raise their voices and to be respected in their difference as a collectivity, particularly against a majority vote to the contrary.[36] The very terms which in the context of homogenous nation states signalled universality, including the key terms 'democracy' and 'equality', can become highly problematic when introduced in supra- or international contexts, or in situations where weak states or former empires are falling apart. The twentieth and twenty-first centuries have been overabundant with conceptual struggles along these lines, within Europe as well as beyond. The comparatively well-studied transnational debates on the meaning of 'human rights' after 1945 are just one example.[37] Those remarks may be sufficient to show that the temporally limited problem Koselleck had in mind when speaking of democratization as a feature of the German *Sattelzeit* may be reformulated in such a way as to open up promising research fields for a European conceptual history project. Most of that research will be focused on the modern age from 1789 onwards. But it may be no less intriguing to investigate analogous contests about striking a balance between universality and particularities, even in earlier periods of European history.

Of all the four basic processes constituting the *Sattelzeit* hypothesis, the temporalization or entiming of concepts (*Verzeitlichung*) is certainly Koselleck's most original discovery. It seems to me that in the precise way he defined it, strong evidence for instances of *Verzeitlichung* are rarely to be found much earlier than in the mid eighteenth century. That periodization seems to be valid not just for the German-speaking academic and political elites, but also, and perhaps even more so, for the French- as well as English-speaking publics all over Europe. Newly coined or redefined older concepts that directly referred to a linear and unitary movement of history towards a new, open-ended and potentially better future only came to the fore in that period – concepts like progress, revolution, evolution/development, emancipation, enlightenment, civilization, education (*Bildung*) and indeed history itself (history in the singular, referring not of course to the activity of storytelling, but to a supposed objective course of history).[38] Using the

French language as a vehicle, and to a lesser extent German and English, the Enlightenment as a transnational intellectual movement supplied European elites with a critical vocabulary that privileged innovation over tradition, the secular over the religious, and (West) European experience over that of all other parts of the world. The invention and spread of temporalized concepts for some time went along with an increasingly eurocentric vision of history.

Within Europe too, that new language of temporalized concepts created a mode of thought in which European states and cultures came to be 'graded' along a hypothetical scale of steps already reached or still to be taken towards what was purported to be, for the time being, the highest degree of civilizational progress. Grading countries in that way was not just a philosophical pursuit. It was directly conducive to political action, mostly in the shape of reforms, in many areas of Europe: in the more peripheral regions of Eastern, Northern and Southern Europe, as well as in those parts of Western and Central Europe considered to be 'backward' or 'not yet cultivated'. Nowhere is Koselleck's claim that concepts are 'factors' that impel into actions and help to restructure the world more evident than in the case of that language of stages, gaps, differentials and progressive comparisons that began to unfold around the key concepts mentioned above.[39] Speaking and acting according to the prescriptions of that progressive language became almost habitual among large sections of European elites all through the long nineteenth century, predominantly among those who called themselves liberals. Socialists of all shades were in general still more radical in this respect. Yet even conservative intellectuals, dispossessed nobles who regretted the old regime, and autocratic rulers who did not share the view that politics and societal relations had to be reformed or revolutionized, found it hard to escape the use of progressive language, if only by rejecting it. Resistance against revolution or reform forced them to position themselves, as well as their concepts, in historical time too. They could not avoid using entimed concepts to describe their own political views. The adoption of a party name, such as 'conservative', implied the acceptance in principle of a developmental vision of history.[40]

While there can be no doubt that key concepts such as 'civilization', 'emancipation' and 'progress' strongly informed the ways in which nineteenth-century European elites – liberals, socialists and conservatives alike – thought and acted, it remains an interesting problem to consider how deeply these concepts took root in the middle and lower strata of European societies. Prima facie one would not expect nineteenth-century small townspeople in Italy or peasants in Russia to have ever used or understood complex terms like civilization, or to have speculated about the progressive course of history. However, English shopkeepers or housewives imbued with the popularized doctrines of political economy, or German workers having learnt some lessons in their local social-democratic *Arbeiterbildungsverein* (workmen's education association) might very well have done so. Moreover, I would contend that the more inconspicuous uses of language that had unfolded around the temporalized key concepts – adverbial formulations like 'being backwards' and 'not yet so far as', and even progressive comparisons with situations of what peasants or small people had achieved or aspired to elsewhere – were indeed within the reach of middle- and lower-class populations all over Europe, including Russian peasants. Mid-nineteenth-century realist literature such as Ivan Turgenev's documentary *Sketches from a Hunter's Album* (1852) contain telling examples.[41]

A change in the method of reading texts – shifting attention away from the abstract nouns and turning instead towards the analysis of sentence constructions – will be necessary to detect such inconspicuous uses of entimed language in social milieux where one would not necessarily expect them. If one would like to attach a label to that methodological turn, I would call it the 'propositional turn'.[42] This would no longer be a history of concepts in the Koselleckian sense, but it is a promising research strategy within the larger field known as historical semantics.

Another interesting question with regard to the entiming of concepts will be, again, the issue of reversibility. The answer is less clear cut than it was in the cases of politicization, ideologization or democratization. As already mentioned, opponents of a progressivist view of history and corresponding actions found it hard to avoid using entimed concepts themselves. An available escape, practised by some political or folklorist movements in nineteenth-century Europe, was to claim the absolute uniqueness of their own, autochthonous culture and flatly reject everything of foreign, usually 'Western', origin. The Russian Slavophiles are a model case. Whether such groups were actually able to frame a language free of entimed concepts and developmental visions, however, is an empirical question still to be explored. In nineteenth-century politics, groups like the Slavophiles generally stood at the margins and were forced to speak and act in a reactive mode; this makes it more likely that they used the concepts against which they actually fought. Conversely, more recent twentieth- and twenty-first-century examples have often shown so-called conservatives or fundamentalists, once in a majority position, to be extremely radical innovators, destroyers of traditions and proponents of policies oriented towards stimulating growth (another entimed concept). Whether 'green' ideologies can avoid the allure of temporalized concepts is equally doubtful. Basically, what happens when policies turn 'green' is a series of conceptual replacements that, however, still appear embedded in entimed modes of argument. Thus, unlimited economic growth as the ultimate goal is replaced by the attunement to nature conceived of in evolutionary terms; utopian visions of endless progress are replaced by dystopian visions of entropy and final destruction, or alternatively by ideas of 'sustainability'; and self-fulfilling prophecies are replaced by prophecies intended to be self-defeating. Yet all these arguments remain within the orbit of a developmental vision of history.[43] In summary, ideologists and politicians of all shades – liberals, socialists, reactionaries, conservatives, fundamentalists and greens – all seem to be drawn into the maelstrom of the entimed 'movement concepts' as defined by Koselleck. These concepts have multiplied around us since the late eighteenth century, the concept 'globalization' being only one of the more prominent examples in recent times.[44]

The unpacking of the *Sattelzeit* hypothesis has resulted in a research programme that stresses recurrent processes (repetitions) instead of a single transition period and, more than before, pays attention to reverse movements countering the four processes described by Koselleck. Such a research programme would be better suited to account for the variety of European experiences without losing sight of the necessity to formulate hypotheses that possess significance beyond single-case studies. To be sure, unpacking the *Sattelzeit* hypothesis in the manner described will lead us away from Koselleck's original leitmotif, the (patho)genesis of modernity as experienced in mid-twentieth-century Germany and Europe. However, that may be no loss. Modernity itself has become an elusive and temporally dislocated concept since it has been split up into 'multiple modernities'.[45] Even with regard to Europe it has lost much of its valency as a meaningful temporal reference frame. Abandoning it will help to shift conceptual historians' focus to some of the more tangible problems affecting Europe and the world in recent decades: problems posed by the increasing speed with which goods, people and ideas are moving around the globe; problems produced by the extent to which social and political entities are constantly reshuffled and reshaped; problems created by repeated clashes between the claims to universality contained in some concepts (mostly of Western origin) and the desires of those who want to see their difference and particularity accepted and respected. In principle, most of these problems are not new but have long histories of their own, the conceptual articulations of which deserve to be explored.

Convergence and Divergence in Europe's Conceptual Space

A controversial question to be raised in a European conceptual history project is to know whether Europeans have ever come close to a shared conceptual universe or, if not, whether such a state could be achieved or is desirable at all. Today's nationalists and promoters of regionalist independence movements would probably reject the latter suggestion out of hand and try to find as many arguments as possible to prove that Europe's languages have always been and continue to be conducive to different concept formations and worldviews. In this conviction they are backed by a number of language philosophers who have held that the semantic relations between, and hence the meanings of, individual concepts are different even in languages bearing strong family resemblances as regards grammar, syntax, morphology, etymology, scripture and pronunciation.[46] Additionally, the friends of cultural-linguistic difference have an obvious point when arguing that most, if not all, European languages contain certain very specific concepts, often quite important ones, that appear to be untranslatable – concepts like *narod* in Russian, *Bildung* in German and *hyggelig* in Danish. Barbara Cassin's dictionary of the 'untranslatables', although in fact suggesting ways of translating such concepts or discussing past attempts at doing so, renders support to that vision – at least as far as the existence of the idiosyncratic concepts is concerned.[47]

Those who oppose the ideas of national-linguistic uniqueness and separateness – let us call them the 'Europeanists' – have good arguments on their side too. In the first place, they might refer to Europe's common Judeo-Christian tradition, which, despite all schisms and denominational conflicts, has given birth to a widely shared network of conceptual relations informing notions of good and evil, the natural and the supernatural, and the course of history. Not only the believers but even those who turned to agnosticism or atheism still share many of these concepts. The Europeanists can also point to the fact that, since the later Roman Empire, derivations from ancient Greek and Latin terms have increasingly become the major building blocks around which vast fields of the moral, political, juridical, economic, aesthetic and scientific vocabularies in all European languages have been arranged. It is indeed hard to deny that both traditions have exerted a unifying influence on European languages and made them distinguishable from non-European ones – at least as long as the non-Europeans did not adapt the Judeo-Christian notions and/or the Greek- or Latin-derived terms for themselves.[48] In addition, from the Middle Ages onwards, educated elites all over Europe were able to communicate by means of three successive, and at times overlapping, linguae francae: Latin up to the eighteenth and in some places into the nineteenth centuries; French from the mid seventeenth to the later nineteenth centuries; and English from the mid twentieth century until today. For all these unifying tendencies, however, understanding and translating terms between European languages still poses difficulties, and language rights in institutions like the European Parliament still remain a potentially contentious issue.[49]

While both sides, the Europeanists and the proponents of cultural-linguistic uniqueness, have good arguments, it is obvious that there can be no either/or answer to the above question. As usual in history, the issue has to be treated as a matter of degree. Conceptual historians should refrain from writing European conceptual history either as a prehistory of European unification or as a history that accentuates nothing but national or regional differences in concept formation. A more meaningful strategy is to search for the historical conditions and processes that made conceptual convergence or divergence more, or less, likely to happen. It is here that timing is again a decisive factor. Language communities in the European space differed widely as to the period from which, the extent to which, and the mode in which they became exposed to Judeo-Christian religious concepts and to the Latin and ancient Greek linguistic heritage. And they also differed as to the time and mode in which the speakers of the European vernacular languages emancipated themselves linguistically from the old or foreign languages that up until a certain moment served as idioms of communication in academia, the law, diplomacy, polite conversation and other social fields.

The latter process, which one might call 'vernacularization', has not received much attention among conceptual historians. This neglect is all the more regrettable as it was probably the most important driving force of semantic change in those language communities that went through it. In abstract terms, vernacularization can be defined as the process whereby speakers of autochthonous spoken languages increase their efforts to adopt, translate and transform the terms of a prestigious written elite language, usually of old or foreign origin, to suit their own purposes. In some cases vernacularization went along with the creation of a written language or its standardization, while in other cases a literature written in the vernacular language already existed. The prime example of the process in medieval and early modern Western, Southern, Central and Northern Europe is of course the gradual replacement of Latin by the respective vernaculars in legal, political, academic, administrative, religious and other everyday contexts. In some parts of south-eastern Europe, old Greek and Old Church Slavonic had played a similar, if more limited, role. Later on, some European vernaculars themselves assumed the role of a prestigious foreign language used by local elites whose spoken, autochthonous language was considered 'uncivilized' or unsuitable for use in administrative, academic or professional contexts: Swedish in Finland, German in large parts of Central Europe, English in the Gaelic-speaking highlands and islands, French in many parts of Europe including Germany, Poland and Russia, and European languages generally in their respective colonial empires.

In all these cases, vernacularization required that speakers of the local languages had to come to terms – literally speaking – with the meanings contained in the Latin, or foreign, words. Finding new terms or redefining existing ones to designate what the Latin or foreign terms purported to mean was no easy task; it could be achieved by simply inserting Latin or foreign words in written texts, by creating loanwords or by enriching the meanings of autochthonous terms. Even more difficult than the merely technical aspects of translation was to figure out what the Latin or foreign terms actually meant or could have meant. Thus, it happened quite often that the Latin political or legal terms found in the rediscovered texts of Roman antiquity, or those of ancient Greek philosophers translated into Latin, did not seem to fit the social realities in the kingdoms or city republics of medieval Europe. When, for instance, from the fourteenth century on, Italian city governors or the learned councillors of the French king tried to make sense of the terms of Aristotle's politics, not least the term *politica* itself, it soon turned out that the meanings they gave to the Aristotelian terms by transferring them in the Italian and French vernaculars differed widely, depending each time on the very concrete environment in which the terms had to be fitted to the social realities encountered.[50] The result was an extreme extension of the horizon of meanings of abstract and obscure Latin terms like *politica*, and, consequently, an increased uncertainty about its meaning.

Generally speaking, as Lucian Hölscher has argued, the concepts referred to by inserted Latin words, or by loanwords derived from Latin, in the European vernaculars were extremely vague concepts.[51] They could be applied to many different usages, and it usually took several centuries until the vernacularized concepts of Latin origin finally got saturated, and were situated in a network of other concepts leading to a mutual stabilization of meanings. Everywhere in Europe this process of semantic stabilization was promoted by bilingual and multilingual dictionaries, by authoritative translations of major texts (above all the Bible), by school education and, from the mid seventeenth century on, by the standardizing activities of academies and state institutions that followed the French model. The transition from Latin to the vernaculars was a gradual process, sometimes lasting for several centuries. As a working hypothesis, one might hold that the process started earlier and lasted longer in countries pertaining to the family of Romance languages, while beginning later and lasting a shorter time in countries pertaining to the Germanic, Slavic and other language families. With regard to parts of northern, central and south-eastern Europe, however, one should consider the fact that in regions where several languages were spoken in one territory, as in the Habsburg Empire, and also in smaller European countries like the Netherlands, Poland and the Nordic countries, Latin was sometimes deliberately upheld far into the nineteenth century – as a matter of fairness to all participants in the transnational republic of letters. Tracing and comparing these different timings and modalities of the transition from Latin into the vernaculars across Europe would be a fascinating as well as necessary theme within a European conceptual history project.[52]

Over centuries the transition from Latin to the vernaculars was a spontaneous, uncoordinated process driven by situational demands in various social fields. It became a voluntary move of language policy, however, from the moment in which it coincided with nation-building or state-building attempts. In France, the deliberative move began early, the famous ordinance of Villers-Cotterêts (1539), which stipulated that French terms had to be used in all legal documents, showing it already in full swing.[53] Similar moves were made earlier in England with the Statute of Pleading (1362), which required that English instead of Law French be used in oral pleadings before courts of law; however, it was only through a statute of 1730 that Law French and Latin were finally eliminated as written languages in English law courts.[54] While both the French ordinance and the English statutes justified the shift to the vernacular in merely practical terms, postulating the understandability of legal proceedings for all subjects, they clearly followed a state- and nation-building agenda. In addition to prohibiting Latin, the French ordinance and later acts of language policy, particularly during the Jacobin phase of the French Revolution, were also targeted against the use of local patois and regional languages such as Occitan, thus accentuating the drive towards national linguistic unity.[55] Similar legislative acts concerning legal and administrative language use can no doubt be found in many European countries. Studying the translation activities of legal terms before and after such legislative acts would be a highly rewarding approach to understand semantic change, because there is hardly any sphere of life in which everyday concepts are unaffected by legal terminology.

Proceeding from the examples of the French and English statutes to promote the national language, conceptual historians might find it useful, for analytical purposes, to introduce a distinction between the uncoordinated process of vernacularization and the conscious moves to achieve, or preserve, national linguistic unity. In a short formula one might call the latter process the 'nationalization' of language use. Nationalization in this sense, again, has two dimensions. The first is directed internally, and aims at suppressing dialects and regional or minority languages in the interest of a unitary nation state in linguistic terms; the second is directed towards the outside world and follows an agenda of purging the national language of foreign vocabulary, whether of Latin or other origin. Examples of both dimensions of nationalizing the use of terms may be found in many European countries. The internal dimension usually came to the fore shortly after nation states had been set up. At such moments, new national governments more or less vigorously sought to consolidate a unity still considered to be precarious by promoting the use of a national standard language, which could either be an ethnic majority language, as in imperial Germany after 1871, or a regional variation enjoying high cultural prestige, as in unified Italy from the 1860s on.

The external dimension of nationalizing language use was particularly prominent in times of war, occupation, (semi)colonial domination or perceived cultural dominance by one of the more powerful European nations and its language. Thus, from the eighteenth century on, and most strongly during and after the Napoleonic imposition of French as the legal, political and administrative language in occupied Europe, nationally minded intellectual and literary elites – particularly in Germany, but also in other parts of the Continent from Spain and Italy to the Netherlands – discovered their own languages as a resource to be protected and purified from French influence.[56] Later in the nineteenth century, similar protective and purifying movements were directed against the use of the German language in countries under Habsburg or German imperial rule and aspiring to form a cultural if not political nation – for example, Bohemia, the northern parts of Italy, and the western parts of Poland.

In most parts of Europe both tendencies of nationalizing language use peaked in the later nineteenth and the early decades of the twentieth centuries, yet attempts to prohibit the use of foreign languages, to proscribe foreign terms and to replace them by more or less artificial autochthonous terms have not been absent in the period after 1945, the main target now being the English language, perceived by some as a threat to national identity and particular cultural values. Contrary to the earlier endeavours to create and stabilize national languages, however, these purely defensive, protectionist efforts have proven to be mostly futile. The calls of French cultural critics to fight so-called 'franglais' – the interspersion of the French language with English, or pseudo-English, terms – are perhaps the most prominent example of such a failure.[57] From a conceptual history perspective, though, even unsuccessful efforts to keep national languages 'pure' from foreign, in this case Anglo-American, influences are worth studying, as they may have given rise to the formation of new, or the redefinition of existing, concepts.

The fact that in the decades since 1945 English has increasingly served as a global lingua franca, spoken by several billion people around the globe as a first, second or third language, creates problems that are in some respects comparable to the use of Latin in medieval and early modern Europe. Then, as now, functional multilingualism was considered a normality by the more mobile social groups, students, businesspeople, diplomats, and so on. Then, as now, the degree to which the lingua franca was mastered determined to a significant extent the opportunities to access knowledge and actively participate in debates going on in a translocal, nowadays increasingly global, public sphere. Then, as now, certain lexical domains linked to professional activities were invaded by the terms of the lingua franca, even if the oral or written communication in question happened to be conducted in one of the vernacular languages. Whether the ongoing anglicization of terms in the worlds of business management, labour relations, academia, mass media, leisure activities and international negotiations of all kinds will result in a durable rapprochement of the conceptual universes in different world regions and languages remains to be seen. At present it seems rather unlikely that global English will suffer the same fate as Latin in early modern Europe: the fate of being eliminated in favour of vernacular languages, themselves subject to nationalization. Yet for good reasons historians are reluctant to forecast events that may, or may not, happen in a very distant future. Our priority as conceptual historians should be to describe and explain the semantic changes that have already been brought about in recent decades by the anglicization of vocabularies in and beyond Europe. Without resorting to dubious historical analogies, the analytical framework for studying the processes of vernacularization and nationalization briefly sketched above, and to be further elaborated, might be of some use for that purpose as well.

Conclusion

It is perhaps no accident that our search for temporal frameworks of a European conceptual history has resulted in a discussion about the changing spatial outreach and functional uses – and also the global cultural significance – of certain languages. This shift of attention reflects present-day problems of conceptual clashes and power asymmetries in a globalized world – clashes and asymmetries which are in part a consequence of the parallel, but uneven, uses of many vernacular (or national) languages in one and the same space. The discussion of the European experience has shown that on a basic level these contemporary problems are not entirely new. A long-term perspective on European conceptual history may therefore be a fruitful way of approaching a global conceptual history still to be elaborated.

A European conceptual history conceived with such an extended vision of its purpose can no longer be bound by the limited, if still inspiring, temporal framework developed by Reinhart Koselleck for the project on German key concepts. Not only should the time span to be investigated be much enlarged, to reach from the Middle Ages to the twenty-first century. More importantly, the very particular and in a way also unilinear view of history and modernity that informed Koselleck's approach in the *Geschichtliche Grundbegriffe*[58] should be abandoned and replaced by an analytical framework that focuses on an array of processes to be studied on a long-term basis and at a micro-diachronic level. In addition, these processes should no longer be regarded as one-way developments towards our own times (modernity), but as movements that are potentially reversible and repeatable, although of course never in an identical fashion, in various historical constellations.

This chapter has briefly discussed seven of these processes: first the four components of Koselleck's *Sattelzeit* hypothesis, namely politicization, ideologization, democratization and the entiming of concepts, and second, three processes related to the issue of cultural or political preponderance of certain languages in a particular territorial space, in this case Europe – namely, vernacularization, nationalization and anglicization. One might be tempted to present all seven processes in a historical model of successive stages. However, bearing in mind that there is no such thing as a standard sequence of linguistic, political or social development, one should refrain from such an attempt. Rather than assuming one normal, or even several typical successions of stages, conceptual historians should content themselves with considering each of the processes individually, assess their importance and timing for various political or linguistic units, and, finally, compare the mechanisms of semantic change at work in the respective constellations. An overall periodization providing one temporal framework, equally valid for all European conceptual histories, is neither possible nor desirable.

Willibald Steinmetz is Professor of Modern and Contemporary Political History at Bielefeld University and was director of the Collaborative Research Centre *The Political as a Communicative Space in History* (2004–2012). He has published extensively on political languages, parliamentary rhetoric and the use of sociopolitical concepts. His current research interests include the history of comparison as a practice in modern and contemporary Europe. Among his publications in English are *Writing Political History Today* (Campus, 2013), *Political Languages in the Age of Extremes* (OUP, 2011, 2nd edition 2012) and *The Force of Comparison* (Berghahn, 2019).

Notes

1. For further reflections on this issue, see Chapter 1 in this volume, by Helge Jordheim.
2. Lucien Febvre, 'Les mots et les choses en histoire économique', *Annales d'histoire économique et sociale* 2 (1930), 233.
3. Lucien Febvre, 'Civilisation. Évolution d'un mot et d'un groupe d'idées', in idem et al., *Civilisation – Le mot et l'idée*, ed. Fondation 'Pour la science', Centre international de synthèse, Première semaine internationale de synthèse, 2e fasc.,

20–25 May 1929 (Paris: La Renaissance du livre, 1930), 10–59; Febvre's article on *civilisation* is remarkable in that it situates the term in a wider semantic field, containing among others the terms *civilité*, *politesse* and *police*, and also because it includes reflections on possible conceptual transfers between France and England as well as on the differences between the Anglo-French notions of *civilisation* and the German concepts of *Bildung* and *Kultur* around 1800 and further into the nineteenth century.

4. Lucien Febvre, *Le problème de l'incroyance au 16e siècle. La religion de Rabelais* (Paris: Michel, 1942).
5. Not without elaborating, of course, much more extensively than Febvre upon the reasons for doing so, cf. Rolf Reichardt, 'Einleitung', in idem and Eberhard Schmitt (eds), *Handbuch politisch-sozialer Grundbegriffe in Frankreich 1680–1820*, vol. 1/2 (Munich: Oldenbourg, 1985), 39–148, esp. 69–78.
6. Reinhart Koselleck, 'Einleitung', in Otto Brunner, Werner Conze and Reinhart Koselleck (eds), *Geschichtliche Grundbegriffe: Historisches Lexikon zur politisch-sozialen Sprache in Deutschland* (hereafter referred to as GG), vol. 1 (Stuttgart: Klett-Cotta, 1972), xiv. This foundational text has been translated into English by Michaela Richter: Reinhart Koselleck, 'Introduction and Prefaces to the Geschichtliche Grundbegriffe', *Contributions to the History of Concepts* 6 (2011), 8.
7. On this, see Niklas Olsen, *History in the Plural: An Introduction to the Work of Reinhart Koselleck* (New York: Berghahn Books, 2012); idem, 'Reinhart Koselleck, Karl Löwith und der Geschichtsbegriff', in Carsten Dutt and Reinhard Laube (eds), *Zwischen Sprache und Geschichte: Zum Werk Reinhart Kosellecks* (Göttingen: Wallstein, 2013), 236–55; Reinhart Mehring, 'Begriffsgeschichte mit Carl Schmitt', in Hans Joas and Peter Vogt (eds), *Begriffene Geschichte: Beiträge zum Werk Reinhart Kosellecks* (Frankfurt/Main: Suhrkamp, 2011), 138–68.
8. Cf. Willibald Steinmetz, 'Vierzig Jahre Begriffsgeschichte – The State of the Art', in Heidrun Kämper and Ludwig M. Eichinger (eds), *Sprache – Kognition – Kultur: Sprache zwischen mentaler Struktur und kultureller Prägung* (Berlin and New York: de Gruyter, 2008), 183.
9. For a critical view: Hans Erich Bödeker, 'Aufklärung über Aufklärung? Reinhart Kosellecks Interpretation der Aufklärung', in Dutt and Laube, *Zwischen Sprache und Geschichte*, 128–74; see also Victor Neumann's Chapter 9 in this volume.
10. See in particular his articles on the concepts emanicpation, progress, history, crisis and revolution: Reinhart Koselleck and Karl Martin Grass, 'Emanzipation', in GG, vol. 2 (Stuttgart: Klett-Cotta, 1979), 153–97; Reinhart Koselleck and Christian Meier, 'Fortschritt', in ibid., 351–423; Reinhart Koselleck et al., 'Geschichte, Historie', in ibid., 593–717; Reinhart Koselleck, 'Krise', in GG, vol. 3 (Stuttgart: Klett-Cotta, 1982), 617–50; Reinhart Koselleck et al., 'Revolution', in GG, vol. 4 (Stuttgart: Klett-Cotta, 1984), 653–788.
11. See Hans Ulrich Gumbrecht, 'Pyramiden des Geistes: Über den schnellen Aufstieg, die unsichtbaren Dimensionen und das plötzliche Abebben der

begriffsgeschichtlichen Bewegung', in idem, *Dimensionen und Grenzen der Begriffsgeschichte* (Munich: Fink, 2006), 7–36.
12. See the argument in Walter Sperling, '"Schlafende Schöne"? Vom Sinn und Unsinn der Begriffsgeschichte Russlands. Ein Diskussionsbeitrag', *Jahrbücher für die Geschichte Osteuropas* 60(3) (2012), 373–405.
13. For Russia, see Walter Sperling, 'Vom Randbegriff zum Kampfbegriff: Semantiken des Politischen im ausgehenden Zarenreich (1850–1917)', in Willibald Steinmetz (ed.), *"Politik": Situationen eines Wortgebrauchs im Europa der Neuzeit* (Frankfurt and New York: Campus, 2007), 248–88; for India, see Margrit Pernau, *Ashraf into Middle Classes: Muslims in Nineteenth-Century Delhi* (New Delhi: Oxford University Press, 2013); and for African countries, see Axel Fleisch and Rhiannon Stephens (eds), *Doing Conceptual History in Africa* (New York: Berghahn Books, 2016).
14. Reinhart Koselleck, '*Begriffsgeschichte* and Social History', in idem, *Futures Past: On the Semantics of Historical Time* (Cambridge, MA and London: MIT Press, 1985), 73–91.
15. Koselleck, 'Einleitung', in GG, XIV; idem, 'Introduction and Prefaces', 8.
16. Steinmetz, 'Vierzig Jahre', 183–88.
17. Reinhart Koselleck, *Preußen zwischen Reform und Revolution: Allgemeines Landrecht, Verwaltung und soziale Bewegung von 1791 bis 1848*, 3rd edn (Stuttgart: Klett-Cotta, 1981); a good review of Koselleck's conceptual approach in the book on Prussia can be found in Olsen, *History in the Plural*, 136–41; for a critical reassessment of this book and its impact, see Marian Nebelin, 'Das Preußenbild Reinhart Kosellecks', in Hans-Christof Kraus (ed.), *Das Thema "Preußen" in Wissenschaft und Wissenschaftspolitik vor und nach 1945* (Forschungen zur Brandenburgischen und Preußischen Geschichte, Beiheft 12) (Berlin: Duncker & Humblot, 2013), 333–84.
18. For an elaboration of this argument, see Jörn Leonhard, 'Erfahrungsgeschichten der Moderne: Von der komparativen Semantik zur Temporalisierung europäischer Sattelzeiten', in Joas and Vogt (eds), *Begriffene Geschichte*, 423–48.
19. In his review of the complete *Geschichtliche Grundbegriffe*, Kari Palonen remarks that in the later volumes 'the original dating of the Sattelzeit has become relativised', particularly with regard to its end; see Kari Palonen, 'A Train Reading Marathon: Retrospective Remarks on Geschichtliche Grundbegriffe' (2006), in idem, *Politics and Conceptual Histories: Rhetorical and Temporal Perspectives* (Baden-Baden: Nomos, 2014), 101; Palonen also writes that Koselleck has 'failed to properly explicate why the Sattelzeit would have come to an end around 1850'; see Kari Palonen, 'The Politics of Conceptual History' (2005), in idem, *Politics and Conceptual Histories*, 114.
20. This is Melvin Richter's precise translation; see Melvin Richter, 'Appreciating a Contemporary Classic: The *Geschichtliche Grundbegriffe* and Future Scholarship', *Finnish Yearbook of Political Thought* 1 (1997), 29.
21. I am aware that this is a slightly modernized redescription of what Koselleck said about *Ideologisierbarkeit*, but I think that it is compatible with his thoughts. For

a concise résumé of Freeden's definition of an ideology, see Michael Freeden, *Ideology: A Very Short Introduction* (Oxford: Oxford University Press, 2003); see also Michael Freeden's Chapter 4 in this volume.

22. Iain Hampsher-Monk used this translation in a paper he gave at a conference on 'Moral Concepts' organized by Edward Skidelsky in London on 16 October 2015. I thank Iain Hampsher-Monk for allowing me to use it in this chapter.

23. See Willibald Steinmetz, 'Some Thoughts on a History of Twentieth-Century German Basic Concepts', *Contributions to the History of Concepts* 7(2) (2012), 87–100.

24. On this debate, see Sabine Marquardt, *Polis contra Polemos: Politik als Kampfbegriff der Weimarer Republik* (Cologne: Böhlau, 1997), 59–84; for the use of the noun *Politisierung* and the verb *politisieren* in nineteenth- and twentieth-century Germany, see also Ulrich Meier, Martin Papenheim and Willibald Steinmetz, *Semantiken des Politischen: Vom Mittelalter bis ins 20. Jahrhundert* (Göttingen: Wallstein, 2012), 78, 82–83 and 102; and Kari Palonen, 'Korrekturen zur Geschichte von "Politisierung"', *Archiv für Begriffsgeschichte* 30 (1989), 224–34. With a few exceptions the verb *politisieren* had formerly only been used in an intransitive mode, meaning something like 'talking insignificantly about politics'; from around 1900 the verb *politisieren* and the noun *Politisierung* were increasingly used in a transitive mode, now meaning 'to make something a political issue, which it had not been before'.

25. An excellent study on new forms of language use and communicative practices generally around 1968 in Germany is: Joachim Scharloth, *1968: Eine Kommunikationsgeschichte* (Munich: Fink, 2011); see also idem, 'Revolution in a Word: A Communicative History of Discussion in the German 1968 Protest Movement', in Ingrid Gilcher-Holtey (ed.), *A Revolution of Perception? Consequences and Echoes of 1968* (New York and Oxford: Berghahn Books, 2014), 162–83.

26. On the example of medical doctors, see Tobias Weidner, *Die unpolitische Profession: Deutsche Mediziner im langen 19. Jahrhundert* (Frankfurt: Campus, 2012); see also his case study on Rudolf Virchow: idem, 'Moving across Boundaries: Rudolf Virchow between Medicine and Politics', in Willibald Steinmetz, Ingrid Gilcher-Holtey and Heinz-Gerhard Haupt (eds), *Writing Political History Today* (Frankfurt and New York: Campus, 2013), 235–49; on the example of economists, see Stefan Scholl, *Begrenzte Abhängigkeit: "Wirtschaft" und "Politik" im 20. Jahrhundert* (Frankfurt and New York: Campus, 2015).

27. Cf. Willibald Steinmetz and Heinz-Gerhard Haupt, 'The Political as Communicative Space in History: The Bielefeld Approach', in Steinmetz, Gilcher-Holtey and Haupt, *Writing Political History Today*, 26.

28. For a succinct overview of the origin of the ideology concept and its reception across Europe and the United States, see Bo Stråth, 'Ideology and Conceptual History', in Michael Freeden, Lyman Tower Sargent and Marc Stears (eds), *The Oxford Handbook of Political Ideologies* (Oxford: Oxford University Press, 2013), 3–19.

29. Ideologization may also proceed in an unintended fashion, and the resulting ideologies can be much more loosely structured; on this, see Michael Freeden's Chapter 4 in this volume.
30. As for example in Stalinist Russia during the 'Great Patriotic War' against Germany; see Sarah Davies and James Harris, *Stalin's World: Dictating the Soviet Order* (New Haven, CT and London: Yale University Press, 2014), 175.
31. The 'end of ideology' debate is resumed in Howard Brick, 'The End of Ideology Thesis', in Freeden, Sargent and Stears, *Handbook of Political Ideologies*, 90–112.
32. On the increasing 'volatility' in the meanings of concepts, see Christian Geulen, 'Plädoyer für eine Geschichte der Grundbegriffe des 20. Jahrhunderts', *Zeithistorische Forschungen / Studies in Contemporary History* 7 (2010), 91–93; and Steinmetz, 'Some Thoughts', 98; but cf. against this argument Michael Freeden's remarks on 'unending ideology': Michael Freeden, 'The Morphological Analysis of Ideology', in Freeden, Sargent and Stears, *Handbook of Political Ideologies*, 123–24.
33. Cf. Ingrid Schierle, 'Semantiken des Politischen im Russland des 18. Jahrhunderts', in Steinmetz, *"Politik"*, 227 and 239.
34. See the Chapter 10 by Henrik Stenius in this volume.
35. A classic study for England is: Gareth Stedman Jones, *Languages of Class: Studies in English Working Class History, 1832–1982* (Cambridge: Cambridge University Press, 1983). Examples from more recent case studies on the Netherlands, Romania, and the Ibero-American world: Joost J. Kloek and Karin Tilmans (eds), *Burger: Geschiedenis van het begrip 'burger' in de Nederlanden van de Middeleeuwen tot de 21ste eeuw* (Amsterdam: Amsterdam University Press, 2002); Victor Neumann, '*Neam* (Romanian for *Kin*) and *Popor* (Romanian for *People*): The Notions of Romanian Ethno-Centrism', in Victor Neumann and Armin Heinen (eds), *Key Concepts of Romanian History: Alternative Approaches to Socio-Political Languages* (Budapest and New York: Central European University Press, 2013), 377–402; Javier Fernández Sebastián and Cristóbal Aljovín de Losada (eds), *Diccionario político y social del mundo iberoamericano: La era de las revoluciones 1750–1850* (Madrid: Fundación Carolina, 2009), 177–304 (*Ciudadano / Vecino*), 849–978 (*Nación*), 1115–1250 (*Pueblo / Pueblos*).
36. Cf. Jörg Fisch, *The Right of Self-Determination of Peoples: The Domestication of an Illusion* (New York: Cambridge University Press, 2016); Jörg Fisch (ed.), *Die Verteilung der Welt: Selbstbestimmung und das Selbstbestimmungsrecht der Völker* [The World Divided: Self-Determination and the Right of Peoples to Self-Determination] (Munich: Oldenbourg, 2011).
37. Stefan-Ludwig Hoffmann (ed.), *Human Rights in the Twentieth Century* (Cambridge: Cambridge University Press, 2011); Jan Eckel and Samuel Moyn (eds), *The Breakthrough: Human Rights in the 1970s* (Philadelphia: University of Pennsylvania Press, 2014); Jan Eckel, *Die Ambivalenz des Guten: Menschenrechte in der internationalen Politik seit den 1940ern* (Göttingen: Vandenhoeck &

Ruprecht, 2014); Bettina Heintz and Britta Leisering (eds), *Menschenrechte in der Weltgesellschaft: Deutungswandel und Wirkungsweise eines globalen Leitwerts* (Frankfurt and New York: Campus, 2015).

38. There is, however, evidence of an emergent language of 'improvement' in England from the mid seventeenth century onwards, which can be seen as anticipating all-European eighteenth-century concepts of 'progress'; on this, see Paul Slack, *The Invention of Improvement: Information and Material Progress in Seventeenth-Century England* (Oxford: Oxford University Press, 2015), esp. 4–8, 242–64. There is also evidence that temporalized visions of history in the Koselleckian sense can be found before the mid eighteenth century: see Stefanie Stockhorst, 'Novus ordo temporum. Reinhart Kosellecks These von der Verzeitlichung des Geschichtsbewußtseins durch die Aufkärungshistoriographie in methodenkritischer Perspektive', in Joas and Vogt (eds), *Begriffene Geschichte*, 359–86; Jan Marco Sawilla, 'Geschichte und Geschichten zwischen Providenz und Machbarkeit. Überlegungen zu Reinhart Kosellecks Semantik historischer Zeiten', in ibid., 387–422; in my opinion these findings do not invalidate the temporalization hypothesis as such.

39. On the unfolding and variations of progressive comparisons in eighteenth- and nineteenth-century Europe, see Willibald Steinmetz, '"Vergleich" – eine begriffsgeschichtliche Skizze', in Angelika Epple and Walter Erhart (eds), *Die Welt beobachten: Praktiken des Vergleichens* (Frankfurt and New York: Campus, 2015), 125–28.

40. So much so that British and German conservatives in the 1960s and 1970s conceived of themselves as the real progressives; see Martina Steber, 'A Better Tomorrow: Making Sense of Time in the Conservative Party and the CDU/CSU in the 1960s and 1970s', *Journal of Modern European History* 13(3) (2015), 317–37.

41. See, for example, the story of 'Khor and Kalinych', two Russian peasants, in Ivan Turgenev, *Sketches from a Hunter's Album* (1852), transl. with an introduction and notes by Richard Freeborn (London: Penguin Books, 1990), 13–28.

42. For an explanation of this method, see Willibald Steinmetz, *Das Sagbare und das Machbare: Zum Wandel politischer Handlungsspielräume – England 1780–1867* (Stuttgart: Klett-Cotta, 1993), 30–40; idem, '"A Code of its Own": Rhetoric and Logic of Parliamentary Debate in Modern Britain', *Finnish Yearbook of Political Thought* 6 (2002), 84–104.

43. On the ambivalences and tensions within green ideologies, see Mathew Humphrey, 'Green Ideology', in Freeden, Sargent and Stears, *Handbook of Political Ideologies*, 422–38.

44. For a first attempt to trace the history of the concept, see Olaf Bach, *Die Erfindung der Globalisierung: Entstehung und Wandel eines zeitgeschichtlichen Grundbegriffs* (Frankfurt/Main: Campus, 2013).

45. The starting point of the debate was Shmuel N. Eisenstadt, 'Multiple Modernities', *Daedalus* 129 (2000), 1–29; different views are summarized in

Wolfgang Knöbl, 'Multiple Modernities and Political Sociology', in Sérgio Costa et al. (eds), *The Plurality of Modernity: Decentering Sociology* (Munich: Hampp, 2006), 215–27; see also Wolfgang Knöbl, 'The Origins of the Social Sciences and the Problem of Conceptualizing "Modernity"/"Modernities"', in Sven Trakulhun and Ralph Weber (eds), *Delimiting Modernities: Conceptual Challenges and Regional Responses* (Lanham, MD: Lexington Books, 2015), 79–96.
46. Prominent among those who argued in that direction were the German linguist Leo Weisgerber (1899–1985) and the American linguists Edward Sapir (1884–1939) and Benjamin Lee Whorf (1897–1941).
47. Barbara Cassin (ed.), *Vocabulaire Européen des philosophies: Dictionnaire des intraduisibles* (Paris: Le Robert/Seuil, 2004); for a (pertinent) critical note on the pertinence of Cassin's notion of 'untranslatable' (*intraduisible*), see Olivier Christin, 'Introduction', in idem (ed.), *Dictionnaire des concepts nomades en sciences humaines* (Paris: Éditions Métailié, 2010), 14–15; for Christin, pretensions of untranslatability as well as claims of easy comparability of terms are ideological operations that conceptual historians need to analyse critically.
48. Cf. Bo Stråth, 'Comparative Conceptual History and Global Translations: An Outline of a Research Agenda' in R. de Cillia et al. (eds), *Diskurs, Politik, Identität – Discourse, Politics, Identity: Festschrift für Ruth Wodak* (Tübingen: Stauffenberg Verlag, 2010), 213–20.
49. For a recent discussion of these problems, see Johann Wolfgang Unger, Michał Krzyżanowski and Ruth Wodak (eds), *Multilingual Encounters in Europe's Institutional Spaces* (London: Bloomsbury, 2014).
50. See Ulrich Meier's discussion of this problem, with examples, in Meier, Papenheim and Steinmetz, *Semantiken des Politischen*, 18–38.
51. I am referring here to thoughts elaborated in an unpublished paper on the concepts of *patria/Vaterland* (fatherland) given by Lucian Hölscher at a workshop on 'Dutch Conceptual History in Comparative Perspective', Amsterdam, 15–16 June 2006.
52. Another interesting problem is to study the constant translational moves between the new professional languages of bureaucrats, academics, politicians and so on, and the vernacular languages.
53. See the text at: https://fr.wikisource.org/wiki/Ordonnance_de_Villers-Cotter%C3%AAts; the relevant articles here are nos. 110 and 111.
54. 36 Edw. III c. 15, see: http://www.languageandlaw.org/TEXTS/STATS/PLEADING.HTM; and 4 Geo. II c. 26, see: http://web.archive.org/web/20050226023444/http://home.freeuk.net/don-aitken/ast/ag2.html#249.
55. Sylvain Auroux, 'Le modèle français de politique linguistique: de la monarchie à la révolution', in Michel Bozdémir and Louis-Jean Calvet (eds), *Politiques linguistiques en Mediterranée* (Paris: Honoré Champion, 2010), 37–54; for similar policies and reactions to them in countries around the Mediterranean, see the other chapters in that volume. Countermovements to such policies in contemporary Europe are discussed in Alistair Cole and Jean-Baptiste Harguindéguy

(eds), *The Politics of Ethnolinguistic Mobilization in Europe: Language Matters* (London: Routledge, 2014).

56. An interesting case study on such language disputes in a northern German Napoleonic satellite state, the short-lived Kingdom of Westphalia, is Claudie Paye, *"Der französischen Sprache mächtig": Kommunikation im Spannungsfeld von Sprachen und Kulturen im Königreich Westphalen 1807–1813* (Munich: Oldenbourg, 2013).

57. The fight was opened by René Étiemble, *Parlez-vous franglais?* (Paris: Gallimard, 1964); more recent contributions to the debate: Paul Bogaards, *On ne parle pas franglais: la langue française face à l'anglais* (Bruxelles: De Boeck Duculot, 2008); Philipp Tody, *Le Franglais: Forbidden English, Forbidden American: Law, Politics, and Language in Contemporary France. A Study in Loanwords and National Identity* (London: Athlone, 2010).

58. In some of his own essays on historical semantics, most notably in his article on asymmetric counterconcepts, Koselleck went far beyond the temporal framework he devised for the authors of *Geschichtliche Grundbegriffe* and stressed the repeatability and reversibility of conceptual developments: see Reinhart Koselleck, 'The Historical-Political Semantics of Asymmetric Counterconcepts', in idem, *Futures Past*, 159–97.

References

Auroux, Sylvain, 'Le modèle français de politique linguistique: de la monarchie à la révolution', in Michel Bozdémir and Louis-Jean Calvet (eds), *Politiques linguistiques en Mediterranée* (Paris: Honoré Champion, 2010), 37–54

Bach, Olaf, *Die Erfindung der Globalisierung: Entstehung und Wandel eines zeitgeschichtlichen Grundbegriffs* (Frankfurt/Main: Campus, 2013)

Bödeker, Hans Erich, 'Aufklärung über Aufklärung? Reinhart Kosellecks Interpretation der Aufklärung', in Carsten Dutt and Reinhard Laube (eds), *Zwischen Sprache und Geschichte: Zum Werk Reinhart Kosellecks* (Göttingen: Wallstein, 2013), 128–74

Bogaards, Paul, *On ne parle pas franglais: la langue française face à l'anglais* (Bruxelles: De Boeck Duculot, 2008)

Brick, Howard, 'The End of Ideology Thesis', in Michael Freeden, Lyman Tower Sargent and Marc Stears (eds), *The Oxford Handbook of Political Ideologies* (Oxford: Oxford University Press, 2013), 90–112

Cassin, Barbara (ed.), *Vocabulaire Européen des philosophies: Dictionnaire des intraduisibles* (Paris: Le Robert/Seuil, 2004)

Christin, Olivier, 'Introduction', in Olivier Christin (ed.), *Dictionnaire des concepts nomades en sciences humaines* (Paris: Éditions Métailié, 2010), 11–23

Cole, Alistair, and Jean-Baptiste Harguindéguy (eds), *The Politics of Ethnolinguistic Mobilization in Europe: Language Matters* (London: Routledge, 2014)

Davies, Sarah, and James Harris, *Stalin's World: Dictating the Soviet Order* (New Haven, CT and London: Yale University Press, 2014)

Eckel, Jan, *Die Ambivalenz des Guten: Menschenrechte in der internationalen Politik seit den 1940ern* (Göttingen: Vandenhoeck & Ruprecht, 2014)
Eckel, Jan, and Samuel Moyn (eds), *The Breakthrough: Human Rights in the 1970s* (Philadelphia: University of Pennsylvania Press, 2014)
Eisenstadt, Shmuel N., 'Multiple Modernities', *Daedalus* 129 (2000), 1–29
Étiemble, René, *Parlez-vous franglais?* (Paris: Gallimard, 1964)
Febvre, Lucien, 'Civilisation: Évolution d'un mot et d'un groupe d'idées', in Lucien Febvre et al., *Civilisation – Le mot et l'idée*, ed. Fondation 'Pour la science', Centre international de synthèse, Première semaine internationale de synthèse, 2e fasc., 20–25 May 1929 (Paris: La Renaissance du livre, 1930), 10–59
——, 'Les mots et les choses en histoire économique', *Annales d'histoire économique et sociale* 2 (1930), 231–34
——, *Le problème de l'incroyance au 16e siècle: La religion de Rabelais* (Paris: Michel, 1942)
Fernández-Sebastián, Javier, and Cristóbal Aljovín de Losada (eds), *Diccionario político y social del mundo ibericoamericano: La era de las revolucciones 1750–1850* (Madrid: Fundación Carolina, 2009)
Fisch, Jörg (ed.), *Die Verteilung der Welt: Selbstbestimmung und das Selbstbestimmungsrecht der Völker* [The World Divided: Self-Determination and the Right of Peoples to Self-Determination] (Munich: Oldenbourg, 2011)
——, *The Right of Self-Determination of Peoples: The Domestication of an Illusion* (New York: Cambridge University Press, 2016)
Fleisch, Axel, and Rhiannon Stephens (eds), *Doing Conceptual History in Africa* (New York: Berghahn Books, 2016)
Freeden, Michael, *Ideology: A Very Short Introduction* (Oxford: Oxford University Press, 2003)
——, 'The Morphological Analysis of Ideology', in Michael Freeden, Lyman Tower Sargent and Marc Stears (eds), *The Oxford Handbook of Political Ideologies* (Oxford: Oxford University Press, 2013), 115–37
Geulen, Christian, 'Plädoyer für eine Geschichte der Grundbegriffe des 20. Jahrhunderts', *Zeithistorische Forschungen/Studies in Contemporary History* 7 (2010), 79–97
Gumbrecht, Hans Ulrich, 'Pyramiden des Geistes: Über den schnellen Aufstieg, die unsichtbaren Dimensionen und das plötzliche Abebben der begriffsgeschichtlichen Bewegung', in Hans Ulrich Gumbrecht, *Dimensionen und Grenzen der Begriffsgeschichte* (Munich: Fink, 2006), 7–36
Heintz, Bettina, and Leisering, Britta (eds), *Menschenrechte in der Weltgesellschaft: Deutungswandel und Wirkungsweise eines globalen Leitwerts* (Frankfurt and New York: Campus, 2015)
Hoffmann, Stefan-Ludwig (ed.), *Human Rights in the Twentieth Century* (Cambridge: Cambridge University Press, 2011)
Humphrey, Mathew, 'Green Ideology', in Michael Freeden, Lyman Tower Sargent and Marc Stears (eds), *The Oxford Handbook of Political Ideologies* (Oxford: Oxford University Press, 2013), 422–38

Kloek, Joost J., and Karin Tilmans (eds), *Burger: Geschiedenis van het begrip 'burger' in de Nederlanden van de Middeleeuwen tot de 21ste eeuw* (Amsterdam: Amsterdam University Press, 2002)

Knöbl, Wolfgang, 'Multiple Modernities and Political Sociology', in Sérgio Costa et al. (eds), *The Plurality of Modernity: Decentering Sociology* (Munich: Hampp, 2006), 215–27

———, 'The Origins of the Social Sciences and the Problem of Conceptualizing "Modernity"/"Modernities"', in Sven Trakulhun and Ralph Weber (eds), *Delimiting Modernities: Conceptual Challenges and Regional Responses* (Lanham, MD: Lexington Books, 2015), 79–96

Koselleck, Reinhart, 'Einleitung', in Otto Brunner, Werner Conze and Reinhart Koselleck (eds), *Geschichtliche Grundbegriffe: Historisches Lexikon zur politisch-sozialen Sprache in Deutschland*, vol. 1 (Stuttgart: Klett-Cotta, 1972), xiii–xxvii

———, *Preußen zwischen Reform und Revolution: Allgemeines Landrecht, Verwaltung und soziale Bewegung von 1791 bis 1848*, 3rd edn (Stuttgart: Klett-Cotta, 1981)

———, 'Krise' in Otto Brunner, Werner Conze and Reinhart Koselleck (eds), *Geschichtliche Grundbegriffe: Historisches Lexikon zur politisch-sozialen Sprache in Deutschland*, vol. 3 (Stuttgart: Klett-Cotta, 1982), 617–50

———, '*Begriffsgeschichte* and Social History', in Reinhart Koselleck, *Futures Past: On the Semantics of Historical Time* (Cambridge, MA and London: MIT Press, 1985), 73–91

———, 'The Historical-Political Semantics of Asymmetric Counterconcepts', in Reinhart Koselleck, *Futures Past: On the Semantics of Historical Time* (Cambridge, MA and London: MIT Press, 1985), 159–97

———, 'Introduction and Prefaces to the Geschichtliche Grundbegriffe' [transl. by Michaela Richter], *Contributions to the History of Concepts* 6 (2011), 1–37

Koselleck, Reinhart, and Karl Martin Grass, 'Emanzipation', in Otto Brunner, Werner Conze and Reinhart Koselleck (eds), *Geschichtliche Grundbegriffe: Historisches Lexikon zur politisch-sozialen Sprache in Deutschland*, vol. 2 (Stuttgart: Klett-Cotta, 1979), 153–97

Koselleck, Reinhart, and Christian Meier, 'Fortschritt', in Otto Brunner, Werner Conze and Reinhart Koselleck (eds), *Geschichtliche Grundbegriffe: Historisches Lexikon zur politisch-sozialen Sprache in Deutschland*, vol. 2 (Stuttgart: Klett-Cotta, 1979), 351–423

Koselleck, Reinhart, et al., 'Geschichte, Historie', in Otto Brunner, Werner Conze and Reinhart Werner (eds), *Geschichtliche Grundbegriffe: Historisches Lexikon zur politisch-sozialen Sprache in Deutschland*, vol. 2 (Stuttgart: Klett-Cotta, 1979), 593–717

Koselleck, Reinhart, et al., 'Revolution', in Otto Brunner, Werner Conze and Reinhart Koselleck (eds), *Geschichtliche Grundbegriffe: Historisches Lexikon zur politisch-sozialen Sprache in Deutschland*, vol. 4 (Stuttgart: Klett-Cotta, 1984), 653–788

Leonhard, Jörn, 'Erfahrungsgeschichten der Moderne: Von der komparativen Semantik zur Temporalisierung europäischer Sattelzeiten', in Hans Joas and

Peter Vogt (eds), *Begriffene Geschichte: Beiträge zum Werk Reinhart Kosellecks* (Frankfurt/Main: Suhrkamp, 2011), 423–48

Marquardt, Sabine, *Polis contra Polemos: Politik als Kampfbegriff der Weimarer Republik* (Cologne: Böhlau, 1997)

Mehring, Reinhard, 'Begriffsgeschichte mit Carl Schmitt', in Hans Joas and Peter Vogt (eds), *Begriffene Geschichte: Beiträge zum Werk Reinhart Kosellecks* (Frankfurt/Main: Suhrkamp, 2011), 138–68

Meier, Ulrich, Martin Papenheim and Willibald Steinmetz, *Semantiken des Politischen: Vom Mittelalter bis ins 20. Jahrhundert* (Göttingen: Wallstein, 2012)

Nebelin, Marian, 'Das Preußenbild Reinhart Kosellecks', in Hans-Christof Kraus (ed.), *Das Thema "Preußen" in Wissenschaft und Wissenschaftspolitik vor und nach 1945* (Forschungen zur Brandenburgischen und Preußischen Geschichte, Beiheft 12) (Berlin: Duncker & Humblot, 2013), 333–84

Neumann, Victor, '*Neam* (Romanian for *Kin*) and *Popor* (Romanian for *People*): The Notions of Romanian Ethno-Centrism', in Victor Neumann and Armin Heinen (eds), *Key Concepts of Romanian History: Alternative Approaches to Socio-Political Languages* (Budapest and New York: Central European University Press, 2013), 377–402

Olsen, Niklas, *History in the Plural: An Introduction to the Work of Reinhart Koselleck* (New York: Berghahn Books, 2012)

———, 'Reinhart Koselleck, Karl Löwith und der Geschichtsbegriff', in Carsten Dutt and Reinhard Laube (eds), *Zwischen Sprache und Geschichte: Zum Werk Reinhart Kosellecks* (Göttingen: Wallstein, 2013), 236–55

Palonen, Kari, 'Korrekturen zur Geschichte von "Politisierung"', *Archiv für Begriffsgeschichte* 30 (1989), 224–34

———, 'A Train Reading Marathon: Retrospective Remarks on Geschichtliche Grundbegriffe' (2006), in Kari Palonen, *Politics and Conceptual Histories: Rhetorical and Temporal Perspectives* (Baden-Baden: Nomos, 2014), 95–109

———, 'The Politics of Conceptual History' (2005), in Kari Palonen, *Politics and Conceptual Histories: Rhetorical and Temporal Perspectives* (Baden-Baden: Nomos, 2014), 111–21

Paye, Claudie, *"Der französischen Sprache mächtig": Kommunikation im Spannungsfeld von Sprachen und Kulturen im Königreich Westphalen 1807–1813* (Munich: Oldenbourg, 2013)

Pernau, Margrit, *Ashraf into Middle Classes: Muslims in Nineteenth-Century Delhi* (New Delhi: Oxford University Press, 2013)

Reichardt, Rolf, 'Einleitung' in Rolf Reichardt and Eberhard Schmitt (eds), *Handbuch politisch-sozialer Grundbegriffe in Frankreich 1680–1820*, vol. 1/2 (Munich: Oldenbourg, 1985), 39–148

Richter, Melvin, 'Appreciating a Contemporary Classic: The *Geschichtliche Grundbegriffe* and Future Scholarship', *Finnish Yearbook of Political Thought* 1 (1997), 25–38

Sawilla, Jan Marco, 'Geschichte und Geschichten zwischen Providenz und Machbarkeit: Überlegungen zu Reinhart Kosellecks Semantik historischer

Zeiten', in Hans Joas and Peter Vogt (eds), *Begriffene Geschichte: Beiträge zum Werk Reinhart Kosellecks* (Frankfurt/Main: Suhrkamp, 2011), 387–422

Scharloth, Joachim, *1968: Eine Kommunikationsgeschichte* (Munich: Fink, 2011)

———, 'Revolution in a Word: A Communicative History of Discussion in the German 1968 Protest Movement', in Ingrid Gilcher-Holtey (ed.), *A Revolution of Perception? Consequences and Echoes of 1968* (New York and Oxford: Berghahn Books, 2014), 162–83

Schierle, Ingrid, 'Semantiken des Politischen im Russland des 18. Jahrhunderts', in Willibald Steinmetz (ed.), *"Politik": Situationen eines Wortgebrauchs im Europa der Neuzeit* (Frankfurt and New York: Campus, 2007), 226–47

Scholl, Stefan, *Begrenzte Abhängigkeit: "Wirtschaft" und "Politik" im 20. Jahrhundert* (Frankfurt and New York: Campus, 2015)

Slack, Paul, *The Invention of Improvement: Information and Material Progress in Seventeenth-Century England* (Oxford: Oxford University Press, 2015)

Sperling, Walter, 'Vom Randbegriff zum Kampfbegriff: Semantiken des Politischen im ausgehenden Zarenreich (1850–1917)', in Willibald Steinmetz (ed.), *"Politik": Situationen eines Wortgebrauchs im Europa der Neuzeit* (Frankfurt and New York: Campus, 2007), 248–88

———, '"Schlafende Schöne"? Vom Sinn und Unsinn der Begriffsgeschichte Russlands: Ein Diskussionsbeitrag', *Jahrbücher für die Geschichte Osteuropas* 60(3) (2012), 373–405

Steber, Martina, 'A Better Tomorrow: Making Sense of Time in the Conservative Party and the CDU/CSU in the 1960s and 1970s', *Journal of Modern European History* 13(3) (2015), 317–37

Stedman Jones, Gareth, *Languages of Class: Studies in English Working Class History, 1832–1982* (Cambridge: Cambridge University Press, 1983)

Steinmetz, Willibald, *Das Sagbare und das Machbare: Zum Wandel politischer Handlungsspielräume – England 1780–1867* (Stuttgart: Klett-Cotta, 1993)

———, '"A Code of its Own": Rhetoric and Logic of Parliamentary Debate in Modern Britain', *Finnish Yearbook of Political Thought* 6 (2002), 84–104

———, 'Vierzig Jahre Begriffsgeschichte – The State of the Art', in Heidrun Kämper and Ludwig M. Eichinger (eds), *Sprache – Kognition – Kultur: Sprache zwischen mentaler Struktur und kultureller Prägung* (Berlin and New York: de Gruyter, 2008), 174–97

———, 'Some Thoughts on a History of Twentieth-Century German Basic Concepts', *Contributions to the History of Concepts* 7(2) (2012), 87–100

———, '"Vergleich" – eine begriffsgeschichtliche Skizze', in Angelika Epple and Walter Erhart (eds), *Die Welt beobachten: Praktiken des Vergleichens* (Frankfurt and New York: Campus, 2015), 85–134

Steinmetz, Willibald, and Heinz-Gerhard Haupt, 'The Political as Communicative Space in History: The Bielefeld Approach', in Willibald Steinmetz, Ingrid Gilcher-Holtey and Heinz-Gerhard Haupt (eds), *Writing Political History Today* (Frankfurt and New York: Campus, 2013), 11–33

Stockhorst, Stefanie, 'Novus ordo temporum: Reinhart Kosellecks These von der Verzeitlichung des Geschichtsbewußtseins durch die Aufklärungshistoriographie in methodenkritischer Perspektive', in Hans Joas and Peter Vogt (eds), *Begriffene Geschichte: Beiträge zum Werk Reinhart Kosellecks* (Frankfurt/Main: Suhrkamp, 2011), 359–86

Stråth, Bo, 'Comparative Conceptual History and Global Translations: An Outline of a Research Agenda' in Rudolf de Cillia et al. (eds), *Diskurs, Politik, Identität – Discourse, Politics, Identity: Festschrift für Ruth Wodak* (Tübingen: Stauffenberg Verlag, 2010), 213–20

———, 'Ideology and Conceptual History', in Michael Freeden, Lyman Tower Sargent and Marc Stears (eds), *The Oxford Handbook of Political Ideologies* (Oxford: Oxford University Press, 2013), 3–19

Tody, Philipp, *Le Franglais: Forbidden English, Forbidden American: Law, Politics, and Language in Contemporary France. A Study in Loanwords and National Identity* (London: Athlone, 2010)

Turgenev, Ivan, *Sketches from a Hunter's Album* (1852), transl. with an introduction and notes by Richard Freeborn (London: Penguin Books, 1990)

Unger, Johann Wolfgang, Michał Krzyżanowski and Ruth Wodak (eds), *Multilingual Encounters in Europe's Institutional Spaces* (London: Bloomsbury, 2014)

Weidner, Tobias, *Die unpolitische Profession: Deutsche Mediziner im langen 19. Jahrhundert* (Frankfurt: Campus, 2012)

———, 'Moving across Boundaries: Rudolf Virchow between Medicine and Politics', in Willibald Steinmetz, Ingrid Gilcher-Holtey and Heinz-Gerhard Haupt (eds), *Writing Political History Today* (Frankfurt and New York: Campus, 2013), 235–49

Chapter 3

Concepts and Debates

Rhetorical Perspectives on Conceptual Change

Kari Palonen

'Koselleck and I both assume that we need to treat our normative concepts less as statements about the world than as tools and weapons of debate', writes Quentin Skinner.[1] In one of his final remarks on conceptual history, Koselleck formulated the same point as follows: 'Gerade wegen ihrer Unersetzbarkeit werden die Grundbegriffe als solche strittig' [It is precisely because of their irreplaceability that key concepts become contested].[2]

Strangely enough, few conceptual history scholars have carried further the idea of relating concepts to debates and debates to concepts. In this chapter my aim is to analyse the inherent links between concepts and debates as the clue to a rhetorical interpretation of conceptual changes.[3] For this purpose I shall first discuss some of the underlying assumptions in Koselleck's and Skinner's research programmes for conceptual history from the perspective of studying debates, and then move on to a closer examination of parliaments as exemplary assemblies that practise the politics of debating. To thematize political aspects in the use of concepts in debates, and concepts as pivots of debates, I will, furthermore, apply my scheme of dividing the concept of politics into four aspects – policy, polity, politicking and politicization – and linking them to the paradigmatic types of parliamentary debates. Finally, I shall discuss the relevance of these aspects of debates for a wider range of politics-related concepts. By means of this chapter, as a thought experiment based on my own studies, I shall discuss the implications of employing the investigation of debates for the analysis of conceptual changes.

Concepts and Debates in the *Geschichtliche Grundbegriffe*

Reinhart Koselleck recognizes the link between concepts and debates in a rather indirect manner. His *Einleitung* (Introduction) to the *Geschichtliche Grundbegriffe* (GG) contains only a minimal, but hardly discussed, typology of source paradigms for the analysis of debates in conceptual history. He first mentions the 'classics' – that is, great political philosophers and widely read scholarly literature in different disciplines including also textbooks, 'Lehrbuchverfasser'.[4] His second type consists of the 'lexica', and he recommends to the authors of GG 'die Mindestlektüre der großen *Wörterbücher*' [to read at least the major lexica and encyclopaedias]. He justifies that in the following terms: 'Auf dieser Ebene hat sich das Wissen und Selbstverständnis der Generationen niedergeschlagen, erst der gelehrten, dann der gebildeten Welt, schließlich der publizistisch gebildeten Öffentlichkeit' [It is at this level that the knowledge and self-understanding of successive generations has been condensed; first that of academic scholars, then that of the educated world, and finally that of the reading publics].[5] This level of sources refers both to the canonization of knowledge and the extension of canonized knowledge from the stratum of independent academics and teachers to the entire reading public.

If we read this GG programme in Skinnerian terms of linguistic action,[6] its paradigmatic sources are lexical and classical. Both sources rely on practices of canonization: in the lexical form through the establishment of an up-to-date understanding of the time aimed at the wider reading public, and in the classical form through the academic canonization of texts that are 'obligatory' both as reading for students and as intellectual references for scholarly debates.

More interesting from the debate perspective, however, is a third type of source materials, a broad middle range of sources, which Koselleck alludes to when he speaks of 'die *Streuweite* der Quellen weit in den Alltag hinein' [the outreach of sources far into everyday life].[7] Consideration of such sources, however, is added on without discussing the politics of their formation or classification: 'Sie erfaßt Zeitschriften, Zeitungen, Pamphlete, ebenso Akten der Stände und Parlamente, der Verwaltung und Politik; schließlich Briefe und Tagebücher' [this level encompasses journals, newspapers, pamphlets, written documentation of assemblies of estates and parliaments, of administration and politics; and finally letters and diaries].[8] The triadic division of sources has implications for the understanding of the form and degree of political agency, and the manner in which sources are documented in the GG. In this respect the GG follows a definite paradigmatic perspective on political action in its view on conceptual changes.

The crucial point is that the broad middle range of sources between lexica and the classics is not canonizable. They remain a matter of dispute: with the exception of very personal documents, the other materials more or less reflect institutionalized and proceduralized situations of communication between the actors, such as parliamentary debates. The problem with the GG is that this middle range of sources hardly receives any independent discussion when conceptual changes are analysed in the individual articles.

The preponderance of the two canonized types of source materials is largely responsible for the lexicon's lack of systematic problematization of the link between concepts and their contexts in debates. The GG's two paradigmatic types of sources correspond to its principle of concentrating on the semantics of conceptual changes, which can well be analysed from the canonized sources, without linking them to the rhetorical uses of the concepts. The political struggles over concepts are indirectly present in the GG, namely between different editions of the same lexica, and to some extent between the different lexica, but the political principles of the formation and selection of the entries in the lexica are never presented and compared with each other.

Of course, there are other writings of Reinhart Koselleck in which the agency dimension in conceptual changes appears more explicitly. This is obviously the case with his 1990s studies concerning the debates on how to commemorate the victims of the Second World War, to which Koselleck himself contributed by entering into polemics against the authorities and thematizing their conceptual commitments. Thus, he exposed their play with the double meaning of the notion *Opfer*, as both making a sacrifice and being a victim.[9] In other words, in this case Koselleck argued against the implicit partisanship of the existing debate and wanted to include additional dimensions. More importantly, in a brilliant article Koselleck criticized the asymmetric use of counter-concepts by showing their dead ends.[10] But he hardly ever analysed debates, in which approximately symmetric uses of counter-concepts would be realizable.

Skinner on Concepts and Debates

In Quentin Skinner's work there is a more explicit link between concepts and debates. Skinner's idea that 'there cannot be any histories of concepts as such; there can only be histories of their uses in argument' can be reformulated in terms of understanding concepts as an inherent part of debates.[11] In other words, the use of concepts cannot be understood without analysing it in context with other uses, and through identifying prevailing conventions and the debates on them. The point is to identify and specify the 'moves' in argument, by which the agents situate themselves within a certain context by aiming to *do* something to it – for example, confirming, supporting, transcending, subverting or parodying the conventions by their interventions in the debate – or by initiating a debate where no previous debate seems to exist.

This is my periphrasis summarizing Skinner's programmatic articles on rhetoric and conceptual change,[12] as well as his discussion of the rhetorical means for conceptual changes, in particular in Chapter 4 of *Reason and Rhetoric in the Philosophy of Hobbes*.[13] They are complemented by his empirical studies on the histories of concepts of the state and liberty.[14] Skinner illustrates the historical role of the rhetorical tradition in his polemics against Rubinstein's Aristotelian interpretation of Lorenzetti's pictorial concepts in terms of Roman rhetoric as well as in his extensive studies on conceptual changes in the work of Thomas Hobbes.[15] In the monograph *Hobbes and Republican Liberty*, he argues against the academic *communis opinio* by emphasizing that Hobbes changed his concept of liberty from *Elements of Law* (1640) to *De Cive* (1642) and to *Leviathan* (1651).[16] While Hobbes, for example, originally denied that citizens are free, he shifted towards accepting that even slaves are free, when freedom is generalized to mean the freedom of bodily movement.

In the original 1999 version of his 'Rhetoric and Conceptual Change', Skinner uses the words 'more contingent' twice in order to emphasize the singularity of his own approach. The first time he does it is when distancing himself from the 'history of ideas' à la Arthur Lovejoy; the second time is when he says: 'I have immersed myself in the writings of the ancient theorists of eloquence who originally spoke of rhetorical redescription, and have come to share their more contingent understanding of normative concepts and the fluid vocabularies in which they are generally expressed'.[17] This second emphasis on contingency marks an insight not only relating to a 'recovery of lost traditions' but also to a comprehensive alternative to the study of conceptual changes, which Skinner had not previously thematized in an equally explicit manner, although he practised it for example in his study on the concept of the state in the conclusion of *The Foundations of Modern Political Thought*.[18]

The two central *topoi* of conceptual change that shape Skinner's *Reason and Rhetoric* and subsequent writings are the *paradiastole* and the principle of *in utramque partem disputare*. The paradiastolic rhetorical redescription refers above all to the normative dimension of the concepts, to the close relationship, known since Aristotle, between virtues and their 'neighbouring vices'. For Skinner this opens up the opportunity to use the conceptual pair as a horizon of possibilities that allows the rhetorical devaluation of virtues and also, to a certain extent, an 'extenuation' of the viciousness of vices. In the article 'Paradiastole', Skinner emphasizes that most Renaissance writers had a tendency to concentrate on the exculpation of vices, whereas the dethroning of virtues was seldom seen as acceptable.[19]

To see a situation or move from the opposite perspectives is for Skinner a condition of the paradiastolic redescription.[20] The rhetorical theory of knowledge (indebted to ancient sophists), according to which it is always possible to invent plausible arguments or interesting perspectives against every proposal or every analysis of the situation, marks a challenge to all uses of concepts and hints at a procedure for a fair treatment of conceptual controversies. In an interview from 2008, Skinner sees a still closer link between concepts and debates: 'I now say to my students on Hobbes's "Leviathan", on which I am giving a course at the moment, think of it as a speech in parliament; all of these great works of political philosophy are recognizably contributions to a debate; interpreting them is uncovering what that contribution was'.[21] Here Skinner recognizes that academic struggles can be better understood if we compare them with the more explicit struggles among parliamentarians. Furthermore, he acknowledges that parliament is not merely a familiar site of debate, but also the closest approximation to the ideal type of a deliberative assembly to have developed a systematic procedure for dealing with opposite viewpoints and arguments. Other fora of dispute can be compared to the parliamentary ideal type, and analogies to the parliamentary manner of debating can also be discussed in academic debates.[22]

The Koselleckian emphasis on the controversial character of concepts is largely limited to the general claim that everything that is regarded beyond dispute can be contested. Skinner's rhetorical approach goes beyond this in illuminating both the instruments and the procedures of an open and fair dealing with controversies.

The Rhetoric of Concepts

By 'rhetoric' I refer to human practices of persuading others to accept or reject certain items on the agenda, to introduce new items to the agenda or to remove them from it without formally rejecting them. The rhetorical vision denies the possibility of sufficient grounds to make any definite move while admitting that a debate is limited in time – that is, a decision on the item must be taken sooner or later.

For the analysis of conceptual changes, rhetoric offers us a comparative perspective in the elementary sense that it does not deal with absolute entities but with debates – the pros and cons of motions and arguments. It analyses the strengths and weaknesses of the items debated as well as the similarities and differences among the concepts included in the items on the agenda. The rhetorical point is seldom found in a straightforward acceptance or rejection, but rather in revisions and modifications of the alternatives themselves in the course of a debate that alter their conditions of acceptance. In the Westminster terminology, an amendment that intends 'to suppress, to add, or to substitute' the original motion well illustrates the rhetoric of conceptual change as part of a debate.[23] Rhetoric offers us clues for comparison, not only for the study of the outcome of the actual disputes over concepts but also for the changes of conceptual constellations during debates.

The capacities of rhetoric to allow comparative studies on the uses of concepts in debates are inherently linked to the historical role of rhetoric in European thought. Rhetoric has been part of 'political life itself' that establishes the problems for the political theorist.[24] The question is which of the numerous possibilities included in the rhetorical styles of thought can and should we use for writing conceptual history or political theory? I shall not discuss here, for example, the rhetoric of *topoi*,[25] but merely refer to conceptual change in relation to the deliberative genre of rhetoric, concentrating on the specific possibilities of its parliamentary variant.

The rhetorical genres provide elementary models for comparison. The rhetorical genres of acclamation (epideictic rhetoric), prosecuting, defending and judging (forensic rhetoric), debating *pro et contra* (deliberative, especially parliamentary rhetoric) and negotiating or bargaining (diplomatic rhetoric) offer us a typology of concepts that regulate political struggles in a definite manner and that are related to different political institutions.[26] The different genres also compete with each other over their validity as procedural rules and models designed to regulate controversies.

Deliberative rhetoric is the only genre for which the debate *pro et con* is constitutive. In deliberative rhetoric there is no superior or external authority to decide on the subject, but it is up to the agents themselves to debate and to decide, although they never have sufficient grounds to do so. The parliamentary form of deliberative rhetoric is its most nuanced procedural and institutional form, developed for the systematic treatment of opposed points of view and proposals.

The link between parliamentary debates and conceptual change can already be found in William Gerard Hamilton's *Parliamentary Logick*, a collection of maxims he collated from the English and Irish parliaments from 1754 to 1796. His major point is the recognition that parliamentarians can alter the meaning or rhetorical tone of concepts as a tool in the debate. One example of this is the following maxim: 'Mark whether your adversary and you use the same word in the same sense; and how much, or how little he includes in his idea of anything. He perhaps considers a principal part as if it were the whole.'[27]

Several of Hamilton's maxims use the *paradiastole*; for example: 'When the person or the conduct you wish to defend, is so absolutely indefensible that it would be quite ridiculous to defend it, you have but one thing left; which is, to extenuate, and shew that though it arose from error or a wrong motive, yet the error is not so great as it is alleged, nor was the motive that to which it is ascribed'.[28] The example indicates how the parliament has become the historically paradigmatic political forum of debating, and the closest approximation to a dissensual assembly of debates without a superior arbiter. The parliament provides an institutional procedure for debating compared to which other debates deviate in some respect or another.[29]

Parliament and Rhetoric

Basically, any parliament deserving the name operates by systematizing dissensus among perspectives and by setting up rules of debate on motions on its agenda. In the parliamentary proceduralism of politics every motion is debated in many stages, both in the plenary sessions and in committees. The parliamentary rules and practices also enable actors to broaden the spectrum of political disputes simply by combining them with respect for the persons of the adversaries and for the parliament itself as an institution, although the criteria for 'unparliamentary language' are historical and controversial in themselves.[30] The corpora of parliamentary debates provide an inventory that can be actualized on new occasions, in parliaments of other periods and of other countries.[31]

Concepts used within parliamentary debates may play different roles.[32] We might undertake histories of specific concepts by using parliamentary sources, which might result in different histories from, for example, those produced by using lexical sources. We can also analyse parliamentary debates directly related to conceptual struggles, such as the disputes over democracy in debates on suffrage reforms or on electoral systems. Or we can analyse debates on the concept of parliamentarism itself, which might occur, for instance, in debates directly related to the opposition between constitutional, presidential, plebiscitary and parliamentary regimes. We can also analyse parliamentarism through *parliament-constitutive* concepts such as the (parliamentary) sovereignty, responsibility, representation and deliberation.[33] Or we can ask how far the parliamentary character of deliberations is possible either in parliaments of semi-presidential regimes – such as the French Fifth Republic – or in non-sovereign, regional or supranational parliaments.

At the next level we can speak of *parliament-conditioning* concepts. Parliamentary debates in their formal and regulated character are based on a variety of freedoms: most generally on freedom from dependence, and more particularly on freedom of speech, the free mandate, free elections and freedom from arrest (parliamentary immunity).[34] All of the latter refer to the opposition between freedom and dependence in the sense of the neo-Roman concept of liberty.[35] The parliamentary freedoms specify the political conditions of the members' independence in a deliberative and representative assembly. Or, in Koselleckian terms, the parliamentary freedoms provide an approximation of the symmetric uses of concepts among the debaters.[36]

Finally, we may look at *intra-parliamentary* concepts. These are concepts either used only in parliaments or having a specific parliamentary interpretation. Thus, when I speak here of, for example, motions, amendments, commitments or the Speaker with a capital 'S', I clearly use the concepts only in their parliamentary sense. It is in the parliamentary procedure, in the standing orders and in the procedure tracts, such as Erskine May's (1844, 1883) or Eugène Pierre's (1887), that we can best analyse such intra-parliamentary concepts.[37]

Aspects of Politics

Which kinds of debates can be found in parliaments? We can distinguish a number of subtypes of debates, such as the opposition between the plenary and committee debates, the debates on budgets, on legislation, on votes of no confidence in the government, and so on. Furthermore, we can distinguish between government-initiated and member-initiated debates. Or we can emphasize the difference between debates concerning items on the agenda and those concerning procedure.

In the remaining part of the chapter, however, I want to employ distinctions that pertain to the different ways of addressing political issues in parliamentary debates by referring to some aspects of my studies on the concept of politics. I use 'politics' as an analytical category independently of the actual history of the polit-vocabulary.[38] As such it is important to nuance it by distinguishing its different aspects. The three English nouns for the political – politics, policy and polity – conceptualize well-known dimensions of the political. I have proposed, however, to split 'politics' into politicking and politicization, which results in four nouns, to each of which I have given a temporal interpretation referring to different aspects of the activity of playing with time.[39] In this typology, policy and polity indicate relatively stable, but limited situations, whereas politicking and politicization allude to the broader horizon of possible activities. I once gave the following interpretation to them: 'Politicisation names a share of power, opens a specified horizon of chances in terms of this share, while politicking means performative operations in the struggle for power with the already existing shares and their redistribution.

Polity refers to those power shares that have already been politicised but have also created a kind of vested interest that tacitly excludes other kinds of shares, while policy means a regulation and coordination of performative operations by specific ends and means'.[40]

Looking at these four aspects of the political from a parliamentary point of view enables us to distinguish four specific types of dispute over concepts in parliamentary politics. In my view, *policy* refers to the coordination between the issues on the parliamentary agenda; *polity* opens up questions of regime, of 'parliamentary government', of electing or dismissing government in a parliamentary manner; *politicking* can be interpreted in the sense of the parliamentary procedure, the question, how the items are debated and regulated in a parliamentary manner; and *politicization*, in the parliamentary sense, refers to putting items on the parliamentary agenda. This fourfold scheme of politics can provide ideal types that thematize the specific discernible forms of political elements evident in conceptual disputes. In a wider sense the scheme enables a mode of political reading of conceptual changes within one of the four aspects, or between them.

The debates about the 'policy' aspect concentrate around the theme of the items. Policies concern all the ministries responsible for the government's proposals, or all committees, through which they pass in their parliamentary itinerary. The policy aspect refers to *directive concepts* that aim at an ideal combination of one normative line and the conditions of its realization in a given situation. Disputes over concepts over the directives concern their normative aims as well as their realizability. The conceptual choices concern not only ends and means but also the possibilities contained in the situation, as well as an assessment of the consequences of relevant action.[41]

Governments tend to present their programme by combining normative declarations of principles and teleological direction statements into a certain line or doctrine. In foreign policy, parliaments can only make resolutions, while it is difficult to legislate on their direction. Friedrich Meinecke claimed that every state has at any moment a singular *Staatsräson* – one best possible line or policy that is not a matter of choice but of finding the best interpretation.[42] This is an extreme version that reifies policy into an entity beyond politics.

In the government's annual budget, the stances on the different policy fields are knit together into a programme about the general policy of the government. The budget policy contains obligatory and optional items, and an annual ranking of priorities. It is itself a result of debates within the ministries, between the ministers and their ministries as well as among the ministers. It is submitted to parliament both in its broad lines and in its details, and budget debates thus allow parliamentarians to combine detailed criticisms with an overall judgment of the government's policy. The procedural principle of reserving enough time for the budget debates in the plenum and in the committees also guarantees that the acceptance of a budget is never a mere ratification of the government's policy, even if the final changes made by the parliament may be marginal.

The 'polity' concepts, understood as *regime concepts*, refer to comparisons between political regime types. Some types of action are considered within the regime as ordinary, unproblematic or even recommendable, others remain just tolerable or matters of dispute and eventual subjects of incorporation into the regime, while the third type of actions is excluded as extravagant, politically impossible or condemnable. Disputes on regime concepts deal with the principles of a regime, what is included and what is excluded, as well as with controversies over interpreting the borderline between the legitimate and the illegitimate.

Parliamentarism is a type of regime that is opposed to non-parliamentary regimes, such as monarchical, presidential and plebiscitarian ones, and can also be contrasted with extra-parliamentary forms of acting politically. The conventional conceptual histories of parliamentarism deal with the criteria that distinguish the parliamentary regime from others.[43] 'Parliamentarism' itself has, of course, also been subject to different interpretations: the 'monistic' model of cabinet government, in which – according to Walter Bagehot – the cabinet is understood as an executive committee of the parliament, was opposed to the 'dualistic' model of Robert Redslob.[44] For the parliamentary responsibility of government the minimum criterion is the parliament's power to dismiss the government by a vote of no confidence. Max Weber, for example, went further and demanded that parliament also should have the power to appoint the government, which is not the case in Britain, and that the ministers' parliamentary responsibility should be more rigorously enforced when as ministers they also remained members of parliament.[45]

Josef Redlich, among others, claimed that if government were to be turned into an executive committee of the parliament, this would make the 'old opposition' between parliament and government obsolete.[46] By contrast, for Weber the crucial political point was the parliamentary control of government against the overwhelming power of officialdom, and he proposed different measures, such as the cross-examination of the officials and the parliamentary control commissions, to submit the allegedly superior knowledge of the officials to detailed parliamentary scrutiny.[47] One might argue, however, that making the parliamentary responsibility of government the only criterion for parliamentarism might rather easily result in unparliamentary forms of conduct while marginalizing the deliberative aspects of the parliament.

Governments are tempted to supersede the proceduralism of parliamentary politics and thorough debate.

The conceptual disputes relating to 'politicking' refer to the *procedure concepts* for conducting and regulating debates. The procedural character of the deliberations themselves is indispensable for the parliamentary form of politics. In no other institution is the dissensus between perspectives so deeply embedded in the entire mode of proceeding as it is in the parliament. Politicking in parliaments has to operate with the insight that the consideration of a motion from the opposite point of view is a necessary condition for the proper understanding of the motion itself.

In parliamentary politics the dissensus between perspectives conceptually precedes the formation of the parties, and the debate *pro et contra* has its point in the very possibility of altering the distribution between adherents and adversaries of a motion, at least of their arguments if not their votes. The formation of a distinct parliamentary procedure has been developed in Westminster since the late sixteenth century and institutionalizes the dissensus and debate into necessary conditions of parliamentary politics as such.[48] The extension of procedural items and the priority of the procedural over substantial questions on the parliamentary agenda allow members to pose a question of 'order' that compels the Speaker of the parliament to consider whether the member currently speaking violates the rules of parliamentary procedure.[49]

The rules of parliamentary procedure remain themselves controversial. The procedural tracts of John Hatsell (1818), Jeremy Bentham (1843) and Thomas Erskine May (1844, 1883) provide repertoires of procedural disputes and their changing histories.[50] May's nine editions of his *Treatise* from 1844 to 1883 illustrate the growing insight that, in the course of the nineteenth century, procedural disputes increasingly concerned the range of application of rules that appeared to oppose each other. The principle of free speech could be limited merely to the content of speeches or could also be valid for their length, thus allowing its obstructive use. Parliamentary procedure designed to deal with time combines spending and saving time in an original manner. The principle of fair play requires a sufficient time to debate the items on the agenda, but parliamentarians have always known that time is a scarce resource. The democratization of the suffrage and the parliamentarization of government greatly increased the number of items on the parliamentary agenda as well as the willingness of members to speak in the plenum. The obstruction campaigns towards the end of the nineteenth century are merely the tip of the iceberg of increasingly scarce parliamentary time. The principle of fair play required a reinterpretation as the fair distribution of parliamentary time.[51]

Detailed histories of parliamentary politics are therefore inherently concerned with debates on seemingly technical concepts of parliamentary procedure. In the practice of parliamentary debating we can distinguish several types of intra-parliamentary concepts of action and debate: concepts referring to parliamentary *moves*, to parliamentary *order*, to parliamentary *time* and to parliamentary *agenda*. They refer to different aspects of parliamentary debate, they have different histories of conceptual changes, and there are explicit disputes surrounding these concepts. In terms of classical rhetoric, moves refer to *elocutio*, their regulation by order and time to *dispositio*, and the agenda to *inventio*.[52]

Finally, with regard to disputes related to 'politicization', I would argue that an item is politicized in the parliamentary sense – that is, exposed to controversy – only when it is put on set to the parliamentary agenda. The politics of agenda can be divided into three moves: putting questions on the agenda, retaining them in the 'possession' of the parliament, and removing questions from the agenda. Disputes related to politicization, then, refer to the *agenda-setting concepts* and to the rhetoric of *inventio*. Conceptual disputes on the agenda-setting are, furthermore, related to the ranking, weight and urgency among the items and to the procedures of the agenda-setting itself. They either concern competition between agents to determine the agenda or the extension of procedural struggles to the agenda-setting controversies. Such agenda-setting disputes may also concern the horizons of the possible of an established regime, or questions related to the existing procedural regulations.

Questions on a parliament's agenda can be divided into obligatory and optional. The obligatory questions are those on the regular agenda of the parliament. The fiscal powers of the state are the oldest conceptual layer of obligatory items, which can be decided only by parliament. They justify its regular summoning, as institutionalized for the first time by the Triennial Act of 1641 in Westminster. Since the Glorious Revolution of 1688–89, the English and later British parliament has met annually to debate and decide on the government's budget. The parliamentarization of government prolonged the list of obligatory items, illustrated by the invention of new ministries or parliamentary committees. For a long time foreign policy remained part of the government's *arcana*, whereas parliament enjoyed considerable budgetary powers also in regimes without a parliamentary government, such as the German Reichstag before 1918. The obligatory items refer to the past politicization of parliamentary questions.

The optional items are based on the initiatives of individual members or on governmental programmes. Members' initiatives are spontaneous moves that aim at setting new questions to the agenda, and they also serve as part of the members' political profiles. All kinds of events in the country and in the world may also oblige the government to introduce items to the agenda that require urgent treatment, independently of its initial programme. From the nineteenth century onwards we can speak of the growing importance of controversies over the politics of parliamentary agenda-setting. The political divides no longer concerned exclusively different answers to the same questions but also controversies over what questions were likewise crucial or urgent. The dissolving of strong party lines and the new opportunities for debates initiated by backbenchers, and the creation of an individual political profile for the parliamentarians, are connected to these debates on the agenda-setting.

Many interpreters, including Josef Redlich, accord the government – as the executive committee of the parliament – priority in agenda-setting, without fearing the reduction of parliamentary powers.[53] When parliamentary agenda-setting is recognized as inherently controversial, this would rather support the possibility of extending the procedure of debating *pro et contra* from the items already on the agenda to the agenda-setting itself. The question remains, how this could be done without further increasing the pressure on parliamentary time. Here the parliamentary imagination of both members and scholars is a desideratum.

Rhetoric, Concepts, Politics

Parliaments are not the only deliberative assemblies in existence today. Deliberations also take place in debating societies and in debating competitions, as well as in many quasi- and semi-parliamentary assemblies, in meetings and in organizations, from the local level up to supranational politics. For example, the Inter-Parliamentary Union can be regarded as a transnational debating society of parliamentarians, and the United Nations General Assembly as an assembly combining parliamentary and intergovernmental aspects. They may not be based on direct elections, or claim any representativeness, and in many cases may not have a decisive vote either. Nonetheless, in all cases we may speak of parliamentary analogies or parliamentary aspects in these assemblies in the sense that the procedural forms of debates and parliamentary principles such as fair play are presupposed to serve as the model to which these debating assemblies are compared, or compare themselves.

Besides the concepts of politics and parliamentarism, many other key concepts could be analysed in political terms by the use of the above outlined typology of directive concepts, regime concepts, procedure concepts and agenda-setting concepts, and their mutual relationships. Possibly some concepts gravitate towards regime-type concepts – democracy as connected with universal and equal suffrage could be a case in point – whereas others are more directive oriented. After all, government as such depends on policies, on acting with certain normative-cum-teleological directives. Indeed, a government might, for example, be characterized as democratic in regime terms or as parliamentary in procedural terms. The criteria and the qualifications of such concepts are subject to disputes and conceptual changes.

Take the example of the German concept of *Herrschaft*, translated as 'rulership' (and no longer 'domination') in current studies. Its traditional meaning refers to the personalized rule by a *Herr*, a prince with a court or a feudal patron with an estate.[54] In the language of Max Weber the concept of *Herrschaft* is, however, neutralized into a special case of *Macht*, of an asymmetric type of power shares,[55] thus abandoning the connotation of a definite regime and referring instead to competition over legitimacy between different regimes.[56] This is emphasized in Weber's letter to Robert Michels on 31 January 1910, when he accuses Michels of employing an all-too-simple concept of *Herrschaft* in his famous book *Zur Soziologie des Parteiwesens in der modernen Demokratie*,[57] one that fails to recognize the omnipresence and instability of the relations of rulership.[58] Or, to put it in Skinnerian terms, Weber has managed a paradiastolic redescription of the concept that allows it to be used both by those who exercise rulership and those who contest it in a specific context.

The Weberian neutralization of the concept has, in other words, transformed *Herrschaft* from a partisan concept into one used by all parties, corresponding to Koselleck's criteria for a *Grundbegriff*. Whereas the feudal *Herrschaft* refers to a stable order, the neutralized Weberian concept of *Herrschaft* thematizes alternative types of rule and asks for their forms of legitimization. The older concept refers to a distinct type of regime, while the Weberian concept makes the choice between regimes a matter of debate as well as subject to different forms of justifying them, as expressed in the Weberian types of legitimacy.

In contemporary debates on the concepts of rulership, both historical layers of its princely or feudal origins and its Weberian neutralization remain controversial. The traditional connotation persists in the usage adopted by Hannah Arendt, for whom *Herrschaft* is a counter-concept of *Macht*, and who misses the point of Weber's conceptual strategy of neutralization.[59] This neutralization is, however, prominent in Weber's other major move, namely that of reformulating the concept of the state as another Weberian *Chance*-concept that is neither to be lauded nor demonized. That aspect is most explicitly presented in his last lecture series in the spring of 1920, which also clearly separates Weber from the German tradition of the concept as exposed by Koselleck and others.[60]

Writing conceptual histories in terms of my scheme for a 'decentring' of the concept of politics can also be used to analyse the political dimension of any concept. To detect the presence of such a dimension is not the point. The point is rather to explore the profile of the four aspects and their changing relations to each other. It is easy to claim that a concept has a political dimension, but we then need analytical tools to illustrate how that is manifested, which aspects are the subject of conceptual controversies, and how the constellations of disputes have shifted in the course of time. In short, conceptual histories are connected to politics through their inherent link to debates, but we also have to render intelligible the specific types of conceptual disputes that express the range of variation to be found in the political aspect of any key concept as they are utilized in debates.

Of course, debate-bound forms of conceptual change cannot provide intelligibility to such radical changes as Koselleck's *Sattelzeit* thesis. Radical changes in the very type of conceptualization, such as post-*Sattelzeit* concepts, can only be introduced from above, in the sense of the tacit adoption of new kinds of conceptualization, circumventing a thorough debate of a parliamentary type. In democratic and parliamentary politics, such a suprapolitical unity of conceptualization is lost. This does not prevent politicians, scholars, journalists or writers from introducing conceptual changes through revising the agenda of debates, although there can be no guarantee of success.

Kari Palonen is Professor of Political Science at the University of Jyväskylä. He is editor-in-chief of the journal *Redescriptions*, and co-chair of the Standing Group 'Political Concepts' of the European Consortium for Political Research. He was co-founder of the 'History of Concepts' group, Academy of Finland Professor, and director of the Finnish Centre of Excellence in Political Thought and Conceptual Change. His books deal with: the history of the concept of politics; the political thought of Max Weber; the principles and practices of conceptual history; and the procedure, rhetoric and concepts of parliamentary politics.

Notes

1. Quentin Skinner, 'Rhetoric and Conceptual Change', *Finnish Yearbook of Political Thought* 3 (1999), 62.
2. Reinhart Koselleck, *Begriffsgeschichten*, ed. Carsten Dutt (Frankfurt/M: Suhrkamp, 2006), 534.
3. See also Kari Palonen, 'Begriffsdebatten und Debattenbegriffe: Das parlamentarische Paradigma des Begriffstreits und –wandels', *Zeitschrift für Politische*

Theorie 1 (2011), 155–72; idem, 'Parlamentarische Politik und parlamentarische Rhetorik: Eine begriffs- und debattengeschichtliche Perspektive', in Andreas Schulz and Andreas Wirsching (eds), *Parlamentarische Kulturen in Europa: Das Parlament als Kommunikationsraum* (Düsseldorf: Droste, 2012), 75–90.
4. Reinhart Koselleck, 'Einleitung', in Otto Brunner, Werner Conze and Reinhart Koselleck (eds), *Geschichtliche Grundbegriffe: Historisches Lexikon zur politisch-sozialen Sprache in Deutschland* (hereafter GG), vol. 1 (Stuttgart: Klett-Cotta, 1972), xxiv.
5. Ibid., xxiv–xxv.
6. Quentin Skinner, *Reason and Rhetoric in the Philosophy of Hobbes* (Cambridge: Cambridge University Press, 1996), 7–8.
7. Koselleck, 'Einleitung', xxiv.
8. Ibid.
9. See, for example, Spiegel-Gespräch, '"Denkmäler sind Stolpersteine": Der Historiker Reinhart Koselleck zur neu entbrannten Debatte um das geplante Berliner Holocaust-Mahnmal, Bußübungen in Stein und die Zukunft der Gedenkkultur', *Der Spiegel* 6 (1997), 190–92.
10. Reinhart Koselleck, 'The Historical-Political Semantics of Asymmetric Counterconcepts', in idem, *Futures Past: On the Semantics of Historical Time* (Cambridge, MA: MIT Press, 1985), 159–97.
11. Quentin Skinner, 'A Reply to My Critics', in James Tully (ed.), *Meaning and Context: Quentin Skinner and His Critics* (Cambridge: Polity, 1988), 283.
12. Skinner, 'Rhetoric and Conceptual Change'.
13. Skinner, *Reason and Rhetoric*; see also, Quentin Skinner, 'Some Problems in the Analysis of Political Thought and Action', *Political Theory* 2 (1974), 277–303; and idem, 'The Idea of a Cultural Lexicon', *Essays in Criticism* 29 (1979), 205–24.
14. On the state: Quentin Skinner, *The Foundations of Modern Political Thought*, 2 vols (Cambridge: Cambridge University Press, 1978), vol. 2, final chapter; Quentin Skinner, 'The State', in Terence Ball, James Farr and Russell N. Hanson (eds), *Political Innovation and Conceptual Change* (Cambridge: Cambridge University Press, 1989), 90–131; Quentin Skinner, 'A Genealogy of the Modern State', *Proceedings of the British Academy* 162 (2009), 325–70. On liberty: Quentin Skinner, 'The Idea of Negative Liberty: Philosophical and Historical Perspectives', in Richard Rorty, J.B. Schneewind and Quentin Skinner (eds), *Philosophy in History* (Cambridge: Cambridge University Press, 1984), 193–221; Quentin Skinner, *Liberty before Liberalism* (Cambridge: Cambridge University Press, 1998); Quentin Skinner, 'Rethinking Political Liberty', *History Workshop Journal* 61(1) (2006), 56–70.
15. Quentin Skinner, 'Ambrogio Lorenzetti: The Artist as Political Philosopher', *Proceedings of the British Academy* 72 (1987), 1–56.
16. Quentin Skinner, *Hobbes and Republican Liberty* (Cambridge: Cambridge University Press, 2008).
17. Skinner, 'Rhetoric and Conceptual Change', 62 and 67.
18. Skinner, *Foundations*.

19. Quentin Skinner, 'Paradiastole', in Sylvia Adamson et al. (eds), *Renaissance Figures of Speech* (Cambridge: Cambridge University Press, 2007), 147–63.
20. Ibid., 158.
21. Quentin Skinner, interviewed by Alan Macfarlane, 10 January 2008, at http://www.dspace.cam.ac.uk/bitstream/1810/197060/1/skinner.txt, 27 July 2010.
22. See Kari Palonen, *'Objektivität' als faires Spiel: Wissenschaft als Politik bei Max Weber* (Baden-Baden: Nomos, 2010); Palonen, 'Begriffsdebatten'.
23. Jeremy Bentham, *Essay on Political Tactics* (1843), in *Collected Works of Jeremy Bentham*, vol. 2, ch. XII, at http://oll.libertyfund.org/title/1921/113915.
24. Skinner, *Foundations*, vol. 1, xi.
25. As I do in Kari Palonen, *The Struggle with Time: A Conceptual History of Politics as an Activity* (Münster: LIT-Verlag, 2006).
26. See also Palonen, *'Objektivität'*, ch. 2.
27. William Gerard Hamilton, *Parliamentary Logic*, with an introduction and notes by Courtney S. Kenny (Cambridge: Heffer, 1927), 88.
28. Ibid., 42.
29. On the difference between controversial and parliamentary debate, see James De Mille, *Elements of Rhetoric* (New York: Harper & Brothers, 1878), 475, at http://www.archive.org/stream/elementsrhetori01millgoog.
30. On the contemporary uses, see Cornelia Ilie, 'Unparliamentary Language: Insults as Cognitive Form of Confrontation', in R. Dirven, R. Frank and C. Ilie (eds), *Language and Ideology*, vol. 2 (Amsterdam: Benjamins, 2001), 235–63.
31. See Pasi Ihalainen and Kari Palonen, 'Parliamentary Sources in the Comparative Study of Conceptual History: Methodological Aspects and Illustrations of a Research Proposal', *Parliaments, Estates & Representation* 29 (2009), 17–34.
32. See Palonen, 'Begriffsdebatten'; Palonen, 'Parlamentarische Politik'; Kari Palonen, 'Towards a History of Parliamentary Concepts', *Parliaments, Estates & Representation* 32 (2012), 123–38.
33. See Pasi Ihalainen, Cornelia Ilie and Kari Palonen (eds), *Parliament and Parliamentarism: A Comparative History of a European Concept* (Oxford: Berghahn Books, 2016).
34. See, for example, Jack H. Hexter (ed.), *Parliament and Liberty* (Stanford, CA: Stanford University Press, 1972); for the free mandate, see Christoph Müller, *Das imperative und freie Mandat* (Leiden: Sifthoff, 1966).
35. See Skinner, *Liberty before Liberalism*; Skinner, 'Rethinking Political Liberty', 56–70.
36. See Koselleck, 'Asymmetric Counterconcepts'.
37. Thomas Erskine May, *A Treatise upon the Law, Privileges, Proceedings and Usage of Parliament* (1844), at http://www.archive.org/stream/atreatiseuponla00may-goog; Thomas Erskine May, *A Treatise on the Law, Privileges, Proceedings and Usage of Parliament* (1883), at http://www.archive.org/stream/treatiseonlaw-pri00maytrichs; Eugène Pierre, *De la procédure parlementaire* (Paris: Maison Quantin, 1887); see Palonen, 'Parlamentarische Politik'; Palonen, 'Towards a History of Parliamentary Concepts'; Kari Palonen, *The Politics of Parliamentary*

Procedure: The Formation of the Westminster Procedure as a Parliamentary Ideal Type (Leverkusen: Budrich, 2014).
38. See Kari Palonen, 'Reinhart Koselleck on Anachronism and Conceptual Change', in Martin Burke and Melvin Richter (eds), *Why Concepts Matter: Translating Social and Political Thought* (Leiden: Brill, 2012), 73–92.
39. See Kari Palonen, 'Four Times of Politics: Policy, Polity, Politicking and Politicization', *Alternatives* 38 (2003), 171–86; Palonen, *Struggle with Time*.
40. Palonen, 'Four Times', 175.
41. Cf. Max Weber, 'Die "Objektivität" sozialwissenschaftlicher und sozialpolitischer Erkenntnis' (1904), in idem, *Gesammelte Aufsätze zur Wissenschaftslehre*, ed. Johannes Winckelmann (Tübingen: Mohr, 1973), 149–50.
42. Friedrich Meinecke, *Die Idee der Staatsräson in der neueren Geschichte* (1924) (Munich: Oldenbourg, 1960), 1–3.
43. See Hans Boldt, 'Parlament, parlamentarische Regierung, Parlamentarismus', in Otto Brunner, Werner Conze and Reinhart Koselleck (eds), *Geschichtliche Grundbegriffe: Historisches Lexikon zur politisch-sozialen Sprache in Deutschland*, vol. 4 (Stuttgart: Klett-Cotta, 1978), 649–76.
44. Walter Bagehot, *The English Constitution* (1867) (Cambridge: Cambridge University Press, 2001); Robert Redslob, *Die parlamentarische Regierung in ihrer wahren und in ihrer unechten Form* (Tübingen: Mohr, 1918).
45. See Max Weber, 'Parlament und Regierung im neugeordneten Deutschland' (1918), in *Max-Weber-Studienausgabe* I/15, ed. Wolfgang J. Mommsen (Tübingen: Mohr 1988), 227; cf. Kari Palonen, 'Der Begriff des Parlamentarismus bei Max Weber', in Olaf Asbach et al. (eds), *Zur kritischen Theorie der politischen Gesellschaft: Festschrift für Michael Th. Greven zum 65. Geburtstag* (Wiesbaden: Springer VS-Verlag, 2012), 195–206.
46. Josef Redlich, *Recht und Technik des Englischen Parlamentarismus* (Leipzig: Duncker & Humblot, 1905).
47. Weber, 'Parlament und Regierung', esp. 235–48.
48. See Redlich, *Recht und Technik*; Palonen, 'Towards a History of Parliamentary Concepts'.
49. See also, Henry Scobell, *Memorials of the Method and Manner of Proceedings in Parliament in Passing Bills* (1656), Early English Books Online (EEBO), 30–31.
50. John Hatsell, *Precedents of proceedings in the House of Commons; with observations* (1818), 4 vols, at http://www.archive.org/details/precedentsofproc01hats, http://www.archive.org/stream/precedentsofproc02hats, http://www.archive.org/details/precedentsofproc03hats, http://www.archive.org/stream/precedentsofproc04hats; Bentham, *Essay* (1843); Erskine May, *Treatise* (1844, 1883).
51. See Redlich, *Recht und Technik*; and Palonen, *Politics of Parliamentary Procedure*.
52. See Palonen, 'Parlamentarische Politik'; Palonen, 'Towards a History of Parliamentary Concepts'.
53. Redlich, *Recht und Technik*, 243.
54. See, for example, Otto Brunner, *Land und Herrschaft* (Brünn: Rohrer, 1942), or the discussion by Dietrich Hilger in Reinhart Koselleck et al., 'Herrschaft', in

GG, vol. 3 (Stuttgart: Klett-Cotta, 1982), 1–102, and the commentary on that in Melvin Richter, *The History of Political and Social Concepts* (Oxford: Oxford University Press, 1995).
55. Max Weber, *Wirtschaft und Gesellschaft* (1922), ed. Johannes Winckelmann (Tübingen: Mohr, 1980), 28.
56. Cf. Reinhart Koselleck, 'Begriffsgeschichte and Social History', in idem, *Futures Past: On the Semantics of Historical Time* (Cambridge, MA: MIT Press, 1985), 91; Hilger, in Koselleck et al., 'Herrschaft', 98–101.
57. Robert Michels, *Zur Soziologie des Parteiwesens in der modernen Demokratie* (Leipzig: Klinkhardt, 1910).
58. Max Weber, *Briefe 1909–1910: Max-Weber-Gesamtausgabe* II/VI, ed. M. Rainer Lepsius (Tübingen: Mohr, 1994), 761.
59. Hannah Arendt, *Crises of the Republic* (Harmondsworth: Pelican, 1971), esp. the essay 'On Violence'.
60. See Max Weber, *Allgemeine Staatslehre und Politik: Mit- und Nachschriften 1920. Max-Weber-Gesamtausgabe* III/7, ed. Gangolf Hübinger (Tübingen: Mohr, 2009); Reinhart Koselleck et al., 'Staat und Souveränität', in GG, vol. 6 (Stuttgart: Klett-Cotta, 1990), 1–154; and my commentary: Kari Palonen, 'The State as a "Chance" Concept: Max Weber's De-substantialisation and Neutralisation of the Concept', *Max Weber Studies* 11 (2011), 99–117.

References

Arendt, Hannah, *Crises of the Republic* (Harmondsworth: Pelican, 1971)
Bagehot, Walter, *The English Constitution* (1867) (Cambridge: Cambridge University Press, 2001)
Bentham, Jeremy, *Essay on Political Tactics* (1843), in *Collected Works of Jeremy Bentham*, vol. 2, ch. XII, at http://oll.libertyfund.org/title/1921/113915
Boldt, Hans, 'Parlament, parlamentarische Regierung, Parlamentarismus', in Otto Brunner, Werner Conze and Reinhart Koselleck (eds), *Geschichtliche Grundbegriffe. Historisches Lexikon zur politisch-sozialen Sprache in Deutschland*, vol. 4 (Stuttgart: Klett-Cotta 1978), 649–76
Brunner, Otto, *Land und Herrschaft* (Brünn: Rohrer, 1942)
De Mille, James, *Elements of Rhetoric* (New York: Harper & Brothers, 1878), at http://www.archive.org/stream/elementsrhetori01millgoog
Hamilton, William Gerard, *Parliamentary Logic*, with an introduction and notes by Courtney S. Kenny (Cambridge: Heffer, 1927)
Hatsell, John, *Precedents of proceedings in the House of Commons; with observations* (1818), 4 vols, at http://www.archive.org/details/precedentsofproc01hats, http://www.archive.org/stream/precedentsofproc02hats, http://www.archive.org/details/precedentsofproc03hats, http://www.archive.org/stream/precedentsofproc04hats
Hexter, Jack H. (ed.), *Parliament and Liberty* (Stanford, CA: Stanford University Press, 1972)

Ihalainen, Pasi, and Kari Palonen, 'Parliamentary Sources in the Comparative Study of Conceptual History: Methodological Aspects and Illustrations of a Research Proposal', *Parliaments, Estates & Representation* 29 (2009), 17–34

Ihalainen, Pasi, Cornelia Ilie and Kari Palonen (eds), *Parliament and Parliamentarism: A Comparative History of a European Concept* (Oxford: Berghahn Books, 2016)

Ilie, Cornelia, 'Unparliamentary Language: Insults as Cognitive Form of Confrontation', in René Dirven, Roslyn M. Frank and Cornelia Ilie (eds), *Language and Ideology*, vol. 2 (Amsterdam: Benjamins, 2001), 235–63

Koselleck, Reinhart, 'Einleitung', in Otto Brunner, Werner Conze and Reinhart Koselleck (eds), *Geschichtliche Grundbegriffe: Historisches Lexikon zur politisch-sozialen Sprache in Deutschland*, vol. 1 (Stuttgart: Klett-Cotta, 1972), xiii–xxvii

———, 'Begriffsgeschichte and Social History' [1972], in Reinhart Koselleck, *Futures Past: On the Semantics of Historical Time* (Cambridge, MA: MIT Press, 1985), 73–91

———, 'The Historical-Political Semantics of Asymmetric Counterconcepts' [1975], in Reinhart Koselleck, *Futures Past: On the Semantics of Historical Time* (Cambridge, MA: MIT Press, 1985), 159–97

Koselleck, Reinhart, et al., 'Herrschaft', in Otto Brunner, Werner Conze and Reinhart Koselleck (eds), *Geschichtliche Grundbegriffe: Historisches Lexikon zur politisch-sozialen Sprache in Deutschland*, vol. 3 (Stuttgart: Klett-Cotta, 1982), 1–102

Koselleck, Reinhart, et al., 'Staat und Souveränität', in Otto Brunner, Werner Conze and Reinhart Koselleck (eds), *Geschichtliche Grundbegriffe: Historisches Lexikon zur politisch-sozialen Sprache in Deutschland*, vol. 6 (Stuttgart: Klett-Cotta, 1990), 1–154

May, Thomas Erskine, *A Treatise upon the Law, Privileges, Proceedings and Usage of Parliament* (1844), at http://www.archive.org/stream/atreatiseuponla00maygoog

———, *A Treatise on the Law, Privileges, Proceedings and Usage of Parliament* (1883), at http://www.archive.org/stream/treatiseonlawpri00maytrich

Meinecke, Friedrich, *Die Idee der Staatsräson in der neueren Geschichte* (1924) (Munich: Oldenbourg, 1960)

Michels, Robert, *Zur Soziologie des Parteiwesens in der modernen Demokratie* (Leipzig: Klinkhardt, 1910)

Müller, Christoph, *Das imperative und freie Mandat* (Leiden: Sifthoff, 1966)

Palonen, Kari, 'Four Times of Politics: Policy, Polity, Politicking and Politicization', *Alternatives* 38 (2003), 171–86

———, *The Struggle with Time: A Conceptual History of Politics as an Activity* (Münster: LIT-Verlag, 2006)

———, *'Objektivität' als faires Spiel: Wissenschaft als Politik bei Max Weber* (Baden-Baden: Nomos, 2010)

———, 'Begriffsdebatten und Debattenbegriffe: Das parlamentarische Paradigma des Begriffstreits und –wandels', *Zeitschrift für Politische Theorie* 1 (2011), 155–72

———, 'The State as a "Chance" Concept: Max Webers De-substantialisation and Neutralisation of the Concept', *Max Weber Studies* 11 (2011), 99–117

——, 'Der Begriff des Parlamentarismus bei Max Weber', in Olaf Asbach et al. (eds), *Zur kritischen Theorie der politischen Gesellschaft: Festschrift für Michael Th. Greven zum 65. Geburtstag* (Wiesbaden: Springer VS-Verlag, 2012), 195–206

——, 'Parlamentarische Politik und parlamentarische Rhetorik: Eine begriffs- und debattengeschichtliche Perspektive', in Andreas Schulz and Andreas Wirsching (eds), *Parlamentarische Kulturen in Europa: Das Parlament als Kommunikationsraum* (Düsseldorf: Droste, 2012)

——, 'Reinhart Koselleck on Anachronism and Conceptual Change', in Martin Burke and Melvin Richter (eds), *Why Concepts Matter: Translating Social and Political Thought* (Leiden: Brill, 2012), 73–92

——, 'Towards a History of Parliamentary Concepts', *Parliaments, Estates & Representation* 32 (2012), 123–38

——, *The Politics of Parliamentary Procedure: The Formation of the Westminster Procedure as a Parliamentary Ideal Type* (Leverkusen: Budrich, 2014)

Pierre, Eugène, *De la procédure parlementaire* (Paris: Maison Quantin, 1887)

Redlich, Josef, *Recht und Technik des Englischen Parlamentarismus* (Leipzig: Duncker & Humblot, 1905)

Redslob, Robert, *Die parlamentarische Regierung in ihrer wahren und in ihrer unechten Form* (Tübingen: Mohr, 1918)

Richter, Melvin, *The History of Political and Social Concepts* (Oxford: Oxford University Press, 1995)

Scobell, Henry, *Memorials of the Method and Manner of Proceedings in Parliament in Passing Bills* (1656), Early English Books Online (EEBO)

Skinner, Quentin, 'Some Problems in the Analysis of Political Thought and Action', *Political Theory* 2 (1974), 277–303

——, *The Foundations of Modern Political Thought*, 2 vols (Cambridge: Cambridge University Press, 1978)

——, 'The Idea of a Cultural Lexicon', *Essays in Criticism* 29 (1979), 205–24

——, 'The Idea of Negative Liberty: Philosophical and Historical Perspectives', in Richard Rorty, Jerome B. Schneewind and Quentin Skinner (eds), *Philosophy in History* (Cambridge: Cambridge University Press, 1984), 193–221

——, 'Ambrogio Lorenzetti: The Artist as Political Philosopher', *Proceedings of the British Academy* 72 (1987), 1–56

——, 'A Reply to My Critics', in James Tully (ed.), *Meaning and Context: Quentin Skinner and His Critics* (Cambridge: Polity, 1988), 231–88

——, 'The State', in Terence Ball, James Farr and Russell N. Hanson (eds), *Political Innovation and Conceptual Change* (Cambridge: Cambridge University Press, 1989), 90–131

——, *Reason and Rhetoric in the Philosophy of Hobbes* (Cambridge: Cambridge University Press, 1996)

——, *Liberty before Liberalism* (Cambridge: Cambridge University Press, 1998)

——, 'Rhetoric and Conceptual Change', *Finnish Yearbook of Political Thought* 3 (1999), 61–73

——, 'Rethinking Political Liberty', *History Workshop Journal* 61(1) (2006), 56–70

———, 'Paradiastole', in Sylvia Adamson et al. (eds), *Renaissance Figures of Speech* (Cambridge: Cambridge University Press, 2007), 147–63

———, *Hobbes and Republican Liberty* (Cambridge: Cambridge University Press, 2008)

———, 'A Genealogy of the Modern State', *Proceedings of the British Academy* 162 (2009), 325–70

Skinner, Quentin, interviewed by Alan Macfarlane, 10 January 2008, at http://www.dspace.cam.ac.uk/bitstream/1810/197060/1/skinner.txt, 27 July 2010

Spiegel-Gespräch, '"Denkmäler sind Stolpersteine": Der Historiker Reinhart Koselleck zur neu entbrannten Debatte um das geplante Berliner Holocaust-Mahnmal, Bußübungen in Stein und die Zukunft der Gedenkkultur', *Der Spiegel* 6 (1997), 190–92

Weber, Max, 'Die "Objektivität" sozialwissenschaftlicher und sozialpolitischer Erkenntnis' (1904), in Max Weber, *Gesammelte Aufsätze zur Wissenschaftslehre*, ed. Johannes Winckelmann (Tübingen: Mohr, 1973), 146–214

———, *Wirtschaft und Gesellschaft* (1922), ed. Winckelmann, Johannes (Tübingen: Mohr, 1980)

———, 'Parlament und Regierung im neugeordneten Deutschland' (1918), in *Max-Weber-Studienausgabe* I/15, ed. Wolfgang J. Mommsen (Tübingen: Mohr 1988), 202–302

———, *Briefe 1909–1910. Max-Weber-Gesamtausgabe* II/VI, ed. M. Rainer Lepsius (Tübingen: Mohr, 1994)

———, *Allgemeine Staatslehre und Politik. Mit- und Nachschriften 1920: Max-Weber-Gesamtausgabe* III/7, ed. Gangolf Hübinger (Tübingen: Mohr, 2009)

Chapter 4
Conceptual History, Ideology and Language

Michael Freeden

In the famous passage in Lewis Carroll's *Through the Looking Glass*, Humpty Dumpty says: 'When *I* use a word, it means just what I choose it to mean – neither more nor less'. 'The question', responds Alice, 'is whether you *can* make words mean so many different things'. 'The question is,' says Humpty Dumpty, 'which is to be master – that's all'. Lewis Carroll's nominalism illuminates the ambiguity – normal and inevitable – we now recognize when handling words and the concepts they apparently signify. For a political theorist, certain striking themes emerge out of that ambiguity. First, the quest for precision has been at the heart of certain logical and rational traditions in Western thought; in political theory they are to be found in some analytical philosophical schools, as well as in some branches of quantitative political science. But how far can precision go? Second, meaning appears to be connected to human agency and to choice. But does meaning not also circumscribe and override agency if it is embedded in social practices? Third, the intentional control over a vast array of potential meanings that can be attached to words indicates one of the power features of language. But what is the effective scope of that power, and to what extent is its exercise already preconstrained by structural limitations? And is intentionality sufficient to account for the semantic field a concept occupies?

From Fixity to Fluidity

Underlying those three issues is a tacit appreciation of the malleability of meaning combined with the impossibility of coping with excessive fluidity when ideas have to be communicated and acted upon. It conjures up a world in which imprecision is normal, yet has continually to be suppressed artificially because we seemingly need clear-cut maps of meaning in order to make political decisions and in order to navigate through our social and political worlds. And as with any map, its function is to offer a manageable level of simplification, even of Gestalt – one of the most fundamental roles of ideologies – without which the world is bewildering, and our capacity to follow collective or individual paths is stunted. The malleability of meaning also presents a state of affairs in which to emphasize intentionality alone is in effect to identify a power-exercising *dictat*, suggestive of an agentic and individualist hubris. The potentially open exercise of choice is thus immediately accompanied by an attempt to withhold it through discursive constraint. That can conceal the fact that a selection, or preselection, of meaning has taken place that may be arbitrary or at least idiosyncratic, and it is further complicated – as we know only too well from reception theory – by a probable loss in transmission of any artificial precision to which it may aspire.[1]

Conceptual historians, as well as analysts of ideologies, know that while their scholarship is inspired by an awareness of the constant mutation of meaning, whether subtle or dramatic, the actual language of politics – comprising a well-known range of concepts that are loosely held together in the semantic packages we call ideologies – is typically characterized by resistance to such mutation. It is concerned with minimizing as far as possible that range of meaning and with choosing a particular interpretation out of the wealth of meanings each of the constitutive concepts of an ideology may contain. The illusion of determinate meanings is vital if a society needs to make the decisions without which social life cannot function. Sometimes – for instance in liberal societies – such determinate meanings are confidently envisioned as a question of reasoned choice. Just as often – and liberal societies are plainly no exception here – such decisions are partly predetermined by historical cultural patterns. To formulate determinate, or quasi-determinate, meanings of social vocabularies is the role of ideologies when they are understood as necessary competitors over the control of political language, without which social action becomes chaotic and amorphous. In that sense, ideologies service the specialized, if unrealizable, drive of the political to provide the decisions that human affairs invite and demand. In that sense, too, competition and conflict over the nature of those decisions, whether as short-term policy or long-term vision, is endemic in social and political discourse.

Conceptual history, as well, needs to take on board some of the central features of language more generally, from which social and political concepts – signified by words – are obviously not excluded. These features include ambiguity, indeterminacy and vagueness, and – on a different level – inconclusiveness; and they all fly in the face of the precision-seekers. It is clear why the obsession with precise meaning is so common. Among *scholars* trained in certain philosophical or scientific modes of thinking, precision is the hallmark of careful argument as well as the key to offering well-thought-out solutions to the problems that social and political concepts address. Among the political *producers* of language, ideologies are attempts to limit the multiple meanings that political concepts always possess. Therefore imposed 'precision', or attempts to impose precision, serves a vital role. That role derives from the features of the practice we call 'thinking politically', with its emphasis on finality, decisions, sovereignty and authority.[2] Language is harnessed to pursue those necessary features. Both for the theoreticians of the political and for those articulating political discourse and ideology in open societies, such forms of semantic control are apparently deliberate and derive from prevalent, if controversial, understandings of human agency as autonomous and purposive. In other societies they may relate to the absolute authority of the supranatural or to the interpretation of foundational texts. The exercise of that semantic control is, however, no symbolic sideshow but a vital means of moulding and directing a society. To monopolize, channel or contain the understandings prevailing in a society's language is also to preside over its practices and processes. Conceptual history is therefore also the history of those attempts at semantic domination, whether successful or not, and the history of opposition to such domination, in the form of alternative proposals for domination – as when sparring ideologies offer their versions of ideational monopolies – or in the form of destabilizing discursive rupture.[3]

Nonetheless, intentionality is always accompanied by what Paul Ricoeur called the 'surplus of meaning'[4] – the fact that we can never be in full command of the messages we produce, let alone the comprehension and consumption of those messages by others. Consequently, the important dimension of unintentionality has to supplement the intentionality that many conceptual historians, rightly, wish to reconstruct. That aspect has occasionally been underplayed by those historians of ideas who wish to reconstruct the intentions of an author, inasmuch as intentions signify agentic control over what one says and does. But the control that ideologies attempt to impose on political language is elusive for two main reasons. First, the linguistic usages that we adopt relate to broad and constantly changing semantic fields in which, though we may endeavour to position ourselves deliberately, we are at least in part already positioned unwittingly. Those fields both enable us to express ourselves in communicable language and debar us from crossing certain semantic boundaries, beyond which we cannot be understood. Second, the concepts that we employ – for reasons associated with their essential contestability – carry more meanings than we can master in any particular utterance. The idea of essential contestability signals the enduring impossibility of achieving discursive closure through settling categorically and authoritatively on any particular meaning of a concept. Two factors account for that: first, the multiple, and occasionally incompatible, content of the conceptions that political concepts contain; and second, the range of interpretations that consumers of our oral and written texts bring to bear on them. In the first case we may indeed be able to choose certain meanings of a concept, though often that choice is unconscious and it superimposes finality on natural linguistic fluidity. In the second case the meaning of our texts is usually beyond our control. Even if we intend to exclude some of those meanings, we will convey meanings that we may not have intended and of which we are unaware. When Machiavelli wrote that Fortuna was a woman who has to be beaten and coerced,[5] he intended to say something unpleasant about princes who do not take energetic and impetuous risks; we now also read him as saying something unpleasant about women in a manner that reflects misogynous attitudes towards them.

Hence ambiguity, indeterminacy and vagueness, as well as inconclusiveness, perpetuate the linguistic variability that lies at the heart of conceptual semantic flexibility, and in a very important sense they are extra-historical, independent of time and space.[6] That is, of course, a constraint within which the historical understandings of conceptual historians have to operate. To illustrate, *ambiguity* is a form of semantic equivocation – a relatively simple and manageable issue. It refers to the possibility of more than one reading of a unit of language, a lack of clarity that may be resolved through contextualization. Thus, race could be contextualized to signify a nationality ('our island race'), an 'ethnic' grouping (the Aryan race), or a competition (the race for the White House). Crucially, ambiguity can be *disambiguated* and removed from contention by surrounding it with additional information that crisply separates those meanings.

That is not the case with another feature of language, *indeterminacy*, which dismisses the possibility of interpretative closure. For example, indeterminacy is a feature of democracy, whose internal components may be arranged in countless ways and in unlimited distributions of relative significance, none of which is final or authoritative, no matter what political scientists, philosophers or ideologists may claim to the contrary. Both logically and in actual usage, democracy contains among others the concepts of liberty (self-determination), equality (one person one vote), community (it is a group practice and attribute, not a concept that relates to individual behaviour), participation (it assumes the activation of its members) and – at least in liberal-democratic understandings – accountability (it is constrained by procedures of monitoring and transparency). Although these five concepts have a quite separate existence, they are also key components of the concept of democracy itself. That makes democracy a super-concept, not in the sense of possessing superior status or appeal, but by dint of the internal complexity of its structure: it acts as a host to a number of additional concepts that also have a separate and recognizable social and historical life of their own. Not least, the conceptual history of democracy cannot be divorced from the conceptual histories of its components.

Vagueness refers to the impossibility of drawing hard and fast boundaries between concepts that may shade into one another. What is the difference, or overlap, between social-democracy and socialism in West European contexts? Is there a clear-cut way of distinguishing between liberalism, neo-liberalism and libertarianism? The issue becomes even more problematic when we realize that political concepts have more than one boundary. The boundaries of those socialisms that aspire to eliminate the state will differ considerably from those socialisms appealing to the power of a centralized state. Hence some socialisms have a vague boundary delimitation in relation to anarchism; others have a vague boundary delimitation in relation to authoritarianism.

Inconclusiveness is a slightly different notion. It is not a direct attribute of language; rather, it is an attribute of argumentation, referring to the impossibility of developing paths of argument that will explore the nuances and micro-elements of a concept in all their details: the human mind is simply too feeble to attempt that, and there can be no point when we can assert: 'nothing else can be said about this concept'. Inconclusiveness suggests that arguments will run out of steam once they move from the general to the particular: the weightiness of an argument, and its attendant concepts, will peter out as we struggle with applying it to specific situations. It is unfeasible to suggest that we will be able to apply the meaning of a concept, such as justice, to all the millions of individual concrete cases where that concept is engaged, particularly when they run up against other concepts – efficiency, loyalty – that may clash with them. Conceptual historians have to accommodate a semantic world in which concepts in mutual competition (e.g. some interpretations of equality versus some interpretations of liberty) cannot gain a decisive upper hand, one over the other. If and when they do so, it is only through manipulating their complex meanings so that one concept is presented in a more attractive, persuasive or effective light than another – and that can only be achieved by silencing many conceptions of each concept.

Ideological Morphology: Fixity amidst Fluidity?

The consequence of those ineliminable features of language and words is the fact of the essential contestability of concepts. It is not only that we cannot agree on ranking what we value for collective life: autonomy or interdependence, stability or revolution; it is also that the complex internal structure of a concept does not permit the utterance of sentences that contain all its possible meanings.[7] All social and political concepts contain more parts than can be used in any given instance, and that raises a fundamental challenge to human thought and practice. For to avoid social entropy or paralysis, decisions have to be made – even if they are short term and unravel at a future point, requiring another decision or set of decisions. That is where the archetypal device of ideologies – semantic decontestation – enters the fray. Thus in employing the concept of equality, I cannot advocate equality of distributive outcomes and equality of need at the same time. I have to abandon one of those meanings when I try to make sense of the idea of equality in making effective political decisions. Hence an inevitable selection process occurs that is *logically* arbitrary – that has no logical necessity attached to it – but that is of great cultural and social significance. It is wholly historical and contextual, occurring in a particular space at a particular time. That is to say, it is not *culturally* arbitrary, for it operates within historical traditions, social conventions, cultural trajectories and ideological frameworks that constrain and direct the logically unlimited range of meaning a concept can signify. In sum, all social and political thought operates within a dual set of conditions and constraints: semantic, referring to meaning, and structural (or morphological), referring to the field of conceptual configurations. The historical contingencies, crises and continuities on which conceptual historians focus are invariably superimposed on those two fundamental features.

The insight derived from the surplus of meaning raises the obvious point that the production of conceptual meaning is accompanied by its consumption, as conceptual historians appreciate. But although conceptual history has been reception sensitive, there is more work to be done on different epistemologies of reception and how they affect diverse meanings of a concept even in the same society. Audiences and readerships are vital determinants of both intended and unintended conceptual meaning, yet we have been somewhat hampered by the past tendency of conceptual historians to focus on 'high' language, in part because it is more easily accessible in books and articles, in part because as scholars we have been trained to be attracted to complex debate. But newspapers, parliamentary debates, popular books, ordinary vernacular expression, and even visual representations of concepts are crucial sources of the understanding of political language.[8] The current generation of conceptual historians, as is evidenced by other contributions to this volume, is more attuned to the role of the vernacular, or vernaculars, and their interflow into more professional languages.[9] And that is not all: as scholars, we too intervene in the meaning of a concept when we apply our own interpretative skills and comprehension, so that in setting out our intellectual wares we add a second layer to the consumption of language. The meanings a concept possesses, for its producers, its consumers and for us, however different, are always incomplete renderings of its content. Concepts are not endowed with neutral meanings.

My main argument is this: with its focus on the genealogy, context, continuity, change, disruption, intertwining, and transmission of the relation between concepts and language, the study of conceptual history has introduced new understandings of temporality and spatiality into the field of intellectual history. But it can be further fertilized by recent developments in the analysis of concepts that have developed since the early 1990s, predominantly as a branch of the study of ideologies. Specifically, in order to flesh out the history of concepts we require a close acquaintance with the properties of a concept; and among its most edifying properties for the purpose of conceptual history is its morphology, both internally and in relation to neighbouring concepts. Hence a closer investigation of social and political concepts (though this will apply to most other fields as well) reveals a three-dimensional structure: the concept as the fundamental dimension (on which conceptual historians focus) can be magnified to disclose the variable internal components – the conceptions – that constitute it; and it can be reduced to appear in an interlocked but usually flexible cluster of concepts.

The internal morphology of a concept – the looseness, variability and plasticity of its components – results in the essential contestability of its conceptions; that is to say, its particular conceptualizations. But the morphological study of ideologies decodes not merely the meanings of a given concept shaped by its internal micro-variations that form its intension, but the interrelationships among concepts. Ipso facto, essential contestability also applies to combinations of concepts as well as to the single concept, introducing in effect two layers of contestability. Those clusters are the fields, or maps, of complex political meaning that we term ideologies. From the viewpoint of conceptual analysis, the distinctions between one ideological family and another reflect changing movements in the meanings, positioning, and relative weight assigned to each of the concepts that make up such an interdependent field. Concepts are not only assessed in terms of their temporal mutability – completely in line with the previous practice of conceptual historians – but also in terms of their relative location vis-à-vis each other in any concrete discursive instance (involving not only geographical and cultural space but semantic space), and in terms of the diverse weight and significance that the same concept, and its selected conceptions, can possess in different settings. For instance, the concept of liberty may be found in almost every ideological family, but the work it does within the conceptual cluster of which it is part will vary in significance, and the conceptions that constitute it (non-constraint, choice, development, emancipation) will compete with one another. Consequently the macro-analysis of concepts looks at the way in which concepts intersect with each other, while the microanalysis of concepts explores how even small changes in their internal structure may shift the way they produce meaning as well as the way they are decontested or consumed in various interpretative codifications.

The Interdependent World of Concepts

In sum, in the most fundamental sense, social and political concepts are never found in isolation from each other. Rather, they are located in an environment of further sustaining or conflicting concepts that serve to endow with a particular meaning the concept on which we have initially decided to focus. The conceptual environment of concepts thus serves as a significant context – as part of a broader semantic field – within which to decode any selected concept. For when we contend that ideologies – whatever else they are – compete over the control of political language, we allude to their attempts to hold together forms of conceptual arrangements or patterns, some more fluid, some less so, that decontest (or attempt to decontest, for it is an exercise that can only be a temporary one) the essentially contested meanings that are a feature of all social and political concepts.

As do conceptual historians, the analysts of ideologies insist on focusing on the empirical, 'real-world' meanings of concepts, not on modelling their ideal types, and thus depart from the more abstract and universalizing conventions of analytical political philosophy. They also claim that, even with respect to purist conceptual historians, it is important to reaffirm that those meanings are always accessed through consciously or unconsciously held ideological patterns. Both in ordinary speech and in professional languages, concepts are always located in mutually sustaining constellations of some complexity, and the examination of an individual concept must always be sensitive to that interplay and avoid the tendency to abstract artificially towards a single ideationally decontextualized concept. One aspiration of a post-Koselleckian age should be to approach concepts not on a single linear trajectory but – however this may complicate our lives as scholars – as constantly bumping into one another, cutting across each other, chipping away at each other, adding and dropping conceptualizations, and all along in those processes changing the meaning each separate concept carries. Of course, the heavy focus of many conceptual historians on the history of single concepts will always remain central to that pioneering intellectual enterprise, and I have no desire to query this, or to belittle its enormous heuristic value. But there are other stories to be told. Concepts do not exist in a conceptual vacuum; they are significantly informed by their proximity to other concepts, and that conceptual environment is changing continuously. The social environment, the historical environment, the cultural environment, we are aware of all these, but as scholars interested in concepts we have paid too little attention to the micro-conduct of the conceptual environment. In particular many conceptual historians have assumed that, although concepts mutate over time and space, they do so as whole concepts rather than as semantic fragments of the concept. The claim here, rather, is that concepts have a built-in propensity to mutate internally, that they are inherently in a state of permanent flux, and that they never possess a holistic, agreed meaning. Their precise meaning cannot be captured even at a point in time or space. Crucially, they always appear in fragmented form in relation to the full semantic potential they are capable of carrying. At best we can indicate two things: the patterns in which that fluidity obtains; and the cultural and ideological attempts to disrupt that fluidity by decontestation – a practice designed to further the (politically necessary) illusion that the fragment represents the whole. That practice, of course, is far from being entirely successful and is invariably matched by many rival decontestative attempts.

Two consequences of employing this approach relate to the intersections and overlaps among concepts, and to the variable tempi of change that occur in a conceptual semantic field:

1. Some concepts occupy a semantic space that is largely external to other concepts with which they are brought into a semantic relationship. When John Stuart Mill advocated the 'free development of individuality',[10] he constructed a link between liberty and human development that is contingent and external: after all, one can be free not to develop or, alternatively, be forced to develop, at least in some senses. That mutual fertilization both enriched the meanings of the concepts in question and served to constrain them into a narrower channel. But many concepts are both external and internal to the concept under investigation: they may have separate existences and spheres of impact, but they are always implied when the investigated concept is invoked – they are logically integral to the concept in question. If some of those internally constitutive meanings are absent in the actual usage of that concept, it is because a specific cultural filter has been deliberately or unconsciously deployed to exclude them, as illustrated above with respect to the concept of democracy.

That said, the analysis of concepts and their history needs to factor in the relative weight of all those conceptual components of democracy in each concrete case. The mere presence of a conception in a concept, or of a concept in a super-concept, fails to supply sufficient information for its scholarly analysis. One way of appreciating the changing meanings of democracy is through exploring the continuous flux in the ranking order of significance that its major conceptual components (namely, liberty, equality, community, participation and accountability) possess or attempt to possess in concrete instances: how much space within the super-concept does each occupy and how do those manoeuvrings crowd out or diminish some of the other conceptual components? We also need to factor in the mutual incompatibility of some interpretations of each conceptual component: thus, maximizing equality and participation is only possible under a highly restricted notion of both concepts, when they meet in the act of voting, while many other conceptions of either equality or participation cannot coexist, as for example when we consider the quality or influence of participation as part of the participatory practice.

Of course, it is highly likely that a *number* of definitions of democracy constitute intellectually valid and politically legitimate interpretations of the relationships among its components. Put differently, each concept is structurally endowed with a range of *plausible* conceptions. That would appear to offer a methodology that endorses the validity of pluralism. But, to return to indeterminacy, it is more than that. It indicates the ineluctable contingency of meaning resulting from the permanent slipperiness of interpretations. Certainty, not uncertainty, is the ephemeral factor in political language, while contingency is the default position of individual and collective lives, even if a spurious certainty is sometimes necessary to engineer the ultimately futile escape from contingency and to make language manageable and decisions possible: that again is what ideologies endeavour to achieve, and what I have termed the phenomenon of 'decontestation'. Of course, not all interpretations of democracy have been acceptable: past attempts to include 'guided' democracies by non-elected elites have proved not to hold water, and the former German Democratic Republic was anything but. There certainly exist both logical and cultural constraints on those extreme relativist interpretations that declare that 'anything goes' semantically. But because we can never nail down the intricate meaning of political concepts once and for all, we need, as scholars, to develop tools that will specifically assist us in coping with the ubiquity of conceptual indeterminacy, rather than force an artificial determinacy on an unwilling subject matter or foster the illusion of fixed universalizable meanings. I believe that our task as conceptual historians will benefit by noting how the term 'democracy' has been filtered through a number of methodologies and epistemologies, each of which locates democracy at a different point in their system. Thus, the exploration of the empirical or moral validity of democracy as a truth assertion is joined by its investigation as a significant rhetorical device with emotional appeal, or by its positioning within a number of ideological fields.

2. The second consequence of this approach introduces the notion of variable speeds of conceptual change that occur in a semantic field. Koselleck brought to our attention that phenomenon of experiencing modern time directly, its future being 'open and without boundaries'. And he added a crucial observation about the acceleration of changes brought about by technology and industry: 'temporalization and acceleration constitute the temporal framework that will probably have to be applied to all concepts of modern social history'.[11] But he did not take up the question of how that is manifested in the actual features and 'conduct' of concepts. For the structure of concepts, the ideational context in which we find them, and their relative weight, all impact on their acceleration or, more accurately, on the interpretations of velocity that we assign them. Some concepts appear to mutate slowly because they are located at the empirically determinable core of a particular discourse; and their rapid change, let alone elimination, is undesirable to those who value that discourse. At least the word assigned to the concept does not seem to change. An obvious example is the concept of liberty: the word is pretty fundamental to liberal (and many other) discourses, which create the impression of durability. That is indeed true in one sense, although the conception of liberty that is in play may undergo (and has undergone in the history of liberal discourse) considerable modification.

Social and political discourse, however, also contains adjacent concepts that may have a more ephemeral relationship with the core concept, and peripheral ones that are even shorter-lived and that reflect historical or cultural contingencies. Take for instance the concept of citizenship – a highly appraised concept in European societies for the past two centuries or so. Its connotations of membership, status, recognition and rights have been durable. But we find it surrounded by a range of different *adjacent* concepts that serve to colour the meaning of the core concept and pull it in this or in that direction: for instance, citizenship and duties versus citizenship and equality, or citizenship and participation, or citizenship and ethnicity, or citizenship and national pride; or citizenship versus residency; or natality versus naturalization. In that adjacent range, change will accelerate more rapidly than in the core. Then there also are *peripheries* of conceptual meaning, or of practices that direct the understanding of a concept on a particular path: evermore fleeting and faster-mutating understandings relating, say, to shifting national boundaries, or to pressures of immigration, or to welfare policies: all these serve to affect further the meanings of the adjacent concepts and to have knock-on impact on the core concept. If we picture the main ideological families as each containing a number of core concepts which they have appropriated as being of central significance to them, and that within each ideology the configurations of core, adjacent and peripheral concepts vary at a different velocity, we can begin to appreciate how this complex conceptual world is constructed and how a semantic field operates. While accepting Koselleck's argument about the acceleration of historical time, we need concurrently to be alert to differentials of acceleration among the components of a concept, differentials that impart considerable additional information to the researcher.

Methodological Overlaps and Disengagements

What I am trying to demonstrate here is an overlap between the analysis of ideologies and conceptual history: different methods obtain similar results, and that is one reason for the insistence that the two branches of scholarship join hands to mutual advantage. The absence of precise conceptual definitions may frustrate the scholarly ambitions of some philosophers and social scientists, and may disappoint those ethicists who pursue the global acceptance of what they see as fundamental social truths. This latter observation runs counter to the agenda of some Western political philosophers, namely, the quest for a moral consensus through stipulating certain rational and deliberative processes of communication. That agenda comes in two versions. The harder version posits the possibility of extra-empirical universal ethical norms with the status of truth statements through which regulative principles and ideals are extracted.[12] The softer version posits empirical multilogues among articulate members of reasonable groups that produce justifiable and reflective decisions in a manner designed to be accepted by others, or at least to be regarded as reasonable, perhaps even compelling.[13] The harder version creates a notable hiatus with the real-world processes through which values are enunciated and circulated. The softer version ostensibly appears to work within the real world, but implicitly demands a high degree of mutual understanding and accuracy for its accounts of deliberative democracy to succeed, let alone a degree of articulation that is not in fact distributed equally among the users of publicly oriented discourse. The world of political language, as I have tried to argue, is – regrettably or not – far murkier than that.

It is therefore worth reflecting on the history of the concept of ideology itself, all too often – both in Napoleonic and in Marxist discourse – indicating falsehoods or distortions masquerading as truths on one dimension, and abstractions remote from the real world on another.[14] The perceived failure of ideological language to capture moral or scientific truths resulted in a serious reputational problem for the notion of ideology, let alone its study. What is striking about the recent convergence of the analyses engaged in the fields of ideology studies and conceptual history is that the truth status of social and political utterances is discounted as irrelevant as far as the task of the scholar is concerned. Whether or not ideologies represent 'real-world' phenomena is distinct from the fact that the existence of ideologies is itself a reality that calls for inquiry. Indeed, the concepts of which ideologies consist are fundamental units of meaning that both refer to something in the world (an act, an event, a thing) and are themselves part of the reality we encounter – they interpret reality and are themselves a component of symbolic reality and a form of thought-practice.[15] Because concepts are ideas it does not mean that they do not exist as much as concrete entities. The same applies to ideologies as imagined and imaginative maps of social reality. They cannot be dismissed as superimpositions on the real world because they are part of it; they too actually and ubiquitously exist as thought-practices and are accordingly an object of empirical analysis. Ideologies are particularly action-oriented, in thought and deed; they continuously engender actions and reactions that aim at conserving, changing or criticizing perceived reality. And human practices are ideology-rich. That growing convergence of two neighbourly fields of research – through postulating conceptual maps and conceptual trajectories as empirically identifiable, and through recognizing both the persistence and the limits of conceptual confrontation – is proving fertile ground for the joining of investigative and analytical forces.

What conceptual history can bring to the study of ideologies is a keen awareness of the mutation of public terminology and the variability of time, as well as a readiness to focus on the vernacular (not always in evidence in the *Geschichtliche Grundbegriffe* tomes) and openness to the plethora of sources on which scholars can draw. What the study of ideologies can bring to conceptual historians is the need to confront a number of challenging phenomena: one is that of complex diachrony, in which fields of meanings, embodied in clusters of concepts, move over time (and across space), mutating *internally* all the while. That offers a more complex conceptual diachrony, as well as focusing on the shifting structures of the components that constitute them. The other is a dual problem of translation: not only the familiar one of moving across cultures and languages, but the less familiar one of translating the conceptual vocabulary within one culture from the vernacular to the professional (including our professional language as scholars) and vice versa. Here traditional political philosophy is at a disadvantage, as it prefers to study those particular professional voices and texts that meet certain criteria of validity, lucidity, consistency, concision and ethical force – in fact the same voices ostensibly employed by the academic students of those voices. But those are not typical human voices; they are quite abnormal in their sophistication. That may account for the occasional impatience of political philosophers with those scholars who study the kind of everyday, or qualitatively 'mediocre', political language that does not always excel in those standards. But as social scientists or as historians our curiosity should know no bounds and our tolerance of research-worthy texts and utterances no limits. The emphasis on the exceptional is revealing at many levels, but it is simultaneously a distortion of the nature of language and discourse. The challenge of distinguishing patterns within the mass of individuating information – as is the wont of students of human conduct and thought-practices – necessitates a focus on the typical and the normal, though never exclusively so. All forms of speech or writing are grist to our mills, and all contain significant information that can be extracted from them. The issue is not just the movement from elite to vernacular languages but the requirement to navigate continuously among a number of different elite languages (parliaments, bureaucrats, journalists and academics all produce distinctive 'elite' languages) and among a number of vernacular languages. We are thus not just looking at vernacularization over time but at an abundance of specialized languages, with the additional concomitant of having, as scholars, to reformulate vernacular idioms in new elite registers when we apply our analytical tools to redescribing the former. That rather distinct dimension is also a major challenge for comparative political thought, as we compare the understandings and interpretations of issues that appear to be similar but that are often articulated in parallel and even divergent terminologies (consider the interplay between 'political obligation', 'allegiance', 'loyalty', 'commitment' and 'trust' in both professional and ordinary language discourses). This *intra*-cultural problem has far less frequently been seen as one of comparison, but that is exactly what it is. Here too are fruitful fields that conceptual historians are beginning to explore.

One of the most important, and complex, aspects of such a project will be not just to explore diachrony and synchrony in a given society, but diatopy: to secure sufficient attention to the continuous flow of meaning across cultural boundaries. Comparison across space requires different analytical frameworks, and comparison over both time and space is complicated and fragmentary. I believe that we should try to offer the next generation of scholars a series of flavours of what can be done with conceptual history. For that we need to be imaginative and move away from some of the too lexical approaches to the field. But no project that emerges from our deliberations can move in all directions simultaneously and with sufficient depth. Instead, we may consider the methods of archaeologists when they excavate a cross-cut, segment or layer. Good scholarship must know its limitations. Attempts at comprehensiveness are bound to be exercises in failure simply by setting unattainable standards of fullness. As experts in temporality, we need to sign off each of our explorations with the coda 'awaiting contrary interpretation', acknowledging the ephemeral nature of our own contributions.

Further Dimensions of Conceptual Decoding

The study of social and political language has enriched our comprehension of concepts in many further ways. Although language is a human product, it has, as noted above, some features that cannot be altered by human will without rendering communication meaningless. But it is also the case that concepts come with additional baggage that does not refer directly to the intellectual contents of their meaning but relates rather to the coating and patina that accompany them. Meaning is not only the product of time, space and structure but of presentation and intensity of attachment. The vital task of the latter two is to add weight and impact to concepts with regard to their communicative and directive roles.

The presentational aspect links concepts to rhetoric. The study of rhetoric enables us to appreciate the aesthetic and persuasive devices employed to embellish the messages imparted by concepts. Rhetoric is not an optional by-product of conceptual arrangements but is embedded in the very acts of speech and writing themselves. Utterances have rhythms and they display both word sequences and ranking orders that contribute centrally to the distribution of significance among concepts, even irrespective of the intellectual persuasiveness of such ranking. Ranking must therefore be considered as one of the relational aspects of concepts. In the American Declaration of Independence, the rhetorical device of attaching the qualifiers 'truth' and 'self-evidence' to human equality, life, liberty and the pursuit of happiness adds maximal weight to their meanings by removing them entirely from rational contention within the cultural conventions of the late eighteenth century. The commonplace attachment of the concept 'natural' to other concepts such as 'rights', 'law' and 'justice' discharges a similar attempt to ratchet up the illocutionary force of language, irrespective of whether that reflects a true belief, a socially inherited opinion or a strategic act. Concepts often appear with that gloss, and their semantics and interpretation cannot be detached from their mode of delivery.

Conceptual history must therefore render account of those rhetorical environments in which a concept, or group of concepts, is to be found.[16] On that dimension the meaning of a concept relates, first, to the rhetorical *discursive priority* it attains ('give me liberty or give me death' [Patrick Henry]; 'Democracy is the worst form of government, except for all those other forms that have been tried from time to time' [Winston Churchill]). Second, it relates to the *form of delivery* with which the concept can be associated, and the cultural flourishes, ornamentations and signals to which it can be (and cannot be) attached. Here the associations the concept possesses in a specific milieu may be critical, as will be the justificatory arguments that accompany their presentation in each case. Thus, the concept of welfare has been valorized in the heyday of welfare state discourse by attaching it to the word 'vision' and associating it with progress, humanism, egalitarianism and social efficiency – in particular by left-liberal and social democratic ideologies; and it has been degraded by employing it in conjunction with 'scrounger' or 'parasite' – in particular by conservative, libertarian and populist ideologies. The recent not-so-subtle switches between 'refugee', 'asylum seeker', and 'illegal immigrant' have created a semantic equalization that blurs conceptual boundaries and raises the rhetorical temperature of a concept. Importantly, social and political concepts reflect not only historical, technological and cultural forces – a topic on which many conceptual historians focus – but shape present and future understandings of the world and serve as guides to action (or deliberate non-action), and their rhetorical persuasiveness, emotional attractiveness and imaginative vigour are central to those tasks. Third, the *performative power* of concepts is considerably enhanced through rhetoric which, in various nuanced ways, can be adapted to different professional and vernacular languages. Concepts are a locus of differential social and political power, and we must take account of the waxing and waning of the illocutionary force[17] of any given concept as it fluctuates over time as well as within different cultural segments of a society. The rhetorical attachment of the word 'red' to the concept of socialism has often signalled a violent and extreme potential, but it is also used as a much more 'technical' modifier to colour-code political parties, as in the current German political scene. A thorough conceptual history will examine the rise and fall of such tropes and the changing utility of metaphors or modulators, while fluctuating standards of fashion, of knowledge and of political correctness make their mark. Associating politics with 'dirty hands', with 'the art of the possible', or referring to 'the politics of envy' offers a rhetorical and emotional environment that impinges heavily on what the concept is understood to signify. Ultimately, rhetoric is not an art or a skill possessed by the initiated, but an ingredient of all language, professional or vernacular. Nor does it have to be intentional. Even the mere construction of a sentence places diverse emphases on the words that constitute it.

The power of language, however, does not merely concern rhetorical devices, but is embedded in the very structure, organization and ideological content of speech and writing. One school of thought that approaches language largely through its oppressive employment of power is critical discourse analysis. Its relevance to conceptual history lies in its assertion that dominant discourses wield detrimental control over their users. That suggests that some of the conflictual elements evident in a Koselleckian view of modernity are regarded as contrary to human interests, inhibiting social emancipation and, as a consequence, removable in principle if not in practice.

The occasional moralizing approach of critical discourse analysis tends to see language as oppressive – which inevitably draws attention to some of its negative political features.[18] But that can be a one-sided and unduly pessimistic interpretation that misses out on empowerment, on the granting of resources to individuals and groups to realize their aims – which is another conception of the concept of power. Beyond that, one attribute of concepts in general is their capacity to wield discursive power in their organizational, directive and interpretative roles, but that power is far from being necessarily pernicious. Positing the normal existence of conflict, competition, arrogation and dissent is a perspective shared with conceptual history, for, as Stråth has put it, '[c]onceptual history is about discursive struggles aimed at appropriating positions of interpretative power'.[19]

Nonetheless, just as the study of concepts benefits from the microanalysis of their structure, so does the study of power benefit from the microanalysis of its manifestations. For, as Austin argued, inasmuch as language is performative it is always an attempt to make a difference. That attempt may either succeed or fail; either way, language acts upon its consumers, and the deployment of certain concepts is a way of focusing on and highlighting specific ideas and practices. The very introduction of a concept into a sentence simultaneously excludes others and diverts our attention towards a given theme. That is the case not just because the articulators of language may be powerful, but because discourse is itself a form of power. In other words, the persuasive characteristics of rhetoric – themselves a form of power – are not only conveyed *through* language but embedded *in* it. For apart from concentrating on a particular concept or set of concepts – as for instance in the sentence 'Justice is the first virtue of political institutions'[20] – we tend to surround concepts with modifiers that intensify their impact. 'Obviously', 'surely', absolutely', 'indisputably' are examples of such adjectival modifiers, and show the need to include the grammatical environment of a concept in the analytical equation.

But there also exist concepts that have themselves served as cultural intensifiers; the most salient of them being 'rights'. The main feature of a right is as a ranking device that gives the highest priority to whatever concept it wishes to endorse and protect, thus overriding other claims and values. Placing the phrase 'the right to' before a valued concept such as life, liberty, property, happiness or welfare assigns to it a power that – at least in European and North American discourses – enshrines it in social and, potentially, legal practice. It hosts a claim to immutability that cannot be countermanded without very serious, dehumanizing, consequences. Indeed the ranking of values through the unequal distribution of their significance is the chief mechanism by which to defuse the struggle among concepts that is such a marked focus of conceptual history, unless more than one concept is couched in terms of a competing right – in which case an intractable conflict ensues.[21]

Finally, languages are not, after all, solely presented in oral or written shape. One current advantage the analysis of ideologies has over conceptual history is the possibility of adopting a more generous understanding of how both conceptualization and ideology proceed. Art, architecture, music and dance are practices with powerful ideological content and alternative means of conceptualizing the world and conveying clear political messages. Focusing on words as carriers of meaning restricts and marginalizes the impact of those central forms of social experience as expressers and conveyers of ideas.

Social and philosophical research has tended in recent years to concentrate on dispute and disruption. That may suit those who still regard ideology as a pejorative concept, and it may sit well with those conceptual historians for whom modernity emerges cloaked in crisis. There is certainly a strong case to be made for the salience of contention in social life, yet, concurrently, the emphasis on the conflictual features of discourse tends to deflect attention away from other aspects of the relationship between ideology and language. Conceptual combinations are extraordinary enabling devices that decode, explore and reinvent the social and political worlds. Ideologies consequently give vent to the human imagination in both exalted and malevolent modes, and even slight changes in their internal conceptual relationships produce discourses that direct perception, understanding and conduct into significantly different channels. Concepts thus not only have a history, they have immediate and long-term impacts on available social space and potential social action, even if that impact may also consist in delaying change, not merely in igniting or furthering it.

Michael Freeden is Emeritus Professor of Politics, University of Oxford, and Professorial Research Associate, SOAS, University of London. His books include *The New Liberalism* (Oxford, 1978); *Liberalism Divided: A Study in British Political Thought, 1914–1939* (Oxford, 1986); *Ideologies and Political Theory: A Conceptual Approach* (Oxford, 1996); *Liberal Languages* (Princeton, 2005); and *The Political Theory of Political Thinking* (Oxford, 2013). He is founder-editor of the *Journal of Political Ideologies*, and a Fellow of the Academy of Social Sciences. He was awarded the Sir Isaiah Berlin Prize for Lifetime Contribution to Political Studies by the UK Political Studies Association, and the Medal for Science, Institute of Advanced Studies, Bologna University.

Notes

1. See, for example, the interesting examination of Weber's 'Politik als Beruf' in J. Borchert, 'From *Politik als Beruf* to *Politics as a Vocation*: The Translation, Transformation, and Reception of Max Weber's Lecture', *Contributions to the History of Concepts* 3(1) (2007), 42–70.
2. See Michael Freeden, *The Political Theory of Political Thinking: The Anatomy of a Practice* (Oxford: Oxford University Press, 2013).
3. For an example of the latter, see Jacques Rancière, 'Ten Theses on Politics', *Theory and Event* 5(3) (2001).
4. Paul Ricoeur, *Interpretation Theory: Discourse and the Surplus of Meaning* (Fort Worth: Texas Christian University Press, 1976).
5. Niccolo Machiavelli, *The Prince* (Harmondsworth: Penguin, 1961), Chapter 25.
6. I have addressed these issues in greater detail in Michael Freeden, 'What Should the "Political" in Political Theory Explore?', *Journal of Political Philosophy* 13 (2005), 113–34; and Michael Freeden, 'Thinking Politically and Thinking about Politics: Language, Interpretation, and Ideology', in David Leopold and Marc Stears (eds), *Political Theory: Methods and Approaches* (Oxford: Oxford University Press, 2008), 196–215.
7. In introducing the notion of essentially contested concepts, W.B. Gallie emphasized the first feature; I have introduced the second feature, which seems to me to account more fundamentally for conceptual contestation. See W.B. Gallie, 'Essentially Contested Concepts', *Proceedings of the Aristotelian Society*, vol. 56 (1955–56), 167–98; Michael Freeden, *Ideologies and Political Theory: A Conceptual Approach* (Oxford: Oxford University Press, 1996), Chapter 2; David Collier, Fernando Daniel Hidalgo and Andra Olivia Maciuceanu, 'Essentially Contested Concepts: Debates and Applications', *Journal of Political Ideologies* 11 (2006), 211–46.
8. See also Michael Freeden, 'Editorial: Ideologies and Conceptual History', *Journal of Political Ideologies* 2 (1997), 3–11.
9. See, e.g., Willibald Steinmetz, 'New Perspectives on the Study of Language and Power in the Short Twentieth Century', in W. Steinmetz (ed.), *Political Languages in the Age of Extremes* (Oxford: Oxford University Press, 2011), 3–51; Willibald Steinmetz and Heinz-Gerhard Haupt, 'The Political as Communicative Space in History: The Bielefeld Approach', in Willibald Steinmetz, Ingrid Gilcher-Holtey and Heinz-Gerhard Haupt (eds), *Writing Political History Today* (Frankfurt: Campus, 2013), 11–33.
10. John Stuart Mill, *On Liberty* (London: Dent, 1910), Chapter 3.
11. Reinhart Koselleck, *The Practice of Conceptual History* (Stanford, CA: Stanford University Press, 2002), 120–21.
12. Habermas's understanding of normativity is of that kind. See Jürgen Habermas, *The Inclusion of the Other* (Cambridge: Polity Press, 1999), 55 [Original: *Die Einbeziehung des anderen*].

13. See, for example, John Rawls, *Political Liberalism* (New York: Columbia University Press, 1996), 45.
14. For an instructive analysis, see Bo Stråth, 'Ideology and Conceptual History', in Michael Freeden, Lyman Tower Sargent and Marc Stears (eds), *The Oxford Handbook of Political Ideologies* (Oxford: Oxford University Press, 2013), 3–19.
15. See also Jan Ifversen, 'About Key Concepts and How to Study Them', *Contributions to the History of Concepts* 6 (2011), 67–70.
16. See Kari Palonen's chapter in this volume. For another discussion, see Alan Finlayson, 'Ideology and Political Rhetoric', in Freeden, Sargent and Stears, *The Oxford Handbook of Political Ideologies*, 197–213.
17. See J. L. Austin, *How to Do Things with Words* (Oxford: Oxford University Press, 1975).
18. See, e.g., Norman Fairclough, *Language and Power*, 2nd edition (Harlow: Longman, 2001).
19. Stråth, 'Ideology and Conceptual History', 3.
20. John Rawls, *A Theory of Justice* (Oxford: Oxford University Press, 1972), 3.
21. For elaboration on these themes, see Freeden, *Political Theory of Political Thinking*, 139–45 and 277–309.

References

Austin, John Langshaw, *How to Do Things with Words* (Oxford: Oxford University Press, 1975)

Borchert, Jens, 'From *Politik als Beruf* to *Politics as a Vocation*: The Translation, Transformation, and Reception of Max Weber's Lecture', *Contributions to the History of Concepts* 3(1) (2007), 42–70

Collier, David, Fernando Daniel Hidalgo and Andra Olivia Maciuceanu, 'Essentially Contested Concepts: Debates and Applications', *Journal of Political Ideologies* 11 (2006), 211–46

Fairclough, Norman, *Language and Power*, 2nd edition (Harlow: Longman, 2001)

Finlayson, Alan, 'Ideology and Political Rhetoric', in Michael Freeden, Lyman Tower Sargent and Marc Stears (eds), *The Oxford Handbook of Political Ideologies* (Oxford: Oxford University Press, 2013), 197–213

Freeden, Michael, *Ideologies and Political Theory: A Conceptual Approach* (Oxford: Oxford University Press, 1996)

———, 'Editorial: Ideologies and Conceptual History', *Journal of Political Ideologies* 2 (1997), 3–11

———, 'What Should the "Political" in Political Theory Explore?', *Journal of Political Philosophy* 13 (2005), 113–34

———, 'Thinking Politically and Thinking about Politics: Language, Interpretation, and Ideology', in David Leopold and Marc Stears (eds), *Political Theory: Methods and Approaches* (Oxford: Oxford University Press, 2008), 196–215

———, *The Political Theory of Political Thinking: The Anatomy of a Practice* (Oxford: Oxford University Press, 2013)

Gallie, Walter Bryce, 'Essentially Contested Concepts', *Proceedings of the Aristotelian Society*, vol. 56 (1955–56), 167–98
Habermas, Jürgen, *The Inclusion of the Other* (Cambridge: Polity Press, 1999)
Ifversen, Jan, 'About Key Concepts and How to Study Them', *Contributions to the History of Concepts* 6 (2011), 67–70
Koselleck, Reinhart, *The Practice of Conceptual History* (Stanford, CA: Stanford University Press, 2002)
Machiavelli, Niccolo, *The Prince* (Harmondsworth: Penguin, 1961)
Mill, John Stuart, *On Liberty* (London: Dent, 1910)
Rancière, Jacques, 'Ten Theses on Politics', *Theory and Event* 5(3) (2001)
Rawls, John, *A Theory of Justice* (Oxford: Oxford University Press, 1972)
———, *Political Liberalism* (New York: Columbia University Press, 1996)
Ricoeur, Paul, *Interpretation Theory: Discourse and the Surplus of Meaning* (Fort Worth: Texas Christian University Press, 1976)
Steinmetz, Willibald, 'New Perspectives on the Study of Language and Power in the Short Twentieth Century', in Willibald Steinmetz (ed.), *Political Languages in the Age of Extremes* (Oxford: Oxford University Press, 2011), 3–51
Steinmetz, Willibald, and Heinz-Gerhard Haupt, 'The Political as Communicative Space in History: The Bielefeld Approach', in Willibald Steinmetz, Ingrid Gilcher-Holtey and Heinz-Gerhard Haupt (eds), *Writing Political History Today* (Frankfurt: Campus, 2013), 11–33
Stråth, Bo, 'Ideology and Conceptual History', in Michael Freeden, Lyman Tower Sargent and Marc Stears (eds), *The Oxford Handbook of Political Ideologies* (Oxford: Oxford University Press, 2013), 3–19

Chapter 5

Transnational Conceptual History, Methodological Nationalism and Europe

Jani Marjanen

Most studies in the history of concepts concern themselves with a nationally delineated space of communication or one language community. The number of studies describing themselves as comparative, international or transnational have, however, increased rapidly in the past two decades.[1] This is also true in the case of normative calls for taking the history of concepts beyond the nation state.[2] Focusing on the demand for European conceptual history is not an attempt to achieve complete coverage of all European countries and regions, but rather these demands are characterized by a quest to broaden the scope of research, transgress the boundaries of national historiography and add a comparative dimension.

In discussing comparative, international or transnational history, there seems to exist a common understanding that moving beyond the nation state is a positive objective. At the same time, it is acknowledged that the nation state remains an important unit of study and a historically important communicative space in debates about politics, economy, culture and social affairs.

What seems to be agreed upon to a lesser degree are the ways in which the national perspective might be a problem and how comparative, international or transnational history can solve these problems. In the following, I will suggest revisiting the recent debates about methodological nationalism and the possibilities of writing the history of concepts on a European level. In doing so, I will suggest looking more closely at the spread of concepts by means of frequency analysis of words in digital corpora as well examining the geographical dimensions of using concepts. In this way we may better understand the transnational dimensions of conceptual change in the past as well as help to bridge the gap between strictly quantitative and charting studies of language and the close reading of individual speech acts. The examples in the fourth and fifth sections have to do with the use of 'nationalism' as a concept in political discourse. The choice of examples is designed to illustrate how one can move towards transnational conceptual history, but is also meant to show how the discourse of methodological nationalism is itself rooted in a long discursive tradition. This tradition is significant for the rhetorical appeal of talking about methodological nationalism in today's academia.

Methodological Nationalism and Transnational History

The phrase 'methodological nationalism' has been a part of the language of social theory since the 1970s.[3] In the last few years it has gained new currency and has also figured in the debate about transnational history. In recent years, talk about 'methodological nationalism' has been associated with Ulrich Beck and the project of a cosmopolitan social science.[4] Beck is, however, not alone in theorizing about methodological nationalism or laying the path to overcome methodological nationalism.[5] Apart from in-depth discussions on the topic, we also encounter an everyday, rather fuzzy, and undefined concept of methodological nationalism that keeps popping up in academic pleas to overcome a national gaze. Here methodological nationalism simply tends to denote any study that is not explicitly international, transnational or comparative.

For Beck, 'methodological nationalism' is the acceptance of a national outlook or gaze in the social sciences. This relates to the common view of equating society with the nation and the failure to look upon the increasingly global world from a perspective other than the dichotomy of national and international. Beck criticizes the taking for granted of the fact that the society that the social sciences study is somehow national or nationally delineated. The problem, according to Beck, is that this unreflected nationally delineated sociology does not sufficiently grasp the increasingly transnational political and social processes that are crucial in today's world. He argues that many (if not all) analytical concepts of the social sciences are embedded in a national outlook. For the cosmopolitan social sciences, we consequently need, according to Beck, to create concepts and theories that grasp the increasingly transnational processes at hand.[6] Beck does not discuss how transnational debates are a way of contributing to the national outlook. In a sense, the national and the transnational coincide in different debates. Translation is an important example of this. The process of translating is in itself the use of transnational material and making it national.[7] Being international, cross-national or national are also to be regarded as rhetorical tools in debates, which is a long-term feature in the formation of scholarly discourse and increasingly evident in the rhetoric of funding agencies of science.[8]

The nationalism that Beck describes through the rhetorically potent phrase 'methodological nationalism' is of a specific type. He describes an unreflected everyday nationalism. A conceptual historian might think of the age of nationalism as an instance in history in which the rhetoric of 'nation' and/or 'nationalism' gained particularly strong currency. For Beck, this is not the case. His nationalism is banal, unpronounced and instinctive.[9] Beck's methodological nationalism is related to the everyday nationalism of global economic competition as described by Pauli Kettunen. One dimension of this nationalism of global economic competition is the self-evident apprehension of a nationally delineated 'we' that needs to keep up in global competition, or the almost innate cheering of corporations that are perceived as 'ours' in the global competition for market shares.[10] Similarly, Beck's methodological nationalism is assuming that data about societal phenomena or the questions regarding these phenomena automatically deploy a national perspective.

What Beck criticizes in particular is how knowledge is organized along national borders.[11] Many of the collections or databases of statistical bureaus, libraries and archives are nationally delineated, thus creating a sort of national epistemology.[12] For some present-day processes, this can cause significant skew in collected data. National statistical bureaus are obviously aware of the global flows of the present and have also in the past shown great interest in international comparison and research collaboration, but still remain trapped in the national outlook that is to a large extent inherent in their methods, points of view and – most importantly for conceptual historians – the categories (or concepts) used to describe units of analysis. It is an equally obvious point that the collection of data is at all times a political move of some sort. Creating a set of data to describe an organization, or describing archives as national, regional or European, are similarly political. This is an unavoidable part of knowledge production – an element we can address only by participating in the politics of knowledge production and by tackling it with reflexivity.

Other theorists of methodological nationalism, Andreas Wimmer and Nina Glick Schiller, point at three connected forms of methodological nationalism. First, they discuss not being perceptive enough to see the transnational elements in the studied processes (the geographically limited variant). Second, they point at the naturalization of the nation state as a unit of study (the naturalized variant). Third, they bring forward sidestepping the nation and nation-building as a topic altogether in social theory (the ignorant variant).[13] The ignorant variant is perhaps to a lesser degree applicable to the field of history. Following their conceptualization, methodological nationalism is not only the lack of cross-country comparisons or contrasting examples, which seems to be the assumption in everyday talk about methodological nationalism, but also assuming that the nation is always a natural unit of analysis, even when the perspective is comparative.

It is important to note that Beck's 'methodological nationalism' does not take issue with history, but rather with the present being more transnational than we are capable of understanding. We may ask if the nationally delineated world that Beck describes even existed in the past, and to what degree.[14] We can certainly claim that certain periods of history (most notably the late nineteenth and early twentieth centuries) have been characterized by a stronger division into nation states, and that these nation states have, perhaps more than before or after, been organizing principles for politics, economy, intellectual life, and the everyday experiences of ordinary people. However, the 'golden age' of the nation state might appear, on closer examination, as surprisingly short.[15] Borders, national or otherwise, have certainly been crossed any time before and after the introduction of the nation state as an organizing unit in international politics. Unlike Beck's programme for the social sciences, the historian's task therefore should not be primarily a theoretical one – creating new concepts for the social sciences – but an empirical one.

In order to inform us about the pitfalls of 'methodological nationalism', historians should instead ask historically relevant questions that uncover the transnational in the past. Transnational history is a label that in itself is quite ambiguous, and caters to a variety of different types of study.[16] First, we need to ask how national borders were crossed in the past, and to what extent. Studies concerning migration, commerce, or intellectual influences in the past have of course provided interesting findings on this point. Conceptual history may be particularly well suited to the study of the transnational in the past, as the use of concepts and words can often be analysed from this perspective. Recent studies have, for example, been prone to take into account the 'travels' of concepts across borders, thus scrutinizing how concepts have been imported and adapted to local contexts, and how the spread of concepts into new political cultures has meant a challenge to the existing vocabulary.[17] Second, we should ask how past agents experienced crossing borders at their time. The study of travel literature provides a plenitude of examples of the mental and political borders in the past. One interesting opening in this field consists of the studies that look particularly at the practices of comparison in the past – that is, seeing comparisons as rhetorical moves in political debates.[18] In terms of concepts and their uses in the past, this point relates especially to how concepts may have carried connotations to other cultures. This is especially evident in Jörn Leonhard's extensive study on liberalism.[19] Third, and perhaps the point least explored, we may want to focus on how the crossing of borders has been described linguistically, thus providing a historically informed picture of the conceptualization or non-conceptualization of the 'transnational' in the past. In other words, we should relate past linguistic expressions to what we might today describe as 'transnational', and discuss potential similarities and differences. In doing this, focus will perhaps be mostly on concepts of political and geopolitical units such as nation, empire, realm, region, and so on, but also on the status of concepts describing the crossing of geopolitical units. For example, the rise of such a prominent concept as 'international' is yet to be profoundly studied from a conceptual history point of view. Concepts that are often used analytically to describe relations between different geographical units – such as periphery, universal, geopolitics, local – may also be revealing if examined from a conceptual-history perspective.[20]

This sort of turn towards the transnational in history is only partly a question of describing the past accurately, but more significantly about participating in the ongoing debate about what is important in history.[21] The aim is to broaden the field of history writing by giving us past examples of 'transnational' experiences, and hence enrich our image of the past with new perspectives. While conceptual history has been able to demonstrate the historicity of language and the contingent character of conceptual change, transnational conceptual history should be able to illustrate the complicated spatial dynamics in how concepts have been used. It can undermine a strictly national and particularistic understanding of politics and culture by showing the concrete transnational links that have been in place through the 'travels' of concepts, and the connotations that these concepts have been given in other cultures, nations or places. Transnational conceptual history can also debunk a more universalistic take on concepts by illustrating how the translation of concepts into new languages or political cultures always entails a reinterpretation and adaptation of the concepts. In other words, transnational conceptual history should be able to describe history in between the provincial particularism of national history writing and the ignorant universalism of much of political philosophy.

The National Limits of Basic Concepts

If assuming the contestability of concepts in political debates is one of the cornerstones of doing conceptual history, then exploring the geographical scope of political debate should be a crucial question for analysing the spatial dimensions of conceptual history. This would, in the end, also help us to assess the possible degree of methodological nationalism in a particular study.[22]

For most studies concerned with conceptual history, the contexts of the debate are either national or linguistic, with good reason. The role of national public spheres should not be overlooked. Trying to assess the limits and the historical meaning of national debates is also central to understanding the transnational elements in political and intellectual life. However, national and the linguistic borders are constantly crossed – and have been in the past. As important as national political debates are, it is remarkably often the case that national political debates are fuelled by outside examples, and that the historical experience of crossing borders has in itself been an important rhetorical reservoir.[23] Here, smaller political cultures have often had a stronger experience of having to adapt to and elaborate on foreign examples, but this aspect is certainly not absent from dominant political cultures either.

For instance, in the published conceptual history projects on Korea and Finland, the debates have an inherent multilingual aspect to them. The history of political concepts in Korea cannot be written without taking into account the interconnectedness between Japanese and Chinese concepts, nor can the Finnish conceptualizations from the late eighteenth century until the present day be studied without taking into account the Finnish reconceptualizations of Swedish, German, French and English concepts.[24] The Finnish project *Käsitteet liikkeessä* explicitly states that one objective for the studies is to deal with how European political concepts were used in a Finnish space of contestation.[25]

Conversely, the German, and especially the Spanish, conceptual history projects have stronger multinational aspects to them, and whereas they are by no means blind to multilingualism in the past, the linguistic communities of German and Spanish languages respectively are the organizing principles in both projects.[26] The index volume of the *Geschichtliche Grundbegriffe* displays the presence of multiple languages in the encyclopedia. Focus there is, however, more on etymology than on the interplay between languages or the way individual actors were able to use the linguistic interplay as resources in their argumentation.[27]

While defining the spaces of contestation of political concepts according to national or linguistic borders is generally defensible – ignoring the nation state is not a way of transcending methodological nationalism – this connection is often assumed too lightly. Defining a coherent space of contestation or, more simply, a debate along lines other than national or linguistic ones, is not an easy task for a historian. Certainly, historical agents have not controlled the scope of the debates they have entered. While they may have had acknowledged opponents in debates, the context in which their arguments may have been reproduced or misinterpreted have been countless.[28] The historian should, however, be attentive to the fact that debates cannot merely be regarded as national, but that the limits set by language or national political entities also provided an opportunity to argue against one's opponents by transcending these borders. In both, the case of multilingualism in debates and the case of multinational languages, the crossings of both linguistic and national borders, have themselves generated an element of play in political debate.[29]

To put the role of the nation state in context, I advocate a stronger focus on debates – not only on particular discussions in parliament or newspapers, but on public discourse at large – and how crossing borders has been used as rhetorical reservoirs in them. The most obvious, and today nearly omnipresent, example of this is saying that a certain idea or a certain author has international qualities, thus using 'international' as a positive label. A particularly interesting example of this is how key figures of nineteenth-century nation-building used to be primarily acknowledged for their endeavours as facilitators in 'national awakening', but are today put on a pedestal for their importance as international figureheads of romanticism, rationalism, or simply political thought. While the reassessment of nineteenth-century thinkers from an international perspective is certainly welcome, the shift in characterization can be very dramatic.[30] As David Armitage has put it, 'if you are not doing an explicitly transnational, international or global project, you now have to explain *why* you are not'.[31] While it is almost self-evident that this pressure has consequences in the way historical agents of all ages are described in present-day historiography, it is not equally accepted that this pressure also has consequences for how historical debates are construed.[32]

One overlooked aspect in the ongoing theoretical debate about the differences of words, concepts and basic concepts is precisely how a debate in which basic concepts are made objects for political struggles is defined.[33] In a sense, I want to point to the rather self-evident fact that basic concepts were not really basic concepts for everyone. Others were participating in the debate, whereas some were not. In one of his last texts on the history of concepts, Reinhart Koselleck defined a basic concept (*Grundbegriff*) as 'an inescapable, irreplaceable part of the political and social vocabulary. ... Basic concepts *combine* manifold experiences and expectations in such a way that they become indispensable to any formulation of the most urgent issues of a given time. Thus basic concepts are highly complex; they are always both controversial and contested'.[34]

Koselleck does not state this, but it seems to me that what he had in mind was a national communicative space. The 'most urgent issues of a given time' seems to denote an 'everyone' or a historical 'we'. In the last of the prefaces to the *Geschichtliche Grundbegriffe*, Koselleck even explicitly writes 'our political and social language'.[35] In assessing how broadly political concepts became objects of struggle, we should therefore also try to assess to what degree this 'given time', 'everyone' or 'we' actually coincides with the nation.

Many of the most contested concepts in Western political thinking were of course not confined to contestation along national borders. 'Democracy' cannot be seen as a concept contested only within a national public debate. However, we must ask to what degree the rhythm of the national public debates defines what 'the most urgent issues of a given time' are, and to what degree it does not. Furthermore, we must ask to what degree foreign developments, debates and examples could be used rhetorically in local national debates, thus transcending a simple dichotomy between national and transnational by also noting how the different forums were elements in debate.

Koselleck did acknowledge the supranational elements of the contestation of concepts. He also had a clear view that concepts could be used differently by different strata in society: 'No political action, no social behavior can occur without some minimum stock of basic concepts that have persisted over long periods; have suddenly appeared, disappeared, reappeared; or have been transformed, either rapidly or slowly. Such concepts therefore must be interpreted in order to sort out their multiple meanings, internal contradictions, and varying applications in different social strata'.[36]

From today's point of view, it appears as if transnational elements of past debates did not as such constitute a blind spot for Koselleck and his team, but it was simply not a big concern for them. Today, there is a much greater demand for understanding the supra-national and the sub-national character of debates in which concepts have been contested.

Methodological Europeanness?

In turning towards Europe as a geographical unit that delineates the spread and the influence of political and social concepts, we encounter another set of problems. These problems are rather different from the problems we encounter when dealing with the nation state as a sort of self-evident conceptual universe.[37]

One major issue is of course the question of coverage. European history is often written through a selection of certain European countries or regions, and with a more or less reflected take on the use of nation states as units of analysis.[38] While a selection of cases is inevitable for the production of readable and publishable books, the selection may at times cause a skewed perspective in omitting different historical perspectives. This is the case particularly in the common form of European history that is written as a combination of German, French and British experiences, which follows a Barrington Moorean logic of regarding small countries as passive receivers of ideas that are economically and politically dependent on the big countries, and thus uninteresting.[39] In a neo-Marxist analysis of modernization, such as Moore's, this logic of choosing cases according to size and international power does make sense to a certain degree, although a small-country critique of Moore's study surfaced immediately after the publication of *Social Origins of Dictatorship and Democracy*.[40] From the point of view of conceptual change and political innovation, there are, however, even greater analytical reasons to criticize the Moorean perspective. It is clear that key agents in the influential regions are generally not ignorant of the spread of their thoughts, policies or models in the more peripheral areas. In a sense, even the most self-assured and universalist ideologist is curious about whether or not there is a reception of his or her thoughts. The spread of ideas and concepts certainly influences any political or intellectual debate. Furthermore, the historical experience in smaller countries is complicated by the negotiation of importing ideas and concepts on the one hand and elaborating them for the purpose of local political struggles on the other, thus adding new perspectives to the discussion in the intellectual centre.[41] In a sense, in a smaller political culture there may be a smaller capacity for including different strands of thought, thus ending up eclectically conflating ideas that might have been seen as rivals in the original debate. This entails a simplification of the debate on the one hand, and a questioning of the premises of the original debate on the other.[42] As debates seldom take place in a strict setting of a 'big' or 'small' country, but rather tend to cross borders, the reality of political and intellectual debate is, of course, even more complex.

The choices made in covering some parts in Europe whereas others are left out (most often due to ignorance) are not really different from similar choices made in writing national histories. The difference lies in the experiences of whether or not these histories are felt as shared ones. These experiences naturally include an element of asymmetry between cities, countries, intellectual centres, and civilizations.

A speculative exercise may be useful here. For example, political history that covers events in Helsinki is generally seen as a natural part of Finnish history. The naturalization of Helsinki as a core stage of national history is fairly uncontested. From a European perspective there is more room for contestation. Inasmuch as the French Revolution can be regarded as 'an event', it is certainly seen as an event that is part of European history. The Balkan Wars of the 1990s may also be seen as part of a common European past, but the degree of sharedness in Europe is perhaps more contested than in the case of the French Revolution. The Finnish Civil War of 1918 is part of European history only in the context of writing the history of the First World War from a European perspective. All of these 'events' were by themselves transnational in terms of causes, involved agents, and ideas, but the historical interpretation of their transnationality or Europeanness is understood through the lens of asymmetrical relations in Europe. I would be prone to think that for the everyday understanding of European history, place and asymmetrical relations are even more significant than for the tradition of national history.[43] Ideas of Europe and a European past are simply incorporated differently to the narratives of national history in different parts of Europe.[44]

From the point of view of European history and the perspective of methodological nationalism there are at least three major problems to discuss: (1) having to legitimize Europe as a unit for study in the first place; (2) not having data collected with Europe as an organizing principle; and (3) not really being able to assess the degree to which we can regard European political culture as having a shared conceptual universe. The first two points are questions of the politics of history and the politics of organizing knowledge, and are far beyond the scope of conceptual history. The third point, however, can be tackled as an empirical question that can be studied by means of conceptual history.

I fear that in an attempt to overcome the national perspective and turning towards European projects, we may fall into the trap of 'methodological Europeanness', not in the sense that the projects are a part of some sort of European Commission-directed Euronationalism, but in the sense that the relation to Europe is partly unreflected. Although we can talk about a Euronationalism or a European identity, the real question is how European identities are incorporated in national and other identity constructions among the peoples of Europe.[45] Here, endless combinations of visions of Europe, the particular nation, the local community, or other cornerstones of individual identities, such as class, religion, gender, ethnicity and ideology, are available. Not reflecting upon the asymmetrical relations entailed in these identity constructions is related to the habit of assuming the nation state to be a container to which society is confined.

To avoid 'methodological Europeanness', we do not have to discuss the ever-present question of what Europe is, but we must discuss the relevance of Europe at different times and sort out the asymmetries in the European intellectual field. This also includes studying how Europe has been conceptualized in different parts of the world. Mapping out asymmetries in intellectual relations will also help us to look at the degree to which we can regard European political discourse as creating a sort of European conceptual universe. Below, I will briefly discuss two ways of approaching this problem, first by looking at the possibilities to map quantitatively the spread of concepts, and, second, by qualitatively analysing the geographical dimensions of using concepts.

Quantifying the European Conceptual Universe

As digital text corpora are constantly expanding and becoming more accessible for the text-oriented researcher we now have improved possibilities to chart the geographical spread of concepts. This helps us to address the spatial dimensions of political and social language. Any study looking into the history of a particular concept should therefore not only consult the appropriate dictionaries to look into first uses and the etymology of particular words, but also consult appropriate digital and searchable text corpora to tentatively chart the spread and frequency of words. While the etymology and first uses of words may be revealing, the frequency and spread of a word will tell us even more about the linguistic context in which a concept has been most intensively deployed.

The obvious objection to this path of research is that the results of this type of searching are often trivial and often correspond to our presuppositions. Another objection is that doing a series of searches and putting together the data from those searches is in fact so quick and easy that anyone can do it. Therefore one might think that there is no need to do these searches at all. This is true, but the power of the databases and their convenient searchability lies precisely in the ease of doing them. The results may not be revolutionary, but they can be an effective way of proving or rejecting our presuppositions of the spread and use of particular concepts, so that we have the opportunity to quickly move forward to detailed analyses. In a sense, the big data provided by databases should go hand in hand with, and pave the way for, in-depth qualitative research.

For instance, by searching in the highly usable, and still problematic,[46] set of texts provided by Google Books for the words nationalism, *nationalisme*, and *Nationalismus* in Google Books English, French and German sets of texts we can get some indicative data on the use of these concepts.[47] Most importantly, it is clear that the breakthrough of the word 'nationalism' is rather late in these languages. Although it was first used in a university context in Germany in the early eighteenth century, and later adapted in French political discourse at the end of the eighteenth century, a frequency analysis in the Google Books Ngram shows that the word really only became popular in the early 1900s in all three languages.[48] The rise in frequency would suggest that the concept of nationalism either became rhetorically more appealing or was included in the vocabulary of a larger group of people, and by examining this perhaps counterintuitive finding in the actual texts we can analyse the phenomenon further.

The lack of interest in the use and spread of the word 'nationalism' is perhaps explained by its frequent use as an analytic category sometimes denoting

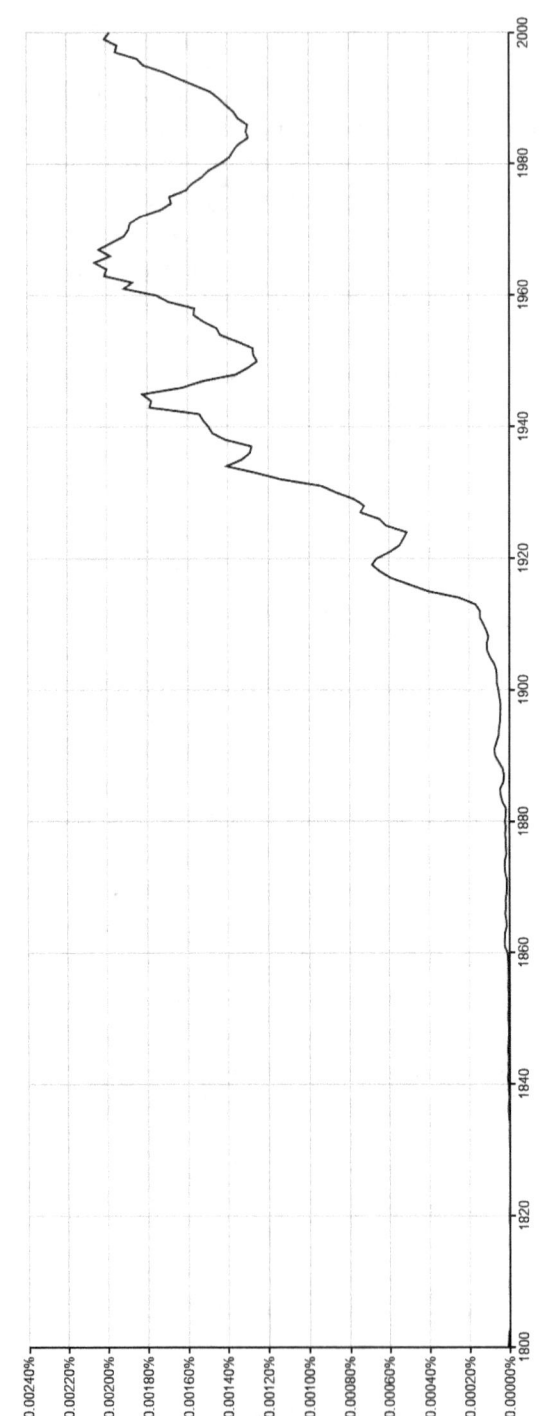

Figure 5.1 In Google Books' set of texts – consisting of books published in the whole of the English-speaking world – the word 'nationalism', with or without capitalization, only started gaining popularity after the turn of the twentieth century. Image taken from Google Books Ngram Viewer, http://books.google.com/ngrams.

a process of the social construction of nation states and sometimes denoting an ideology.[49] In looking into the use of the word nationalism itself, the focus moves to tackling nationalism as an object of conceptual struggle and a rhetorical device in political (and academic) debate.

From the point of view of linguistically or nationally delineated corpora, there is a problem however. It is clear that the words with the same etymology were not equally popular in the three languages. It is clear that *chauvinisme* was often used in French in instances that one would expect *nationalisme* also to have been an option. A similar option to talk about 'jingoism' existed for the English language, but that word was overall used less frequently in the materials contained in Google Books.

One great challenge with the digitized corpora is that they are often built on the presumption that national units are the most natural units of study. Most digitized corpora are somehow nationally or language-wise organized. This relates to the issue of comparability of different series of sources, the problem of methodological nationalism, and what Jörn Leonhard calls 'the trap of semantic nominalism' – that is, assuming that a word with the same etymology has a similar function or meaning in different languages.[50]

By looking further into the semantic field of the words, we find that 'nationalism' appeared in somewhat different discourses. By searching for nationalism and an adjacent adjective in the period 1850–1950 we find that in English 'nationalism' as a word is most often preceded by a preposition like 'of', but if we focus on adjectives only we find that the most popular adjectives preceding 'nationalism' in the English texts in Google Books are (in order of popularity): 'economic', 'German', 'Indian', 'extreme', 'new', 'Arab', 'Jewish', 'narrow', 'Chinese' and 'intense'.[51] These searches point to the fact that the discourse of nationalism often portrayed nationalism in other countries, corresponding well to the well-known idea of 'their nationalism' and 'our patriotism' put forward by Michael Billig.[52] Consequently, instances of 'British nationalism' or 'English nationalism' are mentioned much less frequently than, for instance, 'Chinese nationalism'. This holds also for the books published in Britain only. Apart from other peoples' nationalisms, we also find adjectives that assess the quality of nationalism in terms such as 'new', 'narrow' and 'intense'.

In switching to the German set of texts, we find a similar context for *Nationalismus* with the remarkable exception that *deutsche(n)* and *deutscher Nationalismus* are among the most popular phrases in the search. Similar to the findings in the English corpus, we find economic (*wirtschaftlichen*) as well as modern (*modernen*) and new (*neue*) among the preferred adjectives. French, Russian, Jewish and Indian nationalisms also appear in the texts.

The French findings differ on this point. Among the ten most popular adjectives preceding the word *nationalisme*, we cannot find any references to particular peoples or nations, but only to qualities. The French discussion on nationalism appears to have been more concerned with questions of the authenticity or pureness (for instance in *pur, sain, vrai*) or more broadly the character of *nationalisme* (for instance *nouveau, vieux, certain, étroit, jeune*).[53] The lack of references to other nations or countries, or even the scope (like in economic or *wirtschaftlichen*), enforces the impression that the French discourse on *nationalisme* had a more universalistic character. Naturally, for more certain assertions on the rhetoric of nationalism in English, German and French, the next step would be an in-depth analysis of key texts.

While Google Books and its Ngram searches help us to probe the spread and the frequency of particular concepts and provide some information about the semantic fields of the concepts, the delineation of the sets of texts along linguistic and national lines still remains problematic. Can we make claims about political discourse revolving around the concept of nationalism in these countries based on the searches and, perhaps more importantly, do we expect to make claims about the character of political discourse in a given country in the first place?

Mapping the first appearances of a word in a given language or country, and the frequency of use of that word, should not be seen as more than indications of how the German or French debates functioned; the struggles and different debates in national contexts, as well as those that crossed national and linguistic borders, are not accessible to us through searches. Rather, the mapping of word frequencies is more helpful in determining the spread of the word, which in turn helps us in the qualitative analysis of texts. By mapping the spread of words, we can also find out about the potential border crossings and comparisons in the past. In order to analyse how past actors imported and adapted concepts for the purpose of deploying them at home, it is certainly helpful to have a broader picture of the spread of the words. For instance, the spread of a buzzword into other areas or countries may have also given it special momentum in domestic debates. For the use of the word 'nationalism', for instance, the knowledge that it had been adapted into almost all European languages certainly made it more powerful as a rhetorical tool locally.[54]

Geographical Dimensions of the Use of Concepts

A way to analyse the transnational dimension of the use of concepts is to look into how geographical dimensions are played out in the use of concepts.[55] I suggest analysing especially the countries or areas that the use of a particular concept refers to, bears connotations to, or is borrowed and adapted from. This is perhaps most suitable for series of sources that provide series of similar texts or speech acts, like newspaper material or parliamentary debates. In itself, the material should not be an issue. Franco Moretti, for instance, has looked into the geographical properties of novels and their translations, providing highly interesting results on intellectual centres and peripheries in Europe.[56]

As an example, I have looked at the appearance of the concept of nationalism in Finnish newspapers published before the year 1910. The newspapers are all available digitally and are searchable.[57] The search interface for this corpus does not provide a similar quick tool to analyse the frequency of given words in the text, as the Google Ngram does. However, by counting the number of articles using the words *nationalism* and *nationalismen* (in Swedish) or *nationalismi* (in Finnish)[58] it is easy to determine that the development of the use of nationalism in Finland roughly corresponds to the chronology in the French, German and English texts provided by Google Books. In newspapers published in Finland, the first uses of the term are from the 1860s onwards, and continue appearing sporadically. By the turn of the century, a much more intense debate occurred, and by the year 1906, the concept of nationalism, with its constantly growing number of hits, had become an inseparable part of political discourse in Finland.[59]

In exploring the actual uses of the terminology, it becomes clear that most appearances of *nationalism* or *nationalismen* have to do with news from abroad or are anchored in the context of international power politics. This illustrates how foreign affairs were discussed in Finland at the time, but also how describing foreign affairs was a way of broadening the context of domestic debates, a way of introducing new concepts and ideas, and a way of expressing a political argument by using foreign cases.[60]

The first appearances of the word 'nationalism' in Finnish newspapers already had a non-Finnish context.[61] The first newspaper text describing Finnish nationalism (*den finska nationalismen*) that I have been able to locate is from 1870, and it stresses the fact that the Finnish nationalism did not seek to break up the Russian state, of which Finland 'for the past sixty years [has been an] integrated part'.[62] This was a somewhat exceptional case, as talk of nationalism in the papers of the time seldom referred to Finland or domestic politics. Rather, the term was most often used in descriptions of nationalism elsewhere. New political and theoretical concepts were introduced through descriptions of foreign political affairs.

From the point of view of the geographical dimensions of concepts, the concept of nationalism seems to have been introduced through German,

French, Polish, Danish and Russian examples. The interesting thing here is that Swedish examples are lacking in the early discussion about nationalism, which is to be understood as a form of caution in not introducing political debates from 'the old motherland', although Sweden was self-evidently the primary inspiration for political and social reform.[63] It is difficult to say exactly whether different political factions in the debates gave the concept of nationalism different geographical properties. The sources of inspiration for socialists, liberals and Fennomans differed to a certain extent, but often concrete availability of foreign news and correspondents from abroad steered how foreign news found its way into the papers. For the purposes of this text, it is more important to note that it makes perhaps less sense to quantify the most popular sources of inspiration for Finnish papers debating nationalism than to assess which rhetorical purposes the comparisons or descriptions of foreign models served.

In the Finnish language newspapers the word *nationalismi* had a slightly different introduction. As late as the 1880s, Finnish-language texts were often written in a more patronizing tone, and this was reflected also in the use of nationalism as a concept. In an isolated occurrence from the 1880s the paper *Kotkan Sanomat* called for a life of piety and conformity, and warned against the dangers of nationalism, socialism, and irreligiousness in educating new generations of inhabitants.[64] It was only later, in 1898, that the Finnish-language rhetoric of *nationalismi* started to gain momentum in political discourse.[65] It is also in this instance that foreign models became important in debating the concept.

Despite differences in the Swedish-language and Finnish-language introduction of nationalism and derivate concepts, the intensification of the debate followed a similar pattern in both languages. The Russian Revolution of 1905 brought about an intensified debate over nationality in the empire, which in Finland led to more frequent discussions in which nationalism was used rhetorically as a means of discrediting opponents. This discourse revolved around Finland's position in the empire, but also dovetailed with the increasing tension in the so-called language question.[66]

Often, the use of foreign debates had a domestic audience. Using foreign examples was a way of avoiding censorship. An article in the paper *Nya Pressen* dealing with Finland's position in the Russian Empire may serve as an example. Finland's position as a Grand Duchy was hugely topical at the time, both in Finnish debates but increasingly so also in Russian political life, as the multiethnic reality of the empire clashed with aspirations of national unity.[67] *Nya Pressen* approached the question by summarizing an editorial in the *Frankfurter Zeitung*. Instead of expressing a critique of Russia's policy regarding Finland, the story in the paper presented the news that the German paper critiqued Russia's policy. It was also the tension between Russia's imperial multiethnicity and national unity that provided a context for the rhetoric of nationalism. *Nya Pressen* concluded – and here it is clear the paper is not only paraphrasing the German debate on the topic – that 'Finland's judicial status is clear and has in sufficient degree been illuminated by German and even Russian jurists. There is unfortunately not any hope that these voices of warning should be heard ... so that Russian nationalism would also become informed that it is dangerous to choose the path of violence against foreign peoples in the realm'.[68]

In its discussion on Finland's position, *Nya Pressen* did a number of things by using foreign models. First, it avoided censorship by using the German debate as a way of talking about Finland's position. From 1882 the paper had been a strong defender of Finnish rights to self-government – a position that led to the paper being forced to cease publication in 1900. As was accustomed, the paper was soon established anew, but this new edition wanted to avoid being shut down like its predecessor had been. Second, the German examples were used to introduce Russian debates on nations and ethnicity into a Finnish context. This debate had direct consequences for Finland's self-governance. Third, *Nya Pressen* described 'Russian nationalism' as a stubborn and uninformed movement that was a threat to Finland and the other nations in the Russian Empire. This description served not only to argue against the so-called Russification of Finland and imperial consolidation, but it was also aimed against Fennoman politics (or simply Finnish nationalism) with the ambition of advancing Finnish (as opposed to Swedish) language and culture. *Nya Pressen* and its editor Axel Lille were tightly anchored in the Svekoman (Swedish) movement, and by implicitly associating aspirations towards national unity with Russian nationalism, it followed its Swedish-speaking, liberal and constitutional standing.[69]

The language question overall meant a divide in the use of the concept of nationalism. Swedish-language papers were much more likely to talk about nationalism as a threat, and add pejoratives before using it.[70] Finnish-language papers often shared a negative interpretation of nationalism, especially socialist papers, but they were also more likely to discuss nationalism from a more moderate perspective. For instance, in 1907 the Finnish-language paper *Uusimaa* commented on how a Swedish-language paper had presented an almost 'teary-eyed' plea for agitation before the elections in order to 'avoid the flourishing of "black nationalism"'.[71] Here, nationalism is introduced as a word of abuse used by political opponents. The referral to the blackness of nationalism further emphasizes a sort of victimizing rhetoric in *Uusimaa*'s text. As I have not been able to locate the original Swedish text that is quoted, it is possible that the use of nationalism in this case is an invented quote aimed to agitate by bringing forward the abuse against *Uusimaa*'s readers.

The focus on nationalism as a concept naturally affects which countries appear as models, as warnings, or as useful rhetorical examples. In looking into other concepts, the foreign examples and connotations would certainly appear different. While Finnish political discourse was very much oriented towards Germany (as an intellectual centre),[72] France (as a centre for arts and literature),[73] Sweden (through a shared political culture),[74] and Russia (through the imperial connection),[75] the given debates and the given concepts in conflict opened up for specific rhetorical use of foreign and domestic comparative examples.

Focusing on the geographical dimensions that are present in the use of particular concepts provides insight into the transnational dimensions of past experiences. There are at least four different ways in which geography is present in the use of concepts. First, there are explicit comparisons between a domestic or local debate and another place. Here, the function of the comparison is to provide a new or broader context for the domestic debate, and through that redefinition of the context persuade opponents. Second, the comparisons may be what Jussi Kurunmäki calls 'descriptive comparisons'[76] – simply providing examples without explicitly connecting them to a particular local debate. In the material regarding nationalism in the Finnish press, the introduction of the concept was largely done through such descriptive comparisons. The concept itself was not used to describe Finnish circumstances, but through foreign examples it soon became a part of the political vocabulary in Finland. Third, the concepts themselves may carry connotations to other cultures. In the case of concepts such as the people's home (*folkhemmet*, *kansankoti*) the association is so strong that a Finnish paper still cannot use it without associating it to Sweden.[77] In other cases, the connotation might be weaker or it might disappear over time, like in the example of liberalism in Britain losing its connotations to French political culture during the course of the first half of the nineteenth century.[78] In a sense, the different levels of foreign connotations in concepts are related to the discussion about thick and thin moral arguments or concepts as put forward by Michael Walzer,[79] or even more generally to the perception of concepts as either universal or particular. However, the foreign connotations do not refer to the embeddedness of concepts to a particular culture but rather the perception of the embeddedness of a concept. Fourth, the geographical dimensions attributed to particular concepts are themselves informing the construction of the part of the world a historical 'we' belongs to. In the Finnish case, the comparisons are part of the struggle of which examples and which places belong to 'our' Europe or 'our' West.

In Conclusion

Answering the challenge of methodological nationalism, adding transnational perspectives to writing the history of concepts, and responding to the demand for European history are three very different demands that conceptual history faces today. Let me conclude this discussion by pointing out a few issues that are good to keep in mind while facing these demands.

(1) Overcoming the methodological nationalism is often pointed to as a theoretical problem, but it is also an empirical problem. Historians may benefit from new theoretical concepts produced by social scientists in analysing the transnational dimensions of the past. However, the language of the historical actors can always veto these theoretical concepts.[80] It is the historical language and the transnational dimensions of that language that is of primary interest.

(2) Looking for the transnational elements in past uses of concepts does not really undermine the primacy of national limits of political debates in the nineteenth and twentieth centuries, but rather they highlight how crossing borders in intellectual reasoning has been an argument and an element of game and play in past arguments. The objective of undermining methodological nationalism is not to construct a 'nationless' world, but rather to add a new perspective. This also helps us to better understand the changing role of the nation state in different periods.

(3) In mapping the spread of concepts in Europe (and beyond), the corpora we use are still to a large degree nationally organized. This poses a problem, but can be answered best by reflexivity. Creating new corpora that are defined by Europe or any other entity is a part of the ongoing politics of organizing knowledge. In the end, any organizational principle is a matter of political choice and something that cannot be avoided.

(4) Looking into the geographical dimensions in the use of concepts is one potential way of studying the spatial elements in everyday political struggles. The idea here is not only to map the examples that were important in a particular context, but also to see how these examples were used. In a sense this highlights how comparisons – descriptive or explicit – are political moves in a similar way that history writing is. This also highlights the almost inherent transnationality of political concepts, even in periods when sticking to the national context has been the primary option. It can be argued that in a period with a high level of national closedness, fewer people have been able to use transnational knowledge, use foreign examples, or introduce new concepts from abroad. Paradoxically, in these periods a transnational gaze has implied an even greater power in political debate than in a period of increased global political and intellectual exchange.[81]

If history writing has been (and still is) a form of identity formation, then comparisons are too. We compare to things that are relevant to us, and thus contribute to the construction of identity and political culture.

Jani Marjanen, PhD, is a researcher at the Centre for Nordic Studies in the University of Helsinki. His main scholarly interests concern eighteenth-century economic patriotism and conceptual history. His publications include 'Undermining Methodological Nationalism: *Histoire croisée* of Concepts as Transnational History', in *Transnational Political Spaces: Agents – Structures – Encounters* (2009); and *Den ekonomiska patriotismens uppgång och fall* (2013). Together with Koen Stapelbroek, he edited *The Rise of Economic Societies in the Eighteenth Century: Patriotic Reform in Europe and North America* (2012). He serves as co-editor of the journal *Contributions to the History of Concepts*.

Notes

1. See, e.g., Reinhart Koselleck, Ulrike Spree and Willibald Steinmetz, 'Drei bürgerliche Welten? Zur vergleichenden Semantik der bürgerlichen Gesellschaft in Deutschland, England und Frankreich', in Hans-Jürgen Puhle (ed.), *Bürger in der Gesellschaft der Neuzeit* (Göttingen: Vandenhoeck & Ruprecht, 1991); Norbert Götz, *Ungleiche Geschwister: Die Konstruktion von nationalsozialistischer Volksgemeinschaft und schwedischem Volksheim* (Baden-Baden: Nomos, 2001); Jörn Leonhard, *Liberalismus: Zur historischen Semantik eines Deutungsmusters* (Munich: Oldenbourg, 2001); Jörn Leonhard, *Bellizismus und Nation: Kriegsdeutung und Nationsbestimmung in Europa und den Vereinigten Staaten 1750–1914* (Munich: Oldenbourg, 2008); Pasi Ihalainen, *Protestant Nations Redefined: Changing Perceptions of National Identity in the Rhetoric of the English, Dutch and Swedish Public Churches, 1685–1772* (Leiden: Brill, 2005); Pasi Ihalainen, *Agents of the People: Democracy and Popular Sovereignty in British and Swedish Parliamentary and Public Debates, 1734–1800* (Leiden: Brill, 2010); Marion Eggert and Lucian Hölscher (eds), *Religion and Secularity: Transformations and Transfers of Religious Discourses in Europe and Asia* (Leiden: Brill, 2013).
2. See, e.g., Lucian Hölscher, 'The Theory and Method of German "Begriffsgeschichte" and its Impacts on the Construction of a European Political Lexicon', *History of Concepts Newsletter* 6 (2003), 3–7; Pim den Boer, 'Civilization: Comparing Concepts and Identities', *Contributions to the History of Concepts* 1 (2005), 51–62; Pim den Boer, 'National Cultures, Transnational Concepts: Begriffsgeschichte beyond Conceptual Nationalism', in Javier Fernández Sebastián (ed.), *Political Concepts and Time: New Approaches to Conceptual History* (Santander: Cantabria University Press, 2011), 205–22;

Karin Tilmans, 'Applying Begriffsgeschichte to Dutch History: Some Remarks on the Practice and Future of a Project', *Contributions to the History of Concepts* 2 (2006), 43–55; Jani Marjanen, 'Undermining Methodological Nationalism: *Histoire croisée* of Concepts as Transnational History', in Mathias Albert et al. (eds), *Transnational Political Spaces: Agents – Structures – Encounters* (Frankfurt: Campus, 2009), 239–63; Margrit Pernau, 'Whither Conceptual History? From National to Entangled Histories', *Contributions to the History of Concepts* 7 (2012), 1–11; Bo Stråth, 'Comparative Conceptual History and Global Translations: An Outline of a Research Agenda', in Rudolf de Cillia et al. (eds), *Discourse, Politics, Identity: Festschrift für Ruth Wodak* (Tübingen: Stauffenburg Verlag, 2010), 213–20; 'The European Conceptual History Project (ECHP): Mission Statement', *Contributions to the History of Concepts* 6 (2011), 111–16.
3. Andreas Wimmer and Nina Glick Schiller, 'Methodological Nationalism and Beyond: Nation-State Building, Migration and the Social Sciences', *Global Networks* 2 (2002), 327, attribute the term 'methodological nationalism' to Herminio Martins, 'Time and Theory in Sociology', in John Rex (ed.), *Approaches to Sociology: An Introduction to Major Trends in British Sociology* (London: Routledge & Kegan Paul, 1974), 246. Martins's use is clearly a form of ad hoc usage. 'A kind of methodological nationalism', he writes, 'imposes itself in practice with national community as the terminal unit and boundary condition for the demarcation of problems and phenomena for social science.' The phrase also occurs fairly early in Anthony D. Smith, *Nationalism in the Twentieth Century* (Oxford: Martin Robertson, 1979), 191; Anthony D. Smith, 'Nationalism and Classical Social Theory', *The British Journal of Sociology* 34 (1983), 26; and Anthony D. Smith, *Nations and Nationalism in a Global Era* (Cambridge: Polity Press, 1995), 118. Smith cites Erwin K. Scheuch, who in a 1966 text gives a rather apt description of the problem of using nations as units in cross-country comparisons, but does not use the term methodological nationalism. Instead, he participates in a debate revolving around the 'ecological fallacy' and 'individualistic fallacy' in using aggregate data in the social sciences. See Erwin K. Scheuch, 'Cross-National Comparisons Using Aggregate Data: Some Substantive and Methodological Problems', in Richard L. Merrit and Stein Rokkan (eds), *Comparing Nations: The Use of Quantitative Data in Cross-National Research* (New Haven, CT and London: Yale University Press, 1966), 148–49, 155–56, 166–67. A search in the Google Books (Brigham Young University advanced version) clearly shows how methodological nationalism as a catchphrase grew enormously in popularity in the 2000s: the phrase gets two hits for the 1980s, 17 for the 1990s, and 217 for the 2000s. While Google Books obviously does not include the above-mentioned examples from the 1970s, it is still indicative of the trend in how 'methodological nationalism' is used in English.
4. See particularly Ulrich Beck and Natan Sznaider, 'Unpacking Cosmopolitanism for the Social Sciences: A Research Agenda', *The British Journal of Sociology* 57 (2006), 1–23; Ulrich Beck, *Power in the Global Age: A New Global Political Economy* (Cambridge: Polity, 2005); Ulrich Beck and Elisabeth Beck-Gernsheim, 'Global

Generations and the Trap of Methodological Nationalism for a Cosmopolitan Turn in the Sociology of Youth and Generation', *European Sociological Review* 25 (2009), 25–36.
5. For especially interesting examples, see Wimmer and Glick Schiller, 'Methodological Nationalism and Beyond'; Andreas Wimmer and Nina Glick Schiller, 'Methodological Nationalism, the Social Sciences, and the Study of Migration: An Essay in Historical Epistemology', *International Migration Review* 37 (2003), 576–610; Daniel Chernilo, 'Social Theory's Methodologcal Nationalism: Myth and Reality', *European Journal of Social Theory* 9 (2006), 5–22; Daniel Chernilo, *A Social Theory of the Nation-State: The Political Forms of Modernity beyond Methodological Nationalism* (London and New York: Routledge, 2007), 9–32.
6. Beck and Sznaider, 'Unpacking Cosmopolitanism'; Beck, *Power in the Global Age*, 35–50.
7. For an interesting discussion, see László Kontler, 'Translation and Comparison: Early-Modern and Current Perspectives', *Contributions to the History of Concepts* 3 (2007), 71–102; see also Kontler's Chapter 7 in this volume.
8. For the deployment of international and national qualities as a way of self-fashioning in academia, see Stefan Nygård and Johan Strang, 'Facing Asymmetry', *Journal of the History of Ideas* 77(1) (2016), 75–97.
9. 'Methodological nationalism' is as an expression clearly indebted to 'methodological individualism' – that is, analysing society as a result of individual action. Interestingly, methodological individualism is often presented as a consciously chosen approach, whereas methodological nationalism is not. See also Wimmer and Glick Schiller, 'Methodological Nationalism and Beyond,' 327.
10. Pauli Kettunen, 'Globaalin talouskilpailun nationalismi', in Jussi Pakkasvirta and Pasi Saukkonen (eds), *Nationalismit* (Helsinki: WSOY, 2005), 436–53.
11. Beck and Sznaider, 'Unpacking Cosmopolitanism'; Beck, *Power in the Global Age*, 35–50.
12. For the term 'national epistemology', I am indebted to Henrik Stenius. Henrik Höjer, *Svenska siffror: Nationell integration och identifikation genom statistik 1800–1870* (Hedemora: Gidlunds förlag, 2001), argues that national statistics in the nineteenth century were in fact a crucial element in forging the Swedish nation.
13. Wimmer and Glick-Schiller, 'Methodological Nationalism and Beyond', 302–7.
14. See Wimmer and Glick-Schiller, 'Methodological Nationalism and Beyond'; Daniel Chernilo can convincingly show that Beck's history writing is misleading on this point. Chernilo, 'Social Theory's Methodologcal Nationalism'; Chernilo, *Social Theory of the Nation-State*, 9–32.
15. For a discussion of this, see Michael Mann, 'Globalization, Macro-Regions and Nation-States', in Gunilla Budde, Sebastian Conrad and Oliver Janz (eds), *Transnationale Geschichte: Themen, Tendenzen und Theorien* (Göttingen: Vandenhoeck & Ruprecht, 2006), 21–31.
16. For a discussion on transnational history and further references, see Matthias Middel and Lluis Roura, 'The Various Forms of Transcending the Horizon

of National History', in Matthias Middel and Lluis Roura (eds), *Transnational Challenges to National History Writing* (Basingstoke: Palgrave Macmillan, 2013), 1–35; James Casteel, 'Historicizing the Nation: Transnational Approaches to the Recent European Past', in Joan DeBardeleben and Achim Hurrelman (eds), *Transnational Europe: Promise, Paradox, Limits* (Basingstoke: Palgrave Macmillan, 2011), 153–69; Michael Geyer, 'Where the Germans Dwell: Transnationalism in Theory and Practice', retrieved 17 April 2014 from http://h-net.msu.edu/cgi-bin/logbrowse.pl?trx=vx&list=h-german&month=0610&week=b&msg=6Ipa/qqNnOPa4EWRx1UksA&user=&pw=. Geyer presents three different approaches of transnational history: (1) studying the transnational horizon of the nation – that is, the intermediation of the world within national imaginaries; (2) studying the transnational history of the Nation/State, that is, placing the nation in a larger context of international systems, flows and communication; and (3) studying the histories of transnations – that is, goods, corporations, people, ideas, and others things that cross borders. These obviously differ from my suggestions, but are not incompatible with what I suggest, especially bearing in mind my focus on the historical use of concepts. The field of transnational history is in gestation, although there are already encyclopedic works along the line of Akira Iriye and Pierre-Yves Saunier (eds), *The Palgrave Dictionary of Transnational History* (New York: Palgrave, 2009), that in a sense cement the development of the field. For a general introduction to different approaches placed under the umbrella of transnational history, see Margrit Pernau, *Transnationale Geschichte* (Göttingen: Vandenhoeck & Ruprecht, 2011).
17. For my own take on this, see Jani Marjanen, *Den ekonomiska patriotismen uppgång och fall: Finska hushållningssällskapet i europeisk, svensk och finsk kontext 1720–1840* (Helsinki: University of Helsinki, 2012), 29–33, 77–82.
18. See Jussi Kurunmäki, 'On the Difficulty of Being National Liberal in Nineteenth-Century Finland', *Contributions to the History of Concepts* 8 (2013), 83–95; Pauli Kettunen, 'The Power of International Comparison: A Perspective on the Making and Challenging of the Nordic Welfare State', in N.F. Christiansen et al. (eds), *The Nordic Model of Welfare: A Historical Reappraisal* (Copenhagen: Museum Tusculanum Press, 2006), 31–65; Glenda Sluga, 'The Nation and the Comparative Imagination', in Deborah Cohen and Maura O'Connor (eds), *Comparison and History: Europe in Cross-National Perspective* (New York and London: Routledge, 2004), 103–14.
19. Jörn Leonhard, 'From European Liberalism to the Languages of Liberalisms: The Semantics of Liberalism in European Comparison', *Redescriptions: Yearbook of Political Thought and Conceptual History* 8 (2004), 17–51; Jörn Leonhard, 'Translation as Cultural Transfer and Semantic Interaction: European Variations of Liberalism between 1800 and 1830', in Martin J. Burke and Melvin Richter (eds), *Why Concepts Matter: Translating Social and Political Thought* (Leiden: Brill, 2012), 93–108.
20. Important contributions in exploring the topic are: David Armitage, *Foundations of Modern International Thought* (Cambridge: Cambridge University Press,

2013); Evgeny Roshchin, '(Un)Natural and Contractual International Society: A Conceptual Inquiry', *European Journal of International Relations* 19 (2011), 257–79; Samuel Moyn and Andrew Sartori (eds), *Global Intellectual History* (New York: Columbia University Press, 2013).

21. For a lucid discussion, see Casteel, 'Historicizing the Nation'.
22. See den Boer, 'National Cultures, Transnational Concepts', who even talks of 'conceptual nationalism'.
23. For a convincing argument of this, and examples, see Johan Strang, *History, Transfer, Politics: Five Studies on the Legacy of Uppsala Philosophy* (Helsinki: University of Helsinki, 2010); Stefan Nygård, *Henri Bergson i Finland: Reception, rekontextualisering, politisering* (Helsingfors: Svenska litteratursällskapet, 2011); Nygård and Strang, 'Facing Asymmetry'.
24. Myoung-Kyi Park, 'Conceptual History in Korea: Its Development and Prospects', *Contributions to the History of Concepts* 7 (2012), 36–50; Matti Hyvärinen et al. (eds), *Käsitteet liikkeessä: Suomen poliittisen kulttuurin käsitehistoria* (Tampere: Vastapaino, 2003).
25. Kari Palonen, 'Eurooppalaiset poliittiset käsitteet suomalaisissa pelitiloissa', in Hyvärinen et al., *Käsitteet liikkeessä*, 569–87; Kari Palonen, 'The History of Concepts as a Style of Political Theorizing', *European Journal of Political Theory* 1 (2002), 91–106.
26. Otto Brunner, Werner Conze and Reinhart Koselleck (eds), *Geschichtliche Grundbegriffe. Historisches Lexikon zur politisch-sozialen Sprache in Deutschland*, 9 vols (Stuttgart: Klett-Cotta 1972–97), has Germany in the title as the geographical unit with which it is concerned, but the articles themselves are in practice concerned with the German language. My knowledge of the Spanish and Iberoamerican collaborative studies is regretfully only superficial. Here, both a delineation into Spain, which certainly includes multinational elements, and the Iberoamerican world, with both multinational as multilingual elements, occurs. See Javier Fernández Sebastián and Juan Francisco Fuentes (eds), *Diccionario político y social del siglo XIX español* (Madrid: Alianza Editorial, 2002); Javier Fernández Sebastián and Juan Francisco Fuentes (eds), *Diccionario político y social del siglo XX español* (Madrid: Alianza Editorial, 2008); Javier Fernández Sebastián and Cristóbal Aljovín de Losana (eds), *Diccionario político y social del mundo iberoamericano: La era de las revoluciones, 1750–1850* (Madrid: Sociedad Estatal de Conmemoraciones Culturales, 2009).
27. See Volume 8 of the *Geschichtliche Grundbegriffe*. The division into different languages present in the index volume provides a sort of window to the types of influence the authors of the lexicon were receptive to. Latin words or derivatives from Latin are the most common, but interestingly English words figure nearly as often as French concepts do.
28. Quentin Skinner, 'Motives, Intentions and Interpretations', in Skinner, *Visions of Politics I: Regarding Method* (Cambridge: Cambridge University Press, 2002), 90–93, 96–102.
29. See also Pernau, 'Whither Conceptual History?'.

30. This is particularly evident in comparing articles from Finnish biographical dictionaries from the first half of the twentieth century with modern ones.
31. See Carolien Stolte, 'Itinerario to host on-line discussion with Prof. David Armitage', retrieved 9 April 2014 from http://blog.journals.cambridge.org/2012/11/itinerario-to-host-on-line-discussion-with-prof-david-armitage/.
32. For a case in point, see the discussion on the historical figure of Jesus. Halvor Moxnes, *Jesus and the Rise of Nationalism: A New Quest for the Nineteenth-Century Historical Jesus* (London: I.B. Taurus, 2012), for instance, points out the simultaneous process of nation building in Europe and the emergence of studying Jesus's life historically from the perspective of biography and in the context of a historical Palestine. Moxnes shows how emerging national perspectives became intertwined with the new interpretations of Jesus as a historical agent. In accordance with today's challenges, Moxnes then goes on to suggest a programme for the post-national study of Jesus's life.
33. For concepts and basic concepts, see Jan Ifversen, 'About Key Concepts and How to Study Them', *Contributions to the History of Concepts* 6 (2011), 65–88. For a critique, see Hans-Ulrich Gumbrecht, *Dimensionen und Grenzen der Begriffsgeschichte* (Munich: Wilhelm Fink Verlag, 2006).
34. Reinhart Koselleck, 'A Response to Comments on *Geschichtliche Grundbegriffe*', in Hartmut Lehmann and Melvin Richter (eds), *The Meaning of Historical Terms and Concepts: New Studies on Begriffsgeschichte, Occasional Paper No. 15* (Washington, DC: German Historical Institute, 1996), 64. See also Ifversen, 'About Key Concepts'. Koselleck seems to avoid geographical limits in describing basic concepts. In the introduction to *Geschichtliche Grundbegriffe* he simply describes them as 'defining concepts which must be studied historically' (*Leitbegriffe*). They are 'building blocks for a type of research that considers social and political language ... as causal factors and as indicators of historical change'. In the preface to the seventh volume, Koselleck discusses some of the criticism towards the lexicon and further mentions the possibility of talking about basic concepts when 'all contesting strata and parties find it [a concept] indispensable to expressing their distinctive experiences'. See Reinhart Koselleck, 'Introduction and Prefaces to *Geschichtliche Grundbegriffe*', *Contributions to the History of Concepts* 6 (2011), 7–8, 32, 34; Reinhart Koselleck, 'Einleitung', in Brunner, Conze and Koselleck, *Geschichtliche Grundbegriffe*, vol. 1 (1972), xiii–xiv.
35. The English translation of *unserer* by Michaela Richter is actually 'German-speaking Europe', which is probably an apt translation in the sense that Koselleck probably thought about a German political context. Koselleck, 'Introduction and Prefaces', 34; Reinhart Koselleck, 'Vorwort', in Brunner, Conze and Koselleck (eds.), *Geschichtliche Grundbegriffe*, vol. 8/1 (1997), v.
36. Koselleck, 'A Response', 64.
37. For the term 'conceptual universe', see Henrik Stenius, 'A Nordic Conceptual Universe', in Heidi Haggrén, Johanna Rainio-Niemi and Jussi Vauhkonen (eds), *Multi-layered Historicity of the Present: Approaches to Social Science History*

(Helsinki: Department of Political and Economic Studies, University of Helsinki, 2013), 93–104.
38. I have myself contributed to this. See Koen Stapelbroek and Jani Marjanen (eds), *The Rise of Economic Societies in the Eighteenth Century: Patriotic Reform in Europe and North America* (Basingstoke: Palgrave Macmillan, 2012).
39. Barrington Moore, *Social Origins of Dictatorship and Democracy: Lord and Peasant in the Making of the Modern World* (Harmondsworth: Penguin Books, [1966] 1987), ix–x.
40. Jonathan M. Wiener, 'Review of Reviews: *Social Origins of Dictatorship and Democracy: Lord and Peasant in the Making of the Modern World* by Barrington Moore', *History and Theory* 15 (1976), 169.
41. For a small-state perspective on Moore's approach, see Risto Alapuro, *State and Revolution in Finland* (Berkeley: University of California Press, 1988), 1–2. For the issue of writing history on a European level and the problem of inclusion and exclusion of small nations, see, for instance, Miroslav Hroch, 'Kansallinen historia ja sen vaihtoehdot modernissa eurooppalaisessa historiankirjoituksessa', *Historiallinen Aikakauskirja* 97 (1999), 122–30, which is a lecture presented originally in English, but that I have been unable to locate in English in published form.
42. See Franco Moretti, *Atlas of the European Novel, 1800–1900* (London: Verso, 1999), 168, 171–97.
43. For the sake of simplicity, I will not go into the different traditions of national historiography. For a discussion on the topic of writing European history and regions, see Tibor Frank and Frank Hadler (eds), *Disputed Territories and Shared Pasts: Overlapping National Histories in Modern Europe* (Basingstoke: Palgrave Macmillan, 2011).
44. For the incorporation of European identity to national identity, or the lack thereof, see Thomas Risse, 'A European Identity? Europeanization and the Evolution of Nation-State Identities', in Maria Green Cowles, James Caporaso and Thomas Risse (eds), *Transforming Europe: Europeanization and Domestic Change* (Ithaca, NY and London: Cornell University Press, 2001), 198–216. Risse's account is lucid, but in itself is an example of a study in which the big three – France, Germany and Britain – are chosen as examples for a European comparison. The study does not explicitly claim European coverage, but at the same time it assumes that the three culturally most dominant countries could be informative for anyone studying the smaller countries and their accommodation of Europe in their respective repertoires of national identities.
45. See Risse, 'A European Identity?'; for a very sceptical take on Euronationalism, see Smith, *Nations and Nationalism*, 116–46; and for its ideological foundations, see Heikki Mikkeli, *Europe as an Idea and an Identity* (London: Macmillan, 1998).
46. One particular problem with the Google Books Ngram is that the quality of scanned texts is not as good as desired. Errors occur frequently, which is particularly noticeable for texts from the period before 1900. For instance, searches with the word 'racism' in the English material for the period 1800–1809 will generate

more than thirty hits, all of which are false (Google's search interface interprets words such as 'Græcism' as racism). A search for a longer period does, however, provide information about the frequency of racism as a word, and the scans of the newer material are much more reliable. Mark Davies at Brigham Young University has developed an enhanced version based on the texts in Google Books that is more searchable and more advanced in terms of periodization and data. See http://googlebooks.byu.edu; Mark Davies 'The Corpus of Historical American English (COHA), Google Books (Standard), and the Google Books (BYU / Advanced) corpus', retrieved 18 February 2014 from http://google books.byu.edu/compare-googleBooks.asp. I have used the Google Books Ngram here in order to be able to use also the German and French texts provided by Google, but for the English texts the Brigham Young University version is better adapted for scholarly use. Another particular problem with the Google Books is that the set of texts is constantly growing and is thus not a stable corpus. The inclusion of new material in the set of texts is obviously welcome, but this also causes problems for scholarly discussion as studies cannot easily repeat earlier searches that may be the basis of an interpretation of semantic changes in political and social language. Another problem with the growing set of texts is the explosion in reprints of nineteenth-century material that is no longer copyrighted. These reprints skew the chronology, introducing nineteenth-century vocabulary as present-day vocabulary. Thus, any results for the past few years (but not the period before 2000) include a serious number of anachronisms. See Ben Schmidt, 'Biblio bizarre: who publishes in Google Books', retrieved 15 April 2015 from http://sappingattention.blogspot.fi/2014/04/biblio-biz arre-who-publishes-in-google.html.

47. For now there are texts in Italian, Spanish, Hebrew, Russian and Chinese, but I am not able to assess the usability of these texts. To be sure, an expansion of the sets of text to more languages will provide better opportunities to assess the geographical and linguistic spread of concepts. For searches in Google Books, see https://books.google.com/ngrams; for a description of how to use the Ngram, see https://books.google.com/ngrams/info, and Jean-Baptiste Michel, Yuan Kui Shen, Aviva Presser Aiden, Adrian Veres, Matthew K. Gray, William Brockman, The Google Books Team, Joseph P. Pickett, Dale Hoiberg, Dan Clancy, Peter Norvig, Jon Orwant, Steven Pinker, Martin A. Nowak, and Erez Lieberman Aiden, '*Quantitative Analysis of Culture Using Millions of Digitized Books*', *Science* (Published online ahead of print: 16 December 2010).

48. For early uses of nationalism, see Aira Kemiläinen, *Nationalism: Problems Concerning the Word, the Concept and Classification* (Jyväskylä: Studia Historica Jyväskyläensia III, 1964), 48–53. See also Fritz Gschnitzer et al., 'Volk, Nation, Nationalismus, Masse', in Brunner, Conze and Koselleck, *Geschichtliche Grundbegriffe*, vol. 7 (1992), 398–402; note the low frequency of *Nationalismus* in nineteenth-century German.

49. John Breuilly (ed.), *The Oxford Handbook of the History of Nationalism* (Oxford: Oxford University Press, 2013), is a good example of a book tracing the ideology

of nationalism without showing interest in the word 'nationalism'. See also Andrew Heywood, *Political Ideologies: An Introduction*, 3rd edition (Basingstoke: Palgrave, 2004), 155–87, who does give a first use of nationalism, but does not reflect upon the relation between the use of nationalism as a word and the 'idea of nationalism'. For a sophisticated discussion, see Michael Freeden, 'Is Nationalism a Distinct Ideology?', in Freeden (ed.), *Liberal Languages: Ideological Imaginations and Twentieth-Century Progressive Thought* (Princeton, NJ: Princeton University Press, 2005), 204–24.

50. See Leonhard, 'From European Liberalism'; Leonhard, 'Translation as Cultural Transfer'.
51. For a related query regarding 'the Enlightenment' and related terms, see James W. Schmidt, 'The Fading of "True Enlightenment" (Another Wildcard Search)', *Persistent Enlightenment*, retrieved 17 April 2014 from http://persistentenlightenment.wordpress.com/2013/10/18/the-fading-of-true-enlightenment-another-wildcard-search/.
52. Michael Billig, *Banal Nationalism* (London: Sage Publications, 1995).
53. Discussing the pureness or authenticity is also typical for earlier debates on patriotism. See Jani Marjanen, 'Between "Public" and "Private Economy": The Finnish Economic Society and the Decline of Economic Patriotism, 1797–1833', in Stapelbroek and Marjanen, *Rise of Economic Societies*, 313–38; Marjanen, *Den ekonomiska patriotismens uppgång*, especially 222–34.
54. For a similar argument, see Nygård and Strang, 'Facing Asymmetry'; Kurunmäki, 'On the Difficulty of Being a National Liberal'.
55. For the related idea of ideoscapes, see Arjun Appadurai, *Modernity at Large: Cultural Dimensions of Globalization* (Minneapolis: University of Minnesota Press, 1996), 33–37. For striking examples of radical reinterpretation of concepts due to translation, see Benedict Anderson, *The Spectre of Comparison: Nationalism, South East Asia, and the World* (London, Verso, 1998), 1–26.
56. Moretti, *Atlas of the European Novel*, 171–97.
57. Historical Newspaper Library. The texts are read by an optical character recognition (OCR) programme, the quality of which depends on the original typography and the quality of scans.
58. For the sake of simplicity I have omitted searches on the vernacular forms *kansakunta-aate*, *kansallisuus-aate* and *kansallismielisyys*, and similar words. These had a specific role in adapting the language of nationalism in Finnish, and provided some extra space of manoeuvring in debating nationhood and nationalism.
59. The search interface in the Historical Newspaper Library provided by the National Library in Finland works with different degrees of fuzziness in the search, depending on the chronological scope of a particular search. This adaptive search interface makes is difficult to repeat particular searches and is thus useful for determining a general trend in the use of particular words, but is unreliable in determining exact figures. I have done repeated searches with different scopes and different degrees of fuzziness, which has allowed me to assess the reli-

ability of the searches (by checking the results against originals) and determine the general trend in word use. Simple figures are also misleading in the sense that searches portray the number of articles that include the words *nationalism* and *nationalismen* in Swedish, not actual hits of the words (the use of the Finnish *nationalismi* has a slightly different, but corresponding development). As the number of papers changed over the years and as article lengths were certainly not constant, the figures as such cannot be regarded as proof of shifts of frequency in the use of nationalism and related terms.

60. For the rhetorical use of foreign examples, see Kurunmäki, 'On the Difficulty of Being National Liberal'; Kettunen, 'The Power of International Comparison'; Sluga, 'The Nation and the Comparative Imagination'; Johan Strang, 'Den perifera eklekticismens gränser och potential. Den logiska empirismen i Norden 1930–1970', *Historiska och litteraturhistoriska studier* 86 (2011), 137–58. I also draw from the ongoing research of Mirja Österberg.
61. See, for instance, *Åbo Underrättelser*, 21 July 1864 (describing French politics), and *Finlands Allmänna Tidning*, 27 September 1866 (describing Danish politics).
62. *Finlands Allmänna Tidning*, 7 June 1870. It is worth noting that *Finlands Allmänna Tidning* had semi-official status. It in fact represented the voice of the government.
63. For comparisons and relations to Sweden, see Kurunmäki, 'On the Difficulty of Being National Liberal'; Torkel Jansson, *Rikssprängningen som kom av sig: Finsk-svenska gemenskaper efter 1809* (Stockholm: Atlantis, 2009).
64. *Kotkan Sanomat* no. 47, 24 November 1886.
65. See, for instance, *Isänmaan ystävä*, 6 May 1898; *Uusi Suometar*, 11 May 1900; *Uusi Suometar*, 28 October 1900.
66. For the nationality question, see Andreas Kappeler, *The Russian Empire: A Multiethnic History* (Harlow: Pearson Education, 2001), 328–69; for the language question in Finland, see Henrik Stenius, 'The Language Issue in Finland', in Clive Archer and Pertti Joenniemi (eds), *The Nordic Peace* (Aldershot: Ashgate, 2002), 157–70.
67. See Juliette Cadiote, 'Searching for Nationality: Statistics and National Categories at the End of the Russian Empire (1897–1917)', *The Russian Review* 64 (2005), 440–55; Osmo Jussila, *Suomen suuriruhtinaskunta 1809–1917* (Helsinki: WSOY, 2004).
68. *Nya Pressen*, no. 238, 15 October 1910. Orig.: 'Finlands rättsliga ställning är klar och har tillräckligt belysts af tyska och äfven ryska rättslärda. Tyvärr finnes intet hopp att dessa varnande röster skola höras, ehuru det ock gifves andra viktiga grunder, som äfven för den ryska nationalismen borde göra det klart att det är farligt att skrida vidare på våldets väg mot de främmande folken i riket.'
69. On the development of *Nya Pressen*, see Päiviö Tommila (ed.), *Suomen lehdistön historia* 6 (Kustannuskiila: Kuopio 1988), 168–72.
70. Gschnitzer et al., 'Volk, Nation, Nationalismus, Masse', 398–402, also point towards the predominantly negative use of *Nationalismus* in German twentieth-century discourse. Positive self-descriptions by the radical right provided

in the article are explicitly formulated as redescriptions of the common negative use.
71. *Uusimaa*, 7 January 1907. Orig: 'Lorun loppuna on se, että lehti miltei kyynelsilmin rukoilee waaliagitatsioniin, jottei 'musta natsionalismi' pääse rehottamaan ensi waltiopäivinä.'
72. See, for instance, Elisabeth Stubb, *Rätt som argument: Leo Mechelin och den finska frågan 1886–1912* (Helsinki: Finska Vetenskaps-societeten, 2012); Johan Strang and Stefan Nygård, 'Den moderna filosofin i Finland och Sverige', in Stefan Nygård and Johan Strang (eds), *Mellan idealism och analytisk filosofi: Den moderna filosofin i Fnland och Sverige* (Helsinki: Svenska litteratursällskapet i Finland, 2006); Marja Jalava, *Minä ja maailmanhenki. Moderni subjekti kristillis-idealistisessa kansallisajattelussa ja Rolf Lagerborgin kulttuuriradikalismissa n. 1800–1914* (Helsinki: Suomalaisen kirjallisuuden seura, 2005).
73. See, for instance, Kristina Ranki, *Isänmaa ja Ranska: Suomalainen frankofilia 1880–1914* (Helsinki: Suomen tiedeseura, 2007); Nygård, *Henri Bergson i Finland*.
74. See, for instance, Kurunmäki, 'On the Difficulty of Being National Liberal'.
75. See, for instance, Max Engman, *Lejonet och dubbelörnen: Finlands imperiella decennier 1830–1890* (Stockholm: Atlantis, 2000); Jussila, *Suomen suuriruhtinaskunta*.
76. Kurunmäki, 'On the Difficulty of Being National Liberal'.
77. For the development of *Volk*-terminology in Sweden and Germany, see Götz, *Ungleiche Geschwister*. For a recent re-evaluation of the role of the concept in Swedish, see Nils Edling, 'The Primacy of Welfare Politics: Notes on the Language of the Swedish Social Democrats and Their Adversaries in the 1930s', in Heidi Haggrén, Johanna Rainio-Niemi and Jussi Vauhkonen (eds), *The Multilayered Historicity of the Present: Approaches to Social Science History* (Helsinki: Department of Political and Economic Studies, 2013), 125–50.
78. See Leonhard, 'From European Liberalism'. For a fuller account, see Leonhard, *Liberalismus*.
79. Michael Walzer, *Thick and Thin: Moral Argument at Home and Abroad* (Notre Dame, IN: University of Notre Dame Press, 2002), especially 1–19. See also, Moretti, *Atlas of the European Novel*, 151–71, on the frequency of translations in different European national literatures.
80. See Reinhart Koselleck, 'Archivalien – Quellen – Geschichten', in Koselleck, *Vom Sinn und Unsinn der Geschichte*, ed. Carsten Dutt (Berlin: Suhrkamp, 2010), 78.
81. For a more extensive discussion, see Nygård and Strang, 'Facing Asymmetry'.

References

'The European Conceptual History Project (ECHP): Mission Statement', *Contributions to the History of Concepts* 6 (2011), 111–16

Alapuro, Risto, *State and Revolution in Finland* (Berkeley: University of California Press, 1988)

Anderson, Benedict, *The Spectre of Comparison: Nationalism, South East Asia, and the World* (London, Verso, 1998)

Appadurai, Arjun, *Modernity at Large: Cultural Dimensions of Globalization* (Minneapolis: University of Minnesota Press, 1996)

Armitage, David, *Foundations of Modern International Thought* (Cambridge: Cambridge University Press, 2013)

Beck, Ulrich, *Power in the Global Age: A New Global Political Economy* (Cambridge: Polity, 2005)

Beck, Ulrich, and Elisabeth Beck-Gernsheim, 'Global Generations and the Trap of Methodological Nationalism for a Cosmopolitan Turn in the Sociology of Youth and Generation', *European Sociological Review* 25 (2009), 25–36

Beck, Ulrich, and Natan Sznaider, 'Unpacking Cosmopolitanism for the Social Sciences: A Research Agenda', *The British Journal of Sociology* 57 (2006), 1–23

Billig, Michael, *Banal Nationalism* (London: Sage Publications, 1995)

Breuilly, John (ed.), *The Oxford Handbook of the History of Nationalism* (Oxford: Oxford University Press, 2013)

Brunner, Otto, Werner Conze and Reinhart Koselleck (eds), *Geschichtliche Grundbegriffe: Historisches Lexikon zur politisch-sozialen Sprache in Deutschland*, 9 vols (Stuttgart: Klett-Cotta, 1972–97)

Cadiote, Juliette, 'Searching for Nationality: Statistics and National Categories at the End of the Russian Empire (1897–1917)', *The Russian Review* 64 (2005), 440–55

Casteel, James, 'Historicizing the Nation: Transnational Approaches to the Recent European Past', in Joan DeBardeleben and Achim Hurrelman (eds), *Transnational Europe: Promise, Paradox, Limits* (Basingstoke: Palgrave Macmillan, 2011), 153–69

Chernilo, Daniel, 'Social Theory's Methodological Nationalism: Myth and Reality', *European Journal of Social Theory* 9 (2006), 5–22

———, *A Social Theory of the Nation-State: The Political Forms of Modernity beyond Methodological Nationalism* (London and New York: Routledge, 2007)

Davies, Mark, 'The Corpus of Historical American English (COHA), Google Books (Standard), and the Google Books (BYU / Advanced) corpus', retrieved 18 February 2014 from http://googlebooks.byu.edu/compare-googleBooks.asp

den Boer, Pim, 'Civilization: Comparing Concepts and Identities', *Contributions to the History of Concepts* 1 (2005), 51–62

———, 'National Cultures, Transnational Concepts: Begriffsgeschichte Beyond Conceptual Nationalism', in Javier Fernández Sebastián (ed.), *Political Concepts and Time: New Approaches to Conceptual History* (Santander: Cantabria University Press, 2011), 205–22

Edling, Nils, 'The Primacy of Welfare Politics: Notes on the Language of the Swedish Social Democrats and Their Adversaries in the 1930s', in Heidi Haggrén, Johanna Rainio-Niemi and Jussi Vauhkonen (eds), *The Multi-layered Historicity of the Present: Approaches to Social Science History* (Helsinki: Department of Political and Economic Studies, 2013), 125–50

Eggert, Marion, and Lucian Hölscher (eds), *Religion and Secularity: Transformations and Transfers of Religious Discourses in Europe and Asia* (Leiden: Brill, 2013)

Engman, Max, *Lejonet och dubbelörnen: Finlands imperiella decennier 1830–1890* (Stockholm: Atlantis, 2000)

Frank, Tibor, and Frank Hadler (eds), *Disputed Territories and Shared Pasts: Overlapping National Histories in Modern Europe* (Basingstoke: Palgrave Macmillan, 2011)

Fernández-Sebastián, Javier, and Juan Francisco Fuentes (eds), *Diccionario político y social del siglo XIX español* (Madrid: Alianza Editorial, 2002)

—— (eds), *Diccionario político y social del siglo XX español* (Madrid: Alianza Editorial, 2008)

Fernández-Sebastián, Javier, and Cristóbal Aljovín de Losana (eds), *Diccionario político y social del mundo iberoamericano: La era de las revoluciones, 1750–1850* (Madrid: Sociedad Estatal de Conmemoraciones Culturales, 2009)

Freeden, Michael, 'Is Nationalism a Distinct Ideology?', in Michael Freeden (ed.), *Liberal Languages: Ideological Imaginations and Twentieth-Century Progressive Thought* (Princeton, NJ: Princeton University Press, 2005), 204–24

Geyer, Michael, 'Where the Germans Dwell: Transnationalism in Theory and Practice', retrieved 17 April 2014 from http://h-net.msu.edu/cgi-bin/logbrowse.pl?trx=vx&list=h-german&month=0610&week=b&msg=6Ipa/qqNnOPa4EWRx1UksA&user=&pw=

Götz, Norbert, *Ungleiche Geschwister: Die Konstruktion von nationalsozialistischer Volksgemeinschaft und schwedischem Volksheim* (Baden-Baden: Nomos, 2001)

Gschnitzer, Fritz, et al., 'Volk, Nation, Nationalismus, Masse', in Otto Brunner, Werner Conze and Reinhart Koselleck (eds), *Geschichtliche Grundbegriffe: Historisches Lexikon zur politisch-sozialen Sprache in Deutschland*, vol. 7 (Stuttgart: Klett-Cotta, 1992), 141–431

Gumbrecht, Hans-Ulrich, *Dimensionen und Grenzen der Begriffsgeschichte* (Munich: Wilhelm Fink Verlag, 2006)

Heywood, Andrew, *Political Ideologies: An Introduction*, 3rd edition (Basingstoke: Palgrave, 2004)

Höjer, Henrik, *Svenska siffror: Nationell integration och identifikation genom statistik 1800–1870* (Hedemora: Gidlunds förlag, 2001)

Hölscher, Lucian, 'The Theory and Method of German "Begriffsgeschichte" and its Impacts on the Construction of a European Political Lexicon', *History of Concepts Newsletter* 6 (2003), 3–7

Hroch, Miroslav, 'Kansallinen historia ja sen vaihtoehdot modernissa eurooppalaisessa historiankirjoituksessa', *Historiallinen Aikakauskirja* 97 (1999), 122–30

Hyvärinen, Matti, et al. (eds), *Käsitteet liikkeessä: Suomen poliittisen kulttuurin käsitehistoria* (Tampere: Vastapaino, 2003)

Ifversen, Jan, 'About Key Concepts and How to Study Them', *Contributions to the History of Concepts* 6 (2011), 65–88

Ihalainen, Pasi, *Protestant Nations Redefined: Changing Perceptions of National Identity in the Rhetoric of the English, Dutch and Swedish Public Churches, 1685–1772* (Leiden: Brill, 2005)

———, *Agents of the People: Democracy and Popular Sovereignty in British and Swedish Parliamentary and Public Debates, 1734–1800* (Leiden: Brill, 2010)
Iriye, Akira, and Pierre-Yves Saunier (eds), *The Palgrave Dictionary of Transnational History* (New York: Palgrave, 2009)
Jalava, Marja, *Minä ja maailmanhenki: Moderni subjekti kristillis-idealistisessa kansallisajattelussa ja Rolf Lagerborgin kulttuuriradikalismissa n. 1800–1914* (Helsinki: Suomalaisen kirjallisuuden seura, 2005)
Jansson, Torkel, *Rikssprängningen som kom av sig: Finsk-svenska gemenskaper efter 1809* (Stockholm: Atlantis, 2009)
Jussila, Osmo, *Suomen suuriruhtinaskunta 1809–1917* (Helsinki: WSOY, 2004)
Kappeler, Andreas, *The Russian Empire: A Multiethnic History* (Harlow: Pearson Education, 2001)
Kemiläinen, Aira, *Nationalism: Problems Concerning the Word, the Concept and Classification* (Jyväskylä: Studia Historica Jyväskyläensia III, 1964)
Kettunen, Pauli, 'Globaalin talouskilpailun nationalismi', in Jussi Pakkasvirta and Pasi Saukkonen (eds), *Nationalismit* (Helsinki: WSOY, 2005), 436–53
———, 'The Power of International Comparison: A Perspective on the Making and Challenging of the Nordic Welfare State', in Niels Finn Christiansen et al. (eds), *The Nordic Model of Welfare: A Historical Reappraisal* (Copenhagen: Museum Tusculanum Press, 2006), 31–65
Kontler, László, 'Translation and Comparison: Early-Modern and Current Perspectives', *Contributions to the History of Concepts* 3 (2007), 71–102
Koselleck, Reinhart, 'Einleitung', in Otto Brunner, Werner Conze and Reinhart Koselleck (eds), *Geschichtliche Grundbegriffe: Historisches Lexikon zur politisch-sozialen Sprache in Deutschland*, vol. 1 (Stuttgart: Klett-Cotta, 1972), xiii–xxvii
———, 'A Response to Comments on the *Geschichtliche Grundbegriffe*', in Hartmut Lehmann and Melvin Richter (eds), *The Meaning of Historical Terms and Concepts* (Washington DC: German Historical Institute, 1996), 59–70
———, 'Vorwort', in Otto Brunner, Werner Conze and Reinhart Koselleck (eds), *Geschichtliche Grundbegriffe: Historisches Lexikon zur politisch-sozialen Sprache in Deutschland*, vol. 8/1 (Stuttgart: Klett-Cotta, 1997)
———, 'Archivalien – Quellen – Geschichten', in Koselleck, *Vom Sinn und Unsinn der Geschichte*, ed. Carsten Dutt (Berlin: Suhrkamp, 2010), 68–79
———, 'Introduction and Prefaces to *Geschichtliche Grundbegriffe*', *Contributions to the History of Concepts* 6 (2011), 7–37
Koselleck, Reinhart, Ulrike Spree and Willibald Steinmetz, 'Drei bürgerliche Welten? Zur vergleichenden Semantik der bürgerlichen Gesellschaft in Deutschland, England und Frankreich', in Hans-Jürgen Puhle (ed.), *Bürger in der Gesellschaft der Neuzeit* (Göttingen: Vandenhoeck & Ruprecht, 1991), 14–58
Kurunmäki, Jussi, 'On the Difficulty of Being National Liberal in Nineteenth-Century Finland', *Contributions to the History of Concepts* 8 (2013), 83–95
Leonhard, Jörn, *Liberalismus: Zur historischen Semantik eines Deutungsmusters* (Munich: Oldenbourg, 2001)

———, 'From European Liberalism to the Languages of Liberalisms: The Semantics of Liberalism in European Comparison', *Redescriptions: Yearbook of Political Thought and Conceptual History* 8 (2004), 17–51

———, *Bellizismus und Nation: Kriegsdeutung und Nationsbestimmung in Europa und den Vereinigten Staaten 1750–1914* (Munich: Oldenbourg, 2008)

———, 'Translation as Cultural Transfer and Semantic Interaction: European Variations of Liberalism between 1800 and 1830', in Martin J. Burke and Melvin Richter (eds), *Why Concepts Matter: Translating Social and Political Thought* (Leiden: Brill, 2012), 93–108

Mann, Michael, 'Globalization, Macro-Regions and Nation-States', in Gunilla Budde, Sebastian Conrad and Oliver Janz (eds), *Transnationale Geschichte: Themen, Tendenzen und Theorien* (Göttingen: Vandenhoeck & Ruprecht, 2006), 21–31

Marjanen, Jani, 'Undermining Methodological Nationalism: *Histoire croisée* of Concepts as Transnational History', in Mathias Albert et al. (eds), *Transnational Political Spaces: Agents – Structures – Encounters* (Frankfurt: Campus, 2009), 239–63

———, *Den ekonomiska patriotismen uppgång och fall: Finska hushållningssällskapet i europeisk, svensk och finsk kontext 1720–1840* (Helsinki: University of Helsinki, 2012)

———, 'Between "Public" and "Private Economy": The Finnish Economic Society and the Decline of Economic Patriotism, 1797–1833', in Koen Stapelbroek and Jani Marjanen, *The Rise of Economic Societies in the Eighteenth Century: Patriotic Reform in Europe and North America* (Basingstoke: Palgrave Macmillan, 2012), 313–38

Martins, Herminio, 'Time and Theory in Sociology', in John Rex (ed.), *Approaches to Sociology: An Introduction to Major Trends in British Sociology* (London: Routledge & Kegan Paul, 1974)

Michel, Jean-Baptiste, Yuan Kui Shen, Aviva Presser Aiden, Adrian Veres, Matthew K. Gray, William Brockman, The Google Books Team, Joseph P. Pickett, Dale Hoiberg, Dan Clancy, Peter Norvig, Jon Orwant, Steven Pinker, Martin A. Nowak and Erez Lieberman Aiden, '*Quantitative Analysis of Culture Using Millions of Digitized Books*', *Science* (Published online ahead of print: 16 December 2010)

Middel, Matthias, and Lluis Roura, 'The Various Forms of Transcending the Horizon of National History', in Matthias Middel and Lluis Roura (eds), *Transnational Challenges to National History Writing* (Basingstoke: Palgrave Macmillan, 2013), 1–35

Mikkeli, Heikki, *Europe as an Idea and an Identity* (London: Macmillan, 1998)

Moore, Barrington, *Social Origins of Dictatorship and Democracy: Lord and Peasant in the Making of the Modern World* (Harmondsworth: Penguin Books, [1966] 1987)

Moretti, Franco, *Atlas of the European Novel, 1800–1900* (London: Verso, 1999)

Moxnes, Halvor, *Jesus and the Rise of Nationalism: A New Quest for the Nineteenth-Century Historical Jesus* (London: I.B. Taurus, 2012)

Moyn, Samuel, and Andrew Sartori (eds), *Global Intellectual History* (New York: Columbia University Press, 2013)

Nygård, Stefan, *Henri Bergson i Finland: Reception, rekontextualisering, politisering* (Helsingfors: Svenska litteratursällskapet, 2011)

Nygård, Stefan, and Johan Strang, 'Facing Asymmetry: Nordic Intellectuals and Center-Periphery Dynamics in European Cultural Space', *Journal of the History of Ideas* 77(1) (2016), 75–97

Palonen, Kari, 'The History of Concepts as a Style of Political Theorizing', *European Journal of Political Theory* 1 (2002), 91–106

———, 'Eurooppalaiset poliittiset käsitteet suomalaisissa pelitiloissa', in Matti Hyvärinen et al. (eds), *Käsitteet liikkeessä: Suomen poliittisen kulttuurin käsitehistoria* (Tampere: Vastapaino, 2003), 569–87

Park, Myoung-Kyi, 'Conceptual History in Korea: Its Development and Prospects', *Contributions to the History of Concepts* 7 (2012), 36–50

Pernau, Margrit, *Transnationale Geschichte* (Göttingen: Vandenhoeck & Ruprecht, 2011)

———, 'Whither Conceptual History? From National to Entangled Histories', *Contributions to the History of Concepts* 7 (2012), 1–11

Ranki, Kristina, *Isänmaa ja Ranska: Suomalainen frankofilia 1880–1914* (Helsinki: Suomen tiedeseura, 2007)

Risse, Thomas, 'A European Identity? Europeanization and the Evolution of Nation-State Identities', in Maria Green Cowles, James Caporaso and Thomas Risse (eds), *Transforming Europe: Europeanization and Domestic Change* (Ithaca, NY and London: Cornell University Press, 2001), 198–216

Roshchin, Evgeny, '(Un)Natural and Contractual International Society: A Conceptual Inquiry', *European Journal of International Relations* 19 (2011), 257–79

Scheuch, Erwin K., 'Cross-National Comparisons Using Aggregate Data: Some Substantive and Methodological Problems', in Richard L. Merrit and Stein Rokkan (eds), *Comparing Nations: The Use of Quantitative Data in Cross-National Research* (New Haven, CT and London: Yale University Press, 1966)

Schmidt, Ben, 'Biblio bizarre: who publishes in Google Books', retrieved 15 April 2015 from http://sappingattention.blogspot.fi/2014/04/biblio-bizarre-who-publishes-in-google.html

Schmidt, James W., 'The Fading of "True Enlightenment" (Another Wildcard Search)', *Persistent Enlightenment*, retrieved 17 April 2014 from http://persistentenlightenment.wordpress.com/2013/10/18/the-fading-of-true-enlightenment-another-wildcard-search/

Skinner, Quentin, 'Motives, Intentions and Interpretations', in Quentin Skinner, *Visions of Politics I: Regarding Method* (Cambridge: Cambridge University Press, 2002)

Sluga, Glenda, 'The Nation and the Comparative Imagination', in Deborah Cohen and Maura O'Connor (eds), *Comparison and History: Europe in Cross-National Perspective* (New York and London: Routledge, 2004), 103–14

Smith, Anthony D., *Nationalism in the Twentieth Century* (Oxford: Martin Robertson, 1979)

———, 'Nationalism and Classical Social Theory', *The British Journal of Sociology* 34 (1983), 19–38

———, *Nations and Nationalism in a Global Era* (Cambridge: Polity Press, 1995)

Stapelbroek, Koen, and Jani Marjanen (eds), *The Rise of Economic Societies in the Eighteenth Century: Patriotic Reform in Europe and North America* (Basingstoke: Palgrave Macmillan, 2012)

Stenius, Henrik, 'The Language Issue in Finland', in Clive Archer and Pertti Joenniemi (eds), *The Nordic Peace* (Aldershot: Ashgate, 2002), 157–70

———, 'A Nordic Conceptual Universe', in Heidi Haggrén, Johanna Rainio-Niemi and Jussi Vauhkonen (eds), *Multi-layered Historicity of the Present: Approaches to Social Science History* (Helsinki: Department of Political and Economic Studies, University of Helsinki, 2013), 93–104

Stolte, Carolien, 'Itinerario to host on-line discussion with Prof. David Armitage', retrieved 9 April 2014 from http://blog.journals.cambridge.org/2012/11/itinerario-to-host-on-line-discussion-with-prof-david-armitage/

Strang, Johan, *History, Transfer, Politics: Five Studies on the Legacy of Uppsala Philosophy* (Helsinki: University of Helsinki, 2010)

———, 'Den perifera eklekticismens gränser och potential. Den logiska empirismen i Norden 1930–1970', *Historiska och litteraturhistoriska studier* 86 (2011), 137–58

Strang, Johan, and Stefan Nygård, 'Den moderna filosofin i Finland och Sverige', in Stefan Nygård and Johan Strang (eds), *Mellan idealism och analytisk filosofi: Den moderna filosofin i Fnland och Sverige* (Helsinki: Svenska litteratursällskapet i Finland, 2006)

Stråth, Bo, 'Comparative Conceptual History and Global Translations: An Outline of a Research Agenda', in Rudolf de Cillia et al. (eds), *Discourse, Politics, Identity: Festschrift für Ruth Wodak* (Tübingen: Stauffenburg Verlag, 2010), 213–20

Stubb, Elisabeth, *Rätt som argument: Leo Mechelin och den finska frågan 1886–1912* (Helsinki: Finska Vetenskaps-societeten, 2012)

Tilmans, Karin, 'Applying Begriffsgeschichte to Dutch History: Some Remarks on the Practice and Future of a Project', *Contributions to the History of Concepts* 2 (2006), 43–55

Tommila, Päiviö (ed.), *Suomen lehdistön historia* 6 (Kustannuskiila: Kuopio, 1988)

Walzer, Michael, *Thick and Thin: Moral Argument at Home and Abroad* (Notre Dame, IN: University of Notre Dame Press, 2002)

Wiener, Jonathan M., 'Review of Reviews: *Social Origins of Dictatorship and Democracy: Lord and Peasant in the Making of the Modern World* by Barrington Moore', *History and Theory* 15 (1976), 146–75

Wimmer, Andreas, and Nina Glick Schiller, 'Methodological Nationalism and Beyond: Nation-State Building, Migration and the Social Sciences', *Global Networks* 2 (2002), 301–34

———, 'Methodological Nationalism, the Social Sciences, and the Study of Migration: An Essay in Historical Epistemology', *International Migration Review* 37 (2003), 576–610

Chapter 6

Conceptual History

The Comparative Dimension

Jörn Leonhard

Approaching European Conceptual History: Comparison, Transfer and Entanglement

What is European about Europe? In his preface to the 'Collected Essays on the Sociology of Religion', Max Weber provided the classical formulation of this problem when asking the question: '[W]hat nexus of circumstances led to a situation in which cultural phenomena emerged specifically on the Occident's soil, and only there, that … nevertheless lay within a developmental trajectory of universal significance and validity?'[1] To this day, this crucial question has lost none of its suggestive power. Beyond the challenge it poses to a historical discipline that aims to understand and explain, it reflects the fundamental problem of demarcation and identification: what belongs to Europe or to 'the West', and what lies beyond?[2] The titles of publications and projects dedicated to explaining the specifically European core of Europe from a historical perspective often reveal their retrospective logic as well as the politics of history underlying their analytical frameworks. They tellingly refer to 'the Rise of the West', 'the European *Sonderweg*' or special path, and, in the book series edited by Jacques le Goff, to their intention 'to build Europe'.[3]

Contemporaries referring to Europe and European history often have European unity in mind as an objective, and the integration process as the route to achieving it. Behind the assumed finality of this process one can discern the premise that such a unity is possible on the basis of shared European values, institutions and experiences, which are in turn based on historical developments and learning processes. As a result, phenomena such as the European Enlightenment, the rule of law, the constitutional state and civil society are presented as specific Europeanisms. The crucial problem with this perspective lies in the inherent tension between two tendencies. The first rests on the notion of shared political-constitutional, societal and cultural values as well as the necessity of supranational institutions to solve common problems as a lesson to be derived from European history. The second involves the converse claim that European societies, states and nations exhibit a specific, historically evolved pattern of autonomy and diversity, resulting in a complex variety of conflicting collective self-images. The tension between these convergent and divergent tendencies is at the heart of every attempt to imagine and write European history.[4] And it also has fundamental relevance for conceptual history, whether historians refer to apparently similar meanings of political and social key concepts in different European societies, whether they point to the differences between the analytical use of concepts and their historical meaning or to the diachronic change of meaning and its plurality in different spaces of experience.

Looking at approaches to European history one can distinguish four major ideal-types. European history can, first, be written as an accumulation of national histories that remain more or less isolated from each other. The classical conception, found in many textbooks on European history, is based on the aggregation of quasi-pillarized, disconnected national histories. Often the dimensions of comparison, transfer and entanglement are limited to the introduction or concluding chapter.

Second, European history can be presented as a normative project, as an autonomous history of Europe, a history largely sealed off from other world regions. At best, marginal attention is paid to the relations between Europe and other historical regions, and it is no coincidence that general accounts often make use of chapter headings such as 'Europe and the Rest of the World'.[5]

Third, European history can be written with a focus on internal differentiation on the basis of comparisons, and by various combinations of comparison with the analysis of transfer and entanglement. Narrative compartmentalizations resulting from nation- or nation-state-centred frameworks can be overcome through systematic, sectoral and problem-focused comparisons. They can serve as an equivalent for experiments by which the relevance of certain variables can be distinguished.[6] Comparisons can work from two different angles, focusing either on contrasts and divergences or on generalizations and convergences.[7] In that way they reflect John Stuart Mill's distinction between the 'method of difference' and the 'method of agreement', or Charles Tilly's 'contrasting type' and 'universalizing type'.[8] Comparisons integrate an element of productive alienation by confronting the other.[9] It is, however, important to use the other not only in an asymmetric way to better illustrate one particular case which often tends to foster master narratives. Many histories of European history illustrate that problem by only taking the 'the rest of world' as a useful contrast when working on the supposed particularities of European history.[10]

Despite the high analytical value of many studies stimulated by these perspectives, the costs and problems associated with them have also been discussed: comparisons usually show poor narrative quality. Furthermore, scholars have debated the tension between strict synchronic comparisons on the one hand and research on transfer and entanglement on the other; between statics and dynamics, and between structures and processes. Very often, a comparison already presupposes an implicit relational history, a transfer that is either inherent in the period of the past under examination or else takes place in the imagination of the analysing historian.[11] These problems can be addressed by combining synchronic cross-sections with a long diachronic perspective, a longue durée, in which transfers and entanglements become more visible. Comparative studies in the field of conceptual history are a good example to illustrate that comparisons can help to identify the exact areas of transfer and entanglement, so that a combination of all three approaches is not only possible but fruitful.[12] Another problem inherent in comparisons and histories of transfer and entanglement lies in their focus on a single set of relations. This is especially evident in strictly bilateral comparisons, which often tend to privilege one particular perspective.[13]

The most important requirement when putting comparative frameworks into practice is a clear focus on precisely defined historical problems. In this way, historians have looked at long-term developments conceived in the light of institutions, as in Wolfgang Reinhard's work on the history of the modern state and its particular form of rule, Hartmut Kaelble's works on the origins and varieties of the European welfare state, and Jörg Fisch's analysis of the leitmotif of a coexistence of increased productivity and increased equality in the nineteenth century.[14] Such a matrix may be supplemented by other research fields and analytical explorations, helping to put into practice an 'open internal differentiation' without succumbing to excessive Eurocentrism. Furthermore, the combination of multiple perspectives allows for a better understanding of modes of historical developments, often characterized by a coexistence of structural convergences and divergences in the perception and interpretation of changes. It also affects our understanding of the temporalization of experience. In this field, comparisons help to identify the chronological simultaneity of historically non-simultaneous processes. Reinhart Koselleck's idea of one 'saddle epoch' in the history of modern political and social vocabularies can thus be transformed into the history of a variety of corresponding or divergent saddle epochs at various times.[15]

Fourth of the major ideal-types is that Europe-centred historiographies can be overcome by approaches inspired by global or world history. What underlies these approaches is a dual process of historiographical provincialization, stimulated by the deconstruction of historiographic frameworks like 'special paths' and 'exceptionalisms'. What Dipesh Chakrabarty has called 'provincializing Europe' in the light of global processes was preceded by the internal provincialization of particular European cases through the productive deconstruction of national narratives, as in the case of the German *Sonderweg*, or of the Whig interpretation of history in Britain. Something similar has unfolded with regard to the history of Europe from the perspective of global and world history.[16] Yet this global turn should not replace the many divergent histories within Europe by yet another artificial container-conception of 'Europe'.

As exemplified in the work of Christopher Bayly and Jürgen Osterhammel, these approaches provide a fascinating kaleidoscope of connections, rhythms and interactions, not least between nationalisms and processes of globalization. On the other hand, however, these accounts sometimes seem to open up a possible pitfall: if everything seems interconnected with everything else, causal explanations and hypotheses tend to retreat behind the thick descriptions of similarities and constellations or instances of simultaneity. Our understanding of simultaneity and connectedness of events, so much stimulated by the discovery of 'global moments', is per se no compensation for causal explanation of change over time.[17] This global trend is also obvious in the field of conceptual history, connecting the study of transformations of political and social vocabularies in Europe to global transfers and the complexities of translations.[18] Yet if the complexities and methodological problems of comparison, transfer and entanglement, as explained in this chapter, are evident already in European conceptual history, the project of a global conceptual history confronts historians with even more demanding challenges.

Culture and Experience: Comparing Histories of Meaning

How do these historiographic developments relate to the field of conceptual history? As a starting point one can point to the rise of culture, and more specifically the rise of experience as a paradigm of historical research over the last decades. It reflects a growing distance from the belief in objective social facts and structures, which have dominated much of the historical research and many debates on methodology since the late 1960s. Distancing from the normative contents and deconstructing the myths of socio-economic modernization theories have since gone hand in hand with new approaches to the study of past realities: they seem to no longer be primarily determined by class and socio-economic structures, but also by linguistic constructions of past agents. The discovery of language, performance and space, inter alia, as determining factors of past realities has questioned the long-held belief in the apparently objective meaning of social formations for historical processes. The multiplicity of thematic turns in recent years – from the linguistic to the performative and spatial to the emotional – has thus contributed to a major change in historiographic and methodological debates.[19]

In this context, experience and history of experience have developed as new categories of historical understanding and explanation.[20] They evade a simplistic and mono-causal analytical framework, and take into consideration the importance of language as a prime factor to structure, and articulate and communicate an individual's perception of his or her political, socio-economic and cultural environment. As a paradigm of historical research, experiences are characterized by different aspects.[21] First, in methodological terms the development of historical research methods in the nineteenth century served as a means to analyse the empirical structure of historical experiences. Historical research, in that respect, is to be understood as the sum of analytical operations that reconstruct the empirical structure behind individual expressions of the past. It was in that sense that Johann Gustav Droysen argued that the basic characteristic of the historical method lay in the premise to understand past realities by means of systematic research, and was distinct from speculative or introspective views of the historical past.

Second, in epistemological respect, the analytical concept of experience reflects the conflict between objectivist and constructivist perspectives. Experience relates both to the subjective interpretation of events or facts, which, according to Max Weber, developed their cultural meaning only in the very process of interpretation, and it relates to the predisposed and already existing facts and structures behind experiences. John Dewey, the representative of American pragmatism, underlined this dual nature of experience, with its quasi middle position between subject and object. In other words, not only the content of experiences matters but also the way in which experiences are made. External events derive their historical meaning only by acts of subjective interpretation. Empirical fact, objectivity on the one hand and subjective perception and interpretative integration on the other, do not exclude each other but form different poles of a complex interrelation. Experiences are not mere constructions. Instead they refer to an empirical reality of past events and actions. The past's relevance only becomes visible and communicable by the very act of historical interpretation, by generating meaningful experiences that allow communication. The analytical concept of experience thus allows understanding subjectivity and objectivity not as separated entities but rather as two interrelated dimensions of the same phenomenon.

Experiences refer to both a stream of past events and to the various levels of subjective perceptions and interpretations of these events. In contrast to mere observations, experiences are characterized by the application of interpretative knowledge – a reservoir of linguistic and performative codes, including leitmotifs, topoi, metaphors, dichotomies and arguments. They allow an individual or a group to structure the constant influx of information as generated by events and actions. Structuring information is a basic precondition for generating, formulating and communicating meaning. Hence experiences oscillate between each individual's perspective and collective narratives, making possible individual and intersubjective communication. Experiences, as communicated in concepts, allow meaningful orientation. In that way experience transcends not only the traditional schism between 'real' history, as visible in apparently hard facts and structures, and the way in which past agents dealt with their environment, but also bridges the apparent gap between language and action.[22]

Reinhart Koselleck developed three different categories of human experience: first, primordial experiences of individuals which are *eo ipso* unique and which cannot be repeated; secondly, reiterated experiences which can be communicated between subjects; and thirdly, experiences which are generated *ex post facto*, and thereby through historical reflection. All three categories can be related to different categories of narrations and historiographies, also reflecting the transformation from individual 'histories' to the collective singular of 'history': first, *Aufschreiben*, that is an individual's writing down of unique and personal events in order to explain them; secondly, *Fortschreiben*, a kind of updating, focusing on the interconnection between individual histories; and thirdly, *Umschreiben*, that is a revision in the forms and ways of communicating experiences as they are derived from past sources, referring to an *ex-post-facto* perspective, to a teleological causality by rewriting from the apparent end of historical processes and arguing from the knowledge of historical consequences.[23]

Against this background, innovative research on the relation between experience and language needs to go beyond a classical history of concepts on three levels.[24] First, it needs to concentrate not just on isolated concepts but on semantic fields and clusters, on arguments oscillating between various concepts, topoi, metaphors, basic dichotomies such as 'above/below', 'external/internal', 'earlier/later', which, according to Koselleck, serve as repetitive tools to structure complexity.[25] Secondly, the analysis of semantics needs to take the dimensions of comparison, transfer and entanglement into consideration. In this context translations become important: when and why are concepts exchanged between societies, when and why are they exported or imported, when and why do they become translatable, and how does their meaning change in these processes?

Thirdly, we need to inquire into the methodological and analytical consequences of the tension between the uniqueness of historical experiences that cannot be exchanged, exported or translated, and the repetition, reiteration and application of past experiences through historical analogies. Koselleck's observation of unique experiences, if interpreted dogmatically, would make it almost impossible to apply the study of experiences to whole societies and would limit the possibilities of comparison, transfer and entanglement. It therefore seems more appropriate to speak of a tension between uniqueness and the possible repetition of experiences as formulated and communicated in concepts. As Koselleck himself argued, a minimum of reiteration and analogy is always needed in order to apply old concepts to new experiences, thus underlining the importance of longue durée perspectives. However Koselleck's focus on the uniqueness of individual experiences also helps us to better identify the starting point of comparative historical semantics. There was no universal semantics of political and social key concepts such as 'liberalism' in early nineteenth-century Europe, but rather a spectrum of unique semantics of concepts used in arguments in different societies. We are hence confronted with a dual paradigm of diachronic synchronicity and a pluralism of saddle epochs.[26] But at the same time, repetitive structures are needed – not in the sense of identities, but as analogies in order to integrate new experiences.

Comparative Historical Semantics: Methodical Problems

How can we apply the comparative history of experiences to the historical semantics of concepts? How can we understand different experiences behind seemingly equivalent concepts that contain different semantic structures both in diachronic and synchronic perspective? In what ways does the understanding of translations correspond to comparisons?

Ideologies, Clifford Geertz once remarked, are cognitive maps 'of problematic social reality'.[27] The semantic variations of political and social key concepts in particular contexts represent, like a map, different historical landscapes, based on specific experiences of the past and expectations of the future. Maps imply travel, and travelling in the landscape of ideologies implies contact between speakers, the transfer of interpretative knowledge and hence the semantic transformation of concepts as they are used in arguments. All these elements underline the importance of translational processes for any understanding of semantic change. From that perspective every translation involves a conceptual movement between the translatable and the translated, and indeed translation can be described not only as a metaphor, but as an explanation of comparative semantic analysis. Translations from that perspective have both a diachronic and a synchronic dimension: they stand behind semantic change over time, from 'past past' to 'past present', but they also represent the synchronic export and import of concepts between societies.[28]

A comparative history of concepts brings together both dimensions of translation by stressing the diachronic change over time and the synchronic variations of semantic structures. The former points to translations in one national language community, the other to contact and interrelation, transfer and entanglement between different national languages. Thus comparison cannot only focus on isolated, quasi-pillarized conceptual histories, but needs to take into account processes of semantic transfer, interaction and overlapping.

Two hermeneutical problems are involved here, which the comparative European history of the key concept of 'liberalism' illustrates. First, many comparative studies still tend to equate the meaning of the ideological semantics of a key concept in different countries, as if it meant basically a similar canon of ideas, or movements, or parties. They do not take into consideration the distinct contemporary meanings of such a concept in different historical contexts. The neglect of this semantic aspect results in a trap of semantic nominalism; that is to say, the unconsidered transfer of a concept's semantics from the contemporary political language of one country to the political discourse of another. This implicit equating of contemporary meanings in different contexts conceals an important focus of experiences and expectations – in other words, the possibility of replacing the category of universal European liberalism with a spectrum of distinct histories of contemporary meanings of 'liberal'. This is in contrast to a traditional history of ideas approach, which would point to the singularity of 'European liberalism', quasi distilled from the realm of ideas to which 'liberalism' could be applied *avant la lettre* – that is, before the concept actually existed in contemporary political discourse.[29] Yet the semantics of political concepts are not the same in different countries. Different contexts point to the problem of how distinct experiences of the past and past expectations of the future were translated into distinct political and social discourses, and how that process was stimulated by the import, export and translation of foreign concepts and their semantic fields. In other words, it is not possible to sum up the meaning of French *libéralisme*, German *Liberalismus*, Italian *liberalismo* or English 'liberalism' in a universal concept of 'European Liberalism'. Behind linguistically 'equal' or 'similar' concepts lie essentially different experiences, interests and expectations.

Second, there is what may be called a translational circle. The results of a comparative semantic analysis need to be retranslated into a language that other historians understand and that allows them to comprehend the distinctions between historical meaning and analytical meaning. Theoretically a historian in such a situation would need a meta-language in order to avoid this problem of retranslation, such as a meta-theory which in other comparative analyses often serves as a *tertium comparationis* – for example, modernization theories in social history. However for comparative semantics, there is no such meta-language that always allows distinguishing between the historical and the analytical meaning. Historians engaging in comparative historical semantics are confronted with an aporetic situation, and they need to pay special attention to the way in which their readers can comprehend their analytical operations.[30]

Differentiating the 'Sattelzeit': Semantic Transformation and Translation

Despite these methodological challenges, the perspective of comparison, transfer and entanglement offers important advantages and innovative insights. One of the most important advantages results from the possibility to differentiate Reinhard Koselleck's concept of the saddle epoch (*Sattelzeit*).[31] According to him, a universal semantic change, based on such processes as democratization and the ideological polarization of concepts, took place between 1750 and 1850, and resulted in modern concepts. In contrast to this master narrative, the comparative analysis allows identifying the specific rhythms of conceptual change and thus the lifecycle of concepts in different societies. There was no single period in which the European vocabularies became modern. Rather, that process followed different paths, which nonetheless often connected, interrelated and overlapped.

Looking at the comparative historical semantics of 'liberal', one can describe the diachronic transformation in different stages, which helps to identify the moment when translations can actually influence conceptual change and semantic transformation.[32] First, the pre-political stage of 'liberal' is dominated by the pre-1789 uses of 'liberal' or 'liberality' in the different contexts. As in the case of Immanuel Kant's 'Liberalität der Denkungsart'[33] or Sieyès' 'education libérale'[34] of the Third Estate in France, the concepts reflected an enlightened educational ideal without a fixed political or social meaning. In a second phase, traditional and new semantic elements become fermented, caused by new political, social and cultural experiences, newly articulated interests and new expectations; pre-political and politicized meanings were now beginning to overlap. This process started with the invention of the 'idées liberales' in France in 1799, and their subsequent translation into 'liberale Ideen' in Germany and 'idee liberali' in Italy,[35] but also with the emergence of 'liberales' and 'serviles' as party names in Spain, and the export of this nomenclature to other European countries.

The politicization of concepts as controversial through changing connotations of traditional concepts and the development of new concepts characterized the third phase. Speakers began to structure the semantic field by canonical definitions and semantic clarity, relying on a number of key experiences and expectations. This is the stage in which the import of concepts such as the French 'idées liberales' created a framework for the articulation of new experiences and stimulated conceptual debates, thereby testing the semantic field. In the fourth stage an ideological polarization took place and bipolar or multipolar semantic structures developed. The focus was now on an antagonistic structure of semantics, resulting in a wider field of political and social nomenclatures and their use in arguments. In the case of 'liberal', the semantic field became defined by symmetric counter-concepts such as 'radical', 'conservative' and later 'socialist'.

Translations between national languages played a fundamental role in the second and third stages, when the semantic structure of a concept was still relatively fluid. In this phase the transfer of concepts and their translation

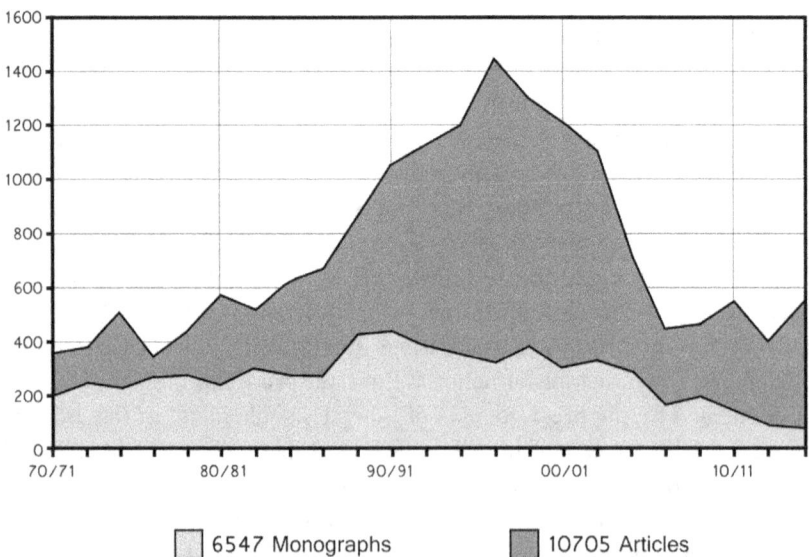

Figure 6.1 A Franco-German Library of Translations, 1770–1815. From Rolf E. Reichardt, *Das Blut der Freiheit. Französische Revolution und demokratische Kultur* (Frankfurt/M.: Fischer, 1998), 292.

served as a stimulating catalyst for politicized discourses. A very good illustration of this constellation is Rolf Reichardt's reconstruction of a virtual library of French–German translations between 1770 and 1815, a quantitative analysis illustrating the importance of translations in the politicization of German concepts and discourses through the translation of French texts. It also underlines the growing importance of journal and newspaper articles in this context, especially during the 1790s.

Such translations presuppose a cultural transfer of concepts that have gained at least a certain degree of universal meaning, before they can be integrated into national discourses. That was the case with the French political connotation of 'libéral' and the Bonapartist 'idées libérales' after 1799. The export of 'libéral' and its translation became a dominating feature in early nineteenth-century German and Italian political discourses. The following table shows the number of monographs containing 'liberal' in the main or subtitle between 1801 and 1880 in European comparison. Again the quantitative analysis underlines the pioneering role of France as a laboratory of political and social language in the early nineteenth century. The export of French concepts and semantic fields to other continental societies was a dominating feature before 1830, especially in German and Italian states.

Following from this merely quantitative analysis, one can identify different stages in the translation between national languages and vocabularies, thereby differentiating various functions of translations. First, imitating translation of characteristic French expressions or texts taken from newspaper articles,

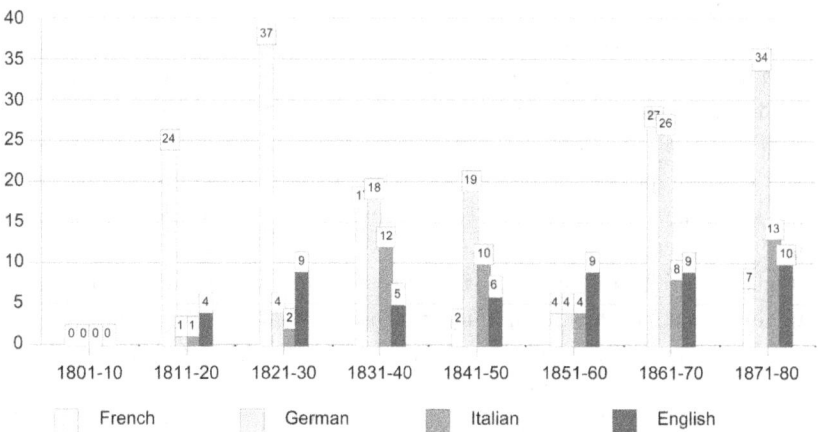

Figure 6.2 Monographs containing 'liberal' in title or subtitle in European comparison, 1801–1880. From Jörn Leonhard, *Liberalismus. Zur historischen Semantik eines europäischen Deutungsmusters* (Munich: Oldenbourg, 2001), 573.

essays, or entries from contemporary dictionaries. This translation usually reflected the direct impact of foreign impressions on a speaker – for instance, a German writer travelling to revolutionary Paris and reading political journals there. In this early stage, there was a characteristic lack of differentiating commentaries that could relate foreign concepts and their semantics directly to the speaker's own political or social context. German Jacobins travelling to Paris translated *principes libéraux* as *liberale Prinzipien*, but focused on the contemporary French context, not on the concept's application to the German political situation.[36]

Second, adapting translation: on the basis of imported foreign concepts, selected semantic elements were applied to a different social and political context. In this phase, the selection of semantics is directed by specific experiences, interests and expectations of the perceiving speakers. Although it still reflected the foreign origins, the concept's original connotation changed. The French *idées libérales* were not only imitated by *liberale Ideen* and *idee liberali* but the translation was applied to the political experiences and constitutional as well as national expectations in Germany and Italy.[37]

Third, discursive integration: in this phase, concepts and their semantic structures, which were now applied to the different political and social contexts of the importing society, were integrated into a society's discourse. This is documented by the emergence of encyclopedic entries of *liberale Ideen*, for instance in the Brockhaus edition of 1817, without any reference to its French origin but with particular references to the German political and constitutional context.[38]

The analysis of the concrete example demonstrated that the French stimulus of the *idées libérales* was fundamental for the development of new political and social concepts in Germany and Italy in the 1820s and early 1830s. In addition, the intensified debates about the French *Charte Constitutionnelle* of 1814 as a *constitution libérale*, and the polarization between *ultras* and *libéraux*, popularized the new concepts well beyond France. Translations of the French import in Germany and Italy changed from imitation through application and adaption to discursive integration. In contrast to Germany and Italy, where the direct import of the *idées libérales* resulted first in translations and direct applications of the French concept to identify and formulate the demands for national unity and constitutional reforms after 1815, the confrontation with the new concept in Britain took a different path: regarding the Spanish *liberales* or the French *libéraux*, the new political adjective was long used to describe the political situation in continental countries. Only after 1815 did the Tories' use of 'liberal' as a derogatory label for their political opponents and the Philhellene movement contribute to a wider diffusion of 'liberal' in the British political public. However, for a long time, 'liberal' retained an un-English tone because it represented political movements and groups in countries other than Britain. Only after 1820, when the reform-oriented Whigs of the Edinburgh Review accepted the new concept as a term with which to label their own position and political strategy, did 'liberal' for the first time become a positive and progressive semantic indicator in English political language, replacing the traditional semantic oppositions between 'court/country', 'Whig/Tory' and 'jacobin/loyalist'.[39]

Conclusion and Outlook

European history should be more than a positivist accumulation of national histories to be 'synthesized' inductively into the history of a larger entity.[40] It should instead be the outcome of a conscious and problem-oriented, lateral thinking. It is necessarily transnational in that it renders the historiographical casing of nation states permeable, thereby deconstructing their essentialisms and historiographic master narratives. From that perspective, comparisons offer a relatively clear and methodologically stringent set of rules, while at the same time incorporating an awareness of relational histories, of transfers and entanglements.

Comparative historical semantics demonstrate how the focus on 'many moving targets' in combination with a longue durée perspective can respond to the inherent problems of static and synchronic comparisons. It centres on processes of transfer and entanglement, not in the traditional sense of one-sided reception but of interactions involving changes in the objects of transfer themselves. Finally, it maintains an awareness of the local modifications occurring when exports are integrated.

Applying comparison, transfer and entanglement to conceptual history offers the possibility to make the different *Sattelzeiten* of European concepts and vocabularies more visible, reflecting distinct rhythms and cycles of past experiences and expectations as they were stimulated and catalysed by the export and import of foreign concepts. These experiences and expectations could not easily be translated, but rather led to complex confrontations with otherness. Translations reflected processes of selective perception stimulating cultural transfers and allowing the articulation of new political and social premises. For the historian, translations serve as a seismographic indicator of how past agents articulated their 'past pasts' and their 'past futures'. Friedrich Nietzsche once stated that a concept that contained in itself a whole history, evaded definition – 'definable is anything that has no history'.[41] However, history necessarily implies translation, whether diachronic or synchronic. The historian, who starts travelling in the landscapes of past experiences and expectations, is well advised to remember that as a traveller he or she will have to rely on translations. The aim of such analytical efforts should be to overcome isolated national histories of concepts by a focus on cultural transfer and semantic interaction between political languages – entangled histories that reflect the synchronic variations of the past.[42]

In that way European history appears as the outcome of multiple complex layers of experience – distinct sediments that cannot be reduced a priori to a single concept of Europe. From an analytical perspective, the goal is to link successiveness and simultaneity: diachronically through the analysis of long-term developmental processes and synchronically by examining the differences between various spaces of experience as well as the interactions and exchanges between them. However, writing modern European history today requires more than this. European history can no longer be the result of a Eurocentric historiography, but requires an intensive dialogue with the writing of global and world history. Dedicated not to the construction but to the deconstruction of apparent exceptionalisms, it must work from a template that is not just transnational but also transcultural.

Jörn Leonhard is Full Professor in Modern European History at the History Seminar of Freiburg University. He received his doctorate (1998) and his habilitation (2004) at the University of Heidelberg. From 1998 to 2003 he taught as Fellow and Tutor in Modern History at Oxford University, and from 2004 to 2006 as Reader in West European History at Jena University before coming to Freiburg. From 2007 to 2012 he was one of the Founding Directors of the School of History of the Freiburg Institute for Advanced Studies (FRIAS). In 2015 he was elected Member of the Heidelberg Academy of Sciences.

Notes

1. Max Weber, 'Vorbemerkung' [1920], in *Gesammelte Aufsätze zur Religionssoziologie*, vol. 1 (Tübingen: Mohr Siebeck, 1988), 1. The German original reads: 'Welche Verkettung von Umständen hat dazu geführt, daß gerade auf dem Boden des Okzidents, und nur hier, Kulturerscheinungen auftraten, welche doch – wie wenigstens wir uns gerne vorstellen – in einer Entwicklungsrichtung von universeller Bedeutung und Gültigkeit lagen?'; cf. Jörn Leonhard, 'Comparison, Transfer and Entanglement, or: How To Write Modern European History Today?', *Journal of Modern European History* 14(2) (2016), 149–163.
2. Heinrich August Winkler, *Geschichte des Westens*, 4 vols (Munich: C.H. Beck, 2009–14).

3. Jacques Le Goff, *L'Europe est-elle née au Moyen Âge?* (Paris: Seuil, 2003); German edition: *Die Geburt Europas im Mittelalter* (Munich: C.H. Beck, 2004). Le Goff served as editor of the book series which was published by C.H. Beck under the title 'Europa bauen'.
4. Jörn Leonhard, 'Europäisches Deutungswissen in komparativer Absicht: Zugänge, Methoden und Potentiale', *Zeitschrift für Staats- und Europawissenschaften* 4(3) (2006), 341–63.
5. Norman Davies, *Europe: A History* (Oxford: Oxford University Press, 1996); Hagen Schulze, *Phönix Europa: Die Moderne. Von 1740 bis heute* (Berlin: Siedler, 1998); Michael Salewski, *Geschichte Europas: Staaten und Nationen von der Antike bis zur Gegenwart* (Munich: C.H. Beck, 2000); Timothy Blanning (ed.), *The Oxford History of Modern Europe* (Oxford: Oxford University Press, 2000); Timothy Blanning and Hagen Schulze (eds), *Unity and Diversity in European Culture* (Oxford: Oxford University Press, 2006).
6. John Breuilly, 'Introduction: Making Comparisons in History', in John Breuilly, *Labour and Liberalism in Nineteenth-Century Europe: Essays in Comparative History* (Manchester: Manchester University Press, 1992), 1–25; Jürgen Kocka, 'Probleme einer europäischen Geschichte in komparativer Absicht', in Jürgen Kocka, *Geschichte und Aufklärung: Aufsätze* (Göttingen: Vandenhoeck & Ruprecht, 1989), 21–28; Jürgen Kocka, 'Comparative Historical Research: German Examples', *International Review of Social History* 38 (1993), 369–79; Heinz-Gerhard Haupt, Geoffrey Crossick and Jürgen Kocka, 'La storia comparata', *Passato e Presente* 28 (1993), 19–51.
7. Heinz-Gerhard Haupt and Jürgen Kocka, 'Historischer Vergleich: Methoden, Aufgaben, Probleme. Eine Einleitung', in Haupt and Kocka (eds), *Geschichte und Vergleich: Ansätze und Ergebnisse international vergleichender Geschichtsschreibung* (Frankfurt/M.: Campus, 1996), 11.
8. John Stuart Mill, *Philosophy of Scientific Method*, ed. E. Nagel (New York, 1881), 211–15; Charles Tilly, *Big Structures, Large Processes, Huge Comparisons* (New York: Russell Sage Foundation, 1984), 80; Otto Hintze, 'Soziologische und geschichtliche Staatsauffassung' (1929), in Hintze, *Soziologie und Geschichte: Gesammelte Abhandlungen*, ed. Gerhard Oestreich, vol. 2 (Göttingen: Vandenhoeck & Ruprecht, 1964), 251.
9. Haupt and Kocka, 'Historischer Vergleich', 15–16; Stephen Kalberg, *Max Weber's Comparative-Historical Sociology* (Cambridge: Polity Press, 1994).
10. See the titles mentioned in Note 6, above.
11. Johannes Paulmann, 'Internationaler Vergleich und interkultureller Transfer: Zwei Forschungsansätze zur europäischen Geschichte des 18. bis 20. Jahrhunderts', *Historische Zeitschrift* 267 (1998), 649–85; Jürgen Osterhammel, 'Transferanalyse und Vergleich im Fernverhältnis', in Hartmut Kaelble and Jürgen Schriewer (eds), *Vergleich und Transfer: Komparatistik in den Sozial-, Geschichts- und Kulturwissenschaften* (Frankfurt/M.: Campus, 2003), 439–66.
12. Jörn Leonhard, *Liberalismus: Zur historischen Semantik eines europäischen Deutungsmusters* (Munich: Oldenbourg, 2001); Jörn Leonhard, *Bellizismus und*

Nation: Kriegsdeutung und Nationsbestimmung in Europa und den Vereinigten Staaten 1750–1914 (Munich: Oldenbourg, 2008).

13. Jean-Jacques Becker and Gerd Krumeich, *Der Große Krieg: Deutschland und Frankreich im Ersten Weltkrieg* (Essen: Klartext, 2010).
14. Wolfgang Reinhard, *Geschichte der Staatsgewalt: Eine vergleichende Verfassungsgeschichte Europas von den Anfängen bis zur Gegenwart* (Munich: C.H. Beck, 1999); Hartmut Kaelble, *Sozialgeschichte Europas: 1945 bis zur Gegenwart* (Munich: C.H. Beck, 2007); Jörg Fisch, *Europa zwischen Wachstum und Gleichheit 1850–1914*, Handbuch der Geschichte Europas, vol. 8 (Stuttgart: Verlag Eugen Ulmer, 2002).
15. Reinhart Koselleck, 'Einleitung', in *Geschichtliche Grundbegriffe: Historisches Lexikon zur politisch-sozialen Sprache in Deutschland*, ed. Otto Brunner, Werner Conze and Reinhart Koselleck, vol. 1 (Stuttgart: Klett-Cotta, 1972), xv; Jörn Leonhard, 'Erfahrungsgeschichten der Moderne: Von der komparativen Semantik zur Temporalisierung europäischer Sattelzeiten', in Hans Joas and Peter Vogt (eds), *Begriffene Geschichte – Beiträge zum Werk Reinhart Kosellecks* (Frankfurt/M.: Suhrkamp, 2011), 423–48; Jörn Leonhard, 'Language, Experience and Translation: Towards a Comparative Dimension', in Javier Fernández Sebastián (ed.), *Political Concepts and Time: New Approaches to Conceptual History* (Santander: Cantabria University Press, 2011), 245–72.
16. Dipesh Chakrabarty, *Provincializing Europe: Postcolonial Thought and Historial Difference* (Princeton, NJ: Princeton University Press, 2000).
17. Erez Manela, *The Wilsonian Moment: Self-Determination and the International Origins of Anticolonial Nationalisms* (Oxford: Oxford University Press, 2007); Michael Goebel, *Anti-Imperial Metropolis: Interwar Paris and the Seed of Third World Nationalism* (New York: Cambridge University Press, 2015), 291.
18. Willibald Steinmetz, 'Vierzig Jahre Begriffsgeschichte – The State of the Art', in Heidrun Kämper and Ludwig M. Eichinger (eds), *Sprache – Kognition – Kultur: Sprache zwischen mentaler Struktur und kultureller Prägung* (Berlin: de Gruyter, 2008), 175–77 and 192–97; Margit Pernau and Dominik Sachsenmaier, 'History of Concepts and Global History', in Pernau and Sachsenmaier (eds), *Global Conceptual History: A Reader* (London: Bloomsbury, 2016), 1–27.
19. Ute Daniel, *Kompendium Kulturgeschichte: Theorien, Praxis, Schlüsselwörter* (Frankfurt/M.: Suhrkamp, 2001); Ute Daniel, 'Geschichte als historische Kulturwissenschaft – Konturen eines Wiedergängers', in Heide Appelsmeyer and Elfriede Billmann-Mahecha (eds), *Kulturwissenschaft: Felder einer prozeßorientierten wissenschaftlichen Praxis* (Weilerswist: Velbrück Wissenschaft, 2001), 195–214.
20. Friedrich Kambartel, *Erfahrung und Struktur: Bausteine zu einer Kritik des Empirismus und Formalismus* (Frankfurt/M.: Suhrkamp, 1968); Alf Lüdtke (ed.), *Alltagsgeschichte: Zur Rekonstruktion historischer Erfahrungen und Lebensweisen* (Frankfurt/M.: Campus, 1989); Jürg Freudiger et al. (eds), *Der Begriff der Erfahrung in der Philosophie des 20. Jahrhunderts* (Munich: C.H. Beck, 1996); Ute Daniel, 'Erfahren und Verfahren: Überlegungen zu einer künftigen

Erfahrungsgeschichte', in Jens Flemming et al. (eds), *Lesarten der Geschichte: Ländliche Ordnungen und Geschlechterverhältnisse. Festschrift für Heide Wunder zum 65. Geburtstag* (Kassel: Kassel University Press, 2004), 9–30.
21. Friedrich Jaeger, 'Erfahrung', in Stefan Jordan (ed.), *Lexikon Geschichtswissenschaft: Hundert Grundbegriffe* (Stuttgart: Reclam, 2002), 75–76.
22. Jörn Leonhard, 'Erfahrung im 20. Jahrhundert. Methodische Perspektiven einer "Neuen Politikgeschichte"', in Norbert Frei (ed.), *Was heißt und zu welchem Ende studiert man Geschichte des 20. Jahrhunderts* (Göttingen: Wallstein, 2006), 156–63.
23. Reinhart Koselleck, 'Erfahrungswechsel und Methodenwandel: Eine historisch-anthropologische Skizze', in Christian Meier and Jörn Rüsen (eds), *Historische Methode* (Munich: dtv, 1988), 13–61; Willibald Steinmetz, 'Nachruf auf Reinhart Koselleck (1923–2006)', *Geschichte und Gesellschaft* 32(3) (2006), 427–31; Reinhart Koselleck, 'Glühende Lava, zur Erinnerung geronnen: Vielerlei Abschied vom Krieg: Erfahrungen, die nicht austauschbar sind', *Frankfurter Allgemeine Zeitung, Beilage 'Bilder und Zeiten'*, 6 May 1995.
24. Heiner Schultz, 'Begriffsgeschichte und Argumentationsgeschichte', in Reinhart Koselleck (ed.), *Historische Semantik und Begriffsgeschichte* (Stuttgart: Klett-Cotta, 1979), 102–19; Hans Erich Bödeker, 'Begriffsgeschichte als Theoriegeschichte – Theoriegeschichte als Begriffsgeschichte: Ein Versuch', in Hans Erich Bödeker (ed.), *Begriffsgeschichte, Diskursgeschichte, Metapherngeschichte* (Göttingen: Wallstein, 2007), 91–119.
25. Reinhart Koselleck, 'Was sich wiederholt', *Frankfurter Allgemeine Zeitung*, 21 July 2005, 6; Reinhart Koselleck, 'Structures de répétition dans la langue et dans l'histoire', *Revue de Synthèse* 127 (2006, 5e série), 159–67; Steinmetz, 'Nachruf', 431–32; Javiér Fenández Sebastián and Juan Francisco Fuentes, 'Conceptual History, Memory, and Identity: An Interview with Reinhart Koselleck', *Contributions to the History of Concepts* 1(2) (2006), 100–104.
26. Ibid., 99–104.
27. Clifford Geertz, 'Ideology as a Cultural System', in Geertz, *The Interpretation of Cultures: Selected Essays* (New York: Basic Books, 1973), 220.
28. Jörn Leonhard, 'Von der Wortimitation zur semantischen Integration: Übersetzung als Kulturtransfer', *Werkstatt Geschichte* 48 (2008), 45–63.
29. Leonhard, *Liberalismus*, 47, 66, 83.
30. Reinhart Koselleck, Ulrike Spree and Willibald Steinmetz, 'Drei bürgerliche Welten: Zur vergleichenden Semantik der bürgerlichen Gesellschaft in Deutschland, England und Frankreich', in Hans-Jürgen Puhle (ed.), *Bürger in der Gesellschaft der Neuzeit* (Göttingen: Vandenhoeck & Ruprecht, 1991), 22; Sebastián and Fuentes, 'Conceptual History', 111–12; Barbara Cassin (ed.), *Vocabulaire européen des philosophies: Dictionnaire des intraduisibles* (Paris: Le Robert/Seuil, 2004).
31. Reinhart Koselleck, 'Richtlinien für das Lexikon politisch-sozialer Begriffe der Neuzeit', *Archiv für Begriffsgeschichte* 11 (1967), 81–99; Koselleck, 'Einleitung', xiii–xxvii.

32. Jörn Leonhard, 'Translation as Cultural Transfer and Semantic Interaction: European Variations of *Liberal* between 1800 and 1830', in Martin J. Burke and Melvin Richter (eds), *Why Concepts Matter: Translating Social and Political Thought* (Leiden: Brill, 2012), 93–108.
33. Immanuel Kant, *Kritik der Urtheilskraft, 1. Theil: Kritik der ästhetischen Urtheilskraft*, in *Kant's Gesammelte Schriften*, ed. Königlich Preußische Akademie der Wissenschaften, vol. 5 (Berlin 1913), 268.
34. Emmanuel Sieyès, *Qu'est-ce que le tiers état? (1789), précédé de l'Essai sur les privilèges*. Édition critique avec une introduction par Edme Champion (Paris 1888), 42.
35. Paolo Vergani, *Le Idee Liberali: Ultimo rifugio dei nemici della religione e del trono* ([Genoa, 1816, 1817] 3rd edn Turin, 1821).
36. Konrad Ferdinand Oelsner's letter dated 10 May 1797, quoted in Klaus Deinet, *Konrad Engelbert Oelsner und die Französische Revolution: Geschichtserfahrung und Geschichtsdeutung eines deutschen Girondisten* (Munich: Oldenbourg, 1981), 285.
37. Leonhard, *Liberalismus*, 191–203.
38. [F.A. Brockhaus] *Allgemeine deutsche Real-Encyclopädie für die gebildeten Stände: Conversations-Lexicon*, vol. 5, 4th edn (Leipzig, 1817), 674–75.
39. Jörn Leonhard, 'From European Liberalism to the Languages of Liberalisms: The Semantics of *Liberalism* in European Comparison', *Redescriptions: Yearbook of Political Thought and Conceptional History* 8 (2004), 17–51; Jörn Leonhard, '"True English Guelphs and Gibelines": Zum historischen Bedeutungs- und Funktionswandel von *whig* und *tory* im englischen Politikdiskurs seit dem 17. Jahrhundert', *Archiv für Kulturgeschichte* 84(1) (2002), 175–213.
40. Leonhard, 'Comparison, Transfer and Entanglement'.
41. Friedrich Nietzsche, *Zur Genealogie der Moral, Zweite Abhandlung: 'Schuld', 'schlechtes Gewissen', Verwandtes*, in Nietzsche, *Sämtliche Werke: Kritische Studienausgabe*, ed. Giorgio Colli and Mazzino Montinari, vol. 5 (Munich: dtv/de Gruyter, 1967, 3rd edn 1993), 317.
42. Steinmetz, 'Begriffsgeschichte', 175–77.

References

[F.A. Brockhaus] *Allgemeine deutsche Real-Encyclopädie für die gebildeten Stände: Conversations-Lexicon*, vol. 5, 4th edn (Leipzig, 1817)
Becker, Jean-Jacques, and Gerd Krumeich, *Der Große Krieg: Deutschland und Frankreich im Ersten Weltkrieg* (Essen: Klartext, 2010)
Blanning, Timothy (ed.), *The Oxford History of Modern Europe* (Oxford: Oxford University Press, 2000)
Blanning, Timothy, and Hagen Schulze (eds), *Unity and Diversity in European Culture* (Oxford: Oxford University Press, 2006)
Bödeker, Hans Erich, 'Begriffsgeschichte als Theoriegeschichte – Theoriegeschichte als Begriffsgeschichte: Ein Versuch', in Hans Erich Bödeker (ed.), *Begriffsgeschichte, Diskursgeschichte, Metapherngeschichte* (Göttingen: Wallstein, 2007), 91–119

Breuilly, John, 'Introduction: Making Comparisons in History', in John Breuilly, *Labour and Liberalism in Nineteenth-Century Europe: Essays in Comparative History* (Manchester: Manchester University Press, 1992), 1–25

Cassin, Barbara (ed.), *Vocabulaire européen des philosophies: Dictionnaire des intraduisibles* (Paris: Le Robert/Seuil, 2004)

Chakrabarty, Dipesh, *Provincializing Europe: Postcolonial Thought and Historial Difference* (Princeton, NJ: Princeton University Press, 2000)

Daniel, Ute, 'Geschichte als historische Kulturwissenschaft – Konturen eines Wiedergängers', in Heide Appelsmeyer and Elfriede Billmann-Mahecha (eds), *Kulturwissenschaft: Felder einer prozeßorientierten wissenschaftlichen Praxis* (Weilerswist: Velbrück Wissenschaft, 2001), 195–214

———, *Kompendium Kulturgeschichte: Theorien, Praxis, Schlüsselwörter* (Frankfurt/M.: Suhrkamp, 2001)

———, 'Erfahren und Verfahren: Überlegungen zu einer künftigen Erfahrungsgeschichte', in Jens Flemming et al. (eds), *Lesarten der Geschichte: Ländliche Ordnungen und Geschlechterverhältnisse. Festschrift für Heide Wunder zum 65. Geburtstag* (Kassel: Kassel University Press, 2004), 9–30

Davies, Norman, *Europe: A History* (Oxford: Oxford University Press, 1996)

Deinet, Klaus, *Konrad Engelbert Oelsner und die Französische Revolution: Geschichtserfahrung und Geschichtsdeutung eines deutschen Girondisten* (Munich: Oldenbourg, 1981)

Fernández-Sebastián, Javier, and Juan Francisco Fuentes, 'Conceptual History, Memory, and Identity: An Interview with Reinhart Koselleck', *Contributions to the History of Concepts* 1(2) (2006), 99–127

Fisch, Jörg, *Europa zwischen Wachstum und Gleichheit 1850–1914*, Handbuch der Geschichte Europas, vol. 8 (Stuttgart: Verlag Eugen Ulmer, 2002)

Freudiger, Jürg, et al. (eds), *Der Begriff der Erfahrung in der Philosophie des 20. Jahrhunderts* (Munich: C.H. Beck, 1996)

Geertz, Clifford, 'Ideology as a Cultural System', in Clifford Geertz, *The Interpretation of Cultures: Selected Essays* (New York: Basic Books, 1973), 193–233

Goebel, Michael, *Anti-Imperial Metropolis: Interwar Paris and the Seed of Third World Nationalism* (New York: Cambridge University Press, 2015)

Haupt, Heinz-Gerhard, Geoffrey Crossick and Jürgen Kocka, 'La storia comparata', *Passato e Presente* 28 (1993), 19–51

Haupt, Heinz-Gerhard, and Jürgen Kocka, 'Historischer Vergleich: Methoden, Aufgaben, Probleme: Eine Einleitung', in Heinz-Gerhard Haupt and Jürgen Kocka (eds), *Geschichte und Vergleich: Ansätze und Ergebnisse international vergleichender Geschichtsschreibung* (Frankfurt/M.: Campus, 1996), 9–45

Hintze, Otto, 'Soziologische und geschichtliche Staatsauffassung' (1929), in Otto Hintze, *Soziologie und Geschichte: Gesammelte Abhandlungen*, ed. Gerhard Oestreich, vol. 2 (Göttingen: Vandenhoeck & Ruprecht, 1964)

Jaeger, Friedrich, 'Erfahrung', in Stefan Jordan (ed.), *Lexikon Geschichtswissenschaft: Hundert Grundbegriffe* (Stuttgart: Reclam, 2002), 74–77

Kaelble, Hartmut, *Sozialgeschichte Europas: 1945 bis zur Gegenwart* (Munich: C.H. Beck, 2007)

Kalberg, Stephen, *Max Weber's Comparative-Historical Sociology* (Cambridge: Polity Press, 1994)

Kambartel, Friedrich, *Erfahrung und Struktur: Bausteine zu einer Kritik des Empirismus und Formalismus* (Frankfurt/M.: Suhrkamp, 1968)

Kant, Immanuel, *Kritik der Urtheilskraft, 1. Theil: Kritik der ästhetischen Urtheilskraft*, in *Kant's Gesammelte Schriften*, ed. Königlich Preußische Akademie der Wissenschaften, vol. 5 (Berlin, 1913)

Kocka, Jürgen, 'Probleme einer europäischen Geschichte in komparativer Absicht', in Jürgen Kocka, *Geschichte und Aufklärung. Aufsätze* (Göttingen: Vandenhoeck & Ruprecht, 1989), 21–28

———, 'Comparative Historical Research: German Examples', *International Review of Social History* 38 (1993), 369–79

Koselleck, Reinhart, 'Richtlinien für das Lexikon politisch-sozialer Begriffe der Neuzeit', *Archiv für Begriffsgeschichte* 11 (1967), 81–99

———, 'Einleitung', in *Geschichtliche Grundbegriffe: Historisches Lexikon zur politisch-sozialen Sprache in Deutschland*, ed. Otto Brunner, Wernere Conze and Reinhart Koselleck, vol. 1 (Stuttgart: Klett-Cotta, 1972), xiii–xxvii

———, 'Erfahrungswechsel und Methodenwandel: Eine historisch-anthropologische Skizze', in Christian Meier and Jörn Rüsen (eds), *Historische Methode* (Munich: dtv, 1988), 13–61

———, 'Glühende Lava, zur Erinnerung geronnen: Vielerlei Abschied vom Krieg: Erfahrungen, die nicht austauschbar sind', *Frankfurter Allgemeine Zeitung*, Beilage *'Bilder und Zeiten'*, 6 May 1995

———, 'Was sich wiederholt', *Frankfurter Allgemeine Zeitung*, 21 July 2005, 6

———, 'Structures de répétition dans la langue et dans l'histoire', *Revue de Synthèse* 127 (2006, 5e série), 159–67

Koselleck, Reinhart, Ulrike Spree and Willibald Steinmetz, 'Drei bürgerliche Welten: Zur vergleichenden Semantik der bürgerlichen Gesellschaft in Deutschland, England und Frankreich', in Hans-Jürgen Puhle (ed.), *Bürger in der Gesellschaft der Neuzeit* (Göttingen: Vandenhoeck & Ruprecht, 1991), 14–58

Le Goff, Jacques, *L'Europe est-elle née au Moyen Âge?* (Paris: Seuil, 2003)

———, *Die Geburt Europas im Mittelalter* (Munich: C.H. Beck, 2004)

Leonhard, Jörn, *Liberalismus: Zur historischen Semantik eines europäischen Deutungsmusters* (Munich: Oldenbourg, 2001)

———, '"True English Guelphs and Gibelines": Zum historischen Bedeutungs- und Funktionswandel von *whig* und *tory* im englischen Politikdiskurs seit dem 17. Jahrhundert', *Archiv für Kulturgeschichte* 84(1) (2002), 175–213

———, 'From European Liberalism to the Languages of Liberalisms: The Semantics of *Liberalism* in European Comparison', *Redescriptions: Yearbook of Political Thought and Conceptional History* 8 (2004), 17–51

———, 'Erfahrung im 20. Jahrhundert: Methodische Perspektiven einer "Neuen Politikgeschichte"', in Norbert Frei (ed.), *Was heißt und zu welchem Ende studiert man Geschichte des 20. Jahrhunderts* (Göttingen: Wallstein, 2006), 156–63

———, 'Europäisches Deutungswissen in komparativer Absicht: Zugänge, Methoden und Potentiale', *Zeitschrift für Staats- und Europawissenschaften* 4(3) (2006), 341–63

———, *Bellizismus und Nation: Kriegsdeutung und Nationsbestimmung in Europa und den Vereinigten Staaten 1750–1914* (Munich: Oldenbourg, 2008)

———, 'Von der Wortimitation zur semantischen Integration: Übersetzung als Kulturtransfer', *Werkstatt Geschichte* 48 (2008), 45–63

———, 'Erfahrungsgeschichten der Moderne: Von der komparativen Semantik zur Temporalisierung europäischer Sattelzeiten', in Hans Joas and Peter Vogt (eds), *Begriffene Geschichte – Beiträge zum Werk Reinhart Kosellecks* (Frankfurt/M.: Suhrkamp, 2011), 423–48

———, 'Language, Experience and Translation: Towards a Comparative Dimension', in Javier Fernández Sebastián (ed.), *Political Concepts and Time: New Approaches to Conceptual History* (Santander: Cantabria University Press, 2011), 245–72

———, 'Translation as Cultural Transfer and Semantic Interaction: European Variations of *Liberal* between 1800 and 1830', in Martin J. Burke and Melvin Richter (eds), *Why Concepts Matter: Translating Social and Political Thought* (Leiden: Brill, 2012), 93–108

———, 'Comparison, Transfer and Entanglement, or: How To Write Modern European History Today?', *Journal of Modern European History* 14(2) (2016), 149–163

Lüdtke, Alf (ed.), *Alltagsgeschichte: Zur Rekonstruktion historischer Erfahrungen und Lebensweisen* (Frankfurt/M.: Campus, 1989)

Manela, Erez, *The Wilsonian Moment: Self-Determination and the International Origins of Anticolonial Nationalisms* (Oxford: Oxford University Press, 2007)

Mill, John Stuart, *Philosophy of Scientific Method*, ed. E. Nagel (New York, 1881)

Nietzsche, Friedrich, *Zur Genealogie der Moral, Zweite Abhandlung: 'Schuld', 'schlechtes Gewissen', Verwandtes*, in Friedrich Nietzsche, *Sämtliche Werke: Kritische Studienausgabe*, ed. Giorgio Colli and Mazzino Montinari, vol. 5 (Munich: dtv/de Gruyter, 1967, 3rd edn 1993)

Osterhammel, Jürgen, 'Transferanalyse und Vergleich im Fernverhältnis', in Hartmut Kaelble and Jürgen Schriewer (eds), *Vergleich und Transfer. Komparatistik in den Sozial-, Geschichts- und Kulturwissenschaften* (Frankfurt/M.: Campus, 2003), 439–66

Paulmann, Johannes, 'Internationaler Vergleich und interkultureller Transfer: Zwei Forschungsansätze zur europäischen Geschichte des 18. bis 20. Jahrhunderts', *Historische Zeitschrift* 267 (1998), 649–85

Pernau, Margit, and Dominik Sachsenmaier, 'History of Concepts and Global History', in Margit Pernau and Dominik Sachsenmaier (eds), *Global Conceptual History: A Reader* (London: Bloomsbury, 2016), 1–27

Reichardt, Rolf E., *Das Blut der Freiheit: Französische Revolution und demokratische Kultur* (Frankfurt/M.: Fischer, 1998)

Reinhard, Wolfgang, *Geschichte der Staatsgewalt: Eine vergleichende Verfassungsgeschichte Europas von den Anfängen bis zur Gegenwart* (Munich: C.H. Beck, 1999)

Salewski, Michael, *Geschichte Europas: Staaten und Nationen von der Antike bis zur Gegenwart* (Munich: C.H. Beck, 2000)

Schultz, Heiner, 'Begriffsgeschichte und Argumentationsgeschichte', in Reinhart Koselleck (ed.), *Historische Semantik und Begriffsgeschichte* (Stuttgart: Klett-Cotta, 1979), 102–19

Schulze, Hagen, *Phönix Europa: Die Moderne. Von 1740 bis heute* (Berlin: Siedler, 1998)

Sieyès, Emmanuel, *Qu'est-ce que le tiers état? (1789), précédé de l'Essai sur les privilèges*. Édition critique avec une introduction par Edme Champion (Paris, 1888)

Steinmetz, Willibald, 'Nachruf auf Reinhart Koselleck (1923–2006)', *Geschichte und Gesellschaft* 32(3) (2006), 412–32

———, 'Vierzig Jahre Begriffsgeschichte – The State of the Art', in Heidrun Kämper and Ludwig M. Eichinger (eds), *Sprache – Kognition – Kultur: Sprache zwischen mentaler Struktur und kultureller Prägung* (Berlin: de Gruyter, 2008), 174–97

Tilly, Charles, *Big Structures, Large Processes, Huge Comparisons* (New York: Russell Sage Foundation, 1984)

Vergani, Paolo, *Le Idee Liberali: Ultimo rifugio dei nemici della religione e del trono* ([Genoa, 1816, 1817] 3rd edn Turin, 1821)

Weber, Max, 'Vorbemerkung' [1920], in *Gesammelte Aufsätze zur Religionssoziologie*, vol. 1 (Tübingen: Mohr Siebeck, 1988)

Winkler, Heinrich August, *Geschichte des Westens*, 4 vols (Munich: C.H. Beck, 2009–14)

Chapter 7
Concepts, Contests and Contexts

Conceptual History and the Problem of Translatability

László Kontler

In his introduction to a collection of studies on translation and the history of concepts, Melvin Richter writes that '[t]here has been relatively little discussion of the distinctive problems involved in converting texts in the human sciences from one language to another; and even less consideration of the obstacles to translating political and social thought, whether restricted to its classics, or extended to its more ordinary forms'. On this basis he goes on to claim that the volume 'breaks new ground in its focus on the theory and practice of translating political and social thought'.[1] While the merits of the collection, especially of its consistent combination of perspectives from the fields of conceptual history and translation studies, are beyond doubt, its originality lies in both synthesizing and innovating an existing research tradition, rather than establishing one. Over the past two, even three, decades scholars have in fact studied translation in cultural and intellectual history, including the history of social and political thought, quite extensively. Some of the books and articles they have produced have directly and explicitly relied on the propositions of conceptual history and/or translation studies, and most of them are helpful in further refining a research agenda concerning translation in the history of social and political thought as well as in answering the central question of the volume mentioned above – 'why concepts matter'. This is what I shall attempt in this chapter by reviewing some of the existing literature.[2] The notions of 'concept' and 'conceptual history' are understood openly, and I shall be referring to a great amount of material from the history of ideas and discourse, as well as cultural transfer, that I find relevant to the current discussion.

Before exploring the field, it is helpful to recall an important barrier to the smooth marriage between the domain of translation and *Grundbegriffe* in the sense in which 'basic concepts' were understood by the classics upon the inception of the project of *Begriffsgeschichte*, albeit now several decades ago. Enshrined in founding documents like Reinhart Koselleck's introduction to the *Geschichtliche Grundbegriffe*, it has been widely accepted by his contemporaries and followers that one of the central distinguishing features of 'basic concepts' is their character of being 'contested' in major public debates, as if in a struggle to control a semantic field and thereby relations of social and political authority.[3] Equally almost by definition, such contests tend to be taking place in specific political situations and cultural, intellectual and other – eminently linguistic – milieux. This apparently imposes serious limitations on the possibility for *Grundbegriffe* to be communicated across linguistic and cultural frontiers through interlingual translation of key texts. Is it therefore at all meaningful to talk about reception or *trans-latio* in the history of concepts?

Most historians who have dealt with the topic of translation have tended to be pragmatic about this dilemma and have not bothered unduly about the 'problem of the translatability of concepts'. Rightly so; in a linguistically and culturally plural world, translation as a communicative practice with negotiation – de- and re-contextualization – as its central feature is a fact of life. Whether or not translators are inspired by a normative ethos of 'faithfulness' to the original, 'losses in translation' must be taken for granted as a result of, among other things, differences in natural vocabulary, in discursive traditions and in conceptual apparatus. Such evidences have, from the 1970s, led scholars in translation studies to a preoccupation with what translators actually do, instead of what they ought to be doing, in pursuing their job. Several of these scholars have demonstrated an acute awareness of the historicity of the constructed and contingent nature of the 'linguistic equivalences' created in translation.[4] Their 'historical turn' has, in turn, inspired cultural historians to initiate their own 'translatorial turn', combining the perspectives of translation studies with those of 'cultural translation' borrowed from anthropologists, who use it to describe the effort of parties involved in a situation of encounter to make sense of one another's behaviour.[5] Under such multiple influences, the tendency among cultural historians has been towards actually celebrating 'losses in translation' whose 'close examination ... is one of the most effective ways of identifying the differences between cultures', and therefore towards commending the study of translation as 'central to the practice of cultural history'.[6]

Among a wide array of topics, students of cultural translation have ventured to explore translation in the history of ideas, including political theory and history, subjects that are also central to conceptual history. These ventures, however, have not always employed an approach compatible with the preoccupations of conceptual history, namely the development, transformation, shift and – in the case of translations and transmissions – ruptures in the fields of meaning denoted by a specific cluster of expressions that are identified as 'concepts'. In his virtuoso study of the reception of Castiglione's *Il Cortegiano* across Europe in the early modern period, Peter Burke follows closely the 'fortunes' of the concept of *sprezzatura* in the intricate web of constraints defined by social values, linguistic determinants, discursive traditions and other contexts. The question of 'how' and with what outcomes Castiglione's peculiar vocabulary is rendered in the different vernaculars is an important one for the argument presented by Burke about the 'Europeanization of Europe, in other words the gradual integration of European culture over the centuries'.[7] In the same author's investigation of translating histories in early modern Europe, however (and somewhat unexpectedly, given cultural historians' preoccupation with the construction of meaning), the semantic implications and consequences of the process of translation receive little, if any, attention. Rather, the above-mentioned goal of identifying cultural difference is pursued through a quest to find answers to 'what', 'where' and 'why' questions: the selection of authors and titles, the directions, and the motivations for intercultural communication by translating histories (together with the assessment of some paratextual elements highlighting especially the last of these factors). Similarly, the conclusions of Geoffrey Baldwin's valuable panorama of the translation of political theory, about the 'intellectual and moral boundaries in early modern Europe' and the 'porous' nature of these boundaries, are based on a catalogue of the most translated texts and genres, and the 'intentions' in executing these translations – but not on a consideration of the actual shifts of meaning that take place via the act of translation.[8]

In spite of such differences of perspective and endeavour, there is a great deal in these studies to be resorted to by scholars of the history of concepts and the history of social and political thought. For an interesting and innovative combination of the approaches of the practice-based study of cultural diffusion and the discourse-based analysis of intellectual reception, one might turn to a recent exploration of 'the politics of translation and transmission' on the example of the confrontations with James VI of Scotland's *Basilikon Doron* in seventeenth-century Hungary.[9] An early modern political bestseller, *Basilikon Doron* was translated into several European vernaculars – remarkably, from the English, not the Latin version. Building on an impressive array of existing literature of this broad history of reception elsewhere, Hanna Orsolya Vincze traces the ways in which the translation of this text, soon after its original publication in English in order to prepare the *translatio* of its author from Scotland to England (as James I), became instrumentalized in the beginnings of 'political theorizing' in the Hungarian vernacular. Vincze's choice of the term 'theorizing' instead of theory is a calculated one: it refers, on the one hand, to the widely accepted and often lamented lack of 'originality' in terms of genuine theoretical contribution to the European canon in the 'less happy regions' of the continent, but on the other hand also to the element of active agency at work in the process of reception. Culturally, it denotes the activity of authorial networking among a number of Calvinist peregrinates belonging to a distinct group 'with similar careers and interests' and embracing a variety of political languages from divine right and civic humanism through neo-stoicism to Old Testament Biblicism and millenarianism. Intellectually, it refers to the significance of the 'local stakes' defining the prospects of translation, which was not to be a vehicle for the mere transmission of ideas, but a realm for creating 'communicative meanings' through 'communicative acts, i.e., meanings created in use'.[10] In the given case, it is convincingly shown how a regional 'Calvinist' rendering of *Basilikon Doron* emerged, envisioning the office of the ruler 'echoing the ideals of further reformation that the Hungarian peregrine students would have met in the Palatinate'. In the process, a book about the office of the king, reassuring his subjects that he understood his duties towards them, assumed a new illocutionary force and became re-articulated as a conduct book warning the prince about the performance of those duties.[11]

While Vincze prefers to study the rendering of 'keywords' to those of 'concepts' in the Koselleckian sense, her book highlights ways in which cultural history, 'Collingwoodianism'[12] and a somewhat reframed and more elastic conceptual history could be combined.[13] From a different angle, her research on the 'fortunes' of *Basilikon Doron* is a recent reminder of a truism that has been prompted again and again in a long line of studies. This is that the '(un) translatability of concepts' may be a misleading term because it suggests that concepts tend to resist translation *in spite of* whatever efforts translators may be making to render them faithfully. The second part of this assumption would clearly be a fallacious one. Regardless of the resisting power of concepts – keywords, vocabularies – to translation, in most historically documented cases translators could hardly have cared less about their faithful rendering. The outcome has sometimes been described as 'mistranslation' or 'misreception', which is technically accurate, but as it has a tendency to represent the agent of translation or reception as guilty of oversight, incompetence or malicious manipulation, it should be used with caution. Its uncompromising use risks association with a tradition of research that understands reception as a unilinear process of 'passing on' ideal-typical meanings from authoritative creators to inferior recipients, whose only task would be faithful copying, but who, out of inability or unwillingness, would only produce faint or distorted replicas. In contrast to this limited perspective, the studies referred to here – even those that employ the 'mis-' words – have led us a long way towards restoring active agency to the translator-recipient and the environment of reception by translation – to the extent that it might be helpful to exchange the term 'reception' for confrontation and negotiation.

A comprehensive account of this literature is beyond the scope of this chapter, but a selection may support my claim. It could have been a challenge beyond the means of Hume's eighteenth-century German translators to find a word in their mother tongue that would consistently and faithfully render the idea of belief. But one wonders how hard they would have ever wanted to try: their own anti-rationalist bent was probably quite happy with *Glaube*, making out of Hume a sort of ally against himself – 'the patron saint of German fideism and irrationalism'.[14] Another famous example on the Scottish–German axis for a confluence between the lack of exact equivalents in the relevant vocabularies and the radical integrity of the agents of translation, is 'civil society' (particularly as analysed by Adam Ferguson) versus *bürgerliche Gesellschaft* (culminating in and enshrined by Hegel).[15] It has been shown that during the early Enlightenment, Jean Barbeyrac took similar liberties in adjusting Samuel Pufendorf's civil philosophy via his translation of the latter's works to his own ends in moral theology;[16] while another classic in the 'unsocial sociability' tradition, Bernard Mandeville's *Fable of the Bees*, seems to have been turned into not merely an economic but a moral and natural defence of commercial society during the French 'luxury debates' of the mid eighteenth century, thanks to Emilie Du Châtelet's translation, with its shift of emphasis from passions and benefit to pleasure and enjoyment as the organizing notions of the text.[17] From a kaleidoscope of case studies offered in a recent volume, one may pick the account of how the *General History of the World* by William Guthrie and John Gray became, through translation, a *Reichshistorie*, a vehicle for academic emancipation in the hands of German scholars, and then a fountainhead of national histories produced in Eastern and Northern Europe.[18]

Before the impression is created that the exploration of translation in social and political thought is a trade mark in Enlightenment studies, let me hasten to point out that the chronological scope is far broader than that, and besides intra-European processes of reception through translation, 'Western / non-Western' contexts have also received considerable attention. Anthony Pym investigates episodes of nearly a millennium of exchanges in the 'intercultures' of Hispanic frontier society, chiefly aimed at answering the question of how cultures *should* interrelate by studying models of how cultures have *actually* interrelated, and by focusing on the roles of translators rather than translations in such relationships. These explorations range from the twelfth-century project of translating the Qur'an into Latin as a means of providing tools for a future disputation that would save souls from the 'heresy of Islam' to the uses of translation for symbolic purposes during the 1992 Barcelona Olympic Games (where Catalan was selected as one of the four official languages). They are all reminders pertinent to the present concerns, namely, the inevitable element of instrumentalization through active agency on the part of the recipient in the translation process.[19] We now have excellent studies on how auto-translations into Latin of Bodin's *République* and Hobbes's *Leviathan* served as a means, and can be now read as a record of rethinking – at places amplifying, at others excising – points made in their own originals, at others still responding to objections, and on the whole attempting to address a different audience by conceptual reframing. All these translatorial practices have been widely adopted in their time and in others by translators of texts by other authors (in Hobbes's case, practices that he himself also employed when translating Homer's epic works).[20] As far as post-Enlightenment times are concerned, one must underline the work of Jörn Leonhard, who in several works has turned the study of the transformations of the meaning of 'liberal / liberalism' through translation to nothing less than revising the chronology of the *Sattelzeit*.[21] Among modern classics of European social science, translations of Max Weber have received considerable attention from students of conceptual history, with the pre-eminence of translatorial agendas in reshaping Weber in the Anglo-American reception given emphasis, albeit from apparently contradicting stances. In one case, it is argued that the translation (of *Politik als Beruf*) stressed the philosophical and ethical aspects of the text at the expense of others geared towards a political sociology of modern society, while in the other case it is suggested that it was exactly through the appropriation of Weber by the new discipline of university sociology (and the identification of his theoretical interests as primarily sociological) that a 'misrepresentation' was reproduced (encouraged?) in the flawed English translation of his works.[22]

Looking at 'the West versus the Rest', the unequal relations of power, at least with regard to the period of colonialism and imperialism, are usually emphasized as a background to the commerce of ideas and concepts through translation, but even allowing for some explanatory power in this assessment, the picture is highly complex. As a matter of fact, while Europeans were at the recipient end of much of this traffic, the active agency of European translators of non-European texts made it possible for the translations to be turned to culturally 'orientalist' and politically colonialist ends – as, for instance, in the case of William de Slane's translation of part of Ibn Khaldûn's *Ibar* as *Histoire des berbères* in the 1850s.[23] Conversely, however, the adoption of

Western social and political ideas that was understood as a condition of prosperity, even mere survival, by Japanese and Chinese intellectuals in the later nineteenth century, also required a creatively domesticating attitude on their part in translating authors of the Western canon from Montesquieu through Smith and Fichte to Mill: in such cases, translation became 'a translingual act of transcoding cultural material' – with consequences for the specific material studied by the authors of the relevant scholarship.[24] In the Chinese case, concepts of the nation and the body politic were moulded through (pseudo-) translations of Fichte; in the Japanese case an idea of liberty and its limitations arose out of the translation of Mill, but contradicted him on several points.[25]

Even a representative selection of the respectable amount of literature could not be attempted in these pages. What is noteworthy is indeed the tendency of much of this literature to emphasize the amount of intellectual and conceptual adjustment, adaptation and transformation occurring as a result of the combination of linguistic and discursive, sociocultural and political parameters with the agency of translators. The one significant exception I am aware of in which the effective adoption of a text (or a body of texts) through translation served as a blueprint for promoting and pursuing agendas and goals by and large identical with the original, is Sophus Reinert's history of economic translations in Europe between the 1500s and the 1800s, especially those of John Cary's 'Essay on the State of England' (1695). Reinert demonstrates how Cary's essay was central to the rise of political economy as an instrument of policy making in France, Italy, Germany, Scandinavia and America, inspiring solutions – interventionism through tariffs and other means – akin to those that were first adopted in England, and that would now be described as nationalist.[26]

In spite of this important divergence, however, Reinert's study shares a fundamental feature of the comparative endeavour inherent in the historical literature on translation that emphasizes the difference arising at the target end of the translatorial process: the focus of attention of virtually all of this literature is the considerable amount we may learn from the comparisons involved in the study of translation about the cultural-intellectual-conceptual milieu into which the text is transferred by translation. In the concluding section of this chapter, as a cautious attempt to put the 'why concepts matter' question in a new light, I would like to suggest and illustrate that the differences of meaning emerging through translation in the recipient environment can be turned to contributing to significant discussions and to sorting out disagreements about the character and status of authors, their texts and their concepts as they exist in their 'home' culture. My premise is a simple one: whatever aspect in the work of an author or in a concept, or whatever thread in a text, is overlooked, neglected or redescribed in order to better suit the purposes of the translator, must be regarded as peculiar to and distinctive of the 'original'. This may sound trivial, but there are cases in which it may have important consequences.

One such case is that of the historian William Robertson, now widely recognized as one of the most important eighteenth-century European figures in the conversion of history into a field emerging as a branch of knowledge with a claim to being a 'science', as well as of the Scottish Enlightenment. During the first phases of the intensive study of this latter phenomenon in the 1970s, Robertson was hailed largely for the efficient marriage of enjoyable and morally compelling historical narrative with the stringent methodological principles of the eighteenth-century 'science of man': the theory of progress based on the study of human moral psychology and the satisfaction of economic needs, and the consequently construed succession of 'stages' of development understood in terms of ever-more sophisticated 'modes of subsistence' and increasingly refined 'manners' and legal-political arrangements. His language and conceptual apparatus built around 'progress and refinement' has also been identified as an attempt to refocus the priorities of patriotic historical discourse in a Scotland whose staunchly defended traditions of political independence were relativized by the 1707 constitutional union with England. More recently, however, a revisionist assessment of Robertson's contribution has also been gaining ground, pointing out that he struggled hard and not always successfully to smoothly integrate the 'modernist' elements of the social science emerging among his celebrated contemporaries into his historical works, which continued to be organized around established notions carried forward from humanist and Calvinist antecedents.

A contextualized re-examination of the published texts of Robertson goes some way towards giving further support to the argument that the perspectives of 'stadial history' not only imbue the select 'avant-garde' sections of his oeuvre, devoted to sociological framing, but are also crucial to the agenda pursued in the bulk of historical narrative offered in them. As a test of the validity of this impression, it is helpful to resort to a study of the German reception of Robertson's works through translation.[27] During the period 1760–95, all of his published texts were translated into German, most of them with astonishing immediacy, some of them by several hands simultaneously, while others were retranslated and re-edited several times over the course of several decades. Translators usually did a good job in rendering the argument, except for the vocabulary of stadial theory and all of its implications for the intellectual and political outlook of Robertsonian historiography (apart from the single case of Georg Forster, who because of his personal itinerary had a privileged access both to the English language and to Scottish social theory). Some of them were prevented from a more nuanced understanding of such aspects of

Robertson's work by the fact of their being simple artisans of the translating business without an independent agenda, while others used the translation to challenge the Scottish historian boldly and provocatively, precisely on the materialistic implications of his output that were apparently quite important for him. Whether it was a lack of comprehension, a lack of a compatible vocabulary and indigenous conceptual apparatus, or a lack of willingness on the part of Robertson's translators that prevented these implications from resonating in the process of reception, one may suggest that the impression gained from the re-examination of the original texts is confirmed by the study of the corpus of German translations: Robertson's distinctiveness lies in those aspects of his work beyond the reach of his local context. While the recent revisionists have a point in stressing the traditionalist elements in Robertson's work, a study of the German translation history re-establishes him as the avant-garde historian who emerged during the renaissance of eighteenth-century Scottish studies over four decades ago.

In this chapter I have attempted to highlight the considerable amount of useful work recently done by scholars on translation in intellectual and conceptual history. Perhaps the most important achievement of this emerging corpus of scholarship is the abandonment of the assumption that translation in all circumstances either is, or should be, pursued with the aim of familiarizing recipient audiences with the original in all of its foreignness, and the outcome of translations that do not stand up to such expectations is 'misreception'. On the contrary, it is now widely acknowledged that the study of translation is an important tool of comparative intellectual and conceptual history *because of* shedding light on the differences of meaning that are produced in the process. On the basis of a specific case study, I also argue that this holds true for *both* sides of the boundary crossed by the translated text: the 'resistance' of a language, a translator, or a full audience to important meanings, which a text and its author can be said to hold, or the incomprehension with which such texts may meet, point to the real *differentia specifica* of an author and her/his text in the original. Further studies may substantiate, refine or challenge this proposition.

László Kontler is Professor of History at Central European University, Budapest. His research ranges across the history of political and historical thought, translation and reception in the history of ideas, and the production and exchange of knowledge, in the early modern period, mainly the Enlightenment. His English language books include *A History of Hungary* (2002) and *Translations, Histories, Enlightenments: William Robertson in Germany, 1760–1795* (2014). Recently, he co-edited, with Antonella Romano,

Silvia Sebastiani and Borbála Zsuzsanna Török, *Negotiating Knowledge in Early-Modern Empires: A Decentered View* (2014). He is one of the editors of the *European Review of History / Revue d'histoire européenne*, and of Europäische Geschichte Online / European History Online.[28]

Notes

1. Melvin Richter, 'Introduction: Translation, the History of Concepts and the History of Political Thought', in Martin J. Burke and Melvin Richter (eds), *Why Concepts Matter: Translating Social and Political Thought* (Leiden and Boston: Brill, 2012), 1.
2. In two earlier articles I attempted to outline an approach to the study of translation in early-modern intellectual history on the basis of a consideration of the theory and practice of translation in the period itself, in combination with the methodological offer in translation studies, linguistic contextualism and *Begriffsgeschichte*. See László Kontler, 'Translation and Comparison: Early-Modern and Current Perspectives', *Contributions to the History of Concepts* 3(1) (2007), 71–102; idem, 'Translation and Comparison II: A Methodological Inquiry into Reception in the History of Ideas', *Contributions to the History of Concepts* 4(1) (2008), 27–56. The endeavour of those two pieces was theoretical and methodological, while the chief concern here is historiographical. For a similar effort to establish a frame for the historical study of translation on the examination of Enlightenment theories of translation in conjunction with the cultural transfer approach, see Stefanie Stockhorst, 'Introduction. Cultural Transfer through Translation: A Current Perspective in Enlightenment Studies', in Stefanie Stockhorst (ed.), *Cultural Transfer through Translation: The Circulation of Enlightened Thought in Europe through Translation* (Amsterdam and New York: Rodopi, 2010), 7–28. Cf. also Douglas Howland, 'The Predicament of Ideas in Culture: Translation and Historiography', *History and Theory* 42 (2003), 45–60.
3. Reinhart Koselleck, 'Einleitung', in Otto Brunner, Werner Conze and Reinhart Koselleck (eds), *Geschichtliche Grundbegriffe: Historisches Lexikon zur politisch-sozialen Sprache in Deutschland*, vol. 1 (Stuttgart: Klett-Cotta, 1972), xiii–xxvii.
4. This specific formulation is from Lydia H. Liu, 'Introduction', in Liu (ed.), *Tokens of Exchange: The Problem of Translation in Global Circulations* (Durham, NC: Duke University Press, 1999), 5. A non-exhaustive list of the relevant literature includes Antoine Berman, *L'Épreuve de l'étranger: Culture et traduction dans l'Allemagne romantique* (Paris: Gallimard, 1984); Theo Hermans (ed.), *The Manipulation of Literature: Studies in Literary Translation* (Beckenham: Coom Helm, 1985); Wilhelm Graeber and Geneviève Roche, *Englische Literatur des 17. und 18. Jahrhunderts in französischer Übersetzung und deutscher Weiterübersetzung: Eine kommentierte Bibliographie* (Tübingen: Niemeyer, 1988); Lawrence Venuti, *The Translator's Invisibility: A History of Translation* (London and New York: Routledge, 1995); Jean Delisle and Judith Woodsworth (eds), *Translators through*

History (Amsterdam: John Benjamin's Publishing Company, 1995); Anthony Pym, *Negotiating the Frontier: Translators and Intercultures in Hispanic History* (Manchester: St Jerome Publishing, 2000).
5. The fountainhead here is E.E. Evans-Pritchard, *Social Anthropology* (London: Cohen & West, 1951); also, Clifford Geertz, *The Interpretation of Cultures* (London: Harper Collins, 1973), and Edmund Leach, *Social Anthropology* (Glasgow: Fontana, 1982). For a recent assessment, see Susan Gal, 'Politics of Translation', *Annual Review of Anthropology* 44 (2015), 225–40.
6. Peter Burke, 'Cultures of Translation in Early Modern Europe', in Peter Burke and Ronnie Po-Chia Hsia (eds), *Cultural Translation in Early Modern Europe* (Cambridge: Cambridge University Press, 2007), 38.
7. Peter Burke, *The Fortunes of the Courtier: The European Reception of Castiglione's Cortegiano* (Philadelphia: Pennsylvania State University Press, 1995), 2. It must be added that most of Burke's investigation is that of cultural diffusion, rather than intellectual transmission and reception via a minute comparison of the vocabularies and other elements of language involved in the translation process. But see the section 'The Rewriting of the Text', ibid., 66–72.
8. Geoffrey P. Baldwin, 'The Translation of Political Theory in Early Modern Europe', in Burke and Po-chia Hsia, *Cultural Translation*, 101–24; Peter Burke, 'Translating Histories', in ibid., 125–41.
9. Hanna Orsolya Vincze, *The Politics of Translation and Transmission: Basilikon Doron in Hungarian Political Thought* (Cambridge: Cambridge Scholars Press, 2012). See also Hanna Orsolya Vincze, 'The Fortunes of Basilikon Doron', in Janet Coleman and Paschalis Kitromilides (eds), *In the Footsteps of Herodotus: Towards European Political Thought* (Florence: Olschki, 2012), 77–92.
10. See Vincze, *Politics of Translation*, xiii–xiv.
11. Vincze, *Politics of Translation*, 115ff.
12. Quentin Skinner's now preferred way of labelling the 'Cambridge school' of intellectual history. Cf. Quentin Skinner, 'The Rise of, Challenge to and Prospects for a Collingwoodian Approach to the History of Political Thought', in Dario Castiglione and Iain Hampsher-Monk (eds), *The History of Political Thought in National Context* (Cambridge: Cambridge University Press, 2001), 175–88.
13. As proposed in Hans Erich Bödeker, 'Concept – Meaning – Discourse: *Begriffsgeschichte* Reconsidered', in Iain Hampsher-Monk, Karin Tilmans and Frank van Vree (eds), *History of Concepts: Comparative Perspectives* (Amsterdam: Amsterdam University Press, 1998), 51–64.
14. Isaiah Berlin, 'Hume and the Sources of German Anti-Rationalism', in *Against the Current: Essays in the History of Ideas* (Oxford: Clarendon Press, 1981), 181.
15. Norbert Waszek, *The Scottish Enlightenment and Hegel's Account of 'Civil Society'* (Dordrecht: Kluwer Academic Publishers, 1988); Fania Oz-Salzberger, *Translating the Enlightenment: Scottish Civic Discourse in Eighteenth-Century Germany* (Oxford: Clarendon Press, 1995).

16. David Saunders, 'The Natural Jurisprudence of Jean Barbeyrac: Translation as an Act of Political Adjustment', *Eighteenth-Century Studies* 36(4) (2003), 473–90. Cf. David Saunders and Ian Hunter, 'Bringing the State to England: Andrew Tooke's Translation of Samuel Pufendorf's De Officio Hominis et Civis', *History of Political Thought* 24(2) (2003), 218–34.
17. Felicia Gottmann, 'Du Châtelet, Voltaire, and the Transformation of Mandeville's *Fable*', *History of European Ideas* 38(2) (2012), 218–32.
18. Mónika Baár, 'From General History to National History: The Transformations of William Guthrie's and John Gray's *A General History of the World* (1736–1765) in Continental Europe', in Stockhorst, *Cultural Transfer through Translation*, 63–82.
19. Pym, *Negotiating the Frontier*.
20. Mario Turchetti, 'Bodin as Self-Translator of his République: Why the Omission of "*Politicus*" and Allied Terms in the Latin Version?'; Eric Nelson, 'Translation as Correction: Hobbes in the 1660s and 1670s', in Burke and Richter, *Why Concepts Matter*, 109–18 and 119–40.
21. Jörn Leonhard, *Liberalismus: Zur historischen Semantik eines europäisches Deutungsmusters* (Munich: Oldenbourg, 2001); Jörn Leonhard, 'Von der Wortimitation zur semantischen Integration. Übersetzung als Kulturtransfer', *Werkstatt Geschichte* 48 (2008), 45–63; Jörn Leonhard, 'Translation as Cultural Transfer and Semantic Interaction: European Variations of Liberal between 1800 and 1900', in Burke and Richter, *Why Concepts Matter*, 93–108.
22. Jens Borchert, 'From Politik als Beruf to Politics as a Vocation: The Translation, Transformation and Reception of Max Weber's Lecture', *Contributions to the History of Concepts* 3(1) (2007), 42–70; Keith Tribe, 'Translating Weber', in Burke and Richter, *Why Concepts Matter*, 207–33.
23. Abdelmajid Hannoum, 'Translation and the Colonial Imagery: Ibn Khaldûn Orientalist', *History and Theory* 42(1) (2003), 61–81.
24. Richter, 'Introduction', 23, characterizing the import of the contributions of Douglas Howland and Joachim Kurtz in Burke and Richter, *Why Concepts Matter*. Cf. Howland, 'Predicament of Ideas in Culture', 45–60.
25. Douglas Howland, *Translating the West: Language and Political Reason in Nineteenth-Century Japan* (Honolulu: University of Hawai'i Press, 2002); Douglas Howland, *Personal Liberty and the Public Good: The Introduction of John Stuart Mill to China and Japan* (Toronto: Toronto University Press, 2005); Douglas Howland, 'The Public Limits of Liberty: Nakamura Keiu's Translation of J.S. Mill', in Burke and Richter, *Why Concepts Matter*, 153–76; Joachim Kurtz, 'Translating the Vocation of Man: Liang Qichao (1873–1929), J.G. Fichte, and the Body Politic in Early Republican China', in Burke and Richter, *Why Concepts Matter*, 177–92. See also Douglas Howland, 'International Law in East Asia: The Concept and Practice of Japanese Neutrality in 1870', in Coleman and Kitromilides, *Footsteps of Herodotus*, 167–80.
26. Sophus A. Reinert, *Translating Empire: Emulation and the Origins of Political Economy* (Cambridge, MA: Harvard University Press, 2011). Cf. Istvan Hont,

Jealousy of Trade: International Competition and the Nation-State in Historical Context (Cambridge, MA: Harvard University Press, 2005).
27. See László Kontler, *Translations, Histories, Enlightenments: William Robertson in Germany, 1760–1795* (Houndmills, Basingstoke: Palgrave MacMillan, 2014).
28. Available at http://ieg-ego.eu/en/ego.

References

Baár, Mónika, 'From General History to National History: The Transformations of William Guthrie's and John Gray's *A General History of the World* (1736–1765) in Continental Europe', in Stefanie Stockhorst (ed.), *Cultural Transfer through Translation: The Circulation of Enlightened Thought in Europe through Translation* (Amsterdam and New York: Rodopi, 2010), 63–82

Baldwin, Geoffrey P., 'The Translation of Political Theory in Early Modern Europe', in Peter Burke and Ronnie Po-Chia Hsia (eds), *Cultural Translation in Early Modern Europe* (Cambridge: Cambridge University Press, 2007), 101–24

Berlin, Isaiah, 'Hume and the Sources of German Anti-Rationalism', in Isaiah Berlin, *Against the Current: Essays in the History of Ideas* (Oxford: Clarendon Press, 1981), 162–87

Berman, Antoine, *L'Épreuve de l'étranger: Culture et traduction dans l'Allemagne romantique* (Paris: Gallimard, 1984)

Bödeker, Hans Erich, 'Concept – Meaning – Discourse. *Begriffsgeschichte* Reconsidered', in Iain Hampsher-Monk, Karin Tilmans and Frank van Vree (eds), *History of Concepts: Comparative Perspectives* (Amsterdam: Amsterdam University Press, 1998), 51–64

Borchert, Jens, 'From Politik als Beruf to Politics as a Vocation: The Translation, Transformation and Reception of Max Weber's Lecture', *Contributions to the History of Concepts* 3(1) (2007), 42–70

Burke, Peter, *The Fortunes of the Courtier: The European Reception of Castiglione's Cortegiano* (Philadelphia: Pennsylvania State University Press, 1995)

———, 'Cultures of Translation in Early Modern Europe', in Peter Burke and Ronnie Po-Chia Hsia (eds), *Cultural Translation in Early Modern Europe* (Cambridge: Cambridge University Press, 2007)

———, 'Translating Histories', in Peter Burke and Ronnie Po-Chia Hsia (eds), *Cultural Translation in Early Modern Europe* (Cambridge: Cambridge University Press, 2007), 125–41

Delisle, Jean, and Judith Woodsworth (eds), *Translators through History* (Amsterdam: John Benjamin's Publishing Company, 1995)

Evans-Pritchard, E.E., *Social Anthropology* (London: Cohen & West, 1951)

Gal, Susan, 'Politics of Translation', *Annual Review of Anthropology* 44 (2015), 225–40.

Geertz, Clifford, *The Interpretation of Cultures* (London: Harper Collins, 1973)

Gottmann, Felicia, 'Du Châtelet, Voltaire, and the Transformation of Mandeville's Fable', *History of European Ideas* 38(2) (2012), 218–32

Graeber, Wilhelm, and Geneviève Roche, *Englische Literatur des 17. und 18. Jahrhunderts in französischer Übersetzung und deutscher Weiterübersetzung: Eine kommentierte Bibliographie* (Tübingen: Niemeyer, 1988)

Hannoum, Abdelmajid, 'Translation and the Colonial Imagery: Ibn Khaldûn Orientalist', *History and Theory* 42(1) (2003), 61–81

Hermans, Theo (ed.), *The Manipulation of Literature: Studies in Literary Translation* (Beckenham: Coom Helm, 1985)

Hont, Istvan, *Jealousy of Trade: International Competition and the Nation-State in Historical Context* (Cambridge, MA: Harvard University Press, 2005)

Howland, Douglas, *Translating the West: Language and Political Reason in Nineteenth-Century Japan* (Honolulu: University of Hawai'i Press, 2002)

———, 'The Predicament of Ideas in Culture: Translation and Historiography', *History and Theory* 42 (2003), 45–60

———, *Personal Liberty and the Public Good: The Introduction of John Stuart Mill to China and Japan* (Toronto: Toronto University Press, 2005)

———, 'International Law in East Asia: The Concept and Practice of Japanese Neutrality in 1870', in Janet Coleman and Paschalis Kitromilides (eds), *In the Footsteps of Herodotus: Towards European Political Thought* (Florence: Olschki, 2012), 167–80

———, 'The Public Limits of Liberty: Nakamura Keiu's Translation of J.S. Mill', in Martin J. Burke and Melvin Richter (eds), *Why Concepts Matter: Translating Social and Political Thought* (Leiden and Boston: Brill, 2012), 153–76

Kontler, László, 'Translation and Comparison: Early-Modern and Current Perspectives', *Contributions to the History of Concepts* 3(1) (2007), 71–102

———, 'Translation and Comparison II: A Methodological Inquiry into Reception in the History of Ideas', *Contributions to the History of Concepts* 4(1) (2008), 27–56

———, *Translations, Histories, Enlightenments: William Robertson in Germany, 1760–1795* (Houndmills, Basingstoke: Palgrave MacMillan, 2014)

Koselleck, Reinhart, 'Einleitung', in Otto Brunner, Werner Conze and Reinhart Koselleck (eds), *Geschichtliche Grundbegriffe: Historisches Lexikon zur politisch-sozialen Sprache in Deutschland*, vol. 1 (Stuttgart: Klett-Cotta, 1972), xiii–xxvii

Kurtz, Joachim, 'Translating the Vocation of Man: Liang Qichao (1873–1929), J.G. Fichte, and the Body Politic in Early Republican China', in Martin J. Burke and Melvin Richter (eds), *Why Concepts Matter: Translating Social and Political Thought* (Leiden and Boston: Brill, 2012), 177–92

Leach, Edmund, *Social Anthropology* (Glasgow: Fontana, 1982)

Leonhard, Jörn, *Liberalismus. Zur historischen Semantik eines europäisches Deutungsmusters* (Munich: Oldenbourg, 2001)

———, 'Von der Wortimitation zur semantischen Integration: Übersetzung als Kulturtransfer', *Werkstatt Geschichte* 48 (2008), 45–63

———, 'Translation as Cultural Transfer and Semantic Interaction: European Variations of Liberal between 1800 and 1900', in Martin J. Burke and Melvin Richter (eds), *Why Concepts Matter: Translating Social and Political Thought* (Leiden and Boston: Brill, 2012), 93–108

Liu, Lydia H., 'Introduction', in Lydia H. Liu (ed.), *Tokens of Exchange: The Problem of Translation in Global Circulations* (Durham, NC: Duke University Press, 1999)

Nelson, Eric, 'Translation as Correction: Hobbes in the 1660s and 1670s', in Martin J. Burke and Melvin Richter (eds), *Why Concepts Matter: Translating Social and Political Thought* (Leiden and Boston: Brill, 2012), 119–40

Oz-Salzberger, Fania, *Translating the Enlightenment: Scottish Civic Discourse in Eighteenth-Century Germany* (Oxford: Clarendon Press, 1995)

Pym, Anthony, *Negotiating the Frontier: Translators and Intercultures in Hispanic History* (Manchester: St Jerome Publishing, 2000)

Reinert, Sophus A., *Translating Empire: Emulation and the Origins of Political Economy* (Cambridge, MA: Harvard University Press, 2011)

Richter, Melvin, 'Introduction: Translation, the History of Concepts and the History of Political Thought', in Martin J. Burke and Melvin Richter (eds), *Why Concepts Matter: Translating Social and Political Thought* (Leiden and Boston: Brill, 2012), 1–40

Saunders, David, 'The Natural Jurisprudence of Jean Barbeyrac: Translation as an Act of Political Adjustment', *Eighteenth-Century Studies* 36(4) (2003), 473–90

Saunders, David, and Ian Hunter, 'Bringing the State to England: Andrew Tooke's Translation of Samuel Pufendorf's De Officio Hominis et Civis', *History of Political Thought* 24(2) (2003), 218–34

Skinner, Quentin, 'The Rise of, Challenge to and Prospects for a Collingwoodian Approach to the History of Political Thought', in Dario Castiglione and Iain Hampsher-Monk (eds), *The History of Political Thought in National Context* (Cambridge: Cambridge University Press, 2001), 175–88

Stockhorst, Stefanie, 'Introduction. Cultural Transfer through Translation: A Current Perspective in Enlightenment Studies', in Stefanie Stockhorst (ed.), *Cultural Transfer through Translation: The Circulation of Enlightened Thought in Europe through Translation* (Amsterdam and New York: Rodopi, 2010), 7–28

Tribe, Keith, 'Translating Weber', in Martin J. Burke and Melvin Richter (eds), *Why Concepts Matter: Translating Social and Political Thought* (Leiden and Boston: Brill, 2012), 207–33

Turchetti, Mario, 'Bodin as Self-Translator of his République: Why the Omission of "*Politicus*" and Allied Terms in the Latin Version?', in Martin J. Burke and Melvin Richter (eds), *Why Concepts Matter: Translating Social and Political Thought* (Leiden and Boston: Brill, 2012), 109–18

Venuti, Lawrence, *The Translator's Invisibility: A History of Translation* (London and New York: Routledge, 1995)

Vincze, Hanna Orsolya, 'The Fortunes of Basilikon Doron', in Janet Coleman and Paschalis Kitromilides (eds), *In the Footsteps of Herodotus: Towards European Political Thought* (Florence: Olschki, 2012), 77–92

———, *The Politics of Translation and Transmission: Basilikon Doron in Hungarian Political Thought* (Cambridge: Cambridge Scholars Press, 2012)

Waszek, Norbert, *The Scottish Enlightenment and Hegel's Account of 'Civil Society'* (Dordrecht: Kluwer Academic Publishers, 1988)

Chapter 8

Conceptualizing Spaces within Europe

The Case of Meso-Regions

Diana Mishkova and Balázs Trencsényi

Conceptual History and the 'Spatial Turn'

The task of creating a European historical culture in line with the European unification project during the last three decades has revealed a number of branches of historiography with an intrinsic potential of transcending the national frameworks of reference. Among these the growing research interest in supranational and sub-national regional frameworks as structuring historical experience was definitely one of the most important venues of innovation.[1] Similarly, the efforts of making a non-nationally based conceptual history, which have been intensified during the last decade, also meant a breakthrough in a branch of historiography that has traditionally been more nation-centred due to its concern with particular national languages. However, there has been much less research linking these two aspects – in other words, turning the analytical toolkit of conceptual history towards the regional notions, and in general towards the problems of symbolic geography. Consequently, our aim in this chapter is to assess the potential benefits of such a match and bring in the methodological and thematic innovation of the 'spatial turn' to the discussion on a trans-European conceptual history.

Along these lines, our aim is to offer an overview of the most important aspects of a possible conceptual history approach to regional terminologies, taking as a point of reference the regions of our primary expertise, namely Central and South Eastern Europe. Rather than being accidental, the focus on these two regional clusters is also due to the particular importance of regional frameworks of reference in the historical cultures of this part of

Europe. Indeed, the relevance of supranational 'meso-regions' in modern Western Europe was relativized, respectively, by the principle of territorial nation-statehood and the European project of unification. Consequently, academic research into transnational meso-regions in Western and Southern Europe has traditionally been stronger for the medieval and early modern periods, while that devoted to 'Iberia', for example, has remained inconsequential. On the other hand, the political relevance of regions in Eastern (but also Northern) Europe, where the nation-state framework was less consolidated and went through a profound reconfiguration in the nineteenth and twentieth centuries, is obvious. It is enough to mention that Norway, Finland, Iceland, Poland, Ukraine, Estonia, Latvia, Lithuania, Czechoslovakia and its successor states, Yugoslavia and its successor states, Bulgaria, Hungary, Romania and Albania all emerged as new states – even if this was often legitimized in terms of the 'recovery' of their erstwhile independence – in the period between 1859 and 1945. What is more, many of these states also disappeared for some time. Consequently, notions of regions and the debates about them remained central to cultural and political discourse. One might even argue that Central and South Eastern Europe are the most paradigmatic and salient European examples of the conceptualization of 'historical regions'.[2]

Other incentives of regionalization transcend the logic of historical inquiry and have originated with the assertive 'spatial turn' in neighbouring disciplinary fields. While theorists of history, among others, have contributed to it by fleshing out the notion of 'mental mapping', it was geographers, anthropologists and economists who undercut the 'container' and 'natural-scientific' concept of space, emphasizing instead the social production of spatial frameworks.[3] Rather than assuming that space exists independently of humans and that historical processes unfold within it as in a closed vessel, and are even predetermined by it, present-day theorists conceive of it as the product of human agency and perception, as both the medium and presupposition for sociability and historicity. The politics and sociology of space and critical geopolitics are usually concerned with fabrication, appropriation and enclosure as empowering practices of ordering and control, of inclusion and exclusion. Crucial to this understanding of space (and borders for that matter) is not so much its material morphology, but the premises of its social production and the ideological underpinnings of its production, as well as the various forms of interpretation and representation that it embodies. This brings to the forefront research questions dealing not only with the active modelling of physical space, but with the norms guiding the structuring of space, the social practices associated with it, and its perception and symbolic codification by humans.[4]

At this overarching theoretical level the concept of region may usefully be approached through a counter-concept – that of territoriality denoting 'space with a border that allows effective control of public and political life', and where effectiveness means 'the exclusion of alternative claims on political or economic or sometimes even cultural outcomes'.[5] Region in this sense appears as the (subversive) 'other' to state sovereignty. These considerations lead to questions concerning the premises and understanding of regions with regard to two historical periods: first, the era of sovereign statehood and nationality as a recognized norm, and second, the more recent situation of undermined nation-state power, (re-)emergence of old or new territorialities (hence insider–outsider definitions) and spatially related identities.

All of this brings out the issue of sub-national regions vis-à-vis supranational ones. Basically, even though their existence has been anchored in more substantial institutional practices than that of meso-regions, Silesia, Dalmatia, Transylvania, Banat, Vojvodina and Bukovina are historical regions in many ways comparable to Central, Northern or South Eastern Europe: both of these categories are historically and spatially contingent – and in this sense 'contextual' – social constructs; both encapsulate the spatial transformation of Europe in history and help us to avoid anachronistic deductions from contemporary political-territorial organizations. Nonetheless, our focus on the latter group has some commonsensical historical and methodological grounds. All the above sub- or transnational regions were eventually nationalized. The pre-existent tension between territoriality (or politically institutionalized space) and national/cultural identity was largely eliminated, while the potential for their continued existence failed to materialize institutionally as territorial entities with 'specific structures of expectations which are constantly being reproduced by social institutions'.[6]

As everywhere in Europe, moreover, the above-mentioned sub-national historical regions had their roots in medieval or early modern times and predated the establishment of the territorial nation state. Supranational regions, on the other hand, emerged simultaneously with and evolved parallel to the rise of the nation state as the European norm. An improved conceptual apparatus is needed to make sense of the implications of this historical convergence and of the complex and varied patterns of spatiality production beyond territorially demarcated and institutionally integrated political entities, where decision space and identity space do not typically overlap.[7] Finally, the so-called 'Europe of regions' and the 'new regionalism' on a sub-national scale have in the last few decades received far more attention both by policy makers and researchers than has its supranational counterpart.[8]

It is important to stress that the counterposition of supranational meso-regions and sub-national micro-regions is much less unambiguous than it might at first seem. In many cases the very same notion could function under both headings, depending on the social, cultural and political context. A case in point is the Baltic region, which in the self-references of the Baltic Germans in the nineteenth century was functioning as a sub-national notion with respect to the German framework, but could also function (in the interwar period) as a transnational framework for the three new nation states; while from the Russian imperial perspective and also during the Soviet years the Baltic region was a sub-imperial micro-region, however with a supra-ethnic referential function.[9]

Normative political and cultural presumptions have been spurring regions on ever since antiquity: the original division of Europe into a 'civilized' South and a 'barbaric' North was later substituted by an equally moralistic East–West divide; nowadays, propelled by the economic crisis, the former division but with the opposite signs is tacitly, and not so tacitly, resurfacing (see the pejorative but broadly used notion of 'PIGS' – referring to Portugal, Italy, Greece and Spain). Religious divides (Catholic Latin, Protestant Germanic and Orthodox Greco-Slavic), often underscored by racial ones, have been similarly powerful engines of 'cultural-spiritual' regionalizations. The great turning time in the spatialization of historical experience, however, coincided with the advent of the era of high modernity, and found its original form in the post-Enlightenment logic of organizing knowledge along civilizational dividing lines. Temporal terms such as 'development', 'progress', 'conservatism', 'stagnation' and 'delay' acquired spatial embeddedness, and spatial terms such as 'the East', 'the West', 'the North', 'the South', as well as 'centre', 'periphery', 'borderlands', or just 'the lands beyond', became historical terms. It was this peculiar merger of cultural-historical and spatial imaginations that inspired a new, symbolic map of Europe, whose taxonomic (and hierarchically graded) units cut across the administrative boundaries of empires and nation states, and the cultural ones of religion.

With the growing interest in the conceptual underpinning of these symbolic geographies it has become clear that some of the most important work on the history of certain geographical concepts, such as the Balkans, Eurasia and *Norden*, even if they are not necessarily framed in terms of conceptual history per se, actually deal with practices of conceptualization of regions.[10] Non-territorial regions, such as the Slavic or German worlds, had also framed their own spaces, as linguistic and cultural continuums, and impacted on the conceptualization of territorial regions (e.g. *Mitteleuropa* or Eastern Europe).

There are, of course, many different mechanisms of spatialization. An obvious one is the conception of national and supranational (imperial) cultural-political entities, where the spatial aspect is intertwined with other (historical, cultural, institutional) concepts. Specific branches of spatializing

Europe related to regionalization (with macro-, meso-, and micro- versions) bring in various conceptualizations. One is that of territorial versus non-territorial (e.g. 'spiritual-cultural', metaphoric) regions and borders; a second refers to alternative spatial concepts to the national space (for example, federalist or pan-ideologies); a third to the conceptualization of delimitations (discourses about where a given region 'ends', or the metaphors of in-betweenness); and a fourth to the discourses of othering through spatialization (Orientalism, Occidentalism, Balkanism, etc.). Needless to say, these aspects all have a different logic and are subject to different research traditions. Reviewing the historiographical developments in all these fields would exceed the scope of a single chapter. Therefore, our intention is to focus on mechanisms of conceptualizing regions while placing them into the broader framework mentioned above. In this context we have to take into account the close relationship between regional, imperial, and national conceptualizations, since many nineteenth- and twentieth-century nation-building projects framed themselves as imperial or federalist ones (such as Russia and Germany) and hence comprised several regions. Conversely, some larger regions (such as Iberia and the Benelux) are understood as being composed of several nations.

On the whole, conceptual history as a branch of research has focused more on temporalization than spatialization. This explains why there is very limited presence of spatial categories in the flagship of conceptual history, the *Geschichtliche Grundbegriffe*. Reinhart Koselleck himself conceded that 'the overwhelming majority of all historians, when confronted with the alternative of space or time, have opted for a theoretical dominance of time'; thereby the term 'space' has remained under-historicized and under-theorized in the general theories of history.[11] This is true even if Koselleck's analysis of asymmetric counter-concepts – where the relationship of the civilized and the barbarian is spatialized – provided a possibility for engaging with the problem of spatial concepts.

In the context of the transnationalization of conceptual history characterizing the last two decades, the notions of space became much more central, both because concepts themselves came to be seen as rooted in spatial frameworks and because transnational transfers have, by default, a spatial dimension. Indeed, comparative conceptual history is inconceivable outside spatial frameworks. At the same time, there still seems to be far less attention paid to these types of notion when compared to the more traditional keywords of politics, such as 'democracy', 'tyranny', 'liberalism', 'civilization', 'citizen', 'fatherland' and 'nation': as a matter of fact, even the conceptual history of the use of 'Europe' and 'European' is rather understudied.[12] In methodological terms, a fruitful venue for this type of study seems to be offered by Hans-Jürgen Lüsebrink and Rolf Reichardt, whose analysis of the symbolic discourse around the Bastille with the toolkit of conceptual history faced similar challenges to the one posed by the study of historical regions, namely the use of a notion linked to a particular topological coordinate in different connotations going well beyond its original and intended context.[13] However, the differences are also obvious as, in contrast to the Bastille, which is more of a disjointed point in space that can be symbolically 'transposed' to other spatial coordinates, the central feature of regional concepts is that they contain within themselves other regional concepts and relations.

While it is hard to point to 'conventional' conceptual histories of regional notions, there are many works that approach the question of construction of regions and offer reconstructions of the conceptual evolution of regionalization. A case in point is Larry Wolff's *Inventing Eastern Europe*, which aimed at localizing the emergence of a new terminology spacing Europe not along the classical North–South axis but rather the East–West one.[14] One can find similar considerations in Iver Neumann's *Uses of the Other* with reference to the politicization of Eastern Europe in the complex interrelationship of Russia and Western Europe throughout the last two centuries.[15] Beyond these obvious examples, one can in fact find a plethora of 'pre-paradigmatic' works mapping the conceptualization of certain European meso-regions, not so much in systematic conceptual history terms but nonetheless registering conceptual shifts, tracing genealogies, and pointing at conceptual clusters.[16] Indeed, from the interwar period onwards, as regional historical narratives became entrenched in most of East and South East European professional historical cultures as well as public discourses, there were considerable efforts at self-documentation and self-canonization (i.e. mapping previous usages of these regional terminologies). This is eminently the case with Balkan studies, and also with the discussion around Central and Eastern Europe, which had a visible upsurge in the 1930s with certain repercussions also in the postwar period.[17]

On the whole, while there are some important examples of applying the toolkit of conceptual history to regional notions, it is clear that a more systematic approach is still to be developed. The potential benefits are clear: spatial categories have a historicity which is not apparent, as their users tend to 'naturalize' them. In this sense the conceptual historical perspective can relativize these notions and open them up for a more reflective historical usage. Becoming aware of the historical contingency of spatial terminology also contributes to the questioning of the underlying assumptions of national historical cultures based on the 'naturalness' of space and the artificiality of time. Regions thus do not emerge as objectified and disjointed units functioning as quasi-national entities with fixed boundaries and clear-cut lines between insiders and outsiders, but rather as flexible and historically changing frameworks for interpreting certain phenomena.

Seeking to substantiate these claims, our chapter will focus first on the objects of study (i.e. different conceptualizations of meso-regions) and second on the potential ways to analyse them. This means applying the key insights of conceptual history to this kind of material, such as the hypothesis of the *Sattelzeit* or the notion of asymmetric counter-concepts, and also looking at the different contexts in which conceptualizations take place, for instance different disciplines.

The Production of Regionalizing Discourses

Obviously, regional categories are far from being stable, and various intellectual and political projects have devised different, partially overlapping, regional frameworks. The geographical coverage of concepts like Central Europe/*Mitteleuropa*, Eastern Europe/*Osteuropa*, East Central Europe/*Ostmitteleuropa*, South Eastern Europe/*Südosteuropa*, the Balkans, the Carpatho-Danubian space and so on changed dramatically over time, and these notions often designated parallel scholarly ventures stemming from various political, academic and disciplinary subcultures. Different generations and national traditions added to this diversity as they framed these geographical entities in markedly different ways, and the ideological implications contained in concepts of geographical entities could also differ greatly.

While, for instance, Central Europe was often equated in Czech and Hungarian historiography with the territories of the former Habsburg Monarchy, this obviously does not fit the historical tradition of the Poles, who often identified it straightforwardly with the lands of the Polish-Lithuanian Commonwealth and the adjacent territories. In turn, a more encompassing narrative can include in Central Europe the three nations with medieval state-traditions (Poland, Bohemia and Hungary), or extend its grasp to all the countries 'between Germany and Russia'. The national connotations of the terms Balkans and South Eastern Europe reveal palpable normative differences: while for the Bulgarians they are more or less overlapping and auto-descriptive terms, for the Romanians they form rather a conflicting conceptual couple where the Balkans is the negative and South Eastern Europe the positive reference; for the Catholic South-Slavs (Croats and Slovenes) the Balkans is primarily a term of othering used to counter-identify themselves, and South Eastern Europe is a notion applied in certain contexts as a metaterm including also Central Europe.

The plurality of the meanings of these regional notions is due not only to the cultural multiplicity of users but also to the variety of perspectives of regionalization. The main sources of conceptualization, which, for analytical purposes, can be isolated, are academic circles, policy makers and expert communities, international organizations (e.g. UN, EU), and the media (as regards the visualization of spatial concepts). To a certain extent, their conceptualizations converge but they are also marked by specific dynamics. Thus, after the 2004–7 accession phase, the term 'Western Balkans' became salient in international relations as a security-related and, to some extent, financial-administrative concept in the vocabulary of international and EU policy, but one with no foot in the humanities and very limited use in local public discourse. As already indicated, moreover, it is important to contextualize conceptualizations in terms of generations, academic subcultures (and institutions), as well as disciplinary traditions.

While political and economic agendas have often instigated spatial constructions and underpinned the institutionalization of regional studies, scholarly regional conceptualizations typically legitimize public or political discourses. What later was named 'the Balkans' or 'South Eastern Europe' was originally known as 'Turkey-in-Europe' or 'European Turkey' – a political term associated not so much with a fixed territory as with the geopolitical implications of the so-called 'Eastern Question'. The geographical terms of the Balkans and South Eastern Europe as well as of Central Europe emerged in the first half of the nineteenth century and were the products of the upsurge of 'scientific geography' and the search for 'natural' geographic boundaries; they soon 'migrated' to, and in turn became informed by, other disciplinary fields: ethnography, linguistics, literature, history. By the end of the nineteenth century, however, all these scholarly concepts had been imbued with strong political meanings, especially in their external usage, usually assimilating previous geopolitical connotations while adding new ones associated with the great European states' growing economic and political interest in these areas. The politicization of regional terminology within the regions themselves, on the other hand, followed a different logic, partly responding to the geopolitical challenge of the 'big powers' but mostly providing a frame for various nationalist or federalist strategies.

The interference of politics with scholarship might seem a foregone conclusion at first sight: academic regionalizations become, as a rule, politicized, and many 'scientific classifications' serve to promote, tacitly or bluntly, political agendas. *Mitteleuropa* was not just the German translation of Central Europe; it included the Balkans and was co-extensive with the German sphere of interest. The Polish historian Oskar Halecki's 'Divisions of European History' can only be understood in terms of the Cold War partition, as can the 'disappearance' of Turkey and Greece from the map of South Eastern Europe at about the same time, much like Central,

Eastern and South Eastern Europe are vanishing from present-day political vocabulary. Pan-Germanism, pan-Slavism and pan-Scandinavianism, even though they had a divergent logic and dynamism, may serve as another set of eloquent examples in a double sense: firstly, as supranational political concepts underwritten by heavy investments in their intellectual substantiation in the face of overpowering nation-state legitimism; and, secondly, as throwing into full relief these concepts' inherently relational, mutually conditioned 'meanings', which would be inconceivable if isolated from one another.

The politicization of scholarly regional concepts results not only from (external or domestic) political pressure and international alignments. Another source is the recurrent fusion of regionalist and nationalist designs that might be played out in the fields of politics, economy or culture. Indeed, there is no clear-cut difference, but a complex relationship, between the conceptualizations of the national and the regional. Nationalist arguments may be adduced to buttress – and give meaning to – a regionalist framework, and the identification of a supranational region may serve to bolster a nationalist project. For instance, while conceptualizing the Balkan Peninsula as an area of great intraregional diversity, the Serbian anthropogeographer Jovan Cvijić saw the Serbs as destined, by virtue of their strategic geopolitical location and ethno-psychological qualities, to form the region's internal 'centre', which would unify the major part of this area and reverse the centrifugal tendencies resulting from its diversity.[18] The prominent Romanian historian Nicolae Iorga was the first to envisage South Eastern Europe (and not the Balkans) as an integral civilizational space, marked by common history, culture and institutions that served as the necessary context and a mediating zone for incorporating the Romanians in world history.[19] Even the methodologically highly sophisticated regionalist school of 'Balkanology' of the 1930s did not shy away from occasionally employing quasi-academic and metahistorical arguments to underwrite a notion of 'Balkanism' closely replicating national autochthonism.[20] Similarly, the Danubian discourse forming part of the broader Central European framework was rarely used to include all countries geographically linked to the river, but functioned more as a concentric notion, always defining some parts of the territory as more central than others, usually focusing on Vienna and Budapest. The crisscrossing of the regional and the national could occur in different settings. Thus certain nationally framed policies had the effect of outlining regions as the valid frame: for instance due to its comparative logic and tendency to organize data in terms of regional subsets, national economics in the late nineteenth century, which functioned as a 'national science', contributed to the remapping of Europe in terms of regions.

It is important to note, however, that even if scholarly argumentation and political objectives often intermingle and feed on each other – politicians selectively picking up on academic arguments, and scholars cladding their political projects in objective knowledge – this does not mean that public and scholarly regionalist discourses and concepts necessarily overlap. Politicians and the media, on the one hand, and academics, on the other, often operate with the same regionalist terminology, but their semantics are rarely identical. As a cultural-historical concept South Eastern Europe emerged right at the time of burgeoning militant nationalism, which culminated with the Balkan Wars and the First World War, and derived both political sobriety and intellectual appeal from an attempt to counteract the visions of endemic conflictuality and nationalist excesses, which were informing the public, predominantly Western, notion of the region. The great intellectual investment in the study of the Balkan's historical-cultural unity and the revaluation of its civilizational legacy in the interwar period, even if inspired by the conclusion of the Balkan Pact (1934), carried a message that potentially went much further than the politicians at the time would have deemed it 'realistic' to follow.

During the last phase of the Second World War and in the immediate postwar years, the discussion around federalism generated a new kind of regionalist approach seeking to eliminate or at least reduce nationalist contestation by creating a truly transnational expertise. This can be seen in the studies published by the Budapest-based *Revue d'Histoire Comparée*, which fused a genuine regional comparativist agenda with an attempt to present the Hungarian perspective on the nationality problem in the region. Similar attempts were discernible in the Czech scholar Josef Macůrek's history of East European historiography,[21] which treated the various nation-building historical traditions in a synoptic vision, and in the study of Balkan federalism by the Bulgarian historian, Ivan P. Ormandzhiev.[22] In our own days the (politically driven) regionalism of the EU draws on a completely different set of 'structural similarities' from that employed by historians, ethnographers, social and even political scientists. We should also bear in mind that identical regional terms, though involving different representations of the regional 'specifics', could stand for diametrically opposed value systems: conservative (or autochthonist), national-liberal, Marxist, social-constructivist, and others. Once again the Balkans serves as a perfect example in this respect: it could be envisaged as the driver of an alternative, anti-European value system, or be referred to as the root of European civilization; it could signify a younger Europe that would resuscitate the old one, or a stigmatizing notion denoting deficiency in civilizational terms, to be overcome by consistent efforts at Europeanization.

Political and scholarly regionalizations, in brief, interact and amalgamate in many ways and on different levels, but this interaction is not tantamount to complete conformity (or opportunism/mimicry on the part of academia), nor should it blind us to the inherent politics of the scholarly concepts themselves.

Conceptualizations emerging inside and outside of the regions in question – what we call here 'internal' and 'external' regionalizations – interact in similarly intricate ways, while the outcome rarely signifies a 'clean victory' for either. Not surprisingly, the original conceptions of the 'Balkan Peninsula', 'South Eastern Europe', 'Central Europe', and the 'Mediterranean region' as geographical notions were of external, mostly German, origin. By the end of the nineteenth century these terms were stabilized as well as 'Orientalized' as political concepts in popular Western parlance. Scholarly paradigms, like the influential *Südostforschung* in the interwar period, on the other hand, came up with regional definitions that neither neatly converged within the frames of the 'discipline' – as economic, socio-structural, ethno-demographic, political and other sub-disciplines carved different South East European geographies – nor were their incentives and implications invariably political. While many German regional 'experts' conceived of interwar South Eastern Europe as a supplementing space for the German Reich in relation to the new term of *Mitteleuropa* or *Zwischeneuropa*, for others it was a 'working concept' (*Arbeitsbegriff*), sensitive to the variability of boundaries in time and space and to historical change.

Local regionalizations to some extent mirrored, but did not replicate, the external ones. As intra-regional and extra-regional (geo)political agendas diverged considerably, so did the justification and vocabulary of regionality. In fact, the force with which regions in the eastern part of Europe were argued for during the interwar period drew on a palpable anti-hegemonic thrust and aimed at counteracting or preventing 'extra-regional' geopolitical reconfigurations. The newly emerged Balkanology of the 1930s, without openly taking issue with the encompassing German concept of South Eastern Europe from Slovakia to Turkey, came up with its own value-grounded spatial frame by promoting the notion of the 'Balkans for the Balkan people'. All in all, powerful as the post-Enlightenment 'Western discourse' (or rather different national Western discourses) of the east and south-east of Europe had been, it should be emphasized that it was neither the sole nor, at all time, the dominant 'agent' of regionalization. There are thus parallel, Western and local, external and internal processes of conceptualization that are not necessarily connected or commensurate.

Émigré communities and centres have often acted either as a bridge between external and internal regionalizations or as an autonomous regionalizing agent. The most spectacular case in point is the work of Halecki, whose works – especially his *Borderlands of Western Civilization*, going back to the interwar debates but reshaped after 1945 in the context of the Cold War – put East Central Europe back on the map as a historical region.[23] Post-Second World War West European and especially American Balkanistics (often produced by scholars with roots in the region, such as Leften Stavrianos, Charles Jelavich, Trajan Stojanovich, Peter Sugar, Maria Todorova, and many others) were far more important in sustaining the Balkans and South Eastern Europe as a unit of historical analysis than the regional institutes for Balkan or South East European studies, despite the considerable state support they had been receiving since the mid-1960s. Post-1945 émigré Slavists, like František (Francis) Dvornik, also offered alternative regional narratives: in his synthetic *The Slavs in Europe* he saw Eastern Europe as defined in the broader regional context of common Slavic political history, civilization, national character, and language.[24] Furthermore, the Russian emigration based in East Central Europe mediated the various 'vintage points' in a more complex way: in the interwar period the Russian émigrés acted as go-betweens the external and the internal ones, often assuming important positions in Eastern European academic centres; after 1945, when most of them moved to the West, they often brought together different external academic traditions (Russian and West European or American) and an internal one (emanating from Prague, Sofia, Belgrade, etc.)

As our survey shows, there has been in the past as well as at present no obvious or unanimous answer to the question of the scholarly definition of regions. The question ultimately boils down to identifying, or rather proposing, what might provide an underlying, or overarching, coherence to the political, religious and linguistic diversity characterizing these areas. Theoretically the answers can be subsumed under two main, often connected, types of analytical ('heuristic', 'academic') conceptualization: one looking at the region as an arena of interaction, of centuries of contact, conflict and coexistence – in brief, of shared history and legacies; the other emphasizing similarities in long-term social (and sociopolitical) practices and processes – property, household and family organization, cultural patterns, state formation, economic growth, social-class profile, and so on. At an empirical level, though, different disciplines and scientific criteria tend to provide different, often discordant, conceptualizations. Even within a single discipline, such as history, sub-disciplinary domains covering military and diplomatic, social and demographic, cultural and intellectual, economic or political history would render very different regional 'definitions'. There is thus never a single history, or historical legacy, that historians can reify – one that might be thought to depend on a specific cluster of characteristics that could legitimately serve to construct a region. What we witness instead are different history-based conceptualizations of a region, different 'stories' and ways of conceiving it as a 'unitary space'. Epistemological transformations are inherent to such semantic plurality: most recently, it was the convergence of the constructivist turn in historiography with the cultural turn in geography that created the conditions for questioning the 'naturalness' of regions.

Moreover, different disciplines participated with different force at different points of time in producing regionalities. Up to the turn of the twentieth century, geography and geopolitics were crucial for the emergence of meso-regional sub-divisions in this part of Europe. In the interwar period the notion of 'Central Europe' propagated by historians had a certain politically driven potential to subvert national frameworks of historiography. On the other hand, until the Second World War, linguistics, folklore, literature and ethnography were much more important than 'history proper' for the original crystallization of 'the Balkans' as a historical region. The upsurge of the social sciences and, concomitantly, of divisions based on socio-economic and political models after 1945, to a large extent subsumed the East Central and South East European frameworks under a common East European umbrella, undermining the Central European and Balkan narratives, which re-emerged with the 'cultural turn' of the 1970s.

Finally, certain disciplinary subcultures have also exhibited a concept-building capacity: Byzantine studies have shaped a kind of 'Byzantine Commonwealth' far exceeding the political realm of the former Eastern Roman Empire, while Slavic studies and historical demography have framed the space of 'Slavic Europe'. Slavdom could be extended to cover the whole of Eastern Europe, as is the case with Slavic Studies in the United States in recent decades, which also cover Romanian and Hungarian themes. The genealogy of the concept of historical (meso-)region as such is connected to a debate among Polish, Czech and German historians in the interwar period about the notion of 'Slavs' and 'Slavdom', which then moved on to the historical concept of 'Eastern Europe'. Nationalism studies and development economics also carved their 'own' regions, captured by terms like 'late-state' (or 'small-state') formation and '(semi-)periphery', respectively.

As for the main constitutive elements for constructing regions, one can identify three main clusters: physical and anthropogeographic conditions framing regions as 'natural formations'; structures, institutions and mentalities resulting from history/legacies/culture, which describe regions as cultural-historical spaces; and (geo)political designs and alignments, which frame regions as political concepts. Of course, this is above all an analytical distinction, and often these clusters merge – as is the case with the notion of 'the Balkans', which could be defined in terms of geo-morphological and anthropogeographic features, of imperial (Byzantine and Ottoman) legacies, and as a geopolitical zone of instability.

Clusters, Counter-Concepts and Historical Turning Points

Following Michael Freeden's description of ideologies characterized by central and peripheral notions, regional terms can be analysed as parts of regionalizing discourses, which means that they do not usually occur individually, but form a complex cluster of concepts. This is clear if one looks at, for instance, the extremely complex set of notions around the concepts of the Balkans and South Eastern Europe. For some authors the Balkans is by and large coterminous with South Eastern Europe, while for others the two are to a certain extent in tension. This also depends on the normative connotation lent to the Balkans – for those who do not consider it a stigmatizing notion there is usually a functional equivalence between the two, while for others the two are in competition. Thus, most Romanian historians in the twentieth century tended to avoid the Balkans as pejorative, and placed Romanian history into a 'South East European' framework. At the same time, the German concept of *Südosteuropa* tended to transcend both the Balkans and the vernacular notions of South Eastern Europe, as it practically included all lands lying south-east of Germany, such as Hungary, Slovenia and, in certain cases, even Slovakia.

In a similar way, Central Europe denotes a cluster of concepts that at certain historical moments reinforced each other, while at other moments entered into conflicts, such as *Mitteleuropa*, *Zwischeneuropa*, East Central Europe, the Masarykian 'New Europe', and the 'Other Europe' of the 1970s and 1980s. Tracing the shift of connotations and adjacent concepts over time, as well as the different local usages and cumulative traditions of usage, makes it possible to historicize these regional keywords and point at the wide variety of often conflicting meanings that they assumed.

A key intuition of Koselleckian *Begriffsgeschichte*, not unrelated to Carl Schmitt's intellectual heritage, was the analysis of certain key concepts not only as tools of political contestation (*Kampfbegriffe*) but as intrinsically conflict-ridden (i.e. organizing reality with the help of counter-positions). In general, counter-concepts are crucial in structuring regionalist discourses. This also confirms our intuition about the relational character of concepts: one regional concept is defined vis-à-vis another, not necessarily a counter-concept but often an adjacent one (e.g. Central – South Eastern Europe; Eastern – Central Europe; Baltic – Scandinavia; Levant –Mediterranean). This typically implies, on the one hand, cross-regional conceptualizations, and on the other, certain overlappings or intermediate/contested zones. Such conceptual interrelationships also imply that we need to take into account both internal conceptualizations and external notions, as certain regional concepts – like the West, Eastern Europe, the Balkans – are actually framed more from the outside than from the inside. Here attention is due to the mutual reinforcement or, conversely, the 'mirroring'/counterpoising of such internal and external spatial constructions. It is remarkable that sometimes the same notion can be both: part of the cluster and a counter-concept. As mentioned above, South Eastern Europe in certain periods could function both as a complementary and as a counter-concept to the Balkans.

A central mechanism of regional conceptualizations, as in the case of other spatial categories, is based on the mechanism of inclusion and exclusion. This does not mean that concepts could by default be inclusive or exclusive, but that they have both sides and yield to different discursive/political moves delimiting the political community. A case in point is the use of the Central European ideologeme: while in its best-known version in the dissident subculture of the 1980s it often excluded the Balkans, this exclusion was not inherent to the discourse, and in other historical moments it functioned as a more inclusive concept. What is more, even in the 1970s and 1980s it offered an inclusive and integrative framework for creating a common ground for conflictual national narratives – such as the cultural reconciliation of Czechs and Hungarians; and the project of Transylvanian Romanian intellectuals after 1989 designed to enter a common framework of post-Habsburg Central Europe and thus also recreate a multiethnic narrative of regional identity.

All this presents an opportunity to rethink the framework of the practice of conceptual history. Looking at spatial concepts we can better understand how different layers of discourse are created by different communities of knowledge production; how in different orders of discourse we find different conceptual temporal layers; how transnational conceptualization – transcending discrete linguistic and political communities – operates; and finally, we can obtain a more theoretically informed picture of the way regionalist terminologies are becoming politicized and ideologized. Looking at the temporal horizons of the conceptualization of regions, one can identify a number of momentous conceptual transformations (*Sattelzeiten*). Thus, in the early nineteenth century we find a proto-conceptual stage: notions without consistency, or concepts without the corresponding notion. This stage is followed by the coexistence of older, often external regional notions and a new scientific thrust for 'natural' regions (and boundaries). The late nineteenth century is marked by the stabilization of disciplinary usages and the expansion of geography as a formative scientific paradigm for explaining social phenomena. Regionalist terminology now permeated a wide array of disciplines, and the upsurge of comparativism was working in the same direction. Continuing this expansion, the context of post-First World War geopolitical reorganization, and the interwar period in general, witnessed a veritable boom in regional concepts, while after the Second World War, in the binary framework of the Cold War, one witnesses their considerable reduction. The 1960s through to the 1980s saw once again the recovery of multiple conceptual frameworks of regionality, while the post-1989 years have been marked by a spatial turn accompanied by questioning the premises of spatializing history and conceptualizing space, as well as devising historical regions. A case in point is the debate on the Balkans after 1989, when it became clear that the core of this concept is not so much a certain localizable spatial entity, but rather a mental construct, a chain of metaphors and asymmetric counter-concepts used for defining the self and the other in highly politicized discursive situations.

Conclusion

To sum up, one can assess the benefits of the study of regional concepts in two ways. On the one hand, turning the toolkit of conceptual history towards spatial concepts makes that toolkit itself more reflective and refined. Regionalization is often an underlying but rather neglected factor of conceptualization: a number of key notions that conceptual historians study (such as civilization or backwardness) imply regionalizing mental operations as their subtext – for instance contrasting the 'civilized' West with the 'uncivilized' East of Europe in the eighteenth century, or promoting the notion of *Norden* identified with a communitarian welfare state as contrasted both with the lands of repressive state socialism in Eastern Europe and the more unfettered capitalism of the Anglo-American world. Second, key notions of political discourses have strong regional dimensions. For instance, the extended family model of collective property ownership (i.e. the *zadruga*) became central to the discourse attributing a specific type of social organization to the South Slavs; and agrarianism, which in the interwar period was a transnational ideological framework mainly moderated by East Central European networks of economic experts and politicians, was instrumental in charting a zone of 'peasant nations'.

On the other hand, the usefulness of conceptual history is evident for questioning the seeming naturalness and self-evidence of many regional constructs. Conceptual history 'denaturalizes' apparently stable notions, and situates concepts in (unstable) regional settings. It points at the inherent ambiguities of most geographical notions that usually define their object with regard to a constitutive other, constructing their community by defining it through, as it were, its borderline. All this became extremely important in the context of the destabilization of the nation-state-based framework of legitimization during the last decades of the twentieth century. Such a historical reflection alerts us to the threatening quasi-nationalization of regions, where regions become substitutes for nations. This is visible in the way Europeanness is often constructed in terms of symbolic and actual administrative exclusion, but also in some of the 'Eurosceptic' regional narratives that construct Scandinavia, the Visegrad countries, or the Balkans as homogeneous entities characterized by certain common patterns of mentality, economic culture, and so on. Instead, the use of conceptual history in analysing processes and projects of regionalization involves intra-regional and cross-regional comparisons, and it is exactly this approach that can make explicit the implicit comparisons inherent to most regional discourses.

We also found that studying regional concepts and discourses provides a particularly rich field for analysing both the interplay of different disciplinary perspectives of knowledge production and the relationship of professional and public discourse. Behind the ostensibly rather stable regional conceptualizations there are significant divergences from a disciplinary point of view: geographic divisions, historical regions, cultural areas, economic regions, geopolitical cores and peripheries all generate different borderlines and also different symbolic connections between national entities.

Last but not least, the prevalence of asymmetrical counter-concepts in all frameworks of regionalization seems to be a central factor of historical dynamics. Similar to other keywords pertaining to political discourse, regions are essentially contested and relational terms. This can best be seen if one looks at the notions of Eastern Europe, Central Europe and the Balkans, all of which have evolved in a complex symbolic geographical negotiation with the West, and with what is perceived to be 'further East' to them. All this does not necessarily imply a self-evident eastward 'slope', as in certain historical periods there were also powerful attempts to subvert this implied hierarchy. A case in point is the interwar period which witnessed various attempts, mostly from an anti-modernist position, to subvert the imbalance and recover the agency of the non-Western cultures exploiting the trope of the 'decline of the West'. Similarly, after the Second World War the attempt to frame socialist Eastern Europe as more progressive than the bourgeois market economy of Western Europe pursued the same goal. Employing the toolkit of conceptual history in these cases also brings to the fore one more important feature, namely the entanglement of external and internal definitions, as in certain historical configurations not only was the East constructed by the West, but it was also through the eyes of Eastern Europe that the West was actually framed as a homogenous entity in contrast to the previously competing German, French, British and American conceptualizations.

As for the current and possible future use of regional conceptualizations in certain disciplinary contexts, such as political science, anthropology, art history and urban history, the last two decades have witnessed a growing consensus over the heuristic value of meso-regional units of analysis. Thus, we can expect to see more studies of Central European cities, South East European socio-cultural patterns or Nordic modernism. At the same time, it has also become clear for most practitioners that rather than being permanent and neatly separable entities, regional frameworks are models of reality that should not be essentialized. Thus, there is a possibility of arranging the same national entity into different spatial frameworks accentuating multiple identities and multilevel interaction. What is more, with the emergence of the European project encompassing also a considerable part of East Central Europe, and the increasing thrust of globalization, it has become possible to create comparative frameworks that go well beyond the scale of meso-regions. For instance, it is now feasible to compare Portuguese and Spanish post-dictatorship consolidation with the post-communist developments in Eastern Europe, or to analyse East Central European populism against the background of Western European or South American phenomena. This continental and global opening obviously undermines the self-contained nature of meso-regional notions, but it does not eliminate them completely; rather than talking about individual national contexts, most research tends to turn to regional units of analysis as a basis of these comparisons. All in all, rather than seeking to create a definitive taxonomy of regional concepts, users of regional notions are becoming more and more aware of the essentially contested nature of their intellectual tools. From this perspective the aim is evidently not to try to fix meanings once and for all, but to be conscious of the underlying assumptions of different regional concepts – and that is exactly what a conceptual history of regional notions can facilitate.

Diana Mishkova is a historian by training and has specialized in modern and contemporary history of South Eastern Europe. She is the Director of the Centre for Advanced Study, Sofia. Her research focuses on comparative Balkan history, history of nationalism, history of modern political ideas, intellectual history, historiography, and methodology of comparative historical research. She is the author, among others, of *Domestication of Freedom: Modernity-Legitimacy in Serbia and Romania in the Nineteenth Century* (Paradigma, 2001), and co-editor of *Entangled Histories of the Balkans*, Vol. II: *Political Ideologies and Institutions* (Brill, 2014) and *Discourses of Collective Identity in Central and Southeast Europe (1789–1945). Texts and Commentaries*. Vol. 4: *Anti-Modernism: Radical Revisions of Collective Identity* (CEU Press, 2014).

Balázs Trencsényi is Professor at the History Department of Central European University, Budapest. His main field of interest is the history of modern political thought in East Central Europe. Among others he is the author of the monograph, *The Politics of 'National Character': A Study in Interwar East European Thought* (Routledge, 2012); co-author of *A History of Modern Political Thought in East Central Europe*, Vol I: *Negotiating Modernity in the 'Long Nineteenth Century'* (Oxford UP, 2016); as well as co-editor of the series *Discourses of Collective Identity in Central and Southeast Europe (1775–1945)* (CEU Press, 2006–14).

Notes

1. For the most recent attempt to provide a systematic overview of different regionalist frameworks of interpretation, see the January 2013 thematic issue of the journal *Regional Studies*, especially John A. Agnew, 'Arguing with Regions', *Regional Studies* 47(1) (2013), 6–17.
2. Stefan Troebst, '"Geschichtsregion": Historisch-mesoregionale Konzeptionen in den Kulturwissenschaften', *EGO | Europäische Geschichte Online* (2010), 1–14; and idem, 'Meso-regionalizing Europe: History versus Politics', in Johann P. Arnason and Natalie J. Doyle (eds), *Domains and Divisions of European History* (Liverpool: Liverpool University Press, 2010), 78–89.
3. Among the standard readings, see in particular Henri Lefebvre, *La production de l'espace* (Paris: Anthropos, 1974); Derek Gregory and John Urry (eds), *Social Relations and Spatial Structures* (Basingstoke: Macmillan, 1985); Edward W. Soja, *Postmodern Geographies: The Reassertion of Space in Critical Social Theory* (London and New York: Verso, 1989).
4. As illustrative of the current state of the art across a wide range of disciplines, we can mention Jörg Döring and Tristan Thielmann, *Spatial Turn: Das Raumparadigma in den Kultur- und Sozialwissenschaften* (Bielefeld: transcript, 2008); Henk van Houtum, Olivier Kramsch and Wolfgang Zierhofer (eds), *B/ordering Space* (Aldershot: Ashgate, 2005); Frithjof Benjamin Schenk, 'Das Paradigma des Raumes in der Osteuropäischen Geschichte', *Zeitenblicke* 6(2) (2007), 1–25.
5. Charles S. Maier, 'Transformations of Territoriality 1600–2000', in Gunilla Budde, Sebastian Conrad and Oliver Janz (eds), *Transnationale Geschichte: Themen, Tendenzen und Theorien* (Göttingen: Vandenhoeck & Ruprecht, 2005), 32–55.
6. Anssi Paasi, 'The Institutionalization of Regions: A Theoretical Framework for Understanding the Emergence of Regions and the Constitution of Regional Identity', *Fennia* 164(1) (1986), 106–46. The notion of institutionalization involves territorial shaping (the making of 'soft'/'hard' boundaries), symbolic shaping (naming/other symbols) and institutional shaping (institutions/ institutional practices that are used in maintaining the territorial and symbolic

shapes, e.g. administrative and legislative organs, press, associations, etc.), and the establishment of the region as part of the regional system and social consciousness – i.e. the region has an 'identity' (referring to features of nature, culture and inhabitants that distinguish it from other regions, and create special 'structures of expectation').

7. For similar reasons we are not concerned here with the 'functional regions' formed by (analyses of) patterns of economic interaction and transaction, where not only a historical dimension is usually missing but it is hard to disentangle region from network.
8. See, among many others, J. Allen, D. Massey and A. Cochrane, *Rethinking the Region* (London: Routledge, 1998); Michael Keating, *The New Regionalism in Western Europe* (Cheltenham: Elgar, 1998); F. Söderbaum and T. Shaw (eds), *Theories of New Regionalism* (London: Palgrave-Macmillan, 2003); Anssi Paasi, 'The Resurgence of the "Region" and "Regional Identity": Theoretical Perspectives and Empirical Observations on the Regional Dynamics in Europe', *Review of International Studies* 35(1) (2009), 121–46. The misbalance applies also to studies explicitly addressed to historical regions, such as Sven Tägil (ed.), *Regions in Central Europe: The Legacy of History* (London: Hurst, 1999).
9. Pärtel Piirimäe and Andres Andresen (eds), *Baltic Regionalism*. Thematic issue of *Ajalooline Ajakiri* 2012/1–2.
10. Holm Sundhaussen, 'Europa balkanica: Der Balkan als historischer Raum Europas', *Geschichte und Gesellschaft* 25 (1999), 626–53; Holm Sundhaussen, 'Was ist Südosteuropa und warum beschäftigen wir uns (nicht) damit?', *Südosteuropa Mitteilungen*, 42(5–6) (2002), 93–105; Maria Todorova, 'The Balkans as Category of Analysis: Borders, Space, Time', in G. Stourzh (ed.), *Annäherungen an eine europäische Geschichtsschreibung* (Vienna: Verlag der Österreichischen Akademie der Wissenschaften, 2002), 57–83; Maria Todorova, *Imagining the Balkans* (New York: Oxford University Press, 1997), 21–61; Mark Bassin, 'Eurasianism "Classical" and "Neo": The Lines of Continuity', *Slavic Eurasian Studies* 17 (2008), 279–94; Bo Stråth, '"Norden" as a European Region: Demarcation and Belonging', in J.P. Arnason (ed.), *Domains and Divisions of European History* (Liverpool: Liverpool University Press, 2009), 198–215.
11. Reinhart Koselleck, *Zeitschichten: Studien zur Historik* (Frankfurt: Suhrkamp, 2002), 81.
12. For a pioneering attempt, see Jan Ifversen, 'Europe and European Culture: A Conceptual Analysis', *European Societies* 4(1) (2002), 1–26. See also, Miroslav Hroch, 'Regional Memory: Reflections on the Role of History in (Re)constructing Regional Identity', in Steven G. Ellis et al. (eds), *Frontiers, Regions and Identities in Europe* (Pisa: Plus-Pisa University Press, 2009), 1–14.
13. Hans-Jürgen Lüsebrink and Rolf Reichardt, *The Bastille: A History of a Symbol of Despotism and Freedom* (Durham, NC: Duke University Press, 1997).
14. Larry Wolff, *Inventing Eastern Europe: The Map of Civilization on the Mind of the Enlightenment* (Stanford, CA: Stanford University Press, 1994). See also Hans Lemberg, 'Zur Entstehung des Osteuropabegriffes im 19. Jahrhundert:

Vom "Norden" zum "Osten" Europas', *Jahrbücher für Geschichte Osteuropas* 33 (1985), 48–91.
15. Iver Neumann, *Uses of the Other: The 'East' in European Identity Formation* (Minneapolis: University of Minnesota Press, 1999).
16. A case in point is the work of the Austrian scholar of South Eastern Europe, with a rather complicated political past, Fritz Valjavec, 'Südosteuropa und Balkan', *Südost-Forschungen* VII (1942), 1–8; Fritz Valjavec, 'Die Eigenart Südeuropas in Geschichte und Kultur', *Südosteuropa-Jahrbuch* I (1957), 53–62. For Central Europe, see Jacques Droz, *L'Europe centrale: Evolution historique de l'idée de 'Mitteleuropa'* (Paris: Payot, 1960).
17. See, for instance, Jovan Cvijić, *La péninsule balkanique: géographie humaine* (Paris: Payot, 1918); Milan Budimir and Petar Skok, 'But et signification des études balkaniques', *Revue internationale des études balkaniques* I (1934), 1–28; Victor Papacostea, 'Avant-Propos', *Balcania* I (1938), iii–vii; idem, 'La Péninsule Balkanique et le problème des études comparées', *Balcania* 6 (1943), iii–xxi; Nicolae Iorga, *Le caractère commun des institutions du Sud-Est de l'Europe* (Paris: Librairie universitaire J. Gamber, 1929); idem, *Ce este Sud-Estul european* (Bucharest: Datina Românească, 1940); Oscar Halecki, 'Qu'est-ce que l'Europe Orientale?', *Bulletin d'information des sciences historiques en Europe Orientale* (Warsaw, 1934), 82–93; Marceli Handelsman, 'Le développement des nationalités dans l'Europe Centrale-Orientale', *L'Esprit International* 6 (1932), 558–75; István Hajnal, 'A kis nemzetek történetírásának munkaközösségéről', *Századok* 1–2 (1942), 1–42, 133–65.
18. Cvijić, *La péninsule balkanique*.
19. See, in particular, Nicolae Iorga, *Byzantium after Byzantium*, translated by Laura Treptow (Iași, Oxford, Portland: The Centre for Romanian Studies, 2000; originally published in 1935 in French).
20. On the political implications of regionalist Balkan scholarship, see Diana Mishkova, 'The Politics of Regionalist Science: The Balkans as a Supranational Space in Late Nineteenth to Mid-Twentieth Century Academic Projects', *East Central Europe* 39 (2012), 266–303.
21. Josef Macůrek, *Dějepisectví evropského východu* (Prague: Historický klub, 1946).
22. Ivan Ormandzhiev, *Федерация на балканските народи. Идеи и пречки* (Sofia: Заря, 1947).
23. Oscar Halecki, *Borderlands of Western Civilization: A History of East Central Europe* (New York: The Ronald Press Co., 1952).
24. Francis Dvornik, *The Slavs in European History and Civilization* (New Brunswick: Rutgers University Press, 1962).

References

Agnew, John A., 'Arguing with Regions', *Regional Studies* 47(1) (2013), 6–17
Allen, John, Doreen Massey and Allan Cochrane, *Rethinking the Region* (London: Routledge, 1998)

Bassin, Mark, 'Eurasianism "Classical" and "Neo": The Lines of Continuity', *Slavic Eurasian Studies* 17 (2008), 279–94

Budimir, Milan, and Petar Skok, 'But et signification des études balkaniques', *Revue internationale des études balkaniques* I (1934), 1–28

Cvijić, Jovan, *La péninsule balkanique: géographie humaine* (Paris: n.p., 1918)

Döring, Jörg, and Tristan Thielmann, *Spatial Turn: Das Raumparadigma in den Kultur- und Sozialwissenschaften* (Bielefeld: transcript, 2008)

Droz, Jacques, *L'Europe centrale: Evolution historique de l'idée de 'Mitteleuropa'* (Paris: Payot, 1960)

Dvornik, Francis, *The Slavs in European History and Civilization* (New Brunswick: Rutgers University Press, 1962)

Gregory, Derek, and John Urry (eds), *Social Relations and Spatial Structures* (Basingstoke: Macmillan, 1985)

Hajnal, István, 'A kis nemzetek történetírásának munkaközösségéről', *Századok* 1–2 (1942), 1–42, 133–65

Halecki, Oscar, 'Qu'est-ce que l'Europe Orientale?', *Bulletin d'information des sciences historiques en Europe Orientale* (Warsaw, 1934), 82–93

———, *Borderlands of Western Civilization: A History of East Central Europe* (New York: The Ronald Press Co., 1952)

Handelsman, Marceli, 'Le développement des nationalités dans l'Europe Centrale-Orientale', *L'Esprit International* 6 (1932), 558–75

Hroch, Miroslav, 'Regional Memory: Reflections on the Role of History in (Re)constructing Regional Identity', in Steven G. Ellis et al. (eds), *Frontiers, Regions and Identities in Europe* (Pisa: Plus-Pisa University Press, 2009), 1–14

Ifversen, Jan, 'Europe and European Culture: A Conceptual Analysis', *European Societies* 4(1) (2002), 1–26

Iorga, Nicolae, *Le caractère commun des institutions du Sud-Est de l'Europe* (Paris: Librairie universitaire J. Gamber, 1929)

———, *Byzantium after Byzantium*, translated by Laura Treptow (Iași, Oxford, Portland: The Centre for Romanian Studies, 2000; originally published in 1935 in French)

———, *Ce este Sud-Estul european* (Bucharest: Datina Românească, 1940)

Keating, Michael, *The New Regionalism in Western Europe* (Cheltenham: Elgar, 1998)

Koselleck, Reinhart, *Zeitschichten: Studien zur Historik* (Frankfurt: Suhrkamp, 2002)

Lefebvre, Henri, *La production de l'espace* (Paris: Anthropos, 1974)

Lemberg, Hans, 'Zur Entstehung des Osteuropabegriffes im 19. Jahrhundert: Vom "Norden" zum "Osten" Europas', *Jahrbücher für Geschichte Osteuropas* 33 (1985), 48–91

Lüsebrink, Hans-Jürgen, and Rolf Reichardt, *The Bastille: A History of a Symbol of Despotism and Freedom* (Durham, NC: Duke University Press, 1997)

Macůrek, Josef, *Dějepisectví evropského východu* (Prague: Historický klub, 1946)

Maier, Charles S., 'Transformations of Territoriality 1600–2000', in Gunilla Budde, Sebastian Conrad and Oliver Janz (eds), *Transnationale Geschichte: Themen, Tendenzen und Theorien* (Göttingen: Vandenhoeck & Ruprecht, 2005), 32–55

Mishkova, Diana, 'The Politics of Regionalist Science: The Balkans as a Supranational Space in Late Nineteenth to Mid-Twentieth Century Academic Projects', *East Central Europe* 39 (2012), 266–303

Neumann, Iver, *Uses of the Other: The 'East' in European Identity Formation* (Minneapolis: University of Minnesota Press, 1999)

Ormandzhiev, Ivan, *Федерация на балканските народи. Идеи и пречки* (Sofia: Заря, 1947)

Paasi, Anssi, 'The Institutionalization of Regions: A Theoretical Framework for Understanding the Emergence of Regions and the Constitution of Regional Identity', *Fennia* 164(1) (1986), 106–46

———, 'The Resurgence of the "Region" and "Regional Identity": Theoretical Perspectives and Empirical Observations on the Regional Dynamics in Europe', *Review of International Studies* 35(1) (2009), 121–46

Papacostea, Victor, 'Avant-Propos', *Balcania* I (1938), iii–vii

———, 'La Péninsule Balkanique et le problème des études comparées', *Balcania* 6 (1943), iii–xxi

Piirimäe, Pärtel, and Andres Andresen (eds), *Baltic Regionalism*. Thematic issue of *Ajalooline Ajakiri* 2012/1–2

Schenk, Frithjof Benjamin, 'Das Paradigma des Raumes in der Osteuropäischen Geschichte', *Zeitenblicke* 6(2) (2007), 1–25

Söderbaum, Fredrik, and Timothy M. Shaw (eds), *Theories of New Regionalism* (London: Palgrave-Macmillan, 2003)

Soja, Edward W., *Postmodern Geographies: The Reassertion of Space in Critical Social Theory* (London and New York: Verso, 1989)

Stråth, Bo, '"Norden" as a European Region: Demarcation and Belonging', in Johann P. Arnason (ed.), *Domains and Divisions of European History* (Liverpool: Liverpool University Press, 2009), 198–215

Sundhaussen, Holm, 'Europa balkanica: Der Balkan als historischer Raum Europas', *Geschichte und Gesellschaft* 25 (1999), 626–53

———, 'Was ist Südosteuropa und warum beschäftigen wir uns (nicht) damit?', *Südosteuropa Mitteilungen* 42(5–6) (2002), 93–105

Tägil, Sven (ed.), *Regions in Central Europe: The Legacy of History* (London: Hurst, 1999)

Todorova, Maria, *Imagining the Balkans* (New York: Oxford University Press, 1997)

———, 'The Balkans as Category of Analysis: Borders, Space, Time', in Gerald Stourzh (ed.), *Annäherungen an eine europäische Geschichtsschreibung* (Vienna: Verlag der Österreichischen Akademie der Wissenschaften, 2002), 57–83

Troebst, Stefan, '"Geschichtsregion": Historisch-mesoregionale Konzeptionen in den Kulturwissenschaften', *EGO | Europäische Geschichte Online* (2010), 1–14

———, 'Meso-regionalizing Europe: History versus Politics', in Johann P. Arnason and Natalie J. Doyle (eds), *Domains and Divisions of European History* (Liverpool: Liverpool University Press, 2010), 78–89

Valjavec, Fritz, 'Südosteuropa und Balkan', *Südost-Forschungen* VII (1942), 1–8

―――, 'Die Eigenart Südeuropas in Geschichte und Kultur', *Südosteuropa-Jahrbuch* I (1957), 53–62

van Houtum, Henk, Olivier Kramsch and Wolfgang Zierhofer (eds), *B/ordering Space* (Aldershot: Ashgate, 2005)

Wolff, Larry, *Inventing Eastern Europe: The Map of Civilization on the Mind of the Enlightenment* (Stanford, CA: Stanford University Press, 1994)

Chapter 9
Conceptualizing Modernity in Multi- and Intercultural Spaces
The Case of Central and Eastern Europe

Victor Neumann

'Centre' and 'Periphery'? Some Preliminary Remarks on a Series of Controversial Notions

Is it possible to explore and assess Europe via the notions of 'centre' and 'periphery'? To what category do these two notions pertain? What can we infer from them? Can the science of history operate with these two notions? Do they imply partisanship? How can one establish the centre and the periphery of a cultural space? Are these notions interchangeable? Provided that we agree on the importance of a civilization's structure, what is the point of introducing a 'centre' – 'periphery' distinction into cultural-historical investigations? Might it not be an illusion that induces us to imagine the relations inside a continent through using formulas derived from geography, an illusion that can be explained due to the notional pair 'we' – 'you'? Or can all this actually stand for an invention carrying an ideological message for which the concepts of 'Europe' and 'the Other Europe' are meant to imply the advance of certain states on the European continent and the backwardness of others, thereby highlighting socio-economic inequalities and their consequences?

These questions are particularly legitimate ones to address since the notions under discussion reflect differences rather than similarities; they point to subordinations and contradictions characteristic of two, or more, cultural geographies rather than the unity in diversity of one and the same continent. In the case of political debates, the use of notions like 'centre' and 'periphery' could be an excuse for those who want to clarify for themselves the meaning of terms and various languages. When this usage becomes part and parcel of the motivation for an academic endeavour, such an approach could be limiting, its advocacy could provoke prejudices, and its results become subordinated to transient ideological interests. Time and space have been differently interpreted depending on individuals' religious traditions, cultural-historical pasts, specific notions and languages; the categories of space and time therefore signal the existence of certain specificities. Nevertheless, they may not offer sufficient justification for historians' usage of dichotomous approaches as tools of investigation. Moreover, the above-mentioned considerations suggest forms of human existence without generating or describing relations (of any possible nature) between an alleged 'centre' and an imaginary 'periphery.' Likewise, a number of seminal contributions over the last couple of decades have promoted an innovative perspective on Eastern Europe and the culture of identity on the European continent as a whole, casting doubt on the limiting approach already mentioned. While a culture manifests itself in a certain socio-political context to which it is related,[1] history is the result of interpretations that can facilitate the understanding of that particular culture, of a system of values, and of people and civilizations. It can lead to the identification of individual and collective mindsets specific to a particular era or location. History can be a narrative about the past, but it is not a linear one, it is not hindered by various religious, ethnocultural, national or economic prejudices on the grounds of which one would seek to justify the present state of affairs.

The endeavours of romanticists and their disciples stand as proof of how the act of moving a political community back in time laid the groundwork for an anachronistic view of the nation and the national state. The conceptualization of modernity did not ignore this form of organization since the technical and economic evolutions of humankind have very rarely been accompanied by an authentic inclusion of cultural-communitarian diversities. What is certain is that it is impossible to define 'centre' and 'periphery' as notions with a clear-cut meaning accepted by the majority of European cultures. When these two notions are actually chosen and used in various locations, their meanings differ in the minds of diverse people and communities; this happens because there are no fixed, unchangeable points of reference presumed by the two notions. Instead, there is a historical process that people can learn about; one in which spiritual, social and economic factors intertwine in order to show who we are at a particular moment in time – an idea well delineated by Giambattista Vico.[2]

Put differently, in the case of Europe, 'centre' and 'periphery' are figments of our imagination. A remarkable example in this respect comes from English and American literatures, which have constructed a genuine imaginary geography of the Balkans.[3] In her book, *Inventing Ruritania*, Vesna Goldsworthy explores the archetypes of the Balkan Peninsula and its worlds disseminated through long-established literary and film productions by famous Western artists. These archetypes emerged in the nineteenth century and have ever since percolated in society. Used by politics and by the mass-media-grounded 'industry of consciousness', these archetypes not only function as clues towards the falsification of realities, but also reveal the manner in which the Balkan region has been exploited as an object of dominant cultures' dialogues about themselves. As a result, the societies – and especially the elites – of the Balkan region have had to learn not only the vocabulary of the West but also the stereotypes it has assimilated. Apparently exonerated from any possible accusation of racism, the cultural and political language of the West has created through the notion of the Balkans an 'other' that could be blamed for anything.[4] In response, Goldsworthy maintains, on the basis of a rich array of arguments, that the Balkan Peninsula is part of Europe despite the fact that the adjective 'Balkan' can mean the opposite of European. Meanwhile, the practice of using the 'Balkan' adjective to refer to one's neighbour has often been the result of ignorance and bigotry.

Deploring nationalist interpretations, conceptual history promotes a comparative and transnational approach to intellectual life by trying to decode both the shared and the separate meanings of notions from one language to another, by exploring the numerous cultural transfers, and the genuine and false ideas contained within languages, discourses and texts. In the case of Central and Eastern Europe, conceptual history is a particularly innovative research method since it has to confront the above-mentioned stereotypes that have been widely perpetuated over the course of time. Europe is a mixture of political and economic systems whose origins lie in multiple religious and cultural values which, in their turn, are a function of the location in which they initially emerged and were later developed. The specificities of Europe derive from its multitude of allegiances including Catholic Rome, the Orthodox Byzantium, the Protestant North, the Mediterranean South, the Anglo-Saxon or French – Dutch West, and the Russian East. Religion has undoubtedly played an important role in these areas. These spaces are associated with several meanings that find a synthesis in the concept of Europe, while an important part of these locations has derived from plural historical legacies, from both oral languages and written texts, from old and new religions alike. What is certain is that modernity was not only connected to discontinuities with the Middle Ages, but also to continuities – to values that were perpetuated from one historical era to another and that bestowed a sense of authenticity on people and the places they inhabited. By examining these latter aspects, we can establish the set of values that permitted the construction of a civilization and, eventually, of a corresponding particular identity.

The foundation of the identity-based culture was originally established at the time when Europe was organized in principalities, kingdoms and empires, when intellectuals imagined cities and regions inhabited by several linguistic and religious groups living free from biases and aspiring to build a *sensus communis*. The modernity of Europe, which dates back to an earlier time than that of the emergence of the idea of 'nation', presupposes a good knowledge of the transnational condition and meanings of the continent's history. On the other hand, we must acknowledge the fact that each region of Europe is to be defined not only on the basis of various communities' economic, political and legal status, but also in light of the traditions, historical legacies and mental reflexes acquired by each of its places of habitation. Political experiences rationalized within some form of procedural thought and the logic of political life make up just one of the initiatives of the modern world. Under the circumstances, at stake is the logic of the state understood on the basis of natural law and covenant-based functioning – a logic implemented due to a constructed rational apparatus and a cultural framework that guarantees an enhanced level of legal constraints.[5] The concept of the state should also be considered in relation to that of culture, as one attesting to the creation of free people beyond socio-economic constraints. As to the concept of culture, it is fundamental not only because it fosters social cohesion, as Reinhart Koselleck has rightly observed, but also because it allows us to decode the communicational and representational peculiarities of human individuals depending on the coordinates of time and space and on the meaning ascribed to their transformation and renewal.

The conceptualization of modernity is not circumscribed to a particular time and geographical area, just as it is not limited to invariable principle (i.e. to one single model of social existence). During the stage of transition towards modernity, but especially after the commencement of modernity proper, the social and liberal understanding of the concept of culture became relatively similar all over Europe. There were intellectual circles, though, such as those of Central, Eastern and South-Eastern Europe, where differences on the basis of social status and profession did not play the same fundamental role as in the West. The process of modernization occurred in default of accurate administrative rules and of an elaborated juridical system. Instead it was founded mainly on cultural encyclopedic minds due to the contributions of a series of remarkable personalities that had been innovative in many areas and that had shown their attachment both to traditional spiritual values and to new intellectual ones, without finding a contradiction between them. The Russian intelligentsia, for example,[6] perfectly illustrates this type of direction since, on the one hand, its members were influenced by and in contact with Western ideas while, on the other hand, they developed a modern cultural concept that intertwined the originality of their own culture, historical-religious and identity-related views, obsessions, or harmonious perspectives with radical, critical viewpoints.

The Specific Realities of Central and Eastern Europe: Multiculturality and Sociocultural Heterogeneity

Frontier cultures and cross-border cultures are not to be analysed only in relation to the geographic coordinates of their particular areas, just as they cannot be completely assimilated to a mindset whose origins lie with the old idea of statehood of the Middle Ages or with that of the nation state as it was constructed and understood in the West. What are the coordinates defining Europe? Where is its centre located, and where can we find its frontier? Do we conceptualize modernity in relation to space, or only in relation to time? If the answer turns towards the latter option, how do we define geographic areas? What degree of importance do we bestow upon meeting places or points, transit areas between Western and Eastern Europe? Could we, for instance, analyse modernity in the regions and sub-regions of Central and Eastern Europe via the notion of *liminality*, a notion derived from the Greek term '*limen*' and signifying the meeting point between the earth and the sea, the idea of a harbour, a transit area, or a so-called grey zone?[7]

There are regions and cities whose histories, cultural-juridical evolutions and administrative structures do not overlap with either those of the 'centre', or those of the 'periphery', their demarcation lines being arbitrary. Bohemia, Silesia and Moravia, as well as Slovenia, Banat, Transylvania and Bukovina, all stand out due to their position in areas of transit, where ambivalences become extremely fertile in points of intra-communitarian communication, collective consciousness, and individual or collective cultural creations. That is why the conceptualization of modernity can be examined in relation to an area's geography and to the results of the cohabitation of two or more linguistic and religious communities therein. This does not constitute the case of speculations in the absence of history, nor does it refer to simple hypotheses meant to enrich the cultural memory of today. This approach involves, instead, the explanation and conceptualization of modernity in relation to social and cultural signposts, real behaviours and a plurality already in existence at the time when the first shoots of the new world sprouted. What is at stake is not the invention of a new theory but the theorization of realities. Following this approach, the multiculturality of Central and East European spaces should no longer be viewed as a premodern given but as a key argument contributing to the conceptualization of modernity.[8] This conceptualization derives from a state's form of organization and administration, from its reforms and political philosophies. It is not a completely new type of construction, but a rethinking of past legacies in light of a strong yearning to be integrated in Europe's system of values at that particular time. In the case of Central and East European regions, the multicultural configuration of the area and its hybrid identities continued to represent a reality that could not be ignored, either by imperial administrative powers or by the ideologists of the ethnonation. This is one reason why, once the ethnonational idea became wide spread, the conceptualization of modernity and, respectively, the models of political and societal thought, had to stand up to different meanings and types of discourses as well as to a series of ideological contradictions.

Is the concept of multiculturality indeed a problem of interpretation derived from socio-communitarian and cultural-linguistic experiences? Are there contradictory meanings of the concept? Long-lasting imperial administrations – as well as conceptual historians following in their footsteps – have admitted that all cultures, irrespective of the time of their genesis or its evolution in different periods of time, should benefit from some sense of integrity, and enjoy respect rather than being silenced on the basis of territorial criterion or the number of people each group represents. Individual and societal ideals bear the traits and ideals of the place in which they were formed. They incorporate external influences but they also maintain cultural-historical legacies. The genesis of modern thought has often been grounded upon the psychological traits of regional communities. As to the sore point of traditional societies, it is different from that of a liberal-democratic society in the sense that the former keeps fostering old manners of multicultural cohabitation while the latter is permanently preoccupied with settling possible inter-communitarian conflicts. In this latter case, the difficulties to be broached involve the need to reconcile the idea of (allegedly superior) cultures with the duty to treat all human beings as equal.[9] This is the argument used by Charles Taylor in order to show that the birth of modern identity was prompted by changes and the end of social hierarchies. He considers that the recognition of differences from one group to another laid the groundwork for asserting collective identities.[10] Filtered through the amount of information we have about North America, a generalization of this idea would be insufficient, to say the least; in fact, such an affirmation does not correspond at all to reality. Likewise, it is unlikely that the theory of identity could reflect a type of nationalism in which, according to Taylor, we could distinguish between its good and bad parts. Just as the act of differentiating between one group and another does not necessarily presuppose showing respect towards the other, one's identification with one group or another does not necessarily entail the embracing of a nationalist ideology. Decoding the meanings ascribed by various cultures to the notions of ethnicity, nationality, nation is therefore important in order to understand the meaning ascribed to the idea of cohabitation involving two or more cultures, bearing in mind the unveiling of the significations of modernization and modernity. Once understood, these notions could contribute to overcoming confusions due to languages that have propagated ethnocentric and nationalist ideologies. As for the concepts of multi- and interculturality, they can help to explain the meanings ascribed to modernity by the inhabitants of the Central and East European regions.

The ethnonation and the ethnonational state were the products of the nineteenth century, emerging under the influence of French-Prussian-German revolutionary and reformist ideologies. Given their location at the crossroads, Central and East European regions cooperated at times with the East and at other times with the West, borrowing sets of values from both cultures and civilizations, giving rise to ties or conflicts with both, constructing themselves under the guise of intercultural harmonies or disharmonies. Hence in the case of the conceptualization of modernity in Central and East Central Europe, one first needs to examine the politics of the House of Habsburg and of the Austrian Empire in the eighteenth and the nineteenth centuries, since the above-mentioned regions had been disputed for centuries by three great empires: the Habsburg, the Tsarist and the Ottoman. As a result, these were societies with multiple legacies that intertwined various languages and cultures, a melting pot that became more and more pronounced after the debut of modernization when the circulation of people was triggered by territorial conquests, administrative reorganizations, economic progress and colonization. Therefore, none of these changes was related to ethnic divisions, which had not actually played any major role before the 1800s. Instead, a certain level of strained tensions characterized these spaces and their inhabitants during a long and complicated process of emancipation and modernization, one which is hard to locate in relation to a single moment in time.

The sense in this part of the world was that it had never represented a 'periphery' but was part of Europe. Many of the technical innovations, literary and artistic creations and administrative-political realities during the eighteenth, nineteenth and twentieth centuries proved not only their closeness to the West, but also their openness for experiment through their own values. This, too, is a reason why determinist assessments should be avoided – namely, those according to which social-economic or political phenomena should always be essential for tracing differences between one region and another.[11] Many Central European cities were comparable to Western cities even if their administrative and economic structures were not similar to those of their Western counterparts. They used to be, and have largely remained, the cultural products of the Austrian Empire, standing for a standard of civilization that was emphatically not lower than that of medieval or modern Europe. These cities bespoke of specificities generated by their different statehood; they showed an appetite for borrowings and crosscurrents, but they did not differ fundamentally from Western urban structures.

The cities of Prague, Budapest, Bratislava, Novi-Sad, Gorizzia, Triest, Cracow, Lemberg, Timișoara/Temeswar and Cernăuți/Czernowitz constructed and developed themselves within modern civilization as self-sufficient identities via plurilingualism and Catholic–Protestant, Orthodox–Catholic (the case of Greek Catholics), Judeo–Christian and Muslim–Christian religious convergences. In other words, they became part of modern civilization thanks to their multiple-coded cultural inheritance. Consequently, they shared a series of similarities with the neighbouring West European cities, while concurrently developing numerous exotic aspects generated by the impact of Enlightenment ideas. We can hence conclude that the modernity of the region under consideration coincided with new scientific, technical and industrial discoveries and trade competitions, as well as with avant-garde literary, artistic and musical movements, all of which propagated unity in diversity. In their turn, South East European cities such as Bucharest, Belgrade, Sofia, Sarajevo and Salonika defined themselves by the cohabitation of various religious communities and not only by their geographic position. They had rarely defined themselves by the name of the Balkans, by the allegedly backward condition of being an outpost of European Christianity or a defensive fortress impeding the advancement of Ottoman civilization. They more likely defined their identity by conservatism, long-term transitions from one historical era to another, or experiments.

Analysing modernity through the lens of multi- and interculturality facilitates a different kind of knowing social and intellectual history, just as it allows one to conceptualize modernity on the basis of cultural transfers and the transnational meaning of urban and regional identities. In his studies, Moritz Csáky has demonstrated the deep connection between official political life and the life generated by diverse cultural, artistic, literary, historical and philosophical forms of expression.[12] This connection corresponds to the general framework of social evolution since the eighteenth and nineteenth centuries, a period of time during which the thought reflexes of the human communities in the regions under discussion became modern. The world of Central and Eastern Europe identified itself with its own behavioural peculiarities transmitted from one generation to another. On the other hand, it accepted change. Its memories and cultural correspondences suggest a space of experiences and a horizon of expectations that can be found in the multiple-cultural code of the populations inhabiting the regions of Central and Eastern Europe. Under the circumstances, the search for essences and their problematization became extremely important, which is why any attempt to 'recontextualize' cultural creations – be they literary, musical or artistic – contributes to our understanding of individual and collective mentalities and mindsets. Even when changes seem to have shared or stimulated the reception and multiplication of ethnonational and national ideas, the assessment and conceptualization of modernity must take into account the specificities of the place under consideration and its history, especially the cultural heterogeneity and the ambivalent signposts of the region.

'Ambivalent cultural legacies'[13] and creations have survived to this day all over Europe. In Central and Eastern Europe they are part and parcel of identity. It is with them that we associate the elements due to the great bureaucratic reforms of the Habsburg state that resulted in a commonly shared culture that can be found in an 'Austrian Germanity'; institutions that led to the formation of behavioural reflexes; empirical terms indicating administrative-juridical, economic and political subordination; the establishment of the ruling royal house as a reference point and a symbol of citizenship; and a German language peppered with expressions originating from the languages of several communities' languages, especially Czech, Polish, Hungarian and Italian – in short, plurilingualism. All these aspects show how individuals and collectivities from these areas acquired similar models; therefore their politics, justice and economy were based on similar principles. Part of the renewals they undertook represented the success of the reforms dreamt up by the Habsburg Emperor Joseph II from as early as 1765, later accepted by Maria Theresia and eventually implemented by the State Council. They were the result of long-lasting disputes that remodelled the system Haugwitz had introduced in 1749.[14] This was a sociopolitical context characterized by the coupling of shared inherited aspects specific to the empire's populations with newly-imposed administrative-financial changes. Such reformist impulses first occurred in Bohemia, and later in Hungary, Banat and Transylvania. They were the result of radical reformist ideas. At first, during his 1773 trip to Banat and Transylvania, the emperor gathered data about the state of the civil and military administration of the regions, their financial situation and the manner of collecting taxes. He then formulated the programme of reforms, which gave priority to the introduction of the civil and criminal codes; the reformation of the magistrature; the establishment of the real-estate register; the archiving of documents and medical checks; the regulation of the activity of representative institutions and their clerks; the regulation of the functioning of craft guilds; the setting up of manufacturing and factories depending upon the raw materials that were exploited; the rise of the clerks' wages and the abrogation of the peasants' obligation to provide their upkeep, and so on.[15] In this respect too, similarities were stronger than differences for the areas under discussion, and these reforms actually constituted the early stage of modernization in these regions.

Over the course of the nineteenth century, the emergence of nationalities, nations and nationalist stereotypes was accompanied by the wish of many intellectuals and politicians to positively highlight 'the motley kaleidoscope represented by the mixture of peoples'. Literature, historiography, political philosophy, music and visual arts of the times focused on the issue of cultural amalgamation – an aspect that has bestowed an air of exoticism on the regions of Central and Eastern Europe. Undoubtedly, the modernity of these places was due, on the one hand, to the reception of Western ideas and, on the other, to the project of a different statehood in comparison to Western Europe. Simultaneously, multiculturality explained the existent realities in these areas. As a result, the conceptualization of multiculturality and modernity in the regions of Central and Eastern Europe had no connection with utopias, 'the Habsburg myth', or the 'emperor's myth'; instead, it was grounded upon historical realities and deeply tied to an inimitable 'heterogeneity of the cultures'[16] functioning in these areas.

Consequently, any theory aimed at the conceptualization of modernity in Central and Eastern Europe must take into consideration the geography of the place, and distance itself from interpretative models borrowed from contemporary postmodern schools and from those subordinated to ethnicist and nationalist ideologies. The analysis of multi- and interculturality in the areas under consideration should constitute a mandatory part of historical investigations – one which is often ignored by studies whose analysis starts from the present-day configuration of states and politics. Located at the crossroads of the West and the East, Central and East European spaces have benefited from the influences of both civilizations, with Western influences prevailing over Eastern ones during the course of the modern era. Some historians have identified these complex sets of influences in the region's structure of organization or in its socio-economic life; others have indicated their presence in cultural ideas or in the set of values pertaining to various religious and linguistic communities.[17] Most importantly, the conceptualization of regional modernity must take into consideration the contributions of the state's administration of the region that led to its socio-economic and organizational progress, such as was the case with the House of Habsburg, the Austrian Empire, and the Austro-Hungarian Monarchy. There are plenty of other examples proving that the Ottoman and the Tsarist empires also reformed the state, drawing inspiration in their endeavours from the Western changes that occurred during the modern era. Regardless of which of these political structures we refer to, we can ascertain that they did not represent the cause of Central and Eastern Europe's backwardness, as has often been contended.[18]

Enlightenment and Modernity

In an article dedicated to the concept of the Enlightenment and the meaning Reinhart Koselleck attributed to it in his book *Kritik und Krise*, Hans Erich Bödeker notes that the absolutist state has been interpreted by historians in highly problematic ways,[19] because the conceptualization of the Enlightenment, and, by extension, of modernity, presupposes a type of understanding that takes into consideration political, social, cultural and civic realities. Unfortunately, at times Koselleck himself extrapolated the data and knowledge he had acquired about the German Principalities, France and other Western countries to wider areas in which things had not happened similarly. As regards the state's agency during the eighteenth century, rather than stressing, as Koselleck did in *Kritik und Krise*, the dialectics between morals and politics, we might as well speak of the ambivalence of Enlightenment ideas – for instance, the conservation of traditions and renewal via the liquidation of illiteracy. The Habsburg colonizations of the eighteenth century were carried out with the help of Catholic populations, whose integration was projected and realized on the basis of religious and moral connections linking the imperial power holders with the Roman Catholic Church representatives. This happened particularly in Banat and Bukovina. The Habsburgs also thought about the establishment of a new church in order to subordinate the newly conquered territories and populations to the representatives of the administration and their interests. Following this line of thought, the Greek Catholic Church was established in Transylvania, a church subordinated to the Vatican but set up on the basis of mixed Orthodox and Catholic values. This is an instance of the cross-fertilization of doctrines, perhaps less often evident in the West, but one which ensured social peace and political stability for quite some time in the region under discussion. This phenomenon resulted from a close cooperation between the state and the church. The same imperial representatives had spread Enlightenment ideas in a top-down manner, thereby keeping control over their consequences. In this equation, the emperor had concurrently to heed church-imposed norms, natural rights and traditional juridical conventions. The autonomy of the Lutheran and Calvinist communities, for example, would not have survived in the eighteenth century unless the Habsburgs had continued to observe old juridical norms, the region's specific form of organizing religious life, or the specifics of its social and institutional hierarchies that had been founded in the previous centuries. Put differently, in the regions of Europe that were integrated into the Habsburg Empire and in which renewals were only partly indebted to Enlightenment ideas, the conceptualization of modernity has to be understood as a mixture of discontinuities and continuities in relation to structures of medieval thought, and not just as the outcome of discontinuities in a vacuum.

The situation of institutions during those times is another complex issue to address. From that perspective it would be misleading to assume that radical, revolutionary views took hold of the entire European continent and led to its modernization; we can note, instead, that in many communities the lure of modernization could become a reality only through the intervention of an organizing power. That is the reason why intellectuals often cooperated with the structures of the absolutist state, hoping thereby to impose their reformist programs regarding justice, economy and politics. Consequently, noblemen's circles, priests, lay intellectuals and merchants were all increasingly in favour of promoting education and emancipation. The books they read, the institutions they founded, the keen interest they showed for the renewal of thought, all these aspects were visible in their high level of individual education, ideas and behaviour, and all suggested the idea of their entering a new historical era. At the same time, the mercantilism of kings and emperors was highly influenced by Enlightenment politics, turning away from revolutionary movements, which were considered dangerous or counterproductive. Not only were the despots of eighteenth-century France thus oriented, but also those of Prussia and Austria. They were generally in favour of reforms and against revolutions or revolutionary reforms as imagined by radical Enlightenment thinkers. As to the differences characterizing the states of the European continent, they become clear if one follows the politics of the rulers in Vienna or the Frankfurt Parliament of 1848, which had not been comparable to those of Paris either in 1789 or in 1848. Unlike the case of Paris, the politics of Vienna and Frankfurt had not been genuinely revolutionary at these two historical moments. Nevertheless, despite the differences between intellectual ideas and the meanings given to sociopolitical events, a type of thought oriented towards renewal functioned during those times in all the regions of the old continent. It had been facilitated by the 'cultural channels' created by the colonizing empires, by the administrators, merchants and intellectuals who had circulated through the continent and had opened up a dialogue between the west, the centre and the east of Europe.[20]

At the beginning of the eighteenth century, the Habsburgs still treated the Roman Catholic Church as a state religion.[21] The new consciousness developing from here had to be an imperial one that implied another form of communication and a different *sensus communis* that was to be constructed by the Catholics. The intention behind this endeavour was to make the inhabitants of the region adhere to one and the same code of cultural and civilizational values. The process of its implementation was a slow one, being deployed over the course of the entire eighteenth century. Latin was the language of the Catholic Church and of the imperial Chancellery. The process of integration was then continued via the German language which was promoted in the regions of the empire in the second half of the eighteenth century. Initially, that promotion was carried out in order to make communication easier with the various populations of the empire, not to bring about a communitarian-linguistic division. The ethnonational idea only appeared later, at the time of the reception and adaptation of romantic literary and historical works to the local context. It benefited from the accumulations of the Enlightenment era but opposed itself to the aspirations formulated by its representatives. Yet, for a long time, multicultural realities continued to exist as a matter of course and were not hindered in any way by the official politics; during this time, the German language spread itself and cultivated the need for a wide dissemination of culture, and especially of the commonly shared interests of the region's inhabitants. At this time, the empire was preoccupied with the organization of individuals, groups, activities and religion, and therefore needed means of communication that were as diversified as possible. As a consequence, the development of education and religious practices in various languages and the establishment of plurilingualism as a natural form of manifestation constituted an important part of the realities of everyday life for the populations of Central and Eastern Europe in the eighteenth and nineteenth centuries.

Thus, enlightened despotism created the 'corridors' for the percolation of books, scholars and artists into the Central and East European regions. Vienna enforced several such reforms in keeping with the ideology of the Enlightenment, an idea we can derive from the contributions of some of its chancellors.[22] Among the Habsburg rulers, Emperor Joseph II was considered to be the most radical reformer of the eighteenth century. Under the circumstances, it is not easy to understand the contradiction raised by the concept of 'despot' that is associated with him, and especially by the title of 'enlightened despot', by which he came to be known. Joseph was 'a revolutionary on the throne'; he gave a new vision to politics, a new meaning to the concept of elites, and he campaigned for a change in mentalities, cultivating social relations enlightened by the philosophical ideas of the times. He did all that by imposing his point of view on his subjects because he believed that the only way to reform the world in which he lived within a reasonable amount of time entailed the use of a top-down approach. The ideas of the

Enlightenment as he understood them undoubtedly gave another meaning to the rapports established between the emperor and papacy, the emperor and monasteries, and the emperor and Freemasons.[23] At the same time, even if the universalization of modern philosophical ideas was present in the region, it did not interrupt the expansion of local particularities. Noblemen represented a segment of the population with the latter type of pursuits, since they were the ones who read, wrote and collected books and pictures – activities for which they needed to bypass the imperial censorship that had banned the circulation of visual and written texts connected to the French Revolution. Besides the nobility, school and culture were the other important sectors of life that made possible the rise and affirmation of intellectual elites in all the regions under discussion.[24]

Even if those intellectuals had not followed the ambivalence of the Enlightenment, as their generational peers from the West often had, they were aware of the novel changes made possible by various sciences and ideologies. When they were lured by high culture, it helped them with their literary, historiographical, philosophical and artistic creations. They did not succumb to the meaning conferred on the concept of the nation by the 1789 French revolution or by the Napoleonic epic; instead, they cared for the measures contributing to the progress of the idea of 'enlightenment'. Their ideal was a *homo novus*, an ideal which, at the time, could only be attained as a result of top-down changes that were in the spirit of enlightened despotism.[25] That explains why the modern ideas circulating in the regions of Central and Eastern Europe were those embraced and spread by Joseph II, and the current so created bore the name of Josephism or Josephinism. Just as in the case of its main promoter, renewal in the area under discussion acquired a meaning that was relatively different from that ascribed to it in the regions of Western Europe. It was a radical reformist meaning that had nothing in common with the idea of a revolution.

Many historical descriptions promoting modernity and a multicultural image were published in Vienna and other cities under Vienna's cultural influence. School textbooks from the first half of the nineteenth century written by German-language authors such as Alfred von Luschin-Ebengreuth, Alfred Dopsch and Ludwig Gumplowitz, as well as books written by Hungarian-language or Czech-language authors like Victor Hornyánszky and Vaclav V. Tomek, claimed that the unity of the empire was based on its linguistic and cultural-communitarian diversity rather than on the dynasty or the myth of the Habsburgs. These types of writings evidently ran counter to anti-monarchic and nationalist penchants. Vaclav Tomek, for instance, maintained that the monarchy was a fantastic political structure that resulted in multiple inter-crossings, intermarriages and a multicultural consciousness, which sustained a commonly shared ideology.[26] Without exaggerating, perhaps the most adequate concept for depicting the region's configuration at that time is that of cultural hybridization. It refers to high culture and the dynamics of social relations, as well as to the relation between the local and the universal. Hence, having as its basis highly diverse cultural-communitarian components, the Austrian state appeared to be dissimilar to the West European state. It thereby facilitated the emergence of several centres in which the symbiosis of cultures predominated, an idea that was then reflected both in social relations and in architectural, artistic, musical, literary and philosophical creations. That is what happened in Brünn/Brno, Prague, Bratislava/Pressburg, Buda/Ofen, Cernăuți/Czernowitz, Novi-Sad/Neusatz, Pécs/Fünfkirchen, Timișoara/Temeswar and other cities, as well as in many villages of the regions that functioned under the administration of the Austrian Empire.

As for the religious life of the region, it was practised in several languages. In the eighteenth and nineteenth centuries, the churches promoted a multicultural and transcultural state of mind. To give just one example, the region of Banat, from the south-eastern part of the monarchy, counted 1,302,807 inhabitants in 1834, of whom 366,841 were Catholic. These latter lived alongside 867,287 Orthodox followers, 26,643 Reformed Church followers, 22,299 Evangelicals, 12,242 Greek Catholic believers and 7,495 Jews. The statistics of the old episcopate of Csanád/Cenad (Temeswar/Timișoara) concerning the Roman Catholic churches of the area illustrated the languages spoken in its various religious communities, namely German, Hungarian, Serbo-Croatian and Romanian. In fifty-seven of the Catholic churches that were situated in Banat in 1834, religious services were performed concomitantly in two or three languages.[27] A similar situation was characteristic for the Catholic schools in the border counties, schools that functioned under the patronage of the same episcopate. Among these, plurilingual schools were the most numerous, and instructors taught in German, Hungarian, Serbian, Czech, Romanian and Slovakian.[28]

This is just one example of what was happening in the border regions of the empire, an example referring to the meaning attributed to cultural plurality that was well understood both in urban and rural environments. Despite centralism and the spread of the Catholic religion, the House of Habsburg of the eighteenth century, the Austrian Empire of the nineteenth century and the Austro-Hungarian Monarchy of the second half of the nineteenth century cultivated multicultural specificities, making an effort to maintain or build inter-communitarian bridges of communication. The successive Habsburg governments generally appreciated the need to protect local languages, religions and cultures, being permanently preoccupied in making the administrative-juridical structure an integrative one. In the meantime, loyalty towards the emperor was recognized as the expression of a citizenship commonly shared by all the inhabitants of the empire. The concept of modernity was therefore expanded inside the empire, in which the various churches and the state acknowledged and promoted multi- and intercultural traits as manifestations of the peaceful coexistence of its inhabitants.

Vienna-run politics not only aimed at consolidating power in the territories annexed to the empire after the wars with the Ottomans, but also at maintaining peace. In places where the communities were well organized and based upon norms observed by believers of various faiths, the authorities agreed to the existence of leading church hierarchies even when they had not been subordinated to the Roman Catholic Church. So it happened with the Slavic-Serbian language church, whose metropolitan seat from Karlowitz/ Sremski-Karlovci was recognized by Vienna authorities as representing the Christian Orthodox creed of the empire. Meanwhile, the Orthodox high priests' attachment to religious dogma was continuously accompanied by scientific study, the reception of new ideas, and their contribution to the formation of modern thought. The idea of attaining progress in knowledge through the cultivation and emancipation of the individual, the reality of a peaceful social cohabitation as well as the acceptance of, or the contribution to, political reforms, conferred a different status on churches in the eighteenth century. At this time, the Austrian Enlightenment was omnipresent due to the churches that were spread throughout the empire. That explains why many of the era's scholars frequented Hungarian, Austrian and German schools, corresponded with one another, and wrote academic studies and books inspired by the most prominent representatives of the Enlightenment. Metropolitan Ștefan Stratimirović (1790–1839) was one of them; he participated actively in cultural and political changes as well as in intercultural and plurilingual communication (in Slavic-Serbian, Hungarian, German and Latin). His writings reveal a constant interest in studying the history of his own community, its relations to neighbouring groups and the relation between the local and the universal.[29]

Jews represented another major group of Central and Eastern Europe promoting the dialogue of cultures; they were a significant presence among the creative elites of the area and amidst the social groups receptive to renewal. This happened in the context in which the practice of the Judaic faith was accepted in the regions under the administration of the Habsburgs and the Ottomans, the Sephardim and Ashkenazim rites having been observed in these areas from the sixteenth to the nineteenth centuries.[30] On the other hand, Jews were a unifying factor everywhere, since they were prone to sustain assimilation, especially after the Austro-Hungarian Monarchy had recognized their rights to citizenship. Jews did not develop ethnonationalist claims, as other communities did in the course of the century of nationalities; instead, they were encouraged to assimilate by the laws of the dualist monarchy.

Romanticism and the Issue of Identity: Continuities and Discontinuities in Multicultural Spaces

Unlike the Enlightenment, which was characterized by a spirit of reform and a quest to keep the equilibrium between the local and the universal, the romanticism of Central and Eastern Europe manifested itself through a strong desire for rapid changes, fuelled by ideals that scarcely corresponded to reality. Philologists, historians and philosophers were those who excelled by imagining the course of events, but they often considered them from an ivory tower, detached from the pulse of everyday life. While Hegel did not pay attention to history proper but only to drawing up a doctrine about the past, Herder enounced the relation between human species and political thought, but not the relationship between the idea of nation and political practice. Karl Popper would later call this way of understanding a 'strange story', 'the story of the rise of German nationalism'.[31] Possessing an encyclopedic type of culture and drawing inspiration from Enlightenment followers, Herder formulated and popularized the ethnonationalist theory in the most accessible possible terms. His historicist essentialism was not actually an instance of doing history. By means of the concept of *Volksgeist* (people's spirit), he developed the idea of Leibniz's monad, with which he impressed a large number of intellectuals. Herder's originality consisted in the application of a biologist doctrine to history. Along with the concept of *Volksgeist*, Herder advanced a vitalist view of the world, which had teleological connotations. He also articulated a theory of the evolution of human history as the repository of overarching meaning.[32] Among his fundamental conclusions – some of which became the highest point of attraction for the learned revolutionaries of 1848 and later nationalists – was to regard the history of humankind as stemming from a supernatural force. Following this line of thought, only the intervention of divinity could inculcate a new life into dead matter at a critical moment.

The existence of independent principalities as a legacy of the Middle Ages and a privileged space for the affirmation of civil society and the urban bourgeoisie was inconceivable for ambitious politicians with intentions to dominate others. Herder had anticipated this state of affairs and pleaded for giving up obsolete forms of administration. Feeling the pulse of the era, he identified himself with the forces announcing change and those whom he believed gave a voice to feelings and consciousness. Yet this type of change did not tally with the British liberal ideal or the British nationalist aspirations that seemed to belong to another historical time. Nor did it correspond to the spirit of post-revolutionary and post-Napoleonic France. Those were different ideas[33] that gave rise to different policies. While in German culture the Enlightenment would above all represent a *time* of transition (the *Sattelzeit* identified by Koselleck with the period from 1750 to 1850), the transition to modernity in the regions of Central and Eastern Europe bore above all the imprint of the *place* where it occurred – a place characterized by the high status of the Catholic Church, the practice of plurilingualism, the heterogeneity and exoticism of cultures, the ever-presence of ambivalences. In this sense, Stefan Jordan is right to state that many scholars have been too easily inclined to adapt or transfer to other areas and cultures a concept like that of *Sattelzeit*, one whose character was vaguely defined even in its original conception.[34] In fact, if we compare the aspirations of German and French romantics, we can see that each of them had their own set of ideals regarding emancipation. We need therefore to understand the importance of investigating and assessing history from the point of view of geography and not only time.

Herder had located the ethnonational issue under the scope of invented laws; hence he spoke of the emergence of a 'fictive ethnicity'.[35] His aspirations actually belonged to the idealist monism professed by the romantics. According to him, only poetry could tell the truth in the highest possible degree and inspire people with 'a sweet tinkling' (*süßem Geklingel*).[36] The truth he spoke about was one according to which individuals had to obey the collectivity. For that to be possible, one had to create a people as an ideal form incarnating the idea of unity. Formulated by the chosen few of the species, this idealism was meant to solve centuries-old frustrations. The poet alone had the power to turn a people's heart in the right direction, and Herder credited him with the role of the opinion maker. As a result, an individual's culture, reason and responsibilities as they had been thought by the Enlightenment figures were abandoned in favour of dreams that had to be turned into reality, but which at that time had no relation to social realities, the administration or the status of an individual or a community. As compared to their predecessors, the romantics had therefore put into effect a second paradigmatic change. Alongside continuities, speculative ideas concerning identity formulated by them gave rise to many discontinuities in all European cultures, especially in the political cultures of the Central and East European peoples.

Consequently, the poet had to be regarded as a god on earth, and the nation was regarded as a poet's creation, its purity being equated with a 'true', 'simple', 'divine', even 'pure' poem. We can read between the lines that this idea was a response to the French encyclopedists, to the French ideals personified by materialist scholars, and to the programmatic ideas of the 1789 revolution. The romantics maintained that if the *Volk* agreed to be guided by the chosen one of the masses, people would no longer have to worry about their success. Following this view, the concept of a political and democratic nation had lost ground in favour of the concept of an organic nation. The idea of the *Volk* – understood as a tribe, a community or an organic representation of a collective being – became the promoter of the future nation. Yet, acknowledging that 'the great therapy' of humanity was, as Herder thought, 'a violent revolt',[37] is the same as making no distinction between good and evil. Claiming that what constitutes power is based on exalted feelings and violence is tantamount to agreeing that reason has no role in human actions. In other words, Herder understood a state's constitution and legislation in relation to piety, religion and chivalrous honour. He sustained the irreducible specificity of each community as well as the necessity to adhere to a mystical metaphysics.[38] This was a speculative type of thought that developed a set of ideas running parallel to reality, and replaced the idea of a rational administrative construction that had been promoted by Josephinism. Following this new perspective, an ethnic community was to become a nation, and the nation of the ethnicity that represented the majority of the inhabitants of that particular area was to be invested with the idea of statehood.

In Lieu of Conclusions: The Conceptualization of Modernity

The earliest conceptualizations of modernity in Central and Eastern Europe were made possible under the influence of Enlightenment ideas. Churches, schools, erudite circles, libraries, publishing houses, books, and especially curious, well-instructed people who were constantly moving from one end of the continent to the other, explored and got to know each other's space. Latin, Slavonic, French and German were means of communication through which ideas and discoveries circulated, and the transfer of knowledge and values was carried out. The relation between a transmitter and a receiver became fundamental in the order of changes of people and things. The Enlightenment era therefore facilitated the formation of a type of cultural elite in which the differences and contradictions between various regions seemed to be levelled. In the case of Central and Eastern Europe, the cooperation between the Austrian state and the Roman Catholic Church ensured a sense of balance, even at moments when the penetration of new ideas in society clearly indicated the necessity for reforms. The Enlightenment cosmopolitanism of the Austrian Empire found its complement in local organisms. The multiculturality of these areas created a 'horizon of expectations' in which the vocabulary of literary, historical, philosophical and political texts indicated the aspirations of the times. The elites of these regions conceived their new condition and status by the formation of reflections that coincided with the cultural and political ideas percolating in society, especially the official and unofficial zeal for change. This was also the era in which Central and Eastern Europe simultaneously took inspiration from the array of local values and the pre-existent cultural heterogeneity of the area. The imperial idea of an inclusive society, understood as a sine qua non principle for the existence of the empire, often had practical results throughout the eighteenth century. The divergence between multicultural inclusion and ethnocentric exclusion that emerged in the following century was one that would deeply affect the second stage of modernity.

A highly important fact is that the Habsburgs did not prevent communities from defining themselves by taking into consideration the level of their fortune and religious allegiance, which were referred to via the notions of nobility and clergy. Yet, starting with the spread and reception of Herder's texts and ideas, cultural differences among communities were encouraged to the detriment of convergences, especially because of the intellectual activism generated by each community in turn. Meanwhile, the German language and the connections with Protestant educational institutions, writers and scholars from the principalities outside Austria, played an important role in the ideological training of the elites from Slavonia, Silesia, Bohemia, Hungary, Transylvania, Banat and Bukovina. Previously, German and not French had been essential in the process of these regions' assertion of identity. 'Austria's German' was then gradually replaced by cultural-ideological messages given in 'Prussia's German' and, later, in 'Germany's German'. Ethnocommunitarian feelings and instincts were thereby encouraged.

Herder's interpretations had thus anticipated an ideal that had been rethought within a very short period of time by cramming together the stages of modernization. They exercised their influence in the region of Central and Eastern Europe through the circulation of some of his works, through translations and popularizations by means of the written press, and through discourses that seduced people with the thesis about people's rights to develop their own culture and 'specificity' on the grounds of linguistic or dialectic particularities, and especially the origins, history, folklore and continued residence on one and the same territory. Even under the given circumstances, it often happened over the course of the nineteenth century that the new elites were confronted with dilemmas about choosing either a monocultural or a traditionally multicultural point of view. Faced with the idea of the supremacy of a cultural ethnonation over another, and with that of recognizing the European modernity in which either inclusion or exclusion predominated, the above-mentioned elites and the collectivities to which they pertained chose to situate themselves at the crossroads for a while, accepting ambiguity and recognizing themselves both as an ethnonation and as a part of the multicultural state. After several decades had elapsed, this act of contesting multicultural realities led to a break of huge proportions, which found its most obvious expression in the events of the First World War, a war centred round the issue of extreme nationalisms. In the interim, the ideologies that encouraged separation and competition among groups gained momentum little by little, and the exotic and warlike theories of identity invented by the romantics imposed themselves on the areas of Central and Eastern Europe to the detriment of communitarian plurality and peaceful cohabitation. Despite this tragic course of events, and despite the tensions resulting from the faulty management of the relations between the mainstream and the minorities of ethno-national states, multicultural realities survived throughout the entire twentieth century. They were, and often remained, a unique ferment for all sorts of creations, one which maintained the bridges of communication among various cultures and state entities in Central and Eastern Europe. This is one more reason why I think that the analysis and assessment of multicultural history significantly contributes to a more objective understanding of the conceptualization of modernity in the region of Central and Eastern Europe.

Victor Neumann is Professor of History at the West University of Timișoara, Romania. His publications include *The Temptation of Homo Europaeus: The Genesis of the Modern Ideas in Central and Southeastern Europe* (New York, 1993); *Between Words and Reality: Studies on the Politics of Recognition and the Changes of Regime in Contemporary Romania* (Washington, DC, 2001); *The End of a History: The Jews of Banat from the Beginning to Nowadays* (Bucharest, 2006); *Essays on Romanian Intellectual History* (Timișoara, 2008 / Iași, 2013); *Key Concepts of Romanian History* (Budapest and New York, 2013), co-edited with Armin Heinen; and *Die Interkulturalität des Banats* (Berlin: Frank und Timme Verlag, 2015).

Notes

1. Reinhart Koselleck, *Begriffsgeschichten: Studien zur Semantik und Pragmatik der politischen und sozialen Sprache* (Frankfurt/M.: Suhrkamp, 2006), 108.
2. Isaiah Berlin, *The Power of Ideas*, ed. Henry Hardy (Princeton NJ: Princeton University Press, 2000), esp. the chapter entitled 'One of the Boldest Innovators in the History of Human Thought', 53–67.

3. On the false representation of the Balkans in the West, see Maria Todorova, *Imagining the Balkans* (New York Oxford: Oxford University Press, 1997); Vesna Goldsworthy, *Inventing Ruritania – The Imperialism of the Imagination* (London: Yale University Press, 1998).
4. Goldsworthy, *Inventing Ruritania*, 232–33.
5. Mario Scattola, 'Begriffsgeschichte und Geschichte der politischen Lehren', in Ricardo Pozzo and Marco Sgarbi (eds), *Typologie der Formen der Begriffsgeschichte (Hamburg:* Felix Meiner Verlag, 2010), 75–76.
6. Berlin, *Power of Ideas*, esp. the chapter entitled 'Russian Intellectual History', 68–78.
7. Mihai Spăriosu defines the term like this: 'The notion of liminality can be an important conceptual tool for choosing not only the way in which cultural (and cognitive) transformations emerge or are produced, but also the way in which these changes can be molded into a peaceful model' (my own translation, according to the study published in Romanian). Cf. Mihai Spăriosu, 'Studiile interetnice contemporane în Europa Centrală: Observații interetnice preliminare' [Contemporary interethnic studies in Central Europe. Preliminary interethnic remarks], in *Armonie și conflict intercultural în Banat și Transilvania* [Harmony and intercultural conflict in the regions of Banat and Transylvania], ed. Vasile Boari and Mihai Spăriosu (Iași: Editura Institutul European, 2013), 66–67.
8. See Peter Niedermüller, 'Der Mythos des Unterschieds: vom Multikulturalismus zur Hybridität', in Johannes Feichtinger, Ursula Prutsch and Moritz Csáky (eds), *Habsburg Postcolonial* (Innsbruck: Studien Verlag, 2003), 69–81.
9. Amy Gutmann, 'Introduction', in Charles Taylor et al., *Multiculturalism: Examining the Politics of Recognition* (Princeton, NJ: Princeton University Press, 1994), 5.
10. Ibid., 30.
11. See such differences in the volume: Peter Gunst, 'Agrarian System of Central and Eastern Europe', in Daniel Chirot (ed.), *The Origins of Backwardness in Eastern Europe: Economics and Politics from the Middle Ages until the Early Twentieth Century* (Berkeley: University of California Press, 1989), 53–92.
12. Moritz Csáky, *Ideologie der Operette und Wiener Moderne: Ein kulturhistorischer Essay* (Vienna: Böhlau Verlag, 1997); Moritz Csáky, *Das Gedächtnis der Städte: Kulturelle Verflechtungen – Wien und die urbanen Milieus in Zentraleuropa* (Vienna: Böhlau Verlag, 2010).
13. Moritz Csáky, 'Ambivalenz des kulturellen Erbes: Zentraleuropa', in Moritz Csáky and Klaus Zeyringer, *Ambivalenz des kulturellen Erbes: Vielfachcodierung des historischen Gedächtnisses. Paradigma Österreich* (Innsbruck: Studien Verlag, 2000), 27–49.
14. See Derek Beales's excellent book *Enlightenment and Reform in Eighteenth-Century Europe* (New York: I.B. Tauris, 2011), 162.
15. See the list of necessary and useful measures to be introduced in Transylvania in Ileana Bozac and Teodor Pavel, *Călătoria împăratului Iosif al II-lea în*

Transilvania la 1773 [Emperor Joseph II's 1773 voyage to Transylvania], vol. I, 2nd edn (Cluj-Napoca: Editura Academiei Române, 2007), 204–2015.
16. Csáky, 'Ambivalenz', 31.
17. Victor Neumann, 'Multiculturality and interculturality: The Case of Timişoara', *Hungarian Studies* (Hungarian Academy of Sciences) 21(1) (2007), 3–18; Victor Neumann, 'Timişoara between "Fictive Ethnicity" and "Ideal Nation": The Identity Profile during the Interwar Period', in *Balcanica* (Serbian Academy of Sciences and Arts), Belgrade, XLIV, 2013, 391–412; Victor Neumann (ed.), *Identitate şi cultură: Studii privind istoria Banatului* [Identity and culture. Studies on the history of Banat] (Bucharest: Editura Academiei Române, 2009), 25–38, 38–48, 77–89, 211–29, 325–47; Victor Neumann, *Die Interkulturalität des Banats* (Berlin: Frank & Timme Verlag, 2015).
18. See Chirot, *Origins of Backwardness*.
19. Hans Erich Bödeker, 'Aufklärung über Aufklärung? Reinhart Kosellecks Interpretation der Aufklärung', in Carsten Dutt and Reinhard Laube (eds), *Zwischen Sprache und Geschichte: Zum Werk Reinhart Kosellecks* (Göttingen: Wallstein Verlag, 2013), 128–74.
20. Răzvan Theodorescu, 'Despre coridoarele culturale ale Europei de Sud-Est' [About cultural channels in South Eastern Europe], in *Memoriile Secţiei de Ştiinţe Istorice* [Memories of the Historical Sciences Department], Romanian Academy, IV, vol. 7, 1982, 7–27; Victor Neumann, '"Cultural Channels" in East-Central Europe: Books and Libraries in Transylvania, Banat, Hungary and Serbia', in Victor Neumann, *The Temptation of Homo Europaeus* (New York: Columbia University Press, 1993), 149–211.
21. The Habsburgs reinstated the domination of the Catholic religion in Transylvania following their own interests. See Lukács Olga and Magyari András, 'Biserică şi stat la maghiari' [Church and State with the Hungarians], in Ioan-Aurel Pop, Thomas Nägler and Magyari András (eds), *Istoria Transilvaniei: De la 1711 la 1918* [The history of Transylvania, 1711–1918], vol. III (Cluj-Napoca: The Romanian Academy, Center for Transylvanian Studies, 2008), 105–6.
22. Franz Szabo, *Kaunitz and Enlightened Absolutism, 1753–1780* (Cambridge: Cambridge University Press, 1994).
23. Beales, *Enlightenment and Reform*, see the chapters 'Joseph II and the Monasteries of Austria and Hungary', 227–56, 'The Origins of the Pope's Visit to Joseph II in 1782', 256–72, and 'Was Joseph II an Enlightened Despot?', 262–87.
24. Domokos Kosáry, *Ujjáépites és polgárosodás 1711–1867* [Reconstruction and civism] (Budapest: Hater Lap és Könyvkiadó, 1990). See also D. Prodan, *Supplex Libellus Valachorum: Din istoria formării naţiunii române* [Supplex Libellus Valachorum. Pages from the history of the formation of the Romanian nation], new edition, (Bucharest, 1984).
25. Cf. Neumann, "Cultural Channels".
26. Csáky, *Gedächtnis der Städte*.

27. See Martin Roos, Die Alte Diözese Csanád, vol. I, part 2b: 1800–1850 (Szeged-Csanád, 2012), 117–18.
28. Ibid., 171.
29. Victor Neumann, 'Principii iluministe și diferențialism etnocultural: Opera cărturarului Ștefan Stratimirovič – mitropolit al ortodocșilor din Imperiul Habsburgic' [Enlightenment principles and ethnocultural differentialism. The oeuvre of scholar Ștefan Stratimirovič – an orthodox metropolitan of the Habsburg Empire], in Neumann, *Identitate și cultură*, 38–48.
30. Victor Neumann, *Istoria evreilor din România: Studii documentare și teoretice* [The history of Romania's Jews. Documentary and theoretical studies] (Timișoara, Editura Amarcord, 1996), 31.
31. K. Popper, *The Open Society and Its Enemies*, vol. 2: *The High Tide of Prophecy: Hegel, Marx and the Aftermath* (London: Routledge, 1996), 49. See detailed explanations at 49–59. About Herder's contribution to the oracular philosophy and to the theory of nationalism, see 52–53. For a more detailed presentation of Herder and Herderianism, see Victor Neumann, 'Peculiarities of the Translation and Adaptation of the Concept of Nation in East-Central Europe: The Hungarian and Romanian Cases in the Nineteenth Century', *Contributions to the History of Concepts* 7(1) (2012), 72–101.
32. Elias Palti, 'The Metaphor of Life: Herder's Philosophy of History and Uneven Developments in Late Eighteenth-Century Natural Sciences', *History and Theory* 38 (1999), 322–23. See also Victor Neumann's comment in *Studia Politica: Romanian Political Science Review* 12(1) (2012), 154–59.
33. See João Feres Jr, 'With an Eye on Future Research: The Theoretical Layers of Conceptual History', in Javier Fernández Sebastián (ed.), *Political Concepts and Time: New Approaches to Conceptual History* (Santander: Cantabria University Press and McGraw-Hill Interamericana de España, 2011) 223–39. See also the comment by Victor Neumann in *Studia Politica: Romanian Political Science Review* 12(1) (2012), 154–59.
34. Cf. Stefan Jordan, 'Die Sattelzeit – Transformation des Denkens oder revolutionärer Paradigmenwechsel?', in Achim Landwehr (ed.), *Frühe Neue Zeiten: Zeitwissen zwischen Reformation und Revolution* (Bielefeld: transcript, 2012), 373–88. I believe that irrespective of which concept we analyse, decoding its meanings or applicability to a certain time and space must take into account context, geography, society, and cultural and religious legacies.
35. Etienne Balibar, 'The Nation Form: History and Ideology', in Etienne Balibar and Immanuel Wallerstein (eds), *Race, Nation, Class: Ambiguous Identities* (London and New York: Verso, 2002), 96–100.
36. J.G. Herder, *Ueber die Wirkung der Dichtkunst*, in Herder's Werke vol. 3 (Weimar: Volksverlag, 1963), 246.
37. Herder, *Ueber die Wirkung*, 253.
38. Palti, 'Metaphor of Life', 322–23.

References

Balibar, Etienne, 'The Nation Form: History and Ideology', in Etienne Balibar and Immanuel Wallerstein (eds), *Race, Nation, Class: Ambiguous Identities* (London and New York: Verso, 2002), 96–100

Beales, Derek, *Enlightenment and Reform in Eighteenth-Century Europe* (New York: I.B. Tauris, 2011)

Berlin, Isaiah, *The Power of Ideas*, ed. Henry Hardy (Princeton, NJ: Princeton University Press, 2000)

Bödeker, Hans Erich, 'Aufklärung über Aufklärung? Reinhart Kosellecks Interpretation der Aufklärung', in Carsten Dutt and Reinhard Laube (eds), *Zwischen Sprache und Geschichte: Zum Werk Reinhart Kosellecks* (Göttingen: Wallstein Verlag, 2013), 128–74

Bozac, Ileana and Teodor Pavel, *Călătoria împăratului Iosif al II-lea în Transilvania la 1773* [Emperor Joseph II's 1773 voyage to Transylvania], vol. I, 2nd edn (Cluj-Napoca: Editura Academiei Române, 2007)

Csáky, Moritz, *Ideologie der Operette und Wiener Moderne: Ein kulturhistorisches Essay* (Vienna: Böhlau Verlag, 1997)

———, 'Ambivalenz des kulturellen Erbes: Zentraleuropa', in Moritz Csáky and Klaus Zeyringer, *Ambivalenz des kulturellen Erbes: Vielfachcodierung des historischen Gedächtnisses. Paradigma Österreich* (Innsbruck: Studien Verlag, 2000), 27–49

———, *Das Gedächtnis der Städte. Kulturelle Verflechtungen – Wien und die urbanen Milieus in Zentraleuropa* (Vinna: Böhlau Verlag, 2010)

Feres Jr, João, 'With an Eye on Future Research: The Theoretical Layers of Conceptual History', in Javier Fernández-Sebastián (ed.), *Political Concepts and Time: New Approaches to Conceptual History* (Santander: Cantabria University Press and McGraw-Hill Interamericana de España, 2011), 223–39

Goldsworthy, Vesna, *Inventing Ruritania: The Imperialism of the Imagination* (London: Yale University Press, 1998)

Gunst, Peter, 'Agrarian System of Central and Eastern Europe', in Daniel Chirot (ed.), *The Origins of Backwardness in Eastern Europe: Economics and Politics from the Middle Ages until the Early Twentieth Century* (Berkeley: University of California Press, 1989), 53–92

Gutmann, Amy, 'Introduction', in Charles Taylor et al., *Multiculturalism: Examining the Politics of Recognition* (Princeton, NJ: Princeton University Press, 1994)

Herder, Johann Gottfried, *Ueber die Wirkung der Dichtkunst*, in Herder's Werke, vol. 3 (Weimar: Volksverlag, 1963)

Jordan, Stefan, 'Die Sattelzeit – Transformation des Denkens oder revolutionärer Paradigmenwechsel?', in Achim Landwehr (ed.), *Frühe Neue Zeiten: Zeitwissen zwischen Reformation und Revolution* (Bielefeld: transcript, 2012), 373–88

Kosáry, Domokos, *Ujjáépites és polgárosodás 1711–1867* [Reconstruction and civism] (Budapest: Hater Lap és Könyvkiadó, 1990)

Koselleck, Reinhart, *Begriffsgeschichten: Studien zur Semantik und Pragmatik der politischen und sozialen Sprache* (Frankfurt/M.: Suhrkamp, 2006)

Neumann, Victor, '"Cultural Channels" in East-Central Europe: Books and Libraries in Transylvania, Banat, Hungary and Serbia', in Victor Neumann, *The Temptation of Homo Europaeus* (New York: Columbia University Press, 1993), 149–211

———, *Istoria evreilor din România. Studii documentare și teoretice* [The history of Romania's Jews. Documentary and theoretical studies] (Timișoara, Editura Amarcord, 1996)

———, 'Multiculturality and interculturality: The Case of Timișoara', *Hungarian Studies* (Hungarian Academy of Sciences) 21(1) (2007), 3–18

——— (ed.), *Identitate și cultură: Studii privind istoria Banatului* [Identity and culture. Studies on the history of Banat] (Bucharest: Editura Academiei Române, 2009)

———, 'Principii iluministe și diferențialism etnocultural: Opera cărturarului Ștefan Stratimirovič – mitropolit al ortodocșilor din Imperiul Habsburgic' [Enlightenment principles and ethnocultural differentialism. The oeuvre of scholar Ștefan Stratimirovič – an orthodox metropolitan of the Habsburg Empire], in Victor Neumann (ed.), *Identitate și cultură. Studii privind istoria Banatului* [Identity and culture. Studies on the history of Banat] (Bucharest: Editura Academiei Române, 2009), 38–48

———, 'Peculiarities of the Translation and Adaptation of the Concept of Nation in East–Central Europe: The Hungarian and Romanian Cases in the Nineteenth Century', *Contributions to the History of Concepts* 7(1) (2012), 72–101

———, 'Timișoara between "Fictive Ethnicity" and "Ideal Nation": The Identity Profile during the Interwar Period', in *Balcanica* (Serbian Academy of Sciences and Arts), Belgrade, XLIV, 2013, 391–412

———, *Die Interkulturalität des Banats* [The interculturality of Banat] (Berlin: Frank & Timme Verlag, 2015)

Niedermüller, Peter, 'Der Mythos des Unterschieds: vom Multikulturalismus zur Hybridität', in Johannes Feichtinger, Ursula Prutsch, and Moritz Csáky (eds), *Habsburg Postcolonial* (Innsbruck: Studien Verlag, 2003), 69–81

Olga, Lukács and Magyari András, 'Biserică și stat la maghiari' [Church and State with the Hungarians], in Ioan-Aurel Pop, Thomas Nägler and Magyari András (eds), *Istoria Transilvaniei. De la 1711 la 1918* [The history of Transylvania, 1711–1918], vol. III (Cluj-Napoca: The Romanian Academy, Center for Transylvanian Studies, 2008)

Palti, Elias, 'The Metaphor of Life: Herder's Philosophy of History and Uneven Developments in Late Eighteenth-Century Natural Sciences', *History and Theory* 38 (1999), 322–47

Popper, Karl, *The Open Society and Its Enemies*, vol. 2: *The High Tide of Prophecy: Hegel, Marx and the Aftermath* (London: Routledge, 1996)

Prodan, David, *Supplex Libellus Valachorum: Din istoria formării națiunii române* [Supplex Libellus Valachorum. Pages from the history of the formation of the Romanian nation], new edition (Bucharest, 1984)

Roos, Martin, *Die Alte Diözese Csanád*, vol. I, part 2b: 1800–1850 (Szeged-Csanád, 2012)

Scattola, Mario, 'Begriffsgeschichte und Geschichte der politischen Lehren', in Ricardo Pozzo and Marco Sgarbi (eds), *Typologie der Formen der Begriffsgeschichte* (Hamburg: Felix Meiner Verlag, 2010), 71–90

Spăriosu, Mihai, 'Studiile interetnice contemporane în Europa Centrală. Observații interetnice preliminare' [Contemporary interethnic studies in Central Europe. Preliminary snterethnic remarks], in *Armonie și conflict intercultural în Banat și Transilvania* [Harmony and intercultural conflict in the regions of Banat and Transylvania], ed. Vasile Boari and Mihai Spăriosu (Iași: Editura Institutul European, 2013)

Szabo, Franz, *Kaunitz and Enlightened Absolutism, 1753–1780* (Cambridge: Cambridge University Press, 1994)

Theodorescu, Răzvan, 'Despre coridoarele culturale ale Europei de Sud-Est' [About cultural channels in South Eastern Europe], in *Memoriile Secției de Științe Istorice* [Memories of the Historical Sciences Department], Romanian Academy, IV, vol. 7, 1982, 7–27

Todorova, Maria, *Imagining the Balkans* (New York and Oxford: Oxford University Press, 1997)

Chapter 10
Concepts in a Nordic Periphery

Henrik Stenius

The Argument

Every actor using a key concept stands inevitably in front of a 'choice' between either using it with universalistic pretentions or conceding that it has been conditioned by its historical context. The word choice is entered in quotation marks to indicate that the kind of decision we speak about is, as a rule, not a conscious intellectual move, but an act of repetition in accordance with ordinary ways of using the concept.[1] Usually, there is no need to reflect on the issue of whether key concepts have, or should have, universally valid definitions. However, we are all aware of the fact that there are certain situations or fields of practice in which strictly harmonized concepts are extremely important, such as, for example, the making of contracts or quantitative research in the natural sciences.

Besides such obvious cases where universality is a self-evident requirement, it is difficult to claim that there are categorically right or wrong ways of approaching the question of whether a key concept has, or should have, a universally valid meaning. For suppressed subjects in an oppressive society, for instance, it is clearly legitimate to defend their own political, cultural and social claims by referring to universal human rights. It is legitimate because it can be an efficient rhetorical tool, but also because talking about universal human rights does not necessarily imply a metaphysical assumption that the whole world is governed by an 'eternal' natural law of which human rights would be a part. The concept of universal human rights can also be used in a more restricted sense, insisting that there is a sociologically, or juridically, established universal applicability of the concept. On the other hand, it can be equally legitimate to deny that key concepts such as 'human rights' have, or should have, a universal content, as, for instance, when historical actors in subcultures or small peripheral nations claim their own right, or even duty, to look upon the world in their own ways – which would imply, among other things, giving key concepts their own particularistic content.

The argument of this chapter is that one essential aspect of the relation between the particular and the universal depends on whether the actor is positioned in the centre or the periphery. This perspective is relevant, irrespective of the historical period we are approaching, but is particularly valid, with regard to Europe, for the early modern period, the period of the formation of modern political languages. The intellectual core regions of the period have fittingly been called 'The Republic of Letters'; implying, among other things, that the core was made up of regions with a high degree of cross-border communication and encounters on a reciprocal basis. Moreover, people in the public life of this 'republic' defined their position as being on the edge of intellectual, political and social thinking. This made them inclined, the argument goes, to invest their own key concepts with essentialist notions and pretend that they could serve to articulate universally valid truths and norms.

We are talking here about tendencies. All cultures claim their right to look upon the world in their own way. But actors in the peripheries usually do this in a more self-conscious way, because the possibility of universalizing one's own particularisms is less likely to succeed. Peripheral actors are forced to navigate between universalisms and particularities. This gives the peripheries a critical potential to reveal the universalist pretensions of the core.[2]

For the purposes of this chapter, the 'Republic of Letters' is comprehended principally in spatial terms, although the term originally did not refer to concrete polities in a programmatic way. When discussing the spatial positioning of actors, there is no need for a social historical definition of what centres and peripheries actually are (or have been). The terms indicate a *relation*, and what matters is the self-understanding of the actor: does (s)he think that her or his position is in the 'catch up' part of the yardstick, or does (s)he experience being part of an ascendant or even dominant culture? Having said that, one has to add that an actor in the core can, of course, make use of a universalistic language without a self-understanding of being part of such a dominant culture.

Generally speaking, my argument is that actors who think that they live in a periphery do not expect much reciprocity in the discursive interchanges between the centre and the peripheries. In a historical perspective, and more particularly with regard to the period of modernization processes in European history, it will be hard to find actors in the peripheries who had the ambition to influence the discourses of the centre, and it might even be more difficult to find people in the centre who felt a need to listen to alternative views expressed in the peripheries.³ There is an asymmetry between the centre and the periphery in the sense that the debate in the core is translated to the peripheries in a way that corresponds to specific interests of specific actors in the peripheries. In this kind of asymmetrical constellation, each periphery created its own kind of intellectual autonomy, a conceptual universe challenging the universalistic ambitions of the actors in the centre's hegemonic culture. Questioning and relativizing the universalisms of the centre could include provocative elements. More often, however, the questioning was timid, acknowledging that there was no reason to expect any serious interest in the centre to listen to the temporalized, particular interpretations of key concepts of the peripheries. In today's academic communities, such arguments on spatiality are often regarded as controversial or even damaging. The reason for such a negative attitude can be tracked down to a misunderstanding that Bourdieu calls an 'illusion': the idea that international intellectual public space is governed by reciprocal interaction between equal partners. Scholars who are inclined to think in that way are equally inclined to disapprove of all talk about centres and peripheries.

Another important argument put forward here is that actors who approved of the idea that concepts had, or should have, particularistic meanings were forced to take a stand between two distinct views. On the one hand they could choose to do without the concord of the Republic of Letters, and create 'parochial' concepts that served the purpose of holistic integration of their own culture. Alternatively, they could try to strike a balance between local conceptions (and contextualizations) of key concepts and the demand for communication across cultural boundaries; the latter could be achieved either by constructing a semi-universalistic vocabulary in a 'third space' (Homi Bhabha) that every partner could accept without betraying his or her own historical experiences, or by using a dead language such as Latin that served as a substitute for a 'meta-language' (Reinhart Koselleck), or by employing other techniques for creating pseudo-universalism.

A Nordic Conceptual Universe

The Nordic societies, particularly in the early modern period, were peripheries outside the Republic of Letters. A Nordic path to modernity, the Nordic *Sonderweg*, was established as a culture of translations, in which the actors who wanted to make sense of European key concepts first had to think their thoughts in a 'central' 'European' language (mostly French, German or English), and only after that might try to articulate their thoughts in their own national contexts – possibly, but not necessarily, in their own vernacular languages. The more sophisticated and elaborated the Nordic conceptual universe became, the more 'European' the universe became, but, at the same time, it never totally lost its own intellectual autonomy. If we may speak of a common European conceptual universe today, it is a mixture of conceptual universes, a complex configuration of parallel regional and country-specific conceptual universes, existing side by side yet overlapping.[4]

When discussing a Nordic *Sonderweg*, the metaphor of the *Sattelzeit* is not particularly illuminating, the main reason being that most political and social key concepts in the early modern Nordic countries were not constructed by a reconceptualization of old Nordic concepts. The situation in German-speaking Europe was different. Here premodern life could rely on a set of autochthonous key concepts with a robust history, some of them with very ancient roots, supplemented by a considerable number of loanwords from Latin and other languages. From the mid eighteenth century onwards that old German conceptual universe entered into an accelerated phase of contestation and reconceptualization, a process that ended about one hundred years later when most key concepts in the German-speaking world finally acquired their modern meanings. An appropriate timeline for the formation of modern key concepts in the Nordic countries should take account of the fact that modernization here did not consist in a reconceptualization of autochthonous concepts, but in an importing of foreign key concepts. One could therefore suggest that, instead of talking about a Nordic *Sattelzeit*, one might talk about a *Trichterzeit*, a funnel period. That metaphor would do justice to the fact that the premodern Nordic countries were in this regard in a 'year zero' situation when, rather suddenly, a large number of 'central' European key concepts were imported and, as if through a funnel, pressed, distilled and poured out as a uniform set of concepts. The funnel functioned as a vehicle for Nordic eclecticism, allowing Nordic actors to choose and combine different elements from European discourses coming from the centres into a new, Nordic set of concepts.

This funnel syndrome was actualized in a political culture that pivoted around two basic principles, more inborn and mechanically accepted than verbally acknowledged and theorized. They can therefore hardly be regarded as concepts. According to the first principle, the gap between worldly and spiritual life should be bridged as much as possible (the Nordic syndrome of one-norm societies); and according to the second one, the different kinds of inclusion mechanisms in different sections of society should serve as a steering principle in *all* discussions on how to organize social and political life.[5] In contrast to the rest of Western Europe, the Reformation in the two Nordic realms, Denmark and Sweden, brought the worldly (King) and spiritual (Church) power into one organic whole where the worldly and spiritual officialdoms were two dimensions of one body of authority. In these societies, no serious rivalry between Church and State existed. There was only one seat of authority, legitimized, of course, by theological arguments, explicated by the members of the 'learned estate', which in these two realms unambiguously meant the clergy – not, as in other Lutheran countries outside Denmark and Sweden, the clergy *and* the faculty of law.

The narrative of conformist, one-norm societies in the North has thus had a long history. It is in this conformism that we can find a fruitful soil for the modern, universalistic practices of the Nordic welfare states. These kinds of narratives on Nordic modernity usually also acknowledge the cultural, ethnic and religious homogeneity that intensified the conformism. However, what seems to be even more decisive for the formation of the Nordic *Sonderweg* are the effective inclusion mechanisms in the two Nordic realms. One should look here at the incorporation of the whole population by forcing every adult to work (instead of relying on philanthropy), the pedagogical programme that efficiently rectified the ideological thinking of the subjects (the Nordic ability to read, which did not go hand in hand with the ability to write), the integration of the male population into local decision making (local democracy), the people's army based on duty and coercion instead of a paid army, and the opening up of possibilities for as broad a populace as possible to take part in the production and distribution of useful knowledge about how to make life more productive.[6]

With irrepressible historical experiences such as these – a life in a one-norm society with strong inclusion mechanisms – policy makers in the Nordic countries looked at the rest of Europe. Did they find practices, models or concepts there that they wanted to copy, avoid or amend in one way or another? And, in studying the adoption of 'central' European key concepts in the Nordic countries, can one identify efforts to signal specific Nordic or national definitions and usages of those key concepts? Alternatively, can one discern strategies that held it more advantageous to emphasize a universalistic use/content of the concept? In the following paragraphs I shall select a couple of European key concepts, and briefly, only catchword-wise, indicate different Nordic ways to answer these questions.

The list of the adoption of modern key concepts starts, awkwardly enough, with concepts that were 'unimportant', that had no use in the Nordic countries. 'Fraction' and 'party' were key concepts in early modern Europe, especially in England, but as a rule with strong negative connotations. The idea of a legitimate opposition, dissenting without being disloyal to the whole, became vindicated by political writers in England and the United States during the eighteenth century.[7] The word 'opposition' did not appear in a newspaper in Finland until as late as 1867.[8] One might call this a conscious refusal to adopt European key concepts. In the Nordic one-norm societies, the ideas of parties and fractions found no resonance, nor did that of opposition. The religious dissensions too were not of a harrowing kind. The Reformation was led from above rather than originating in protests from below. And the Reformation was successful in the sense that it stopped the Nordic societies from splitting up in antagonistic subcultures, as was the case in Germany, Poland, the Netherlands, Hungary, England and many other European countries.[9] Neither did the 'second Reformation', the pietistic movement at the beginning of the eighteenth century, polarize the Nordic societies.[10]

'Pietism' and 'enlightenment' were two concepts, also denoting political movements, in eighteenth-century Europe that – more than many other movements – polarized and mobilized the citizenry in different camps. These two concepts were not only neutralized in the Nordic countries, but worked according to another logic quite different from the polarizing and mobilizing logic the concepts possessed south of the Baltic and the North Sea. In the northern realms, both concepts referred to features that every person had to a higher or a lower degree. By this logic, the concepts acquired a pedagogical character pointing at a potential: each man or woman could be more, instead of less, devoted and enlightened. Within Nordic societies, the concepts could thus only with difficulty be used for distinguishing 'us' and 'the other'.[11]

Similarly, the ethnic and religious differences were small compared to the situation in the more southern parts of Europe where the concept of 'tolerance' became part of the modern conceptual universe, indicating a particular strategy of how to deal with difference. In the Nordic realms, there was little need for such exercises. Instead, tolerance, like the concept of enlightenment, gained a moral and pedagogical aspect, which emphasized the importance of patience: little by little people would understand what was best for themselves.[12]

The cluster of early modern European concepts dealt with so far consisted of concepts that were all future oriented in the core as well as in the peripheral North. In the Nordic countries the concepts were particularistic in that they did not reproduce a common European element of mobilization and polarization. They were, however, 'universal' in another sense, by referring to features that could potentially be shared by every subject. The consensual culture in the Nordic one-norm societies became manifest also in concepts such as 'knowledge' and 'opinion', which in the Nordic countries came to be closely connected to each other. They were introduced as eighteenth-century neologisms in the European languages in order to make a distinction between what is, and what ought to be. This distinction became and remained blurred in the Nordic countries. In Finnish sources dating from the end of the nineteenth century we find quotations arguing that good 'statistics' should substitute for 'politics'.[13] Looking at concepts such as opinion, knowledge, education, culture and enlightenment as parts of a common cluster, they were all expressing an uncontested crucial value of education and culture, art and science.

The influence of the consensual culture is easily traceable also in the way key concepts were introduced and adopted in the period following the turbulent years of the French Revolution. While scouting out new, alternative or complementary ways for a legitimate political order, and while substituting the supremacy of old dynastic principles, the political public in Western Europe focused on universal practices and universal concepts monitoring the new practices. In the two old Nordic countries, Denmark and Sweden, as well as the two new ones, Finland and Norway, the concepts of 'people' and 'nation' became focal concepts of political thinking too. However, they came to be interpreted in a slightly different way, affording the regimes new options for legitimacy, and ultimately a new content of the concept of the 'state'. The concepts of people and nation were pliable, accommodating a tension that marked the political culture of the Nordic countries. As in the rest of Europe they carried with them a tension between a holistic morale and a republican deliberative ideal. On the one hand there was a discussion about who had the right to define what was in accordance with the interest of the whole; yet on the other hand the concepts were laden with republican values. In both cases the concepts could be used in a democratic as well as an anti-democratic rhetorical manner. This second alternative signalled the possibility of loosening up the one-norm ideal. The Nordic concept of people was particularly Nordic because the peasantry constituted such a decisive element of the concept.[14]

Another, very particular expression of inclusion and the one-norm condition is the fact that the concepts of 'state' and 'society' became interchangeable.[15] The counter-concept to 'society' was not the 'state' but 'nature', which, in the Nordic culture, signified the idea of authenticity. In order to construct a harmonious one-norm society, the individuals of the citizenry were expected to regularly replenish authenticity by spending some time in nature. It was regarded as a medicine on which all citizens were dependent. They needed it because it was believed that it would cure the alienation that accompanied urban civilization. Nor did 'democracy' and 'parliamentarianism' destroy the one-norm ideals. Workers' rights (the right to strike), universal suffrage and parliamentarianism – and the concepts relating to them – were innovations that did not provoke any strong reactionary mobilization, partly because the Nordic societies profited from the benefit of being latecomers. Democracy was accommodated to old consensual one-norm ideals. Social democracy became a secularized version of Lutheran practices.

In a narrative of Nordic universalisms, the 1930s constitute a decisive break. That break consisted in the introduction of the Nordic model as a third way, an alternative to capitalism and socialism. According to this rhetoric, universalism means that the Nordic societies from the 1930s on were no longer categorically at the receiving end of the history of conceptual transfers. The Nordic model was considered worth copying in the rest of the world. In the 1930s, social democrats in Sweden in particular successfully also launched and colonized the concept of 'Nordic democracy', and made it a conceptual node that served to forge an anti-totalitarian movement.[16]

This very short account about the transfer of modern key concepts into the Nordic countries is no more than an impressionistic sketch identifying issues to be further investigated in empirical studies. There is no attempt at forming any kind of a typology of different ways in which terms were used, either as universal or particularistic concepts. In the following section the conceptualization of 'citizen' in the Finnish language will be looked at in a more detailed way, as one example of how actors in a Nordic periphery found ways to balance between distancing themselves from the universalisms of the core and, at the same time, partaking in or creating universal discourses of their own.

Citizen

Transfers of concepts always create opportunities for rumination. One can benefit from being a latecomer. 'Catching up' strategies in particular engender a momentum for learning from others' well doings and misdoings, generating a constructivist frame of mind and making it difficult to assume that there is a definition of a key concept that can be regarded as the 'right' definition.

The empirical case in focus here is the translation of the concept of 'citizen' from the Swedish language into Finnish in the most prestigious law manual of the time, written by the most reputable expert on Finnish law, Johan Philip Palmén (*Juridisk handbook för medborgelig bildning*, published in 1859, and translated by the most esteemed Finnish linguist, Eljas Lönnrot (*La 'in-opillinen käsikirja Yhteiseksi sivistykseksi*, published in 1864). Lönnrot revealed a pronounced independence in his treatment of the Swedish original. The concept of 'citizen' is a case in point. Palmén uses the Swedish word *medborgare* thirty-three times, and Lönnrot uses a great deal of ingenuity in finding Finnish equivalents. He uses neologisms created by other philologists; he also creates one for himself, as well as frequently avoiding the word by using various kinds of circumlocution. The neologisms in the Finnish political vocabulary were the products of a translation process, a continuous adjustment of Finnish experiences to European ways of using and defining central political concepts. An analysis of the Finnish concepts is thus only possible by references to major European languages, a point of departure that is not necessary in more self-sufficient languages of the core of Europe. None of the Finnish neologisms that were suggested for the concept of citizen made any references either to European urban history or to the discourse on rights that was connected to the common semantic field of the concept of 'citizen'. One has to regard these linguistic solutions as a decisive effort by those who participated in political debates to create a Finnish political language based on peculiarly Finnish premises.[17]

Only after the emergence in 1809 of Finland as a political unit of its own were political and social debates in the Finnish language set in motion. Before the 1820s, Finnish words for 'citizen' occurred occasionally in print, but each time more or less as spontaneous neologisms. The three serious candidates for expressing the concept of 'citizen' after the 1820s were: (1) *kans(s)alainen*, which was the most common word and could be interpreted either as a 'member of the people' (from the noun *kansa* meaning *Volk* or people) or as 'a person with (us)' from the postposition *kanssa* meaning 'with' as an incomplete word-for-word translation of the Swedish *medborgare*, extending the urban terms *borgare/Bürger* to include a general notion of belonging. As there were no codified rules for spelling with a single or double 's', both interpretations were possible, even though it is reasonable to think that the Fennomane philologists themselves had in mind the idea of *Volk*/people, which means that a word-for-word translation from Finnish to German, English or Swedish would be *Völker*, *peoples* and *folkare* respectively. The two other neologisms were: (2) *yhteiskuntalainen*, derived from the word *yhteiskunta* (society), and (3) *kansajäsen*, which in a word-for-word translation means 'member of the people'. Why was Lönnrot unsatisfied with the word *kansalainen*?

Famous for compiling the national epos *Kalevala* and for becoming the most prestigious authority on questions regarding the consolidation of a written Finnish language, Lönnrot conceptualized 'citizen' in a particular way. Palmén's book demonstrates the skills of an ideological equilibrist, writing about Finland's autonomy with a constitution, legislation and public economy of its own in a way that satisfied not only the Russian rulers but also the nationalist political elite. This balancing act became possible because Palmén, when dealing with the question of citizenship, consistently avoided talking about Finnish *politics*. The target was not the Finnish *homo politicus*.[18]

Lönnrot, like Palmén and the Fennomane thinkers in general, had a Hegelian appreciation of a strong – and benevolent – state. This common philosophical background did not hinder him from endowing the concept of 'citizen' with a meaning very much different from that in Palmén's original text.

The German term *Bürger* was among those German words that until the 1840s had taken on so many overlapping meanings that it had become almost useless as an exact description of social groups, and was accordingly avoided in legal texts.[19] When Lönnrot used the word *kansalainen*, which he did only three times in his translation, he had on his mind a *citizenship in a limited sense*. He used the word in contexts where Palmén talked about the inhabitants of Finland, the members of the state, as people that in reality had the same legal rights and duties. In one of the passages Palmén defined what a Finnish citizen was, according to a *ius sanguinis* principle: a person who, regardless of birthplace, had descended from Finnish parents or had a Finnish citizen as a stepfather.

In all the other cases, talking about citizenship in a broad sense, Lönnrot emphasized the non-universalist context, and elaborated a differentiated vocabulary, including a couple of neologisms. For instance, when Palmén talked about citizens as an abstract category of belonging, regardless of what kind of society the person in question belonged to, Lönnrot introduced his own neologism *kansanjäsen* (member of a people). As Lönnrot used this term it could also be used in connection with primitive societies that did not possess a state apparatus. Lönnrot was quite aware of the fact that, according to the sociological and judicial realities of the time, individuals were not autonomous and not equal in their relation to the state authorities. The universalist principle was the complete opposite of the system of privileges, which was the glue of society at the time he wrote. Lönnrot was comfortable with the fact that rights and duties were unequally shared in society. But, in his keenness to make himself clear, he elaborated a concept of citizenship that was universalist and not just quasi-universalist. His insistence on logical consequence in this regard makes him rather unique in this regard.

Lönnrot's conceptual exercise drove him straight into heated debates on equality in contemporary European political discourse. The year 1848 changed the political language, especially in Germany, moving it away from the old revolutionary rhetoric of liberty and equality. Just as the Germans replaced the word *Bürger* with various other terms or circumlocutions, so Lönnrot also found the Swedish word *medborgare* inexact. Like the Germans, he wanted to formulate a real universalist concept of citizen – citizen in a narrow, restricted sense (*kansalainen*) that fitted into a discourse on *Gleichberechtigung*.[20] For those who had the political initiative, in Finland as well as in Germany, it became important to discover new rules and codes for a new class-based society that worked without corporations and privileges, but in which social and economic differences were still profound sociological facts.

Lönnrot had a special kind of gradation of 'citizen' words. When the reference concerned the ultimate aim of the state, the state as an educational project, corresponding to the Hegelian notion of *Sittlichkeit*, Lönnrot talked about 'a member of the state' (*valtiojäsen*). Palmén himself sometimes used the Swedish equivalent expression, *medlem i staten*, in contexts of the same elevated kind. 'Member of the state' had thus a higher status than 'member of a people' (*kansajäsen*). In more trivial contexts, Lönnrot just talked about 'inhabitants' (*asukkaat*).

But this type of gradation was very different from the traditional European discourse on citizenship. In Europe the discursive struggle had, since the Middle Ages, been focused on rivalry between different groups of (towns) people; between *cives simpliciter*, which refers to independent people who take part in the decision making of the community, and *cives sequndum quid*, which refers to people who are dependent on others, masters, and who therefore do not take part in the decision making.[21] Lönnrot, for his part, did not single out or grade different types of people according to their different rights and duties. Rather, Lönnrot's words referred to different types of *characteristics* that could be ascribed to every Finnish subject/inhabitant.

The distinction Lönnrot made implied that a *kansalainen*, a citizen in a narrow sense, had very limited rights; above all, a *kansalainen* had no political existence as a decision-making member of the *res publica*. On the other hand, the rights and duties of a *valtiojäsen* (member of the state) were wide, because a *valtiojäsen* had the opportunity to take part, on a voluntary basis, in the (educational) nation-building project. These were the windows of opportunity that explain why the Finnish citizen, regardless of his or her reserved character, accumulated a social and human capital, which was of considerable size when one looks upon this *Sittlichkeit* project from a comparative perspective. This became a lasting, positive element of the Finnish concept of citizen. Lönnrot's concept of citizen strengthened in its own particular way the Nordic, but especially Finnish, connection between citizenship and education in the sense of *Bildung*. This process is connected with Finland not being an independent political state during the formative period of a modern political culture. Under these circumstances the main strategy of consolidating the nation focused to a high degree on *Bildung* and an ambitious civil society.

The argument here is not that the Nordic or Finnish citizens are nice compared to other citizens. On the contrary, within the Fennomanian tradition one can easily find examples of cultural solipsistic absolutism, some of them with fatal consequences. By references to the *ius sanguinis* elements in the Finnish concept of citizen, one could grade the citizens into 'more valuable' and 'less valuable' groups in Finnish society. Thus there were politicians making a distinction between the 'Finnish people proper' and the Swedish-speaking 'population'. The concept of citizen often became a diffuse concept of inclusion. By the end of the nineteenth century, even groups east of the Finnish border – in parts of Russia that had never been part of Finland (or Sweden) – came to be recognized as Finnish citizens simply because they spoke Finnish. The Finnish discourse of authenticity became particularly fatal in the polarized situation that ended up in a desperate civil war in 1918, which broke out as a sequel to the dissolution of the Russian Empire. One consequence of the brutal bloodshed was the division of the citizenry into antagonistic camps that lasted for decades; it was expressed, for instance, in the fundamental disagreement over whether the war should be named a war of independence, a war of liberation, a class war, a revolution or a war between brethren. Certain Fennomanian traditions of neglecting republican values, combined with negations of the idea of deliberation that acknowledged competing interests, carried with it the belief that only those who represented the 'authentic' people were able to handle controversies. In turn, that made them unable to solve the political conflict by any means other than force.

Conclusions

Christopher Hill has argued that the universalization of concepts takes place in the peripheries through a process in which the 'parochial' universalisms of the core are adopted by reconceptualizations according to which the meanings of transferred concepts are tailored so that they correspond to the context and needs of the periphery.[22] This is an important argument and a reasonable way of what could be understood by the term 'universal concept'. The focus of this chapter has been, however, on a different meaning of the term. Here the term means that the use of a key concept presupposes that the concept has a universally valid content or definition. My aim has been to show that a person who wants to move together and converge on a common stand, by using key concepts that she or he thinks have commonly accepted definitions, looks upon the world differently in comparison to a person who has a perspectivist approach to political and social questions, and an attitude that implies an acknowledgement that key concepts are always contestable, have their historical layers, and not least get their meanings through the context in which they are being used. The argument in this chapter has been that in a peripheral culture there is generally less temptation to regard key concepts in an ahistorical way as unities that are universally valid than there is in a core culture.

The case study of the Nordic and Finnish concept of citizen has a normative element. The linkage between citizenship and *Bildung* has not only been strong, but has also been of great benefit for the Nordic and Finnish societies.[23] The implication of this normative element of the Finnish concepts of 'citizen' is that one has to regret that the educational system in Finland has capitulated in favour of the European harmonization of higher education, and through that accepted a diluted view of higher education (efficiency and vocational skills). Sadly, we are now approaching a system that no longer encourages students to broaden and deepen their outlook.

My argument is not that one should avoid universalisms altogether when one wants to understand social and political phenomena. Progressive modernism requires the use of universalisms. The judicial apparatus in a state governed by law, treaties in all sections of society, as well as important knowledge-producing practices, all need well-defined concepts with universalized meanings. Even more important is the philosophical fact that good political argumentation too needs universalisms, not only because they can be rhetorically effective tools, but because political and moral argumentation cannot do without universalistic elements.

The main argument of this chapter, however, is that progressive modernism includes the counter principle: the principle that arguments have to be anchored in unique contexts comprehensible only with the help of particularistic concepts. Normatively, one can talk about an obligation to come forward with one's own way of looking at the world, one's own way of conceptualizing life and society. Small nations have a special role in coming forward with critical remarks against the imperialism of universalism.

The balance between these two doctrines is as important today as it was two hundred years ago. Each of us can choose either to strengthen our political/ideological position by arguing that we have the right universalistic understanding of the concept on the agenda, or to the contrary, by trying to convince our audience that we are justified and even obliged to contextualize our key concepts in terms of our own particular social and political situation, thus giving the concept a particularistic content. If we want to strengthen international integration on a basis of democratic values, we had better not ignore the second alternative. There is an emancipatory potential in the historicization of the mental structure governing a discourse.[24]

Henrik Stenius, PhD, has been the Research Director of the Centre for Nordic Studies (CENS) at the University of Helsinki, Professor at the Department of History at the same university, and the Director of the Finnish Institute in London. His field of research has been mobilization and voluntary association, and conceptual history. He was an inaugurating member of the International Research School in Conceptual History and Political Thought (Concepta), the international History of Concepts Group (HCG), and the European project for publishing the book series on European conceptual history.

Notes

1. Cf. Bourdieu's notion of 'illusion', according to which every field of social life is governed to a large extent by certain principles, visions and rules, which are accepted through practice and routine rather than by explicit values about what can be said and what not: Pierre Bourdieu, *Médiations pascaliennes* (Paris: Seuil, 1997), 122–23.
2. It is no coincidence that a Finn, Martti Koskenniemi, working in the field of international law, persistently insists on making visible the structural biases and hegemonic pretentions in international law as a universalistic discourse. Or for that matter, the Argentine Ernesto Laclau's discussion of the universal and the particular as 'tools in the language games that shape contemporary politics'. See Martti Koskenniemi, 'The Politics of International Law: Twenty Years Later', *European Journal of International Law* 20 (2009), 7–19; Ernesto Laclau, *Emancipation(s)* (London: Verso, 1996), 47–48.
3. Stefan Nygård and Johan Strang, 'Facing Asymmetry', *Journal of the History of Ideas* 77(1) (2016), 75–97.
4. Henrik Stenius, 'A Nordic Conceptual Universe', in Heidi Haggrén, Johanna Rainio-Niemi and Jussi Vauhkonen (eds), *Multi-layered Historicity of the Present* (Helsinki: University of Helsinki, 2013), 93–104.
5. Henrik Stenius, 'Nordic Associational Life in a European and Inter-Nordic Perspective', in Risto Alapuro and Henrik Stenius (eds), *Nordic Associations in European Perspective* (Baden-Baden: Nomos, 2010), 29–86.
6. In other parts of premodern Europe you find recesses of life outside the hierarchically organized society, patches of exceptional life among 'fratres', 'cognatos' and 'amicos', communities organized on a more equal basis than in the rest of society; Otto Dann, *Gleichheit und Gleichberechtigung. Das Gleichheitspostulat in der alteuropäischen Tradition und in Deutschland bis zum ausgehenden 19. Jahrhundert* (Berlin: Duncker & Humblot, 1980), 100. Unintegrated groups such as these were very rare in the Nordic societies of the time.
7. Terence Ball, 'Political Parties and the Legitimacy of Opposition', in Hans Bödeker et al. (eds), *Discourses on Tolerance and Intolerance in European Enlightenment* (Toronto: University of Toronto Press, 2009), 77–99.
8. The newspapers, which at this point were predominantly printed in Swedish, spelt the word both as 'opposition' and 'oppositition'. In Finnish print the word 'oppositio' occurred for the first time in 1872, and only began to be used more frequently from the 1880s onwards; www.digi-lib.fi.
9. On the Reformation in different parts of Europe, see Diarmaid MacCulloch, *Reformation: Europe's House Divided* (London: Penguin Books, 2003); about Poland, see esp. 190–92.
10. It is illuminating to turn to the situation in Swedish Pomerania, which followed German, not Swedish, practices: Pomerania had several competing judicial authorities. It was also severely affected by a series of religious controversies, and in this part of the Swedish realm pietism had a decisive polarizing effect.

Contemporary observers, too, were aware of the differences between Swedish Pomerania and the rest of the Swedish realm in this regard. Pomeranian commentators belittled the conforming religious climate in Sweden, claiming that there were no debates or original thinkers in Sweden; Andreas Önnerfors, *Svenska Pommern: Kulturmöten och identification 1720–1815* (Lund: Lunds Universitet, 2003).

11. Unlike in Germany, the Pietist movement of the eighteenth century did not evolve into distinct, Low Church subcultures. Erik Pontoppidan (1698–1754), archbishop of Denmark, is a seminal figure in this regard. He reformed the Danish state church into a form that could accommodate the Low Church faction. In his hands the two major mobilizing and polarizing European concepts of the eighteenth century, Pietism and Enlightenment, became emasculated process concepts with educational connotations no longer useful as rallying points for popular movements separating fractions of the subjects from each other. An analogous diagnosis of the state of affairs in Denmark was presented already in 1694 by the English ambassador to Denmark, Robert Molesworth, in his *Account of Denmark*. From a perspective of a parliamentary government (Molesworth was a friend of Locke), he pictured Denmark as a cautionary example of a country that lacked debate and opposition. In Denmark he found the peace of the grave: 'there are no factions, nor Disputes about Religion which usually have a great influence on any Government', a situation that inevitably leads to stagnation (quoted by Terence Ball in the article mentioned above); Henrik Stenius, 'Är konsensuspolitiken i Finland ny eller gammal? En jämförelse mellan konsensuskulturens rötter i Finland och Österrike' [Is the consensual culture in Finland young or old? A comparison of the roots of consensus culture in Finland and Austria], in T. Gullberg and K. Sandberg (eds), *Medströms: Motströms. Individ och struktur i historien* (Pieksamäki: Atlantis, 2005), 226–43. For further references to the Danish consensual culture of the early modern period, see the literature mentioned in Stenius, 'Nordic Associational Life', 33–34.

12. The formation of the civil society in the premodern Nordic countries that pivoted around a vast and vigorous flora of voluntary associations focused constantly on convergence and consensus. More than in other countries, even England, the movement of secret societies, the main expression of Enlightenment endeavours, became in the Nordic countries pillars of the established society, defenders of King and Church. The voluntary associations established a matrix for dealing with differences in beliefs and judgments: a matrix for attaining convergence and consensus; Stenius, 'Nordic Associational Life', 29–52.

13. 'Hyvä statistiikki korvaa politiikin', quoted in: Pauli Kettunen, *Globalisaatio ja kansallinen me: Kansallisen katseen historiallinen kritiikki* (Tampere: Vastapaino, 2008), 69.

14. Tuija Pulkkinen, 'Valtio' [State], in Matti Hyvärinen et al. (eds), *Käsitteet liikkeessä: Suomen poliittisen kulttuurin käsitehistoria* [Concepts in motion: The conceptual history of the Finnish political culture] (Tampere: Vastapaino, 2003), 213–55; Ilkka Liikanen, 'Kansa' [People], in ibid., 257–307.

15. Pauli Kettunen, 'Yhteiskunta' [Society], in Hyvärinen et al., *Käsitteet liikkeessä*, 167–212.
16. Jussi A. Kurunmäki and Johan Strang, *Rhetorics of Nordic Democracy* [Studia Fennica Historica 17] (Helsinki: Suomen Kirjallisuuden Seura, 2010).
17. Henrik Stenius, 'Kansalainen' [Citizen], in Hyvärinen et al., *Käsitteet liikkeessä*, 309–62. Henrik Stenius, 'The Finnish Citizen: How a Translation Emasculated the Concept', *Redescriptions. Yearbook of Political Thought and Conceptual History* 8 (2004),172–88.
18. E.G. Palmén, *Till hundraårsminnet af Johan Philp Palmén 1811 31/X 1911. II. Lefnadsteckning* (Helsingfors, 1915).
19. Willibald Steinmetz, '"Speaking is a Deed for You": Words and Actions in the Revolution of 1848', in Dieter Dowe, Heinz-Gerhard Haupt, Dieter Langewiesche and Jonathan Sperber (eds), *Europe in 1848: Revolution and Reform* (New York and Oxford: Berghahn Books, 2001), 830–68.
20. Dann, *Gleichheit und Gleichberechtigung*, 18–19, 95, 211–13; Steinmetz, 'Speaking is a Deed for You', 833.
21. Reinhart Koselleck and Klaus Schreiner, 'Einleitung: Von der alteuropäischen zur neuzeitlichen Bürgerschaft. Ihr politisch-sozialer Wandel im Medium von Begriffs-, Wirkungs- und Rezeptionsgeschichten', in Reinhart Koselleck and Klaus Schreiner (eds), *Bürgerschaft: Rezeption und Innovation der Begrifflichkeit vom Hohen Mittelalter bis ins 19. Jahrhundert* (Stuttgart: Klett-Cotta, 1994), 11–42.
22. Christopher Hill, 'Conceptual Universalization in the Transnational Nineteenth Century', in Samuel Moyn and Andrew Sartori (eds), *Global Intellectual History* (New York: Columbia University Press, 2013), 134–58.
23. Thomas Paine, who more than any other person moulded the concept of citizen in England and the United States, very seldom talked about education (never of *Bildung*, of course). Thomas Paine, *Political Writings*, ed. Bruce Kuklik (Cambridge: Cambridge University Press, 2007), 233–37, 247–51, 295–300.
24. Cf. Bourdieu, *Médiations pascaliennes*; Pierre Bourdieu, *Les règles de l'art: Genèse et structure du champ littéraire* (Paris: Seuil, 1998); and again, Koskeniemi, 'The Politics of International Law'.

References

Ball, Terence, 'Political Parties and the Legitimacy of Opposition', in Hans Bödeker et al. (eds), *Discourses on Tolerance and Intolerance in European Enlightenment* (Toronto: University of Toronto Press, 2009), 77–99

Bourdieu, Pierre, *Médiations pascaliennes* (Paris: Seuil, 1997)

———, *Les règles de l'art: Genèse et structure du champ littéraire* (Paris: Seuil, 1998)

Dann, Otto, *Gleichheit und Gleichberechtigung: Das Gleichheitspostulat in der alteuropäischen Tradition und in Deutschland bis zum ausgehenden 19. Jahrhundert* (Berlin: Duncker & Humblot, 1980)

Hill, Christopher, 'Conceptual Universalization in the Transnational Nineteenth Century', in Samuel Moyn and Andrew Sartori (eds), *Global Intellectual History* (New York: Columbia University Press, 2013), 134–58

Kettunen, Pauli, 'Yhteiskunta' [Society], in Matti Hyvärinen et al. (eds), *Käsitteet liikkeessä: Suomen poliittisen kulttuurin käsitehistoria* [Concepts in motion: The conceptual history of the Finnish political culture] (Tampere: Vastapaino, 2003), 167–212

——, *Globalisaatio ja kansallinen me: Kansallisen katseen historiallinen kritiikki* (Tampere: Vastapaino, 2008)

Koselleck, Reinhart, and Klaus Schreiner, 'Einleitung: Von der alteuropäischen zur neuzeitlichen Bürgerschaft. Ihr politisch-sozialer Wandel im Medium von Begriffs-, Wirkungs- und Rezeptionsgeschichten', in Reinhart Koselleck and Klaus Schreiner (eds), *Bürgerschaft: Rezeption und Innovation der Begrifflichkeit vom Hohen Mittelalter bis ins 19. Jahrhundert* (Stuttgart: Klett-Cotta, 1994), 11–42

Koskenniemi, Martti, 'The Politics of International Law: Twenty Years Later', *European Journal of International Law* 20 (2009), 7–19

Kurunmäki, Jussi A., and Johan Strang, *Rhetorics of Nordic Democracy* [Studia Fennica Historica 17] (Helsinki: Suomen Kirjallisuuden Seura, 2010)

Laclau, Ernesto, *Emancipation(s)* (London: Verso, 1996)

Liikanen, Ilkka, 'Kansa' [People], in Matti Hyvärinen et al. (eds), *Käsitteet liikkeessä: Suomen poliittisen kulttuurin käsitehistoria* [Concepts in motion: The conceptual history of the Finnish political culture] (Tampere: Vastapaino, 2003), 257–307

MacCulloch, Diarmaid, *Reformation: Europe's House Divided* (London: Penguin Books, 2003)

Nygård, Stefan, and Johan Strang, 'Facing Asymmetry', *Journal of the History of Ideas* 77(1) (2016), 75–97

Önnerfors, Andreas, *Svenska Pommern: Kulturmöten och identification 1720–1815* (Lund: Lunds Universitet, 2003)

Paine, Thomas, *Political Writings*, ed. Bruce Kuklik (Cambridge: Cambridge University Press, 2007)

Palmén, Ernst Gustaf, *Till hundraårsminnet af Johan Philp Palmén 1811 31/X 1911. II. Lefnadsteckning* (Helsingfors, 1915)

Pulkkinen, Tuija, 'Valtio' [State], in Matti Hyvärinen et al. (eds), *Käsitteet liikkeessä: Suomen poliittisen kulttuurin käsitehistoria* [Concepts in motion: The conceptual history of the Finnish political culture] (Tampere: Vastapaino, 2003), 213–55

Steinmetz, Willibald, '"Speaking is a Deed for You": Words and Actions in the Revolution of 1848', in Dieter Dowe, Heinz-Gerhard Haupt, Dieter Langewiesche and Jonathan Sperber (eds), *Europe in 1848: Revolution and Reform* (New York and Oxford: Berghahn Books, 2001), 830–68

Stenius, Henrik, 'Kansalainen' [Citizen], in Matti Hyvärinen et al. (eds), *Käsitteet liikkeessä: Suomen poliittisen kulttuurin käsitehistoria* [Concepts in motion: The conceptual history of the Finnish political culture] (Tampere: Vastapaino, 2003), 309–62

——, 'The Finnish Citizen: How a Translation Emasculated the Concept', *Redescriptions: Yearbook of Political Thought and Conceptual History* 8 (2004), 172–88

——, 'Är konsensuspolitiken i Finland ny eller gammal? En jämförelse mellan konsensuskulturens rötter i Finland och Österrike' [Is the consensual culture in Finland young or old? A comparison of the roots of consensus culture in Finland and Austria], in Tom Gullberg and Kaj Sandberg (eds), *Medströms: Motströms. Individ och struktur i historien* (Pieksamäki: Atlantis, 2005), 226–43

——, 'Nordic Associational Life in a European and Inter-Nordic Perspective', in Risto Alapuro and Henrik Stenius (eds), *Nordic Associations in European Perspective* (Baden-Baden: Nomos, 2010), 29–86

——, 'A Nordic Conceptual Universe', in Heidi Haggrén, Johanna Rainio-Niemi and Jussi Vauhkonen (eds), *Multi-layered Historicity of the Present* (Helsinki: University of Helsinki, 2013), 93–104

Conclusions

Setting the Agenda for a European Conceptual History

Javier Fernández-Sebastián

Europeanisms: In Search of a European Conceptual Space

What exactly is the European identity? Those who have spent the past two or three decades trying to answer this thorny question have tended to highlight certain cultural traits shared by a large proportion of Europeans, particularly in the modern age, only finally to acknowledge the plural, shifting and elusive nature of this supposed identitary code. Without debating here the pertinence of applying the analytical tool of collective identity to the case of Europe, from our perspective, 'Europeanness' might be described as a constellation of concepts that historically have characterized European civilization. Whilst there have been, and still are, many 'Europes' and many ways of understanding Europeanness, there appears to be no doubt that Europeans' self-awareness, insofar as such a feeling exists, is usually to be found in a handful of particularly cherished notions, values and principles – such as freedom, democracy, humanity and tolerance – regarded as genuinely, though not exclusively, European.

Many of the tongues spoken in Europe include in their vocabulary, with greater or lesser variants, a certain number of words referring to life in society, the meaning of which is relatively clear to the speakers of these different languages. Almost two centuries ago, the Italian poet Leopardi noted that educated Europeans from all countries employed a 'piccola lingua' formed by certain terms that were mutually understandable by all of them, which he called 'Europeanisms'.[1] This basic nomenclature from culture and political and civil life, to which other authors of the age also alluded, might indeed be seen as a mini lingua franca – not in the sense of a bridge language that facilitates communication between speakers of different mother tongues (as Latin was for centuries, and English is today), but rather as a translingual terminological core resulting from the intersection between the various European scientific and sociopolitical dialects.

Even beyond the purely lexical level, we could speak metaphorically of a European 'grammar', in reference to certain characteristic ways of coining, articulating and combining those basic concepts in the public sphere, upon the basis of related historical experiences. Although the capacity to devise concepts with a degree of coherence, flexibility and durability is a characteristic common to all cultures, certain conceptual networks and modes of conceptualization seem to have been specific to European culture. Confronted by the need to tackle similar problems, the various communities of speakers would have forged different conceptual tools, but which retained certain similarities. Why not call these conceptual tools Europeanisms too, even if the words used to designate them are not directly related in an etymological or morphological sense?

Nonetheless, it would be difficult to compile an exhaustive inventory of those concepts and values that together would define the European *logos* and *ethos*, thus establishing the limits of this common conceptual space; and it would be absolutely impossible to provide a list of precise definitions of all of them. A rudimentary knowledge of the nature of language and of the most elementary bases of conceptual history is sufficient in order to rule out such a suggestion. To seek to package the 'European spirit' into dozens or hundreds of conceptual items would be an arduous if not unwise task; as would be, and even more so, to aspire to an unequivocal definition of terms like tolerance, freedom, humanism and democracy, to mention but a few. Quite simply, there is no single European, transtemporal, definition of such terms. Nor is there a French, English or Spanish definition of those same concepts, let us say, in the eighteenth century. Although by reducing the spatial–temporal focus one narrows the range of use of words, there is not even any guarantee that one single author will attribute the same meaning to these words each time he or she employs them in his or her writings.

Historical-conceptual analysis of documents tends to demonstrate the contrary: what we find in the textual sources of medieval, modern and contemporary Europe is a plethora of often incompatible interpretations of these and other fundamental terms. Frequently used in polemics and ideological debates, and often in conflictive contexts, the great words referring to collective life usually carry multiple and contested meanings. And, the more bitter the dispute over the meaning of a word, the greater tends to be its conceptual relevance. The plurality of pragmatic uses of the expressions that stand for basic concepts, whether in the spheres of religion, law, morals or politics, is normally fuelled by the very semantic history of the vocabularies in which they are placed. Diachronic semantical change is linked to historical experiences that vary considerably from one political-linguistic area to another.

One understands, therefore, that such diversity in the use of terms and the ineradicable complexity of their meanings dooms to failure any attempt to determine a network of fundamental concepts by means of a quintessential and uniform definition of each of them. However, it is precisely this vagueness and semantic variability in space and in time of such typically European concepts as freedom, tolerance, democracy, individual and society, as well as notions representative of the darker side of modernity, like racism, colonialism, communism, totalitarianism and genocide, that offers the possibility of historical-conceptual research, as is proposed here.

After all, however diverse these meanings might be, some similarities between them are plain to see. How could this not be the case if we bear in mind the shared roots of a cultural heritage that can be traced back to Greek-Latin and Judeo-Christian Antiquity, and to Romano-Germanic medieval times, to mention but some of its most obvious sources? We are speaking of a rich cultural heritage, transmitted, extended and increased, diversified, transformed and re-elaborated with the passing of the centuries throughout Europe, and one which – not without fractures and discontinuities – has endured until today. Although it is clear that in the history of the subcontinent there have also been periods of fragmentation and semantic distancing between its elites and its constituent parts, what is beyond doubt is the existence of numerous points of contact and of a common substratum – to a large extent Latin – which, despite all the difficulties, permit one to expect substantial and rewarding results from a project like the one presented in this book. The reader has been able to find in the preceding chapters a comprehensive array of methodological tools, but also of the theoretical obstacles and challenges facing the practitioners of conceptual history, as well as a bundle of reflections upon the specific application of those methodologies to the case of Europe, and indeed to the wide range of spaces and times, including different temporalities, asymmetries, discontinuities and changing frontiers, that the adjective 'European' is capable of embracing.

In this final chapter I will briefly return to a point already considered in the introduction to this volume, namely the raison d'être and the objectives of this intellectual adventure; but above all I shall provide some clues as to the questions and topics eligible for inclusion in the project. It is not a case of making an exhaustive list of themes and titles destined to fill the catalogue of the European Conceptual History collection in the near future, but rather of casting a forward-looking glance, inevitably conjectural, at the variety of tasks that potentially await a research project like this. In other words, we will try to explore the vast territory of European sociopolitical conceptuality, and sketch out a map of some of its main provinces. In this way readers will be able to form some idea of the type of book that will continue this series, as well as the kind of proposal for new volumes that is likely to be favourably received by the editorial board.

European Conceptual History: What It Is, and What It Is Not

In order to avoid raising false expectations, it might be appropriate to begin by stating what the project is *not*, and then proceed to describe some positive aspects thereof.

First of all, it should be made clear that the main objective of this collaborative enterprise is not the production of a multilingual pan-European lexicon that might represent for our continent as a whole something similar to what the famous *Historical Dictionary of Fundamental Concepts* (*Geschichtliche Grundbegriffe*), edited by Reinhart Koselleck, meant for the German-speaking world. Unlike the outline for a historical dictionary of European political concepts proposed some time ago by Lucian Hölscher,[2] and other lexicographical or encyclopedic projects already completed or under way, the European Conceptual History book series will not offer a collection of alphabetically ordered histories of individual political concepts. The reasons for ruling out this methodological option were detailed in the Introduction. Apart from the technical difficulties implicit in the adoption of a semasiological starting point in a project necessarily involving several languages, we believe that in this instance the approach via conceptual networks might prove to be far more productive. A broadening of the focus permits one to observe, instead of an isolated term, a fairly wide lexical-semantic area around a theoretical-practical problem related with human interaction. Thus it is possible to perceive what is common and what is particular to the diverse conceptual solutions that each political or linguistic community offered in the light of their historical experiences – particular, but also partly shared with other areas of Europe – to address these basic problems. Meanwhile, the focus upon groupings of concepts enables one better to observe the mutual tensions and relations – of opposition, complementariness, hierarchy – that normally accompany their insertion into ideologies, discourses, theories and arguments.

Closer to the focus we advocate than the *Geschichtliche Grundbegriffe* would be various works that, from linguistics, history or philosophy, have shed light on different aspects of the ancient and modern European cultural lexicon. To name a few French works of this type with which our book series would have some degree of affinity, I would recall Émile Benveniste's pioneering comparative study on the vocabulary of Indo-European institutions[3] as well as some other, more recent, transnational works – for instance, Barbara

Cassin's studies on 'untranslatable' European terms in philosophy, or Olivier Christin's book on 'nomadic concepts' in the social sciences.[4] Scholars from other national and linguistic backgrounds, of course, have also made valuable contributions in recent years to the study of these issues.[5]

A typical question with regard to a European history of concepts would be the search for reasons why some political concepts such as state, republic, federation and citizen, among others, are absolutely central in certain languages, countries and political cultures, whilst in others they have nothing like the same relevance. Sensitivity towards cultural differences, heightened in these years of accelerated globalization, is also increasing among historians and social scientists. Cross-analysis of methods and analytical categories requires students belonging to different national academic cultures to make an effort to appreciate their colleagues' vantage point. As well as favouring mutual knowledge, this intellectual exercise stimulates the reflexive nature of social sciences.

The target of our book series is not limited, however, to academic circles. Its main objective is to study, through a comparative prism, the evolution of a series of complex conceptual structures linked with certain key words in several languages and in different spatial–temporal contexts. The volumes that will be published in the collection will not consist, of course, in a simple juxtaposition of national cases, nor limit themselves exclusively to case studies within the vague geographical boundaries of Europe. On the contrary, without underestimating the importance of political and semantic interactions between countries, it is to be hoped that a transnational and global perspective profoundly informs all the volumes in the series.

As is suggested by the preceding chapters, the collection will not be subject to any orthodoxy as far as methods are concerned. A glance at the list of authors and contents of this volume shows that the project is the fruit of collaboration by a group of scholars from various countries and specialities, all with varied interests and research styles. The fact that this is a bottom-up initiative – led in its early stages, with great determination and contagious enthusiasm, by Henrik Stenius – is in itself revealing of the growing interest that the historical-semantic approach to the study of the past arouses among experts from very diverse fields, as well as the variety of methods gathered today under the banner of conceptual history.

This volume, in which we have attempted to trace the outline of a renovated conceptual history, in addition to an ambitious programme that we hope gradually to complete, is the result of that teamwork. The editing of the book was preceded by many meetings, exchanges of texts, and discussions. And this will continue to be the way of proceeding in the future: each book will be the final product of the sustained efforts of a group of scholars working together on a theme from different spatial–temporal perspectives. Although there are a handful of common sources of inspiration – the name of Reinhart Koselleck immediately springs to mind – each academic tradition, each methodological current has developed its own analytical tools to apprehend its favourite objects of study, be these concepts or languages, discourses, ideologies, translations, images, metaphors, or arguments in debates. And all these studies will be done from no less plural – often eclectic – perspectives, which vary from those which focus upon the long-term evolution of semantic formations and others that prefer to illuminate rhetorical uses in specific contexts. The increasingly popular annual conferences of the History of Concepts Group (HCG) from its foundation in London in 1998 to the present day, and the thematic and methodological variety of articles published in the journal *Contributions to the History of Concepts*, bear witness to the well-stocked toolbox and the growing interest in this branch of historiography.

Mention has been made above of that cross-border civil vocabulary that some authors two or three centuries ago saw as a European quasi-metalanguage; a miniature lingua franca useful in order to understand at first glance many philosophical and scientific, social and political texts, written in different languages of the continent. It is appropriate now to qualify the scope of this analogy of transparency. This small lexicon is indeed an incomplete and often misleading vocabulary, which may lead to significant errors if one takes too seriously the homologies and formal similarities between words. Various studies have evidenced the diversification of the linguistic-national trajectories of certain concepts in different spaces of modern Europe. Let us consider in this respect how mistaken we should be if we were to take that millenary terminological chain that connects the *koinonia politike* of the Ancient Greeks with the modern *civil society*, *société civile* or *bürgerliche Gesellschaft*, passing through the Roman *societas civilis*, as solid proof of the permanence of a supposed semantic nucleus impervious to the passage of time. On the contrary, comparison of the semantics of Germany, England and France have revealed important temporal and spatial discontinuities, to the point of shaping in reality three clearly differentiated modern 'bourgeois worlds'.[6] And British *liberalism*, French *libéralisme*, Italian *liberalismo* and German *Liberalismus* – not to mention their Spanish counterpart – were far from equivalent concepts during their formative stage, in the early decades of the nineteenth century.[7] Neither does the word Enlightenment cover the same type of historical realities as *Aufklärung*, *Lumières*, *Ilustración* or *Iluminismo*, and nor may the cognate ancient and modern concepts *polites*, *civis*, *Bürger*, *medborgare*, *kansalainen*, *citoyen*, *citizen*, *ciudadano* or *cittadino* be regarded in any shape or form as interchangeable.

These and many other examples of false friends that we could cite show once again the degree to which each country and each linguistic zone sometimes manifests very noticeable distinctive features. Paradoxically, seen from the opposite angle, European 'cultural identity' is fuelled by these contrasts and historical distances, given that, globally speaking, these vernacular variations present a family likeness. It is perhaps difficult to find features that are truly common to all linguistic zones, macro-regions and national subcultures. What do the Nordic countries have in common with Mediterranean Europe, and East Europeans with those of the West? Contemplating the whole – particularly if from outside Europe – one nevertheless perceives in all the regions undeniable similarities (not only semantic), which overlap and are distributed in apparently random fashion.

So, whilst continuing to underline the distinctive characteristics of national cultures and of certain linguistic, religious or regional areas, the European Conceptual History project assumes as a working hypothesis the existence of that 'European language' I referred to at the beginning of this chapter. A shared code, elastic and in constant flux, could be interpreted as the symbolic sediment – always provisional – of a long sequence of (partially) common experiences and asymmetric transfers between different zones. At the same time, the unfolding of that European language is an ongoing history, which in recent years has seen the intensification of contacts and the sharpening of trends towards homogenization. The fundamental reasons for this resemblance of experiences and concepts are far from mysterious. Several centuries of migrations, conflicts and all kinds of exchanges between a multitude of individual and collective agents (empires, monarchies, cities, states, nations, churches, armies, corporations, universities, traders, writers, travellers, exiles, clerics, soldiers, scientists, students, workers), all moving within a not particularly wide space, have gradually established a sort of 'conceptual heritage' – an interactive conceptual heritage: unsteady, blurred and polycentric, but nonetheless real.

This constant flow of human beings and, with them, of languages and texts, traditions and ideas in transit has made Europe a crucible and a true conceptual laboratory of modernity – or rather, of the more expansive versions of modernity – since via the great geographical discoveries, conquests and migrations of the last five centuries, many of those concepts forged in Europe have been exported to the rest of the world and remoulded there through complex processes of reception, appropriation and reaction. Consider, for instance, the intense Europeanization of America several centuries prior to the current process of the Americanization of Europe. All this makes the European case a fascinating testing ground for conceptual history. The result of these processes of interaction as far as our approach and purpose is concerned is that from the Atlantic to the Urals and from the Baltic Sea to the Mediterranean – not to mention other places very far from Europe – we can detect here and there a set of typical notions and shared keys by means of which Europeans have given meaning to the world and can recognize themselves historically, irrespective of their nationalities. These common patterns of comprehension, compatible as we have said with clear idiosyncratic differences, some of which cause EU translators no end of headaches, open a communicative space for the expression of their political and cultural disagreements. Europe, then, as we understand it, should be conceived as a single and at the same time extremely diverse space that lends itself to analysis via relational approaches, including studies of transfers and comparative, connected, shared or crossed histories.

The originality of the European Conceptual History collection lies in a set of methodological options that deliberately stray from the paths trodden by customary historiography. Thus, rather than the usual emphasis upon unity and the consensual aspects of European identity, we are interested in shedding light on the plurality of debates and the ideological fracture lines regarding the interpretation of certain concepts. In fact, debates regarding the naming, meaning, scope and normative colour of concepts constantly appear in every sphere of society life – in morals and in science, in politics and in the academic world – and such valuable institutions of modern European culture as freedom of expression, scientific societies, and parliaments respond to the need to channel these never-ending controversies and disagreements. At an international level, these tensions, deeply embedded in languages, often hinder communication across boundaries and establish irreducible limits to the harmonization of vocabularies.

Furthermore, as opposed to the traditional history of ideas, which has tended to attribute excessive importance to the great thinkers, our approach will pay particular attention to everyday political settings, as reflected in sources like the press, parliamentary debates, pamphlets, and so on. Analysis of these speech acts and discursive performances is now considerably easier thanks to the increasingly efficient digital tools for research in the humanities, including large corpora of texts online, databases, parliamentary proceedings and documentary collections. Without abandoning general visions regarding the flow and transfer of ideas, the book series takes in other approaches focused on the uses agents made of these ideas in particular historical contexts and with different objectives in mind. We believe that the interest in the phenomena of reception, cultural appropriation and conceptual adaptation permits old diffusionist approaches applied to intellectual history to be transcended, and may merge with the research agenda of historians of culture interested in problems of translation, circulation of texts and other communicative practices in order thus to obtain a richer, more complex and more nuanced understanding of the political-intellectual dynamic than that currently reflected in most university manuals. At the same time, as suggested by Paul Ricoeur via his notion of 'surplus of meaning', agents also unconsciously and unintentionally transmit additional messages over which they have little control but that may be picked up by their recipients.[8] And, needless to say, these surpluses of meaning continue to have an influence on the fluid and layered meanings of given concepts.

It is likely that this leap in scale, from national history to the sub-, supra- and transnational levels of inquiry, will have significant consequences vis-à-vis our understanding of Europe. The comparative historical study of certain key notions might bring into question some long-standing convictions. Cross-examination of processes of interaction, semantic convergence and divergence could give rise to new narratives and alternative periodizations of the intellectual history of Europe.

From the spatial point of view too, the attempt to map the evolution of a number of conceptual variants throughout Europe may reveal unexpected interregional connections, and even give rise to new units of analysis that do not necessarily coincide with the reductionist frameworks to which we are accustomed. These often misidentify 'Europe' with either Western Europe or even with a few countries like France, Germany and the United Kingdom.

Mapping Europe's Conceptual Legacy

The books to follow this volume will cover liberalism, regions, democracy and federalism, as well as the asymmetric Eastern/Western cleavage. A volume on parliamentarism has already been published.[9] Having received the corresponding proposals, the Editorial Board will entrust each volume to one or several editors who in turn will count on the collaboration of leading experts from all over Europe. By means of these and other works that will gradually be incorporated into the collection, we will attempt to map semantic fields or cluster concepts of a political and sociocultural nature. Among the major conceptual domains to be included in the collection may be the following (listed in each section are some individual concepts, by way of examples):

1. *Disciplines and Areas of Knowledge*: Knowledge, Science, Theory, Philosophy, History, Literature, Humanities, Politics, Economics, Science and Arts, etc.
2. *Spaces and Territories*: Territory, Continent, Europe, Empire, Colony, State, Nation, Region, Province, Frontier, East, West, etc.

3. *Time, Temporality*: History, Modernity, Future, Crisis, Reform, Revolution, Progress, Civilization, Evolution, Transition, Periodization, etc.
4. *Population, Social Classifications and Categories*: Person, Individual, Society, Family, People, Nation, Citizen, Civil Society, Class, Bourgeoisie, Proletariat, Race, Ethnicity, etc.
5. *Religion*: God, Providence, Church, Sect, Cult, Heresy, Tolerance, Confession, Christianity, Paganism, Catholicism, Reform, Judaism, Islam, Secularization, etc.
6. *War, Violence*: Army, Militia, Conquest, Civil War, Rebellion, Mutiny, Terror, Terrorism, etc.
7. *Law*: Justice, Jurisprudence, Right, Privilege, Civil Rights, Political Rights, Social Rights, Constitution, Code, Legality, etc.
8. *Politics*: State, Government, Administration, Civil Servant, Regime, Power, Sovereignty, People, Democracy, Parliament, Legitimacy, Representation, Ideology, etc.
9. *Political Ideologies*: Liberalism, Progressivism, Conservatism, Republicanism, Socialism, Anarchism, Nationalism, Communism, Fascism, Totalitarianism, Populism, etc. (and the conceptual networks accompanying each of these ideologies).
10. *Economy*: Work, Wealth, Production, Agriculture, Industry, Commerce, Services, Market, Capitalism, Treasury, Development, etc.
11. *Culture, Education, Communication*: Language, Symbol, Myth, Rhetoric, Enlightenment, Information, Critique, Intellectual, Journalism, etc.
12. *Emotions and Feelings*: Love, Hate, Sadness, Joy, Compassion, Gratitude, Happiness, Pain, Anger, Well-Being, Guilt, Shame, Hope, Fear, Admiration, etc.

To this tentative list of major thematic areas, another section could be added for those emerging notions which might be termed 'concepts of the present time', such as Globalization, Governance, Postmodernity, Post-colonialism, Memory, Identity, Gender, Empowerment, Resilience, Political Correctness, Inclusion/Exclusion, Social Cohesion, Ecologism, Multiculturalism, Biopolitics, and others of this nature.

It goes without saying that the concepts listed within each major block, and the range of questions addressed by individual volumes, may in turn be subdivided into numerous smaller subsections. Each concept in some way represents by itself a semantic field composed of other subordinate concepts. And these fields and subfields, of course, often intersect. Hence, individual volumes in the series will often cover areas belonging to two or more blocks. The 'maximum programme' of the project would also include the historicization of disciplines, subdisciplines and their principal analytical categories, particularly in the domain of the *sciences de l'homme*, the social sciences or the *Geisteswissenschaften*. The comparative history of the formation of operational concepts of modern social sciences – including colligatory concepts and chrononyms – already boasts valuable contributions that might now be extended, deepened and systematized.[10] At a time of full-blown internationalization and increasing globalization of scientific research, such as the present, clarifying the historicity of these instruments of analysis and periodization will certainly facilitate dialogues between colleagues in different countries and academic fields. By shedding a critical light on the actual theoretical visions and traditions of research, it is to be hoped that this reflexive work will help to remove the barriers that hinder or prevent the consideration of truly transnational objects of study.

It seems reasonable to expect that the book series will contribute not only to knowing more about some historical variants of the plural European identity, but also to a greater appreciation of Europe's cultural diversity, especially if these results are included within the university curricula, thus advancing the Europeanization of national histories. But that is not all. If, as some theorists argue, one of the main goals of current political philosophy should be the analysis of the mechanisms of innovation, obsolescence and conceptual change, the European Conceptual History series can be remarkably useful in the design of new concepts: the knowledge acquired regarding the coining of new notions in the past will allow for a more confident approach to the design of those new intellectual tools so essential in order to deal with the demands of the knowledge society.

These challenges seem particularly daunting in such uncertain times as the present, in which – to borrow the words of Gramsci and Ortega y Gasset – it is difficult to rid oneself of the old ideas that have not quite died in order to embrace the new conceptions not yet born, new conceptions from which may arise unusual courses of action that could provide solutions impossible to conceive of via the rather worn-out current conceptual parameters. After all, coining a new concept bestows the surrounding reality with an alternative meaning that enables one to treat it differently.

Conceptual History and the Construction of Europe

One of these embryonic notions that is constantly in doubt and never quite takes shape is the very concept of Europe. That is the case *a fortiori* of the EU, an entity impossible to define, famously described by Jacques Delors as an 'unidentified political object' many years before its failed attempt to provide itself with a constitution.[11] These lines are being written in the midst of a long crisis in which Europe's long-term future is probably at stake. It is no secret that the European project, in all of its versions and dimensions – economic, political and moral – is enduring difficult times. According to those in the know, the time has come to choose, without further delay, between a much closer union or else clear and simple disintegration. And, beyond the consequences of this decision within the EU, the outcome of this crisis will almost certainly determine the relevance or irrelevance of Europe as a political actor on the world stage.

It is not our task as scholars to take decisions or engage in political discussions of this theme. However, as professionals aspiring to do our job as well as possible, we believe that we can make some contribution to this civic debate. Our commitment to a new European conceptual history, aware of both the internal complexity of our continent and the developments, variations and extensions of those same concepts beyond Europe, could illuminate certain important issues at this delicate juncture. It is no coincidence that the problems Europe experiences in thinking of itself historically eventually translate into conceptual difficulty. Now too, with the return of the old demons of national stereotypes and separatist impulses, the debates over the future of the EU mobilize an entire conceptual vocabulary in the shape of some crucial dilemmas: federation versus disintegration, welfare state versus neoliberalism, solidarity versus national egoism, policies of austerity versus expansive policies, and so on. European historians and political scientists, and in particular specialists in historical semantics, have something to say with regard to these questions. They can show, for instance, the extent to which certain conceptual systems are inextricably woven into the construction of Europe, but also into the most dramatic and destructive periods of its history.

This approach could be of enormous benefit to the European scientific community, thanks not only to its analysis of the complex interplay between sociopolitical change and conceptual innovation on a continental scale, but also its capacity to clear certain categorical obstacles that hinder mutual understanding between scholars educated in different languages, disciplines, schools and national research traditions. Beyond academic circles, our European Conceptual History project can contribute to the clarification of the vocabularies of politics; not via the search for a purely formal and unequivocal definition for each term as advocated by some representatives of analytic philosophy, but precisely by showing the historical depth of their meanings and the dynamics of disagreements. By unearthing the various strata of meaning, indicating the fracture lines of the debates and the inescapably rhetorical nature of political languages, the work we propose raises the historical and linguistic awareness of political actors.

This new form of writing European history is also well equipped to break the double straitjacket – spatial and temporal – that has constrained historiography for nearly two centuries. I refer to 'methodological nationalism', on the one hand, and teleological visions based in one way or another on the philosophies of progress, on the other. With regard to the first, as has been shown, the European Conceptual History collection aims to transcend national frameworks in the quest for a multilingual and transnational approach to social and political concepts. In the second highlighted aspect, the need to reconsider the European conceptual vocabulary appears today to be particularly pressing in view of the crucial shift in the temporal patterns of comprehension that for so many decades have dominated our academic circles. This shift entails a move away from teleological and determinist master narratives, which tended inexorably in the direction of rationalization, modernization and progress, and towards adopting a more realistic perspective in which contingency, indetermination, fragility and openness should be regarded as distinctive characteristics of political language.

Concluding Remarks. Conceptual European History and Global History

All that remains is to add a few words about the sense of this proposal for a European semantic history in today's world, a globalized world that for a long time now has been witnessing the gradual decline of Europe and, more recently, the rapid emergence of new powers in Asia and Latin America. What place should correspond to this Western appendix of the Eurasian continent in a global history of concepts? Do European – or Euro-American – concepts perhaps enjoy some privilege of universality in renewed social sciences in which some theorists have not only raised well-argued questions over the idea of one single modernity, but have on occasions openly denied the validity of their own analytical tools when they are applied to the study of extra-European cultures?

Although it seems undeniable that modern historical awareness and history as a 'scientific' discipline were born in Europe just over two centuries ago, in today's world it would be unacceptable to infer from this a sort of permanent epistemic primacy over the entire planet. Neither are the old historical-philosophical schemas that assigned a direction to history and situated Europe – or to be more accurate, certain Euro-American areas – in the vanguard of the progress of humankind any longer credible. The discredit of those metanarratives provides the opportunity to write a less simplistic history, more balanced and unbiased; an emerging history capable of paying every continent equal attention and taking seriously the temporalities and conceptualities of worlds beyond Europe. In this new historiographical scenario, with the manifest rise of various forms of transnational history, the figure of the contemporary professional historian increasingly resembles that of a mediator between cultures, and historical semantics attains unexpected prominence.

Conceptual history has sometimes been described, and with good reason, as a methodologically sophisticated form of 'translation' between ages and cultures. Like good interpreters, the conceptual historian helps us to familiarize ourselves with the unknown, but also to be surprised by what initially seemed familiar. This is a complex intellectual exercise, of closeness and distance at one and the same time, extraordinarily formative, as Samuel Wineburg so clearly saw: '[T]he sustained encounter with this less-familiar past teaches us the limitations of our brief sojourn on the planet, and allows us to take membership in the entire human race'.[12]

In short, the potential benefits for Europeans of conceptual history, and in particular of this book series – especially for academic circles – are summarized *hic et nunc* in the following points. First, as far as the linguistic and communicative dimension is concerned, the project may lead to a better understanding of the historical background of many conceptual controversies among European citizens; it may help to clear misunderstandings and bring national academic communities closer to one another. Secondly, from the historical-methodological point of view, the project offers alternative approaches to the exaggeratedly teleological and presentist visions that continue to impregnate much of historiography. Thirdly, with regard to reflexivity, so necessary in an accelerated world immersed in a chronic crisis, historicization and cross-analysis of the constellations of concepts and categories through which we perceive the world favour a much more distanced and critical vision of our own conceptual lenses and filters. Finally, from a global perspective, the gradual completion of the book series' programme might give rise to very positive consequences for the international community of historians that is slowly forming. The emphasis on diversity and on the various circles or levels of 'otherness' – cultural, political, linguistic – with which we Europeans perceive each other, places the participants in the project in an advantageous position in order to address other types of otherness and global comparisons with a greater radius, be they cross-linguistic, cross-cultural or cross-civilizational.

While the intention in the early volumes of the European Conceptual History collection is to dedicate various chapters to describing the developments of some European concepts on other continents, when the project is more advanced it will be able to delve deeper in a cross-dialogue with other transnational projects, such as the Ibero-American Conceptual History

Project (*Iberconceptos*), or the Project of Intercommunication of East Asian Basic Concepts, or incipient projects on the history of political concepts in modern Indian and African languages. The results of this and other ongoing joint efforts could provide us with valuable keys in order better to appreciate the plurality of lifestyles that are the legacy of history within and beyond Europe, and thus tackle more efficiently the difficulties of intercultural dialogue. This promises to be a long but stimulating journey towards the gradual construction of a global conceptual history, which might greatly enhance our knowledge of the world.

Javier Fernández-Sebastián is Professor of History of Political Thought at the Universidad del País Vasco (Bilbao, Spain). He has published extensively in the field of intellectual and conceptual history of modern politics. Among his recent books are the edited volumes *Concepts and Time: New Approaches to Conceptual History* (2011) and *La Aurora de la Libertad. Los primeros liberalismos en el mundo iberoamericano* (2012), as well as the *Diccionario político y social del mundo iberoamericano. Conceptos políticos fundamentales* (2009–14, 11 vols), which is the result of an ongoing transnational project on conceptual comparative history in the Iberian Atlantic (*Iberconceptos*).

Notes

1. Giacomo Leopardi, 'Lo Zibaldone di pensieri' (24 June 1821), in *Pensieri di varia filosofia e di bella letteratura* (Florence: Le Monnier, 1921), 1213–16. More recently several scholars have proposed other terms for this kind of word, such as 'internationalisms', 'European internationalisms' and 'transnationalisms'. Peter Braun, *Internationalismen: Studien zur interlingualen Lexikologie und Lexikographie* (Tübingen: Niemeyer, 1990). Peter Braun, Burkhard Schaeder and Johannes Volmert (eds), *Internationalismen II: Studien zur interlingualen Lexikologie und Lexikographie* (Tübingen: Niemeyer, 2003). Joachim Grzega, 'Europäische Internationalismen: Manchmal "falsche Freunde" ... auch bei Nationen "gleicher" Sprache', in *EuroLinguistischer Parcours: Kernwissen zur europäischen Sprachkultur* (Frankfurt: IKO, 2006), 115–38. Pim den Boer, 'Hacia una historia comparada de los conceptos: El ejemplo de *civilisation/beschaving*', *Revista de Estudios Políticos* 134 (2006), 101.
2. Lucian Hölscher, 'Hacia un diccionario histórico de los conceptos políticos europeos: Aportación teórica y metodológica de la Begriffsgeschichte', *Ayer* 53(1) (2004) [Dossier: Historia de los Conceptos, eds. Javier Fernández-Sebastián and Juan Francisco Fuentes], 97–108.
3. Émile Benveniste, *Le vocabulaire des institutions indo-européennes, vol. 1: Économie, parenté, société; vol. 2: Pouvoir, droit, religion* (Paris: Éditions de Minuit, 1975).

4. Barbara Cassin (ed.), *Vocabulaire Européen des philosophies: Dictionnaire des intraduisibles* (Paris: Le Robert/Seuil, 2004); Olivier Christin (ed.), *Dictionnaire des Concepts Nomades en Sciences Humaines*, 2 vols. (Paris: Éditions Métailié 2010 and 2016).
5. Darrin M. McMahon and Samuel Moyn (eds), *Rethinking Modern European Intellectual History* (Oxford: Oxford University Press, 2014). Margrit Pernau and Dominic Sachsenmaier (eds), *Global Conceptual History: A Reader* (London: Bloomsbury, 2016).
6. Reinhart Koselleck, Ulrike Spree and Willibald Steinmetz, 'Drei bürgerliche Welten: Zur vergleichenden Semantik der bürgerlichen Gesellschaft in Deutschland, England und Frankreich', in Hans-Jürgen Puhle (ed.), *Bürger in der Gesellschaft der Neuzeit: Wirtschaft – Politik – Kultur* (Göttingen: Vandenhoeck & Ruprecht 1991), 14–58.
7. Jörn Leonhard, *Liberalismus: Zur historischen Semantik eines europäischen Deutungsmusters* (Munich: Oldenbourg, 2001).
8. Paul Ricoeur, *Interpretation Theory: Discourse and the Surplus of Meaning* (Fort Worth: Texas Christian University Press, 1976).
9. Pasi Ihalainen, Cornelia Ilie and Kari Palonen (eds), *Parliament and Parliamentarism: A Comparative History of a European Concept* (New York and Oxford: Berghahn Books, 2016).
10. L.B. Cebik, 'Colligation in the Writing of History', *The Monist* 53(1) (1969), 40; C. Behan McCullagh, 'Colligation and Classification in History', *History and Theory* 17(3) (1978), 270; Paul Bacot, Laurent Douzou and Jean-Paul Honoré, 'Chrononymes: La politisation du temps', *Mots: Les langages du politique* 87 (2008), 5–95.
11. Speech by President of the European Commission, Jacques Delors (Luxembourg, 9 September 1985), in *Bulletin of the European Communities*, No. 9, September 1985 (Luxembourg: Office for Official Publications of the European Communities, 1985). http://www.cvce.eu/obj/speech_by_jacques_delors_luxembourg_9_september_1985-en-423d6913-b4e2-4395-9157-fe70b3ca8521.html
12. Samuel Wineburg, *Historical Thinking and Other Unnatural Acts* (Philadephia: Temple University Press, 2001), 7.

References

Bacot, Paul, Laurent Douzou and Jean-Paul Honoré, 'Chrononymes: La politisation du temps', *Mots: Les langages du politique* 87 (2008), 5–95

Benveniste, Émile, *Le vocabulaire des institutions indo-européennes, vol. 1: Économie, parenté, société; vol. 2: Pouvoir, droit, religion* (Paris: Éditions de Minuit, 1975)

Braun, Peter, *Internationalismen: Studien zur interlingualen Lexikologie und Lexikographie* (Tübingen: Niemeyer, 1990)

Braun, Peter, Burkhard Schaeder and Johannes Volmert (eds), *Internationalismen II: Studien zur interlingualen Lexikologie und Lexikographie* (Tübingen: Niemeyer, 2003)

Cassin, Barbara (ed.), *Vocabulaire Européen des philosophies: Dictionnaire des intraduisibles* (Paris: Le Robert/Seuil, 2004)

Cebik, L.B., 'Colligation in the Writing of History', *The Monist* 53(1) (1969), 40–57

Christin, Olivier (ed.), *Dictionnaire des Concepts Nomades en Sciences Humaines*, 2 vols. (Paris: Éditions Métailié, 2010 and 2016)

den Boer, Pim, 'Hacia una historia comparada de los conceptos: El ejemplo de *civilisation/beschaving*', *Revista de Estudios Políticos* 134 (2006), 97–124

Grzega, Joachim, 'Europäische Internationalismen: Manchmal "falsche Freunde" … auch bei Nationen "gleicher" Sprache', in *EuroLinguisticher Parcours: Kernwissen zur europäischen Sprachkultur* (Frankfurt: IKO, 2006), 115–38

Hölscher, Lucian, 'Hacia un diccionario histórico de los conceptos políticos europeos: Aportación teórica y metodológica de la Begriffsgeschichte', *Ayer* 53(1) (2004) [Dossier: Historia de los Conceptos, eds. Fernández-Sebastián, Javier and Fuentes, Juan Francisco], 97–108

Ihalainen, Pasi, Cornelia Ilie and Kari Palonen (eds), *Parliament and Parliamentarism: A Comparative History of a European Concept* (New York and Oxford: Berghahn Books, 2016)

Koselleck, Reinhart, Ulrike Spree, and Willibald Steinmetz, 'Drei bürgerliche Welten: Zur vergleichenden Semantik der bürgerlichen Gesellschaft in Deutschland, England und Frankreich', in Hans-Jürgen Puhle (ed.), *Bürger in der Gesellschaft der Neuzeit: Wirtschaft – Politik – Kultur* (Göttingen: Vandenhoeck & Ruprecht 1991), 14–58

Leonhard, Jörn, *Liberalismus: Zur historischen Semantik eines europäischen Deutungsmusters* (Munich: Oldenbourg, 2001)

Leopardi, Giacomo, 'Lo Zibaldone di pensieri' (24 June 1821), in *Pensieri di varia filosofia e di bella letteratura* (Florence: Le Monnier, 1921), 1213–16

McCullagh, C. Behan, 'Colligation and Classification in History', *History and Theory* 17(3) (1978), 267–84

McMahon, Darrin M., and Samuel Moyn (eds), *Rethinking Modern European Intellectual History* (Oxford: Oxford University Press, 2014)

Pernau, Margrit, and Dominic Sachsenmaier (eds), *Global Conceptual History: A Reader* (London: Bloomsbury, 2016)

Ricoeur, Paul, *Interpretation Theory: Discourse and the Surplus of Meaning* (Fort Worth: Texas Christian University Press, 1976)

Speech by President of the European Commission, Jacques Delors (Luxembourg, 9 September 1985), in *Bulletin of the European Communities*, No. 9, September 1985 (Luxembourg: Office for Official Publications of the European Communities, 1985). http://www.cvce.eu/obj/speech_by_jacques_delors_luxembourg_9_september_1985-en-423d6913-b4e2-4395-9157-fe70b3ca8521.html

Wineburg, Samuel, *Historical Thinking and Other Unnatural Acts* (Philadephia: Temple University Press, 2001)

Index

above / below. *See under* Koselleck, Reinhart
absolutism, 246–49
academia, 5–6, 8, 13, 16–18, 21–22, 27–29, 69, 71, 73, 78–79, 82, 96–97, 99–100, 108, 110, 119, 123, 125–127, 129–31, 140–41, 151, 177, 197–99, 201, 203–5, 213, 218–24, 237, 248, 251, 253–55, 265, 285–86, 288, 291–94. *See also* university
accountability, 24, 121,127
administration, 9, 15, 29, 69, 78, 80–81, 89n52, 97, 131, 215, 219, 228, 230n6, 239–48, 250–54, 290
Africa, 3, 295
agency, 8, 10, 16, 22, 31, 97–98, 101, 107, 118–20, 142, 144–45, 147–48, 163n32, 179–80, 187, 200–3, 213, 222–23, 228, 246, 287–89
agenda, 6, 66, 80, 102–4, 106–8, 129, 197, 202–5, 219, 221–22, 275, 288–89
 -setting, 100, 104, 107–8, 110
agrarianism, 227
d'Alembert, Jean Le Rond, 18
America, 52–53, 56, 81, 132, 134, 179, 202–3, 223–24, 227–28, 238, 241, 267, 287. *See also* Latin America
Americanization, 287
Anderson, Benedict, 53
anglicization, 7, 82–83
anti-imperialism, 53. *See also* imperialism
antiquity, 14, 19, 50, 52–53, 77–79, 99–100, 215, 283–84, 286
Arendt, Hannah, 109

argumentation, 17, 23–24, 30–31, 75, 98–101, 106, 122, 144, 153, 156–57, 180–81, 184, 221, 265, 267, 275, 284, 286
Aristotle, 79, 99
arts, 9, 53–54, 135, 156, 242–45, 249–50, 289
Asia, 3, 293, 295
asynchronicity / synchronicity, 4, 6–7, 49–50, 53, 57–58, 63, 68, 181
 of linguistic plurality, 48–50, 55–57
 of meaning, 48–53, 55
 of use, 48–50, 53–56
Austria, 10, 242–43, 244–45, 247, 250–52, 254–55
authenticity, 152, 237, 239, 269, 274
authority, 26, 70, 79, 98, 101, 120–22, 198, 200, 251, 266–67, 271–72, 276n10

backwardness, 18, 48, 54, 246
 concept of, 74–75, 227, 236, 243
the Balkans, 56, 147, 221, 238
 concept of, 8, 215–28, 238, 243 (*see also under* Europe)
Baltic region, 215, 225, 268, 288
Banat, 214, 240, 244, 246, 250, 255
Barbeyrac, Jean, 201
Basilikon Doron, 199–200
Beck, Ulrich, 140–42
Belgrade, 223, 243
Benelux states, 216
Bentham, Jeremy, 106
Bielefeld, 62, 150, 213
Bloch, Ernst, 54
Bödeker, Hans Erich, 246
Bodin, Jean, 202

Bohemia, 81, 218, 240, 244, 255
borders, 8–9, 11–12, 26, 105, 133, 139,
142, 199, 213–16, 219, 226–28,
230n6, 250, 285
  crossing of, 14, 70, 142–45, 147, 152,
157, 161n16, 205, 240, 264, 274,
286
  cultural, 55, 131, 215, 223, 228, 265
  linguistic, 11, 13, 55, 120, 144–45, 152,
205, 288
  national, 12, 14, 31, 128, 139, 141–42,
144–46, 152, 215, 217, 228
  political, 142, 145
Bourdieu, Pierre, 265, 276n1
Bratislava, 243, 250
Britain, 12, 24–25, 47–48, 105, 107, 146,
151, 156, 164n44, 178, 186–87, 228,
253, 286, 289
Brunner, Otto, 4
Bucharest, 243
Budapest, 220–21, 243, 250
Bukovina, 214, 240, 246, 255
Bulgaria, 12, 213, 218, 221
bureaucracy. *See* administration
Burke, Peter, 13, 199, 207n8

Calvinism, 200, 204, 246
Cambridge school of intellectual history,
28–29, 207n12. *See also* Skinner,
Quentin
Canetti, Elias, 12–13
canonization, 19, 97–98, 182, 184, 200,
203, 217
capitalism, 53, 64, 227–28, 270, 290
Carroll, Lewis, 118
Cary, John, 203
Cassin, Barbara, 77, 285
Catalonia, 9, 202
Catherine II, 10, 71
Catholic Church, 13, 215, 218, 238, 243,
246–48, 250–51, 253–54, 290
'the Celtic fringe', 9
Cernăuți, 243, 250
Chakrabarty, Dipesh, 20, 178
China, 3–4, 20, 144, 151, 165, 203
Christianity, 4, 19–20, 22, 77–78, 243, 251,
283, 290
church, 11–12, 68, 78, 246, 250–51, 254,
266–67, 277n11, 287, 290

citizenship, 99, 244, 251–52, 268–69, 274,
294
  concept of, 68, 72, 128, 216, 270–74,
278n23, 285–86, 290
civilization, 74, 78, 147, 220–21, 223,
236–37, 239, 242–43, 244, 248, 269,
281, 294
  concept of, 19, 55, 57, 64, 73–74, 83n3,
215–16, 227, 290
civil society, 252, 273, 277n12
  concept of, 201, 247, 251, 286, 290
clergy, 13, 255, 267
Cold War, 219, 223, 227
colonialism, 3, 8, 14, 20, 78, 81, 202, 242,
246–47, 283, 289, 290
collective singular. *See under* Koselleck,
Reinhart
Communism, 51, 53, 229, 283, 290
community, 7–8, 18, 22, 27, 38n51, 48,
53–55, 70, 75, 121, 127, 180, 187,
226–27, 237, 239–43, 247, 249–50,
252–53, 255–56, 273
  émigré, 222–23
  ethnic, 121, 254–55
  expert, 69, 219, 265, 292, 294
  imagined, 53, 55
  language, 2, 10–12, 14, 17–20, 63,
67–68, 70, 78, 140, 144, 182, 226,
240, 244–45, 248, 282, 284
  local, 148, 241
  national, 63, 159n3, 182, 254, 274
  political, 3, 49, 226, 237, 284
  religious, 200, 239–40, 243, 245–46,
250–51
  social, 13, 49, 81, 241, 272
comparison, 1, 6, 11, 17–20, 23, 28–29,
51, 74–75, 79, 81, 98, 100–2, 105,
108, 131, 139–42, 151–52, 154,
156–58, 159n3, 163n30, 164n44,
185, 203, 207n7, 214, 220–21,
227, 242, 245, 247, 253, 273–74,
284
  and conceptual history (*see under*
conceptual history)
  diachronic, 30
  synchronic, 2, 52, 177, 187
concepts, conceptual
  absence of, 2, 24–25, 27–28
  ambiguity 15, 119, 121

basic, key (*Grundbegriffe*), 2, 4–5, 10, 67–68, 71–72, 74–75, 82, 96, 108, 110, 145–46, 163n34, 176, 181–82, 198, 225, 263–67, 269–70, 274–75, 282, 284, 295 (*see also under* Koselleck, Reinhart)

change, 2, 4, 6–7, 16, 24, 26, 29–30, 52, 57, 63, 67, 96–101, 104, 107, 109–10, 124–26, 128, 130, 139, 143, 147, 180–81, 183, 199, 217, 225–26, 268, 291–92

cluster, field, 3–4, 24, 26–28, 30, 124–25, 128, 130, 132, 180, 199, 217, 225–26, 266, 269, 281, 284, 289, 294

connotation, 16, 24–25, 109, 128, 142–43, 153, 156, 184–86, 217–19, 225, 252, 267, 277n11

contestation / decontestation of, 6, 17, 27, 29–30, 68–72, 96, 100, 120, 122–27, 143–47, 198, 225, 228–29, 266, 274, 282

formation of, 69–70, 77–78, 81

illocutionary force of, 2, 133, 200

inconclusiveness, 119, 121–22

indeterminacy, 25, 119, 121–22, 127

intertwinement, 26, 124, 215, 240

and metaphor, 5, 9, 25–26, 52, 67, 133, 180, 182, 216, 227, 266, 286

morphology, 27, 123–24, 213

network, 24, 26, 79, 125, 282–84, 290

non-verbal, 2, 8–9, 28, 99, 123

normative, 96, 99, 104, 269

paired, 9, 24–25, 99, 218, 236

pattern, 4, 21, 27, 32, 125

performativity of, 2, 28, 133

political, 2, 4, 6–7, 9, 25–26, 30, 67, 71–72, 103–6, 108, 110, 119–25, 127–28, 133, 143–46, 153, 157, 176, 181–82, 184, 186, 220, 222, 224, 254, 266, 268–70, 283–85, 289, 293, 295

regional, 213–17, 219–29

relations, 77, 108, 124, 125–26, 132, 135, 144, 220, 225–26, 284

and semantic fields, 16–17, 22, 25–27, 57, 72, 118–19, 121, 125–26, 128, 152, 180, 182, 184–85, 198, 271, 289–90

social, 2, 4, 6–7, 25–26, 28, 30, 67, 71–72, 119–20, 123–25, 128, 133, 146, 176, 181, 184, 186, 266, 283, 289, 293

spatial, 9, 25, 213, 215–16, 218–19, 226–27, 238

structure, 2, 7, 25–26, 29–30, 49, 51–57, 122, 124–29, 134, 184, 186, 226, 285

temporal, 4–5, 25, 265

theoretical, 153, 157

traditional, 16–17, 184, 266

transfer, 3, 8, 16, 18–19, 57, 70, 84n3, 142–44, 147, 152, 180–82, 184–87, 202–3, 270, 274

universal / particularistic, 10, 68, 72, 76, 127, 143, 156, 181–82, 185, 263–65, 267, 269–70, 272, 274–75, 293

universe, 4–5, 11, 16, 18, 20–21, 28, 63, 67, 82, 129, 146, 148, 265–66, 268

use of, 2–3, 7, 11, 29, 52–56, 70, 72, 100–101, 103, 126, 139, 142–43, 146, 148–49, 152–53, 155–57, 161n16, 176, 263, 267, 270, 274

vagueness, 79, 119, 121–22, 283

conceptual history

comparative approach, 1–2, 12, 17–24, 28, 30, 52, 65, 67, 69, 72, 79, 83, 100–101, 131, 139–40, 175–78, 180–83, 185, 187, 205, 216, 228–29, 238, 273, 284–86, 288–89, 291

development of, 1–2, 4–5, 49–50, 64–65, 124, 286

in the digital age, 1, 32n, 139–40, 149–53, 157, 159n3, 164–65nn46–47, 166n59, 288

and Europe, 1, 3–13, 15, 17, 19–21, 23–24, 32, 48–51, 55–58, 63, 65–68, 71–73, 76–83, 139, 144, 146, 148–49, 157, 175–76, 178, 181–83, 187–88, 212, 216–17, 265–68, 270, 281–89, 291–95

global, 3–4, 19, 73, 82, 178, 188, 285, 293–95

and globalization, 7, 21, 76, 82, 229, 285, 290–91, 293

and language, 2–3, 6–7, 10–21, 25–26, 31, 50–51, 55–57, 71, 78–82, 119, 123–24, 133–34, 139, 143–44, 180–82, 188, 197–99, 202, 205, 212, 238, 282, 285, 287, 293–94

conceptual history (*cont.*)
  macro-analysis, 125
  microanalysis, 125, 134
  national, 13, 63–64, 139, 144, 188, 212, 285, 293
  onomasiological approach, 22–24, 39n65
  semasiological approach, 19, 21–24, 72, 284
  source material, 6, 17, 32n, 65, 97–98, 102, 123, 130, 151, 153, 288
  spatial approach, 7–12, 143, 149, 157, 212–18, 226–29, 264–65, 289, 293
  transnational, 4, 15, 31, 65, 139–43, 152, 157, 216, 238, 284–85, 289, 291, 293–94 (*see also* transnational history)
conceptualization, 2, 5, 9, 20–21, 23–28, 31, 54, 56, 64, 103, 110, 124–25, 135, 141, 143–44, 148, 212–13, 215–20, 222–29, 236–37, 239–47, 254, 256, 270–71, 275, 282
  reconceptualization, 144, 266, 274
conflict, 9, 24, 47, 51, 54–55, 57, 77, 119, 134–35, 156, 179, 221, 223, 225, 241–42, 274, 287
consensus, 129, 229, 268–69, 277n12, 288
conservatism, 24, 55, 74–76, 88n40, 133, 184, 215, 221, 243, 290
constitution, 4–5, 47, 102, 155, 175–76, 186, 254, 271, 290–91
context, 2, 10, 19–21, 23, 27–30, 47–48, 50–52, 54, 56–57, 73, 98, 109, 121, 123–25, 128, 142, 144, 149, 151–53, 155–57, 181–83, 186, 197–99, 201, 204–5, 214–15, 217–20, 223, 229, 237, 244, 248, 259n34, 263, 265, 272–75, 282, 285–86, 288
contingency, 4, 16, 30, 47, 68, 99, 123, 126–28, 143, 198, 214, 217, 293
Conze, Werner, 4
Counter-concepts, 98, 109, 184, 214, 218, 225, 227–28. *See also under* Koselleck, Reinhart
  Christians / heathens, 22
  'civilized' / 'uncivilized', 22, 74, 78, 215–16, 227
  East / West, 215, 217, 227–28, 240, 242–43, 245, 247, 287, 289
  North / South, 215, 217
  society / nature, 269

Cracow, 243
crisis, 47–48, 64, 123, 135, 215, 292, 294
  concept of, 4–5, 34n14, 48, 84n10, 290
Croatia, 218
Csáky, Moritz, 243
cultural history, 13, 197–200, 215, 221, 224, 236–37, 241, 224, 288
culture, 1–3, 6–8, 11, 14, 16, 18, 24–28, 30–31, 50, 54–57, 64, 77, 81–83, 119, 123–24, 126–28, 130–34, 139, 142–43, 155–56, 175–76, 178–79, 183, 198–203, 212–18, 220–21, 224, 226, 228, 231n6, 236–56, 259n34, 263–65, 267–69, 273–74, 281–83, 285, 287–89, 293–94
  concept of, 19, 239, 290
  European, 1, 8, 49, 74–75, 199, 212, 237, 253, 282, 284, 287–88, 291
  high, 249–50
  hybridization of, 250
  identity-based, 237, 239 (*see also under* identity)
  political (*see under* politics, political)
  subculture, 226, 264, 268, 277n11, 287
Cvijić, Jovan, 220
Czechia, 218, 221, 224, 226
Czech language, 244, 249–50
Czechoslovakia, 213

Dalmatia, 214
Danube, 12
debate, 23–24, 28–29, 52, 57, 69, 71, 73, 81–82, 96–110, 123, 139–40, 142–47, 151–57, 186, 198, 201, 213, 223–24, 227, 237, 265, 271–72, 277n11, 282, 286, 288, 292
Delors, Jacques, 291
democracy, 102, 109–10, 121, 127, 129, 132, 147, 254, 267, 269, 275, 281
  concept of, 4–5, 19, 52, 73, 108–9, 121–22, 126–27, 146, 216, 269–70, 282–83, 289–90
democratization, 5–6, 21, 67–68, 71–73, 75, 83, 106, 183
Denmark, 77, 154, 266–67, 269, 277n11
development, 3, 5–7, 18, 21, 47, 58, 65, 68, 74–76, 83, 124, 146, 175, 177, 188, 204, 224, 229, 248, 294
  concept of, 5, 73, 124, 126, 215, 290

Dewey, John, 179
diachrony, 2, 17, 21, 30, 50–52, 66, 130–31, 176–77, 181–83, 187–88, 283
dictionary, 1, 17–19, 70, 77, 79, 97, 144, 149, 186, 254, 284. *See also* lexicography
Diderot, Denis, 18
discourse, 1–2, 5, 7, 22–23, 28–29, 52–55, 57, 128, 131, 133–35, 151–52, 199, 216–17, 222, 241, 255, 264, 266, 270–71, 274–75, 284, 286
 political, 27, 119–20, 128–29, 140, 148–49, 152–54, 156, 182, 185, 204, 213, 219, 227, 272–73
 public, 20, 129, 145, 217, 219, 228
 scholarly, 140, 220–21, 226–28
 social, 27, 119, 128, 182, 186
discourse analysis, 29
 critical (CDA), 29, 133–34
Droysen, Johann Gustav, 179
Du Châtelet, Émilie, 201
Dvornik, František (Francis), 223

earlier / later. *See under* Koselleck, Reinhart
early modern period, 7, 13–14, 20, 77–79, 81–82, 199, 213–14, 264–68
'the East', 8, 215, 217, 219, 222–24, 227–28, 238, 242, 287, 289. *See also under* counter–concepts
economics, 31, 48, 213, 220, 222, 224, 227, 289
economy, 6, 11, 14–15, 48, 58, 64, 67, 75, 77, 139, 141–42, 147, 204, 214–15, 219–20, 223–24, 228, 237–39, 242, 244, 247, 272, 292
 concept of, 4, 19, 151–52, 290
 political (*see* political economy)
education, 75, 77, 79, 97, 154, 247–48, 255, 272–75, 281, 292
 concept of, 19, 73, 183, 269, 290
Eisenstadt, Shmuel N., 48
elites, 6, 9, 11, 13, 31, 51, 73–74, 77–78, 81, 127, 131, 238, 248–49, 251, 254–56, 271, 283
emancipation, 73–74, 124, 133, 242, 247, 251, 253, 275
emotion, 1–2, 9, 127, 133, 179, 290

empire, 9–12, 72–73, 77–79, 81, 154–56, 215–16, 224–25, 239, 241–51, 254–55, 274, 287
 concept of, 8, 52–53, 143, 289
encyclopedia. *See* dictionary
England, 21, 80, 88n38, 101, 107, 200, 203–4, 267–68, 277, 286. *See also* Britain
English language, 3–4, 7, 10–11, 14–15, 19–20, 73–74, 77–78, 80–82, 103, 144, 149–53, 182, 187, 199, 202, 204, 265, 271, 282
Enlightenment, 5, 52, 65, 69, 71, 73–74, 175, 183, 201–2, 204, 243, 246–49, 251–54, 268–69, 286
entanglement, 17, 26, 50, 56–57, 124, 175–78, 180–83, 187–88, 228, 237, 242
equality / inequality, 25–26, 68, 73, 121–23, 127–28, 132, 177, 202, 236, 241, 263, 265, 272
ethnicity, 6, 12–13, 24, 53, 81, 121, 148, 154–55, 215, 226, 242, 245, 254, 267–68. *See also under* nationalism
 concept of, 128, 242, 253, 290
Eurasia, 293
 concept of 215
Eurocentrism, 18, 23, 74, 177, 188
Europe, 1, 3–8, 11, 13–15, 23, 63, 146, 175–78, 199, 212–15, 221, 236, 238–39, 264, 281–82, 287, 293–95
 Central, 8–9, 12, 74, 78–79, 212–14, 217–20, 222, 224–26, 228–29, 238–46, 248–49, 251–56, 266
 concept of, 148, 188, 216, 225, 236, 238, 289
 conceptual convergence / divergence, 19–21, 76–82, 239, 265–66, 284–87
 and conceptual history (*see under* conceptual history)
 East Central, 218, 223–25, 227, 229, 242
 Eastern, 8–9, 12, 74, 201, 213, 215, 217–18, 220, 222–29, 237–240, 243–46, 248–49, 251–56, 289
 multiple temporalities, 47–50, 53, 55–58, 63, 67–68, 76, 183, 187(*see also* asynchronicity / synchronicity)
 Northern, 12, 74, 78–79, 201, 213–14, 268–74 (*see also* Nordic countries)

Europe (*cont.*)
  South Eastern, 9, 12, 78–79, 212–14, 218–23, 225–26, 239 (*see also under* the Balkans)
  Southern, 74, 78, 213, 268 (*see also* the Mediterranean)
  Western, 12, 21, 66, 74–75, 78, 122, 201, 213, 217, 228, 240, 242–43, 245–46, 249–50, 266, 269, 289
European history, 7, 9–10, 20, 49, 58, 73, 146–48, 157, 175–77, 182, 187–88, 219, 264, 285, 293
European integration, 6, 21, 32, 47, 58, 212–13, 291–92
Europeanisms, 'European language', 77, 176, 281–82
Europeanization, 20, 199, 221, 287, 291
Europeanness, 228, 281
  methodological, 146–148
European Union, 8, 15, 47–48, 58, 77, 288, 291–92
evolution. *See* development
expectation, 4, 7, 25, 30–31, 53, 56, 145, 181–84, 186–87, 205, 214, 244, 264–65. *See also under* Koselleck, Reinhart
experience, 4, 7, 13, 15, 48, 50, 52–57, 64, 74, 76, 82, 135, 142–47, 156, 175–84, 186–88, 212, 215, 239, 241, 244, 264–65, 267, 270, 282–84, 287, 292. *See also under* Koselleck, Reinhart

Febvre, Lucien, 64, 67
federalism, 216, 219, 221, 289
Fennomans, 154–55, 271, 273–74
Fichte, Johann Gottlieb, 203
Finnish language, 11, 144, 153–55, 270–74
Finland, 71, 78, 144, 147, 153–56, 213, 267, 269–74
First World War, 14, 147, 221, 227, 256
framing, 17, 48–49, 56, 66, 75, 123, 178, 200, 202, 204, 215–16, 218–20, 222, 224, 226–28, 270
France, 13–14, 20–21, 48, 52, 64, 79–80, 102, 146, 156, 183–86, 201, 203, 238, 242, 246–47, 249, 253–54, 286, 289,
freedom, 99, 102–3, 281, 288
  concept of, 54, 56, 282–83
  See also liberty

French language, 3, 5, 10–11, 14, 57, 64, 67, 69, 71, 73–74, 77–81, 144, 149, 151–54, 182, 184–86, 254–55, 265, 282, 284–85
French Revolution, 48, 51, 64, 68–69, 80, 147, 249, 269

generation, 28, 51, 53–54, 65, 97, 154, 218–19, 243, 249
geography, 3, 8, 10, 50, 55, 124, 139, 141, 143, 146, 148–49, 152–54, 156–57, 163n34, 212–13, 215, 218–20, 222, 224–28, 236–40, 243, 245, 253, 285, 287
German language, 2, 4, 9–12, 14–15, 19–20, 57, 71, 73–74, 77–79, 81–82, 109, 144, 149, 153–55, 184–85, 201, 204–5, 244, 248–51, 254–55, 265–66, 271–72, 284
Germany, 5–6, 9, 49, 54–57, 64–65, 67–72, 74, 76, 78, 81, 107, 127, 133, 149, 151–52, 155–56, 184–86, 201, 203–4, 215–16, 218–20, 222, 224–25, 242, 246, 252–53, 255, 268, 272, 286, 289
Geschichtliche Grundbegriffe (GG), 2, 5, 14, 22, 31, 48–52, 64–66, 82, 97–98, 130, 144–45, 162n26, 198, 216, 284
globalization, 7, 21, 76, 82, 178, 229, 285, 290–91, 293
Goldsworthy, Vesna, 238
government, 9, 19, 54, 80, 103–9, 132, 155, 290
Gramsci, Antonio, 291
Greece, 47–48, 50, 52, 215, 219, 283, 286
Greek language, 4, 7, 12, 19–20, 71, 77–78, 240
Gumplowicz, Ludwig, 249
Guthrie, William, 201

Habsburg Empire, 9, 12, 79, 81, 218, 226, 242, 244–51, 255. *See also* Austria
Halecki, Oskar, 219, 223
Hamilton, William Gerard, 101–2
Hatsell, John, 106
Hegel, Georg Wilhelm Friedrich, 56, 201, 252, 271, 273
Herder, Johann Gottfried, 9, 252–55
hierarchy, 16, 23, 26, 215, 228, 241, 247, 251, 284

historical change, 22, 30, 48–50, 66, 128, 175, 177–79, 222, 241–42, 244, 248–49, 251, 292
historical semantics, 23, 65, 75, 181, 183, 187, 292, 294. *See also* conceptual history
history, 23, 47, 49, 143, 157, 175–76, 187, 204, 216, 223–24, 227, 237, 252
  concept of, 4–5, 73–74, 180, 289–90
  developmental vision of, 5, 65–66, 68, 73–76, 82
history of ideas, 28, 31, 99, 182, 197–98, 288. *See also* ideas
Hobbes, Thomas, 99–100, 202
Hölscher, Lucian, 79, 284
Homer, 202
humanism, 13–14, 133, 200, 204, 282
human rights, 72–73, 241, 263
Hume, David, 201
Hungarian language, 200, 244, 249–51
Hungary, 199–200, 213, 218, 221, 224–26, 244–45, 250–51, 255, 268

Iberia, 162n26, 294
Ibn Khaldûn, 202
ideas, 25–26, 29–30, 118, 120, 128, 130, 134–35, 147–48, 182, 200–203, 243–247, 251, 254–55, 288. *See also* history of ideas
identity, 8–9, 11, 81, 148, 158, 214, 218, 226, 229, 237, 239–41, 243–44, 252–53, 255–56, 290
  European, 148, 281, 287–88, 291
ideologization, 6, 67–71, 75–76, 83, 226–27
ideology, 24, 49, 55, 65, 68–70, 87n29, 119–20, 124–30, 133, 135, 147, 151, 181–84, 249–50, 255–56, 267, 271, 275, 286, 290
  Ideologiekritik, 30
  political, 8, 19, 75–76, 133, 216, 236, 241–42, 245, 248, 290
  and political concepts, 24, 26, 29–31, 119–20, 122–24, 183, 225, 284, 288
imperialism, 3, 20, 53, 78, 81, 155, 202, 215, 241, 275, 283. *See also* anti–imperialism
India, 20, 151, 295
industrialization, 5, 14, 54, 128, 243, 290
in / out. *See under* Koselleck, Reinhart
institution, 4, 9, 14–15, 19, 58, 71, 77, 79, 101–2, 106, 134, 175–77, 214–15, 219–20, 224, 244, 247, 255, 284, 288
institutionalization, 98, 106–7, 214, 219
intellectual history, 1, 28, 124, 197, 243, 288–89
intellectuals, 8–9, 11, 13, 28, 64–65, 69–71, 74, 81, 142, 144, 147, 198–99, 203–5, 225–26, 239–40, 245, 247, 249, 252, 255, 264–66, 290
intentionality / unintentionality, 6, 10, 16, 28, 52, 54–55, 68–70, 118–21, 125–26, 133, 199, 263–64, 267, 289
interculturality, 199, 242–43, 245, 251, 295
international history, 2, 15, 73, 82, 139–43, 145, 153, 219–20, 294
interwar period, 4, 215, 217, 220–24, 227–28, 270
in utramque partem disputare. *See under* Skinner, Quentin
Iorga, Nicolae, 220
Islam, 52, 202, 243, 290
Italian language, 79, 81, 244
Italy, 20–21, 74, 79, 81, 182, 184–86, 203, 215, 281, 286

James VI and I, 199–200
Japan, 3–4, 144, 203
Jordan, Stefan, 253
Joseph II, 244, 248–49, 254
journal. *See* newspaper
Judaism, Jews, 4, 12, 19–20, 77–78, 151, 243, 250–52, 283, 290
judiciary. *See* law
justice, 244, 247
  concept of, 24, 122, 132, 134, 290

knowledge, 2, 17, 19, 27, 49, 53–54, 81, 97, 100, 105, 133, 141, 148, 152, 157, 180–81, 204, 215, 221, 226, 228, 251, 254, 267–69, 275, 289, 291
Korea, 3–4, 144
Koselleck, Reinhart, 1–2, 4–6, 17, 22–23, 31, 48–52, 55, 64–68, 70–76, 82–83, 96–98, 100, 103, 109–10, 125, 128–29, 133, 145–46, 180–81, 183, 198, 200, 216, 225, 239, 246, 253, 265, 284, 286

Koselleck, Reinhart (*cont.*)
  above / below, 23, 180
  on basic/key concepts (*Grundbegriffe*), 2, 68, 82, 96, 109, 145–46, 163n34, 198, 225
  collective singular, 67–68, 71, 180
  on comparison, 19–20, 22–23, 181, 183, 265
  on counter–concepts, 22, 98, 216, 218, 225
  earlier / later, 23, 180
  on experience, 180–81
  in / out, 22–23, 180
  movement concepts, 5, 76
  repetitive structures (*Wiederholungsstrukturen*), 4, 23, 48, 52, 76, 180–81
  Sattelzeit, 5–6, 49–50, 52, 64–76, 83, 110, 177, 181, 183, 187, 202, 218, 226, 253, 266
  simultaneity of the non–simultaneous (*Gleichzeitigkeit des Ungleichzeitigen*), 2, 29, 50, 54, 177
  on space, 216
  space of experience / horizon of expectation, 50–51, 55–56
  temporal layers (*Zeitschichten*), 51–53

language, 3, 6–7, 9–17, 25–27, 29–30, 31, 50–51, 71, 76–77, 118–122, 124, 127, 132–35, 155, 179–80, 205, 281–82
  body, 2
  and conceptual history (*see under* conceptual history)
  and cultural prestige, 11, 81
  elite / professional 7, 15, 25, 69, 78, 82, 89n52, 123, 125, 130–31, 133, 219, 222, 228
  family resemblance, 19, 77, 79, 287
  homogenization of, 4, 12–14, 287
  hybridization of, 13–14
  lingua franca, 4, 13, 20, 77, 81–82, 281, 286
  meta–language, 9–10, 20, 183, 265, 286
  multilinguality, 9, 12–16, 18, 81, 144–45, 243–44, 248, 250–51, 253, 284
  nationalization of, 6, 14, 80–83
  standardization of, 13–14, 78–81

  vernacular, vernacularization, 7, 12–13, 20, 25, 29, 78–80, 82–83, 123, 130–31, 133, 199–200, 225, 287
Latin, 4, 7, 13–14, 19–21, 71, 77–82, 162n27, 199, 202, 248, 251, 254, 265–66, 281–83
Latin America, 162n26, 229, 293–94
law, 4, 13–15, 24–25, 56, 69, 78–81, 132, 134, 155, 175, 204, 239, 263, 267, 270, 272, 275, 282, 290
legitimacy, 52–53, 105, 109, 127, 220, 267, 269, 290
Leibniz, Gottfried Wilhelm, 252
Lemberg, 243
Leopardi, Giacomo, 281
lexicography, 14, 18, 97, 186, 254, 284. *See also* dictionary
liberalism, 25, 122
  concept of, 4, 19, 21, 26, 56, 122, 142, 156, 181–86, 202, 216, 286, 289–90
liberty, 126
  concept of, 27, 67, 99, 103, 121–22, 124, 127–28, 132, 134, 203, 272
  See also freedom
liminality. *See* transit area
literature, 12–14, 16–17, 27, 53, 69, 71, 75, 78, 81, 142, 156, 219, 224, 238, 242–45, 248–50, 253, 255, 281, 289
Lithuania, 213, 218
Locke, John, 28, 277
London, 13, 286
longue durée, 2, 8, 52, 58, 66, 82, 119, 135, 177, 181, 187–88, 223, 243, 286
Lönnrot, Elias, 270–73
Lovejoy, Arthur, 99
Lutheranism, 11, 246, 267, 269

Macůrek, Josef, 221
Mandeville, Bernard, 201
Mannheim, Karl, 54
Maria Theresa, 244
Marxism, 129, 147, 221
Masaryk, Tomáš Garrigue, 225
May, Thomas Erskine, 103, 106
meaning, 2, 13, 16, 19, 21, 24–30, 51–52, 55, 68–70, 77–79, 118–128, 130, 132, 135, 151, 176, 180–83, 185, 199–200, 220, 225, 229, 237, 263, 265–66, 275, 281–83

change of, 2, 5, 8, 13–18, 29, 49–57,
    63–64, 67, 72, 79, 101, 109, 119,
    124–28, 130–31, 176, 199, 202–3,
    205, 248–49, 274, 291–92
  surplus of, 51, 120, 123, 289
  and translation (*see under* translation)
  the media, 53, 70, 82, 219, 221, 238
  the Mediterranean, 238, 287–88
  concept of, 8, 222, 225
Meinecke, Friedrich, 104
metaphor, 5, 9, 22, 25–26, 29, 52, 67, 133,
    180, 182, 216, 227, 266, 282, 286. *See
    also under* concepts, conceptual
Michels, Robert, 109
Middle Ages, 4, 7–8, 13–14, 19–20, 50,
    77–79, 81–82, 213–14, 218, 238, 240,
    243, 247, 252, 273, 282–83
migration, 3, 14, 47–48, 128, 133, 142,
    223, 287
Middle East, 3
military, 11, 52–53, 223, 244, 290
Mill, John Stuart, 126, 176, 203
minority, 13, 73, 80, 256
mobilization, 268–69, 292
modernism, 229, 275
modernity, 3–5, 10, 52–53, 64–66, 76,
    82–83, 133, 135, 215, 238–40, 243,
    245–49, 253, 255, 265, 267, 283, 287,
    293
  concept of, 48–49, 76, 237, 240–43, 251,
    254, 290
  multiple modernities, 48, 76
modernization, 147, 178, 183, 239, 242,
    245, 247, 255, 264, 266, 293
Molesworth, Robert, 277
Montesquieu, 203
Moore, Barrington, 146–47
Moravia, 240
movement, 5, 14, 48, 69–70, 72–76, 81, 83,
    124, 131, 155, 182, 186–87, 243, 247,
    268, 270
multiculturality, 9, 240–41, 245, 248–50,
    252, 254–56, 290

Napoleonic era, 68–69, 81, 129, 249, 253
narrative, 27, 48–50, 56, 148, 176, 178,
    180, 204, 217–18, 223–24, 226, 228,
    237, 267, 270
  master, 21, 176–77, 183, 187, 289, 293

nation, 8–9, 14, 18–19, 49, 56, 58, 73, 81,
    128, 140–42, 157, 176, 186, 212, 218,
    220, 227–29, 237, 271, 273, 275
  concept of, 8–9, 53, 55, 68, 72, 146,
    203, 216, 239, 242, 249, 252–54, 269,
    289–90
national history, 12, 50, 56, 139, 143,
    147–48, 176, 187–88, 201, 289, 291
nationalism, 8–10, 14, 76, 141, 178, 203,
    219–21, 224, 238, 241–42, 245, 249,
    252–53, 256, 271
  concept of, 140–41, 149–56, 166n59,
    290
  and ethnicity, 8–9, 128, 148, 155, 215,
    226, 241–45, 248, 252–56, 267–68,
    290
  and language (*see under* language)
  methodological, 8, 18, 139–144, 148,
    151, 157, 293
nationalization, 6, 80–83, 214, 228
nation-building, 6, 11, 80, 141, 145, 216,
    221, 273
nation state, 6, 8–9, 12, 14, 18, 63, 72–73,
    80, 139–42, 144–48, 151, 157, 176,
    187, 213–15, 220, 228, 240
National Socialism, 54–55, 70
Netherlands, 79, 81, 238, 268
Neumann, Iver, 217
newspaper, 24, 53, 97, 123, 145, 153–56,
    166n59, 185, 255, 267, 288
Nietzsche, Friedrich, 54, 187
nineteenth century, 8–11, 14, 19, 23, 57,
    64, 69, 71, 74–75, 77, 79, 81, 106,
    108, 142, 145, 156–57, 177, 179, 181,
    185, 203, 213, 215–16, 219–20, 222,
    226, 238, 242–43, 245, 248–51, 255,
    268–69, 274, 286
nobility, 74, 247, 249, 255
Nordic countries, 10–11, 79, 265–70
  concept of, 8
Nordic model, 8, 48, 229, 270, 273–74
Norway, 52, 57, 213, 269,
Novi-Sad, 243, 250

opinion, 132, 253
  concept of, 268–69
opposition, 23, 103, 105, 120, 187, 238,
    284
  concept of, 11–12, 267–68, 276n8

Ortega y Gasset, José, 291
Orthodox Church, 215, 238, 243, 246, 250–51
Ottoman Empire, 9, 12, 225, 242–43, 245, 251

Palmén, Johan Philip, 270–73
paradiastole. *See under* Skinner, Quentin
Paris, 10–11, 13, 186, 247
parliamentarism, 102, 105–108, 269, 289
parliament, parliamentary, 9–10, 14–15, 19, 77, 96–110, 131, 247, 288, 290
   agenda, 104, 107–8
   debate, 29, 96, 98, 100–3, 107, 110, 123, 145, 153, 288
   procedure, 102–4, 106–7, 109
   rhetoric (*see under* rhetoric)
participation, 23, 68, 71, 81–82, 121, 127–28, 141, 143, 251, 271
patriotism, 56, 151, 204
peasantry, 12, 74–75, 227, 245, 269
Pécs, 250
pedagogy, 55, 57, 79, 183, 247–48, 255, 267–69, 274–75
people, 9, 13, 68, 73–75, 142, 151–52, 156, 237, 239, 242, 255, 267
   concept of, 51, 72, 222, 252–54, 269, 271–74, 290
performativity, 2, 28–29, 103–4, 133–34, 179–80, 288
periodization, 5–7, 49, 63, 66–67, 73, 83, 289–91
periphery / centre, 6, 10–13, 49–50, 74, 128, 147, 153, 228, 264–65, 268, 270, 274
   concept of, 8, 10, 143, 215, 224–25, 236–242
pietism, 268, 277n11
Pinder, Wilhelm, 54
Poland, 78–79, 81, 154, 213, 218, 224, 244, 268
polarization, 183–84, 186, 268, 274
policy, 96, 103–5, 107, 119, 154–55, 203, 214, 219, 267
political economy, 48, 70, 74–75, 141–42, 201, 203–4, 220, 228, 290
political history, 23, 147, 223

political philosophy, 27, 29–31, 71, 97, 100, 118, 121, 125, 129–30, 143, 201–2, 241, 245, 248–49, 252, 255, 271, 275, 284–85, 291–92
political thought, 1, 99, 123, 131, 145–46, 197, 199, 201, 252, 269
politician, 8, 11, 29, 76, 110, 221, 227, 245, 252, 273
politicization, 6, 8, 21, 67–71, 75, 83, 96, 103–4, 107, 183–85, 217, 219–20, 226–27. *See also under* debate
   depoliticization, 68–70
   repoliticization, 68
politicking, 96, 103–4, 106
politics, political, 15, 31, 53, 74–5, 79, 96–97, 102, 106–8, 110, 119, 139, 142–43, 153, 155, 213, 216, 219–20, 238, 242, 245–48, 251, 282, 288
   action, 29, 74, 97, 146
   concept of, 4, 19–20, 29, 96, 103–4, 108, 110, 133, 268–69, 271, 289–90, 292
   culture, 21, 50, 142–44, 147–48, 156, 158, 253, 266, 269, 273, 285
   international, 142, 153
   parties, 11–12, 74, 108, 133, 184, 267
   procedure, 100, 102–4, 106–8, 121
polity, 66, 73, 96, 103–5
Pomerania, 276n10
Pontoppidan, Erik, 277n11
Popper, Karl, 252
Portugal 3, 215, 229
postmodernism, 245, 290
postwar period, 14, 50, 217, 221
power, 11, 26, 29, 81–82, 103–5, 107–9, 118–19, 122, 133–35, 147, 152–53, 157, 202, 213–15, 219–20, 222, 241, 247, 253–54, 266, 290
Prague, 223, 243, 250
progress / decline, 30, 48–50, 53, 55–56, 58, 76, 228, 242, 245, 249, 251, 293
   concept of, 4–5, 54, 56, 73–74, 133, 204, 215, 290
progressivism, 18, 20, 23, 74–75, 187, 228, 275, 290
Protestantism, 215, 238, 243, 255
Protestant Reformation, 64, 200, 266, 268

Prussia, 66, 242, 247, 255
public, 7, 14, 20, 25, 30, 68, 71–72, 81–82, 97, 129–30, 144–46, 186, 198, 214, 217, 219, 221, 228, 264–65, 269, 273–74, 282
Pufendorf, Samuel, 201

race, 68, 72
  concept of, 121, 290
racism, 164n46, 238, 283
radicalism, 74–75, 184, 244, 247–49
rationalism, 12, 145, 201, 293
reality, 12, 25–26, 31, 47, 79, 125, 129–30, 147, 154, 178–81, 225, 229, 238, 240–42, 245–48, 251–54, 256, 272, 286–87, 291
Redlich, Josef, 105, 108
reform, 23–24, 71, 74, 102, 154, 186–87, 242, 244–45, 247–49, 251–52, 254, 290
regime, 55–56, 70, 74, 102, 104–5, 107–9, 290
region, 7–10, 56, 78, 147, 264
  concept of, 4, 8–9, 143, 214–16, 231n7, 289
  European, 6, 9, 13, 20, 68, 72, 74, 79–81, 139, 146, 200, 212–229, 238–256, 264–67
  Sub-national, micro-, 8–9, 102, 212, 214–16, 238–56, 266
  supranational, meso-, 8–9, 102, 212–229, 238, 267
  territorial / non-territorial, 215–16
  world, 3–4, 82, 176
regionalism, 4, 76, 214, 220–21, 225
regionalization, 213, 215–19, 222–23, 225, 227–28
Reichardt, Rolf, 64, 184–85, 217
Reinert, Sophus, 203
religion, 1, 4, 19, 52, 64, 67–68, 72, 74, 78, 148, 154, 175, 215, 223, 237–40, 243, 245–48, 250–51, 254–55, 267–68, 282, 287, 290
Renaissance, 13, 64, 100
repetitive structures. *See under* Koselleck, Reinhart
Republic of Letters, 10, 79, 264–65
Republicans, Republicanism, 52–53, 269, 274, 290

revolution, 48, 51, 64, 68–69, 74, 80, 107, 147, 154, 184–86, 242, 247–49, 254, 269, 274
  concept of, 4–5, 19, 51, 73, 290
  of 1848, 69, 247, 252, 272
rhetoric, 28–29, 47, 51–54, 56, 96, 98–103, 107–8, 132–34, 140–2, 144–46, 149, 152, 154–56, 263, 269, 272, 275, 286, 290
  deliberative, parliamentary, 101–3, 108
rhetorical redescription. *See under* Skinner, Quentin
Richter, Melvin, 197
Ricoeur, Paul, 51, 120, 289
rights, 52, 73, 77, 128, 155, 246, 251–52, 255, 263, 269, 271–73
  concept of, 132, 134, 263, 290
Robertson, William, 204–5
Romance languages, 20, 79
Romania 12, 213, 218, 220, 225–26
Romanian language, 12, 250
Romanticism, 12, 14, 54, 145, 237, 248, 252–56
Rousseau, Jean-Jacques, 53–55
rulership (*Herrschaft*), 109, 200, 248
Russia, 6, 9–10, 20, 66, 70–71, 74–75, 78, 151, 153–56, 215–18, 223, 238, 240, 271, 274
Russian Language, 3, 11–12, 77

Salonika, 36n35, 243
Sarajevo, 243
Sattelzeit. See under Koselleck, Reinhart
Scandinavia, 56, 203, 220
  concept of, 8, 225, 228
Schmitt, Carl, 225
science, 4, 6–7, 15, 19, 53–55, 64, 69, 77, 120, 204, 219–20, 223, 226, 243, 249, 251, 269, 288–89
  natural, 1, 213, 219, 263
  social, 129, 131, 140–42, 157, 202, 204, 220–21, 224, 229, 285, 291–93
scientization, 6–7, 219, 226
Scotland, 199–201, 204–5
Second World War, 14, 98, 221, 224, 227–28
secularization, 21, 74, 269, 290

semantic change, semantical change, 2, 4, 6–7, 16, 21, 30, 57, 63, 65–67, 78, 80, 82–83, 96, 98–99, 101, 110, 128, 147, 176, 181–83, 283, 291
   micro–diachronic (situational), 52, 66, 82–83, 125–26
   synchronic (comparative), 2, 177, 182
semantic field, 3, 16–18, 21, 26–27, 29–30, 57, 64, 69, 72, 77, 120, 124–29, 151–52, 180, 182, 184–85, 198, 271, 289–90
semantic nominalism, 118, 151, 182
semantic structure, 52, 181–82, 184, 186
Serbia, 220
Serbian language, 250–51
Serbo–Croatian language, 250
Silesia, 214, 240, 255
simultaneity of the non–simultaneous. *See under* Koselleck, Reinhart
Skinner, Quentin, 17, 28–30, 51, 54, 96–100, 109, 200
   in utramque partem disputare, 99
   paradiastole, rhetorical redescription, 54, 99, 102, 109
Slavic languages, 20, 78–79, 223–24, 251, 254
Slavonia, 255
Slavophiles, 6, 75
Slavs, 215, 218, 220, 223–24, 227
Slovakia, 213, 222, 225
Slovakian language, 250
Slovenia, 225, 240
Smith, Adam, 203
social constructivism 179, 221, 224, 270
social democracy, 75, 122, 133, 269–70
social history, 66, 128, 183
socialism, 70, 74, 76, 122, 154–55, 227–28, 270, 290
   concept of, 26, 133, 184
society, 54, 56, 66, 119–20, 123, 133, 146, 148, 175–76, 186, 202, 238, 241, 252, 255, 263, 266, 273, 275, 277n12, 291
   concept of, 19, 140, 201, 269, 271–73, 283, 286, 290 (*see also under* counter-concepts)
   one-norm-society, 266–69
Sofia, 223, 243
Sonderweg, 56
   European, 175

German, 48–49, 178
Nordic, 48, 265–67
sovereignty, 68, 102, 120, 214, 290
space, 3, 7–9, 11, 22, 28, 49, 121, 123–24, 131–32, 135, 144–45, 179, 215–17, 222, 224, 236–40, 254, 265, 282–83, 289
   concept of, 213–14, 216, 227
Spain, 81, 184, 215, 229
Spanish language, 3, 12, 144, 282, 286
spatialization, spatiality production, 3, 7–9, 26, 49, 82, 124, 143, 149, 157, 214–17, 219, 222, 226–29, 264–65, 288
spatial turn, 212–13, 227
speech act, 28–30, 54–55, 69, 100, 132–33, 140, 153, 288
state, 8–9, 13–14, 18, 25, 68, 71–74, 79–80, 104, 107, 122, 139, 141–42, 146, 148, 176–77, 213–15, 218–20, 223–24, 237, 243–47, 250, 256, 267, 273, 275
   concept of, 99, 109, 239–42, 254, 269, 271–73, 285, 289–90
   welfare, 1, 128, 133–34, 177, 227, 267, 292
status, 68, 128, 239, 251, 253, 255, 273
stereotype, 238, 245, 292
Stråth, Bo, 19, 134
Stratimirović, Ștefan, 251
Sweden, 47, 156, 266–67, 269–70, 274, 246n10
Swedish language 71, 78, 144, 153–55, 167n59, 270–73
synchronicity. *See* asynchronicity / synchronicity

Taylor, Charles, 241
temporality, temporalization, 5–6, 48, 50–52, 56–57, 68, 73–75, 88n38, 124, 128, 131, 177, 216, 226, 265, 283, 290, 293
territoriality, 8–9, 213–16, 230n6, 289
text, 13, 16, 29–30, 79, 97–98, 120–21, 203, 249, 282, 287–88
   study of, 2, 16–17, 19, 27–28, 75, 130–31, 149–53, 164n46, 199, 202, 204–5
Third Reich. *See* National Socialism

thought–practices, 26, 74, 101, 123, 130–31, 241, 254
Tilly, Charles, 176
time, 2, 4–7, 17–20, 23, 31, 47–58, 63, 67–68, 71, 73–76, 79, 82, 100, 103, 105–7, 128–30, 145–46, 181, 215–17, 226, 237, 240–42, 253, 266, 293–94. *See also* asynchronicity / synchronicity
  concept of, 4–5, 290
Timişoara, 243, 250
Tindemans, Leo, 58
tolerance, toleration
  concept of, 52, 268, 281–83, 290
Tomek, Vaclav Vladivoj, 249–50
Toynbee, Arnold Joseph, 22
transfer, 3, 8, 16–19, 57, 70, 79, 177–78, 181–82, 184–85, 187–88, 216, 238, 243, 254, 270, 274, 287–88. *See also under* concepts, conceptual
transit area, 9, 240
translation, 3, 8, 10–17, 19, 21, 27, 71, 77–80, 109, 130, 140, 143, 153, 180–88, 197–205, 255, 265, 270–2, 286, 288, 294
  and meaning, 57
  retranslation, 19, 183
  translatability / untranslatability, 19, 77, 89n47, 181–82, 198–200, 285
transnational history, 4, 15, 56, 65, 139–146, 157, 161n16, 294. *See also under* conceptual history
Transylvania, 9, 214, 226, 240, 244, 246, 255
Trichterzeit (funnel period), 266
Triest, 243
Turgenev, Ivan, 75
Turkey, 219. *See also* Ottoman Empire
Turkish Language, 12, 14–15
twentieth century, 6–9, 11, 20, 23, 55, 64–65, 67, 69–70, 73, 75–77, 81, 142, 150, 157, 213, 216, 225, 228, 242, 256

twenty-first century, 7–8, 11, 48, 52, 70, 73, 75, 82

Ukraine, 51, 213, 222
United States. *See under* America
universality, 10, 18, 26–27, 29–30, 57, 68, 72–73, 76, 125, 127, 129, 143, 147, 152, 156, 175–76, 181–82, 185, 249–52, 263–265, 267–70, 272, 274–75, 276n2, 293
university, 13, 15, 149, 202, 287. *See also* academia
urban area / rural area, 12–13, 54, 74, 243, 250, 252, 269, 271

values, 18, 81, 129, 175–76, 199, 254–55, 269, 274–75, 281–82
  religious, 238–39, 246
  sets of, 16, 30, 122, 134, 221, 237, 239, 241–42, 245, 248
Vico, Giambattista, 237
Vienna, 13, 220, 247–49, 251
Vincze, Hanna Orsolya, 199–200
vocabulary, 7–8, 15, 18–20, 23–24, 28, 31, 63, 68–69, 74, 77, 80, 82, 99, 130, 142, 145, 153, 177–78, 198–201, 204–5, 222, 238, 265, 281, 284–86, 288, 293
  political, 2, 103–4, 156, 219–20, 270, 292
  social, 2, 4, 72, 119, 271–2
Vojvodina, 214

Weber, Max, 105, 109, 175, 179, 202
'the West', 3, 6, 18, 20, 23, 52, 54, 56, 66, 71, 74–75, 201–3, 215, 217, 222–23, 238, 240, 242–43, 245–46, 249–50, 289
  concept of, 8, 156, 175, 215, 226–28 (*see also under* counter–concepts)
Westminster, 101, 106–7
Wolff, Larry, 217

www.ingramcontent.com/pod-product-compliance
Lightning Source LLC
Chambersburg PA
CBHW072145100526
44589CB00015B/2093